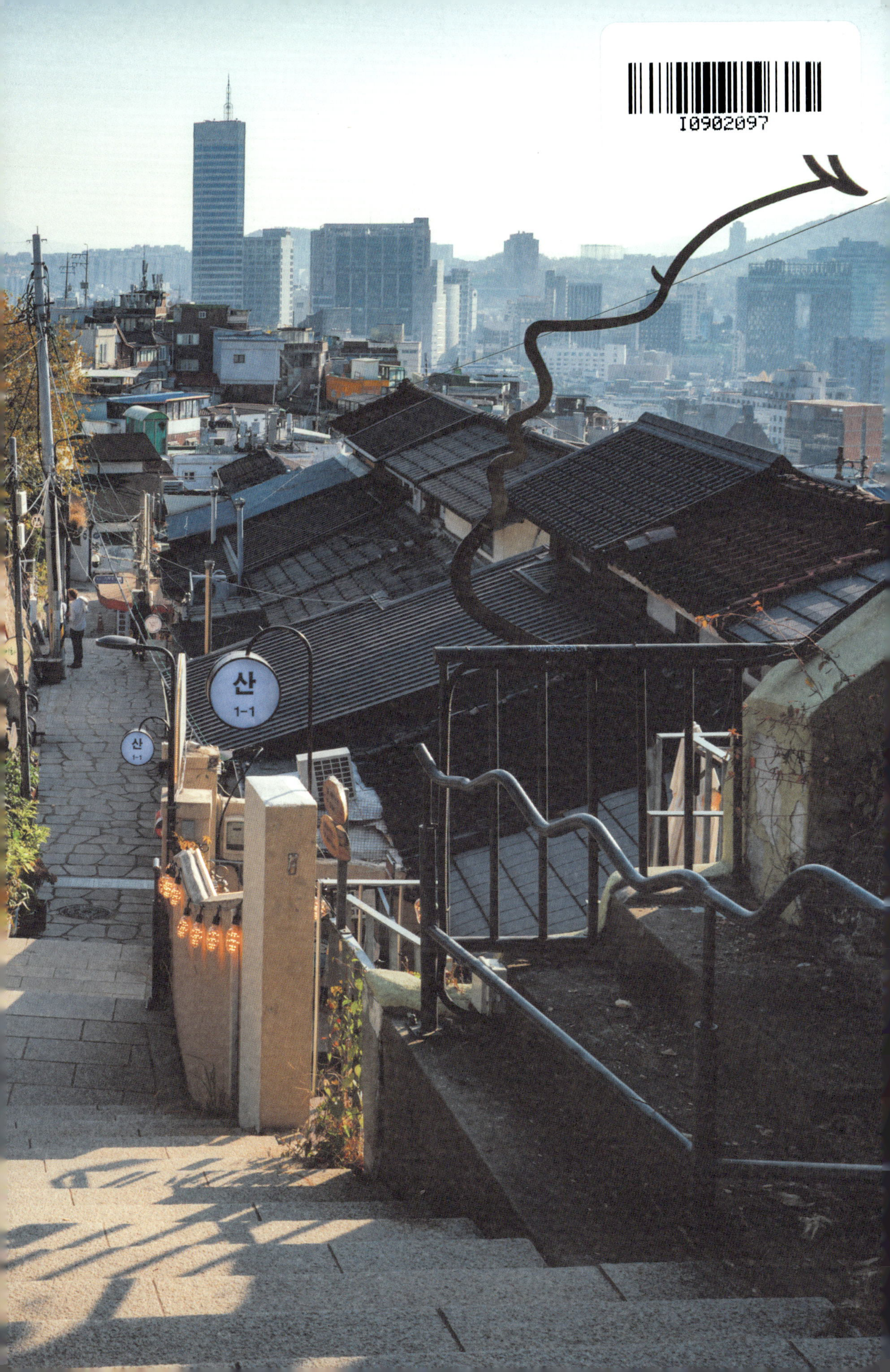
산
1-1

성

# SEOUL DAYS & NIGHTS

Photography by
James Choi
Sangjun Kim
Sam Landers

Essays by
James McPherson
Sam Landers
James Choi

Edited by
Jihyun Kim

Trope Publishing Co.
Chicago

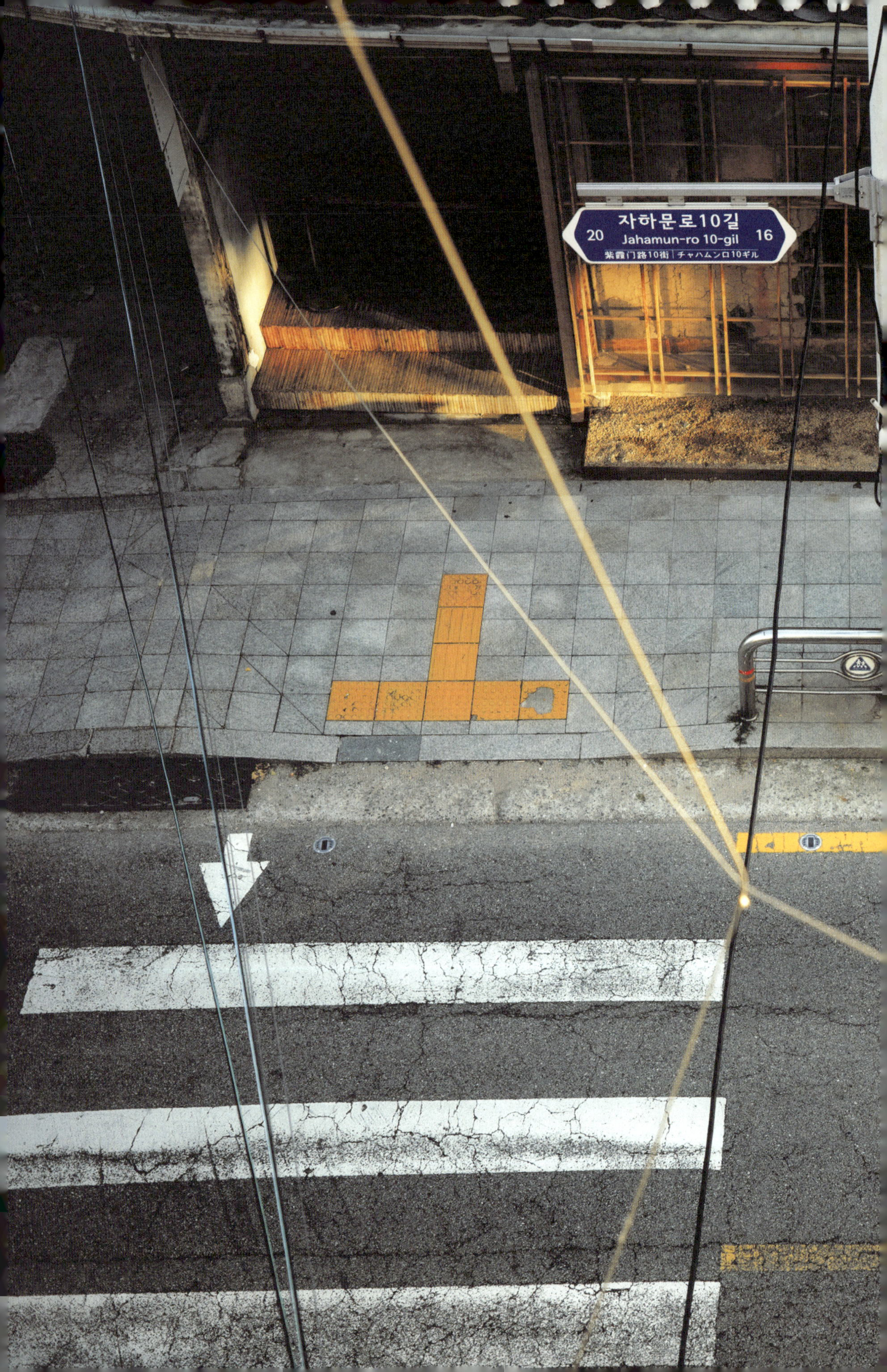

자하문로10길
20
Jahamun-ro 10-gil
16
紫霞门路10街 | チャハムンロ10ギル

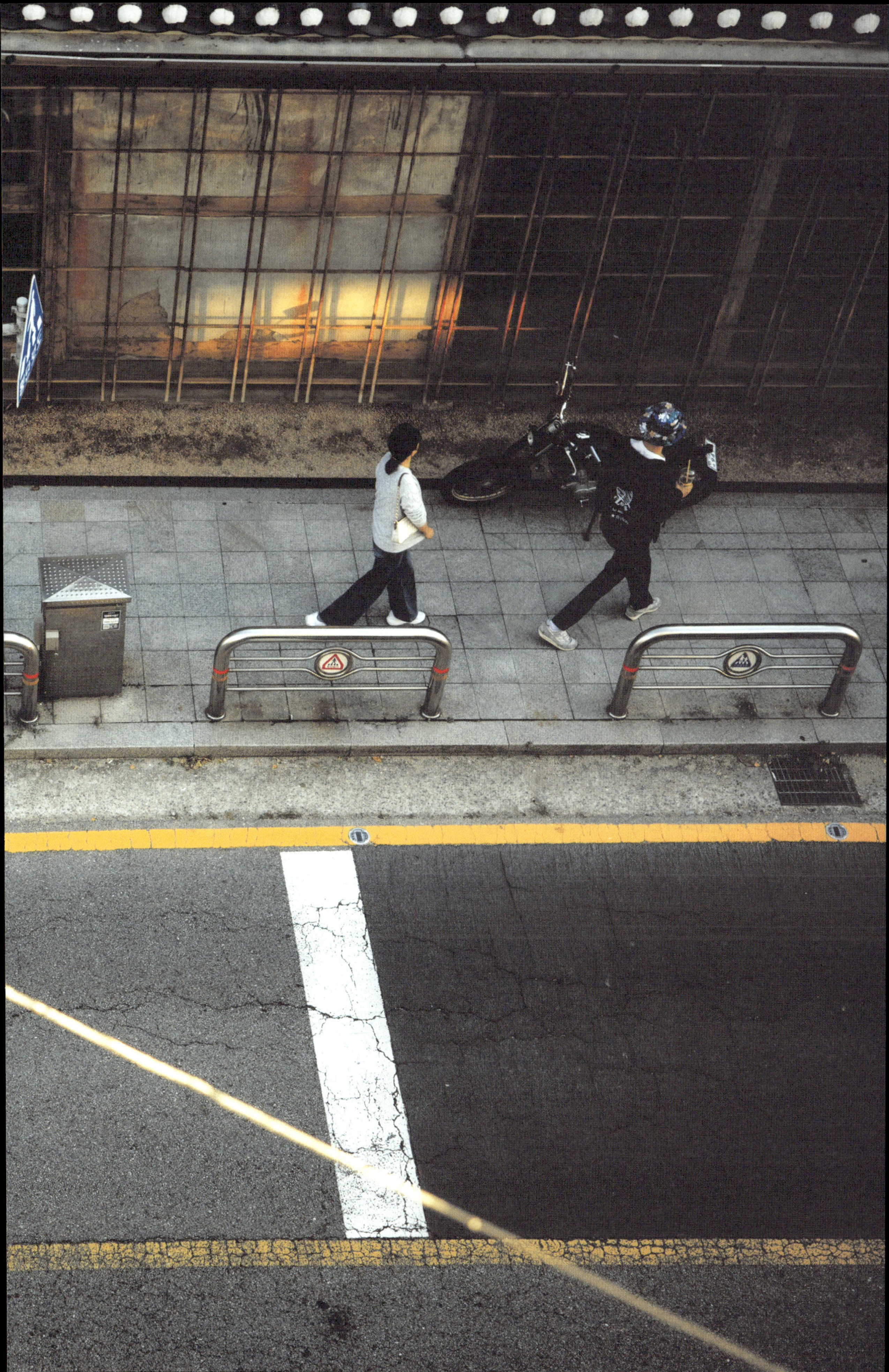

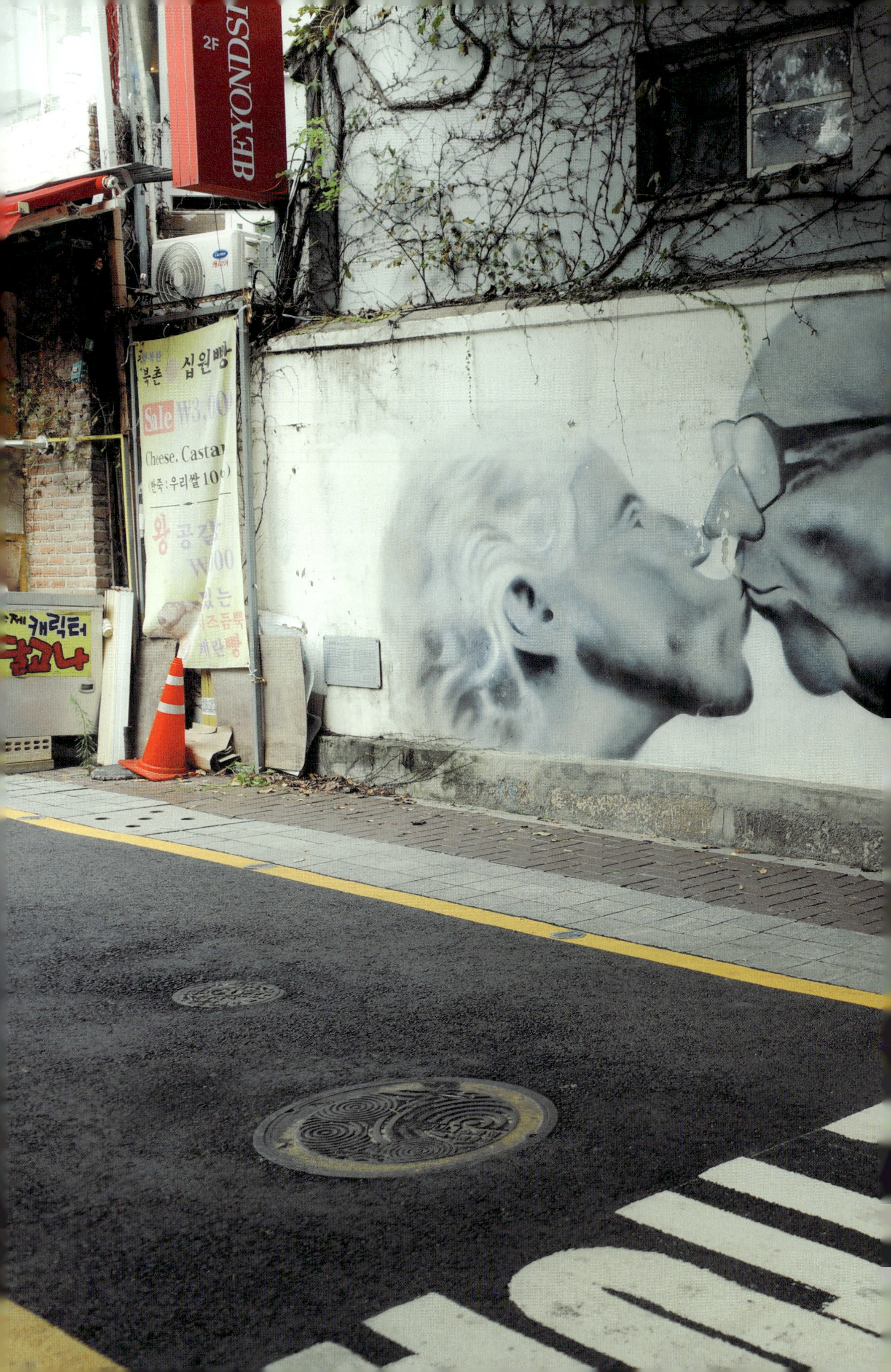

2F
북촌
십원빵
Sale
캐릭터
달고나

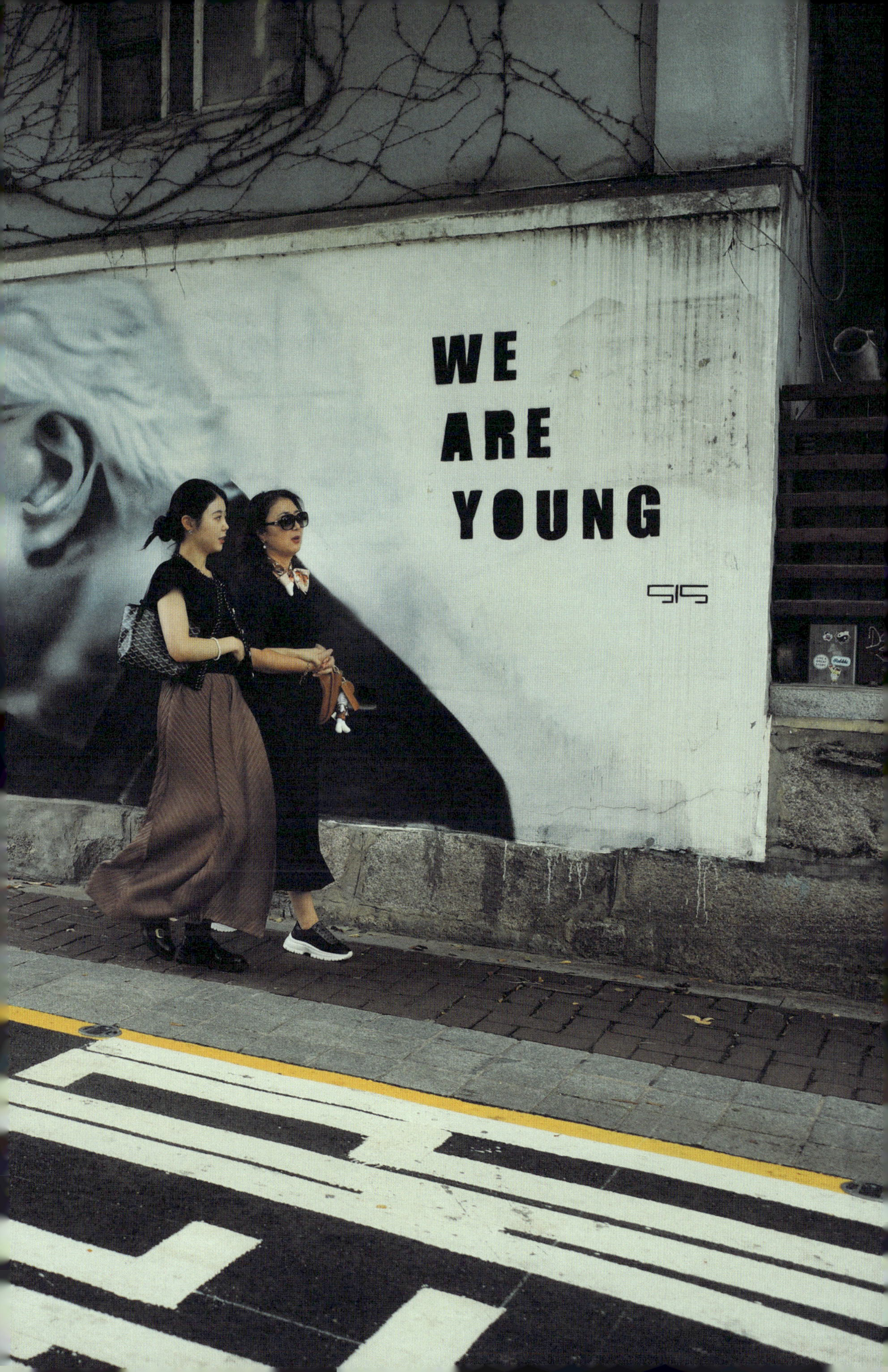
WE
ARE
YOUNG

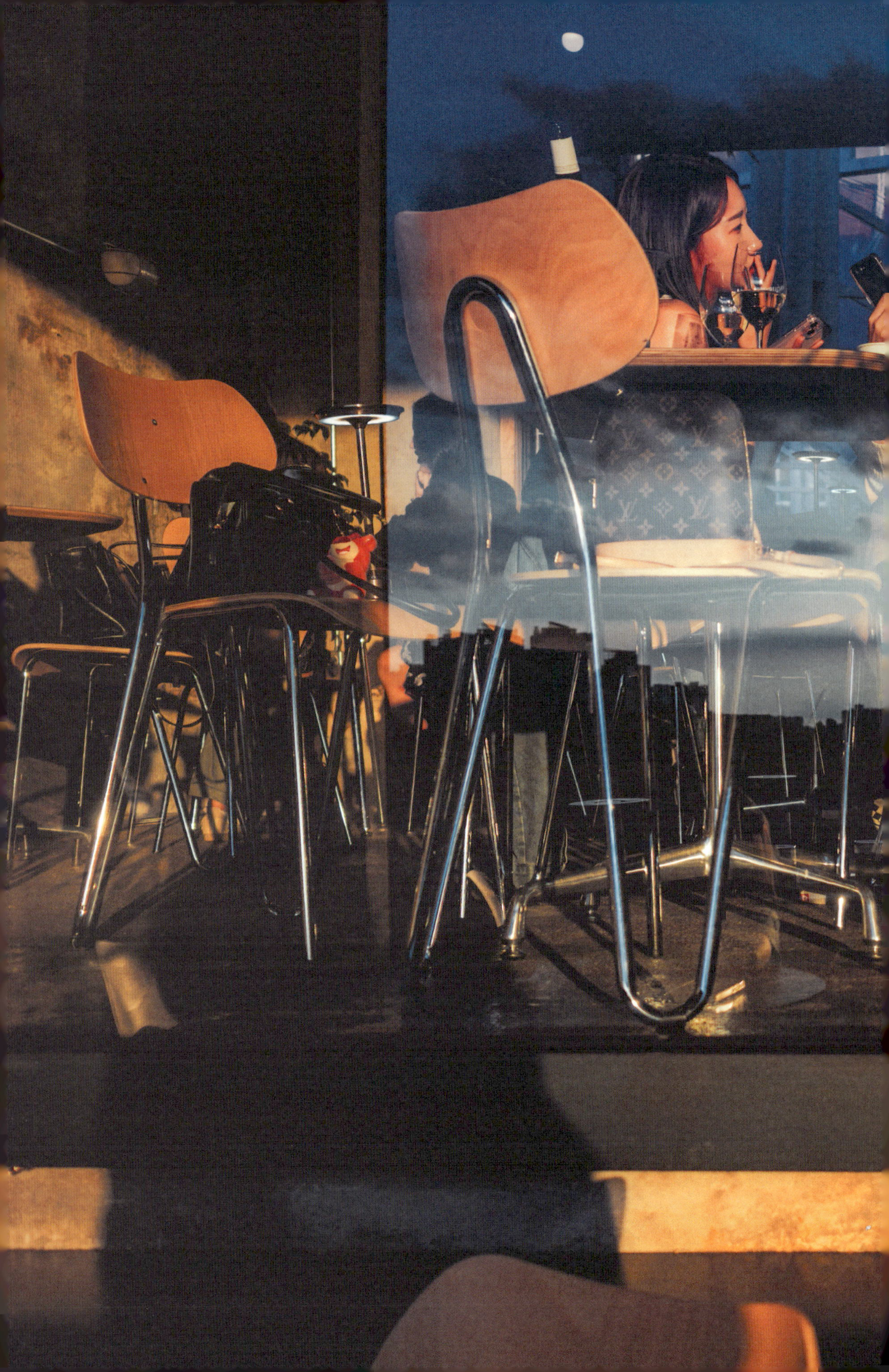

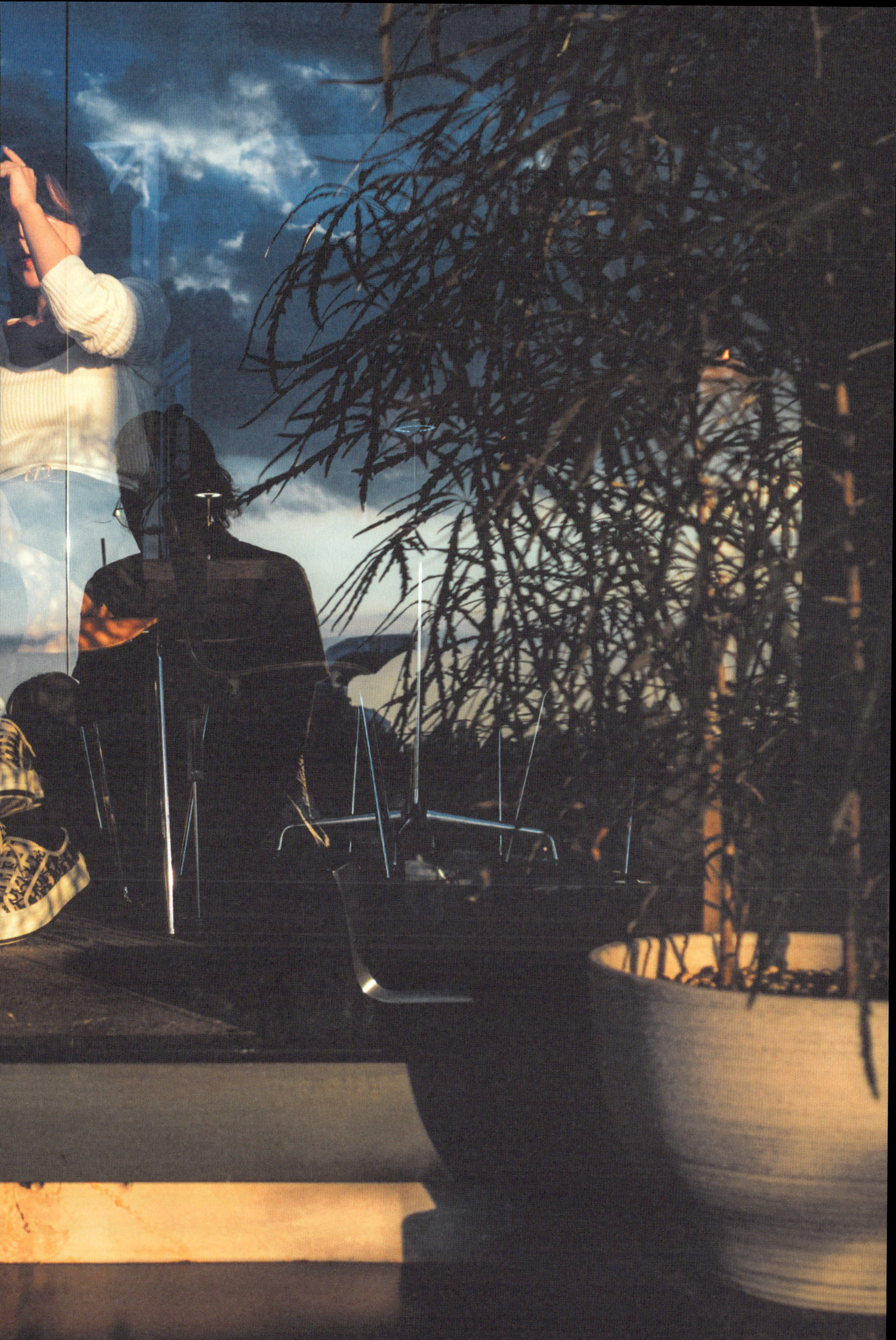

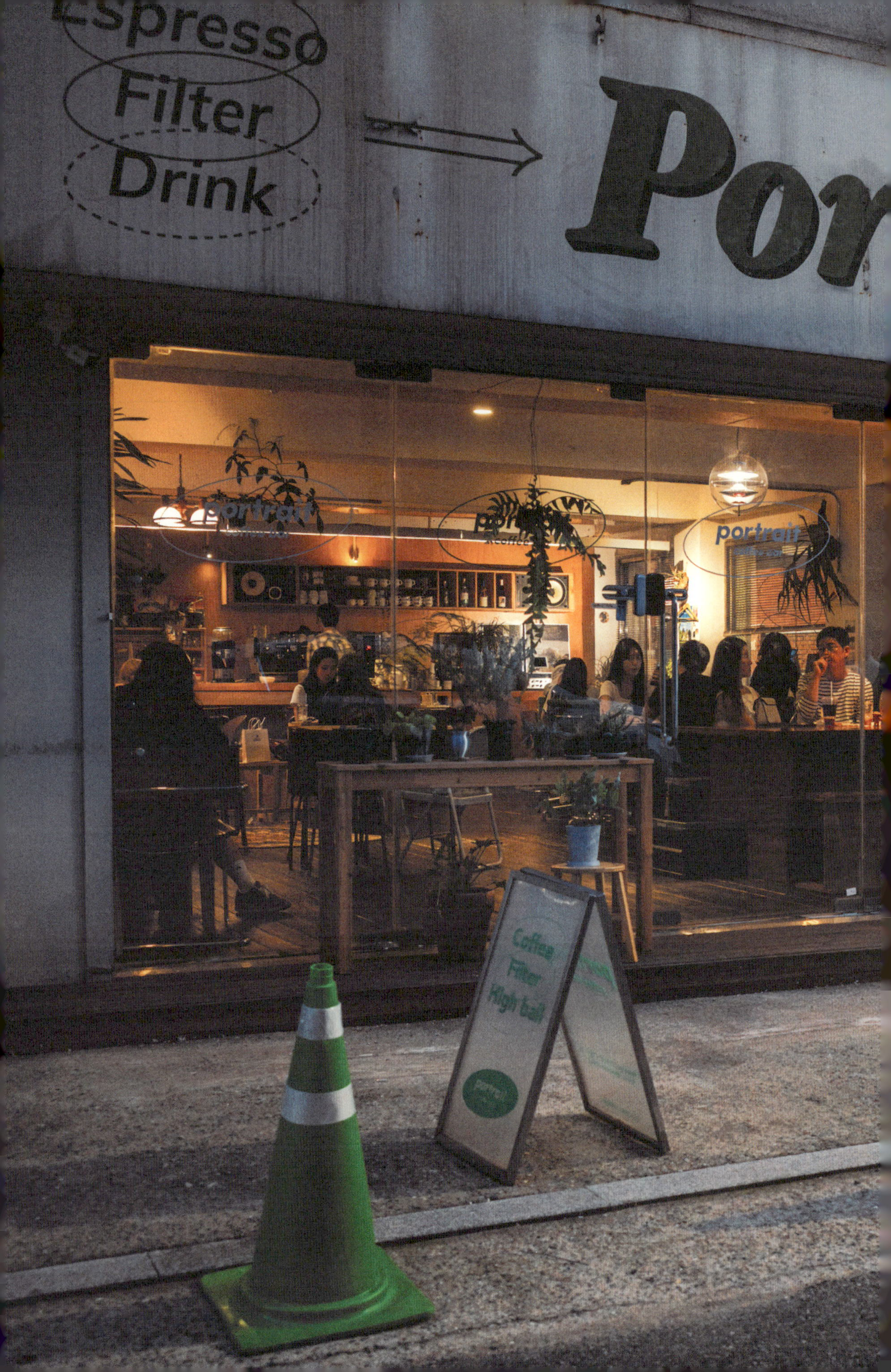
Espresso
Filter
Drink
Por
portrait
portrait
Coffee
Filter
High ball

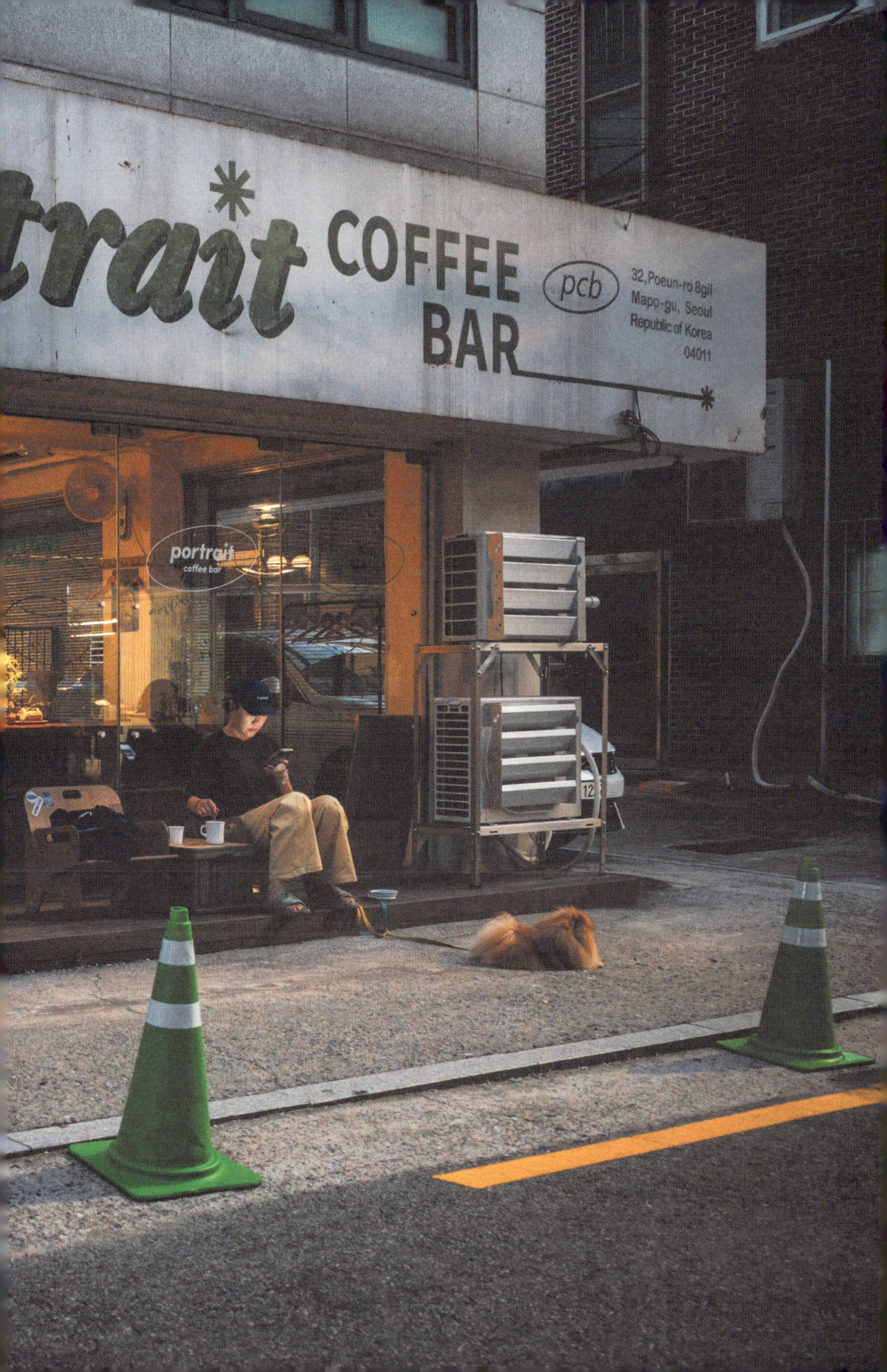
trait
COFFEE
BAR
pcb
32, Poeun-ro 8gil
Mapo-gu, Seoul
Republic of Korea
04011
portrait
coffee bar

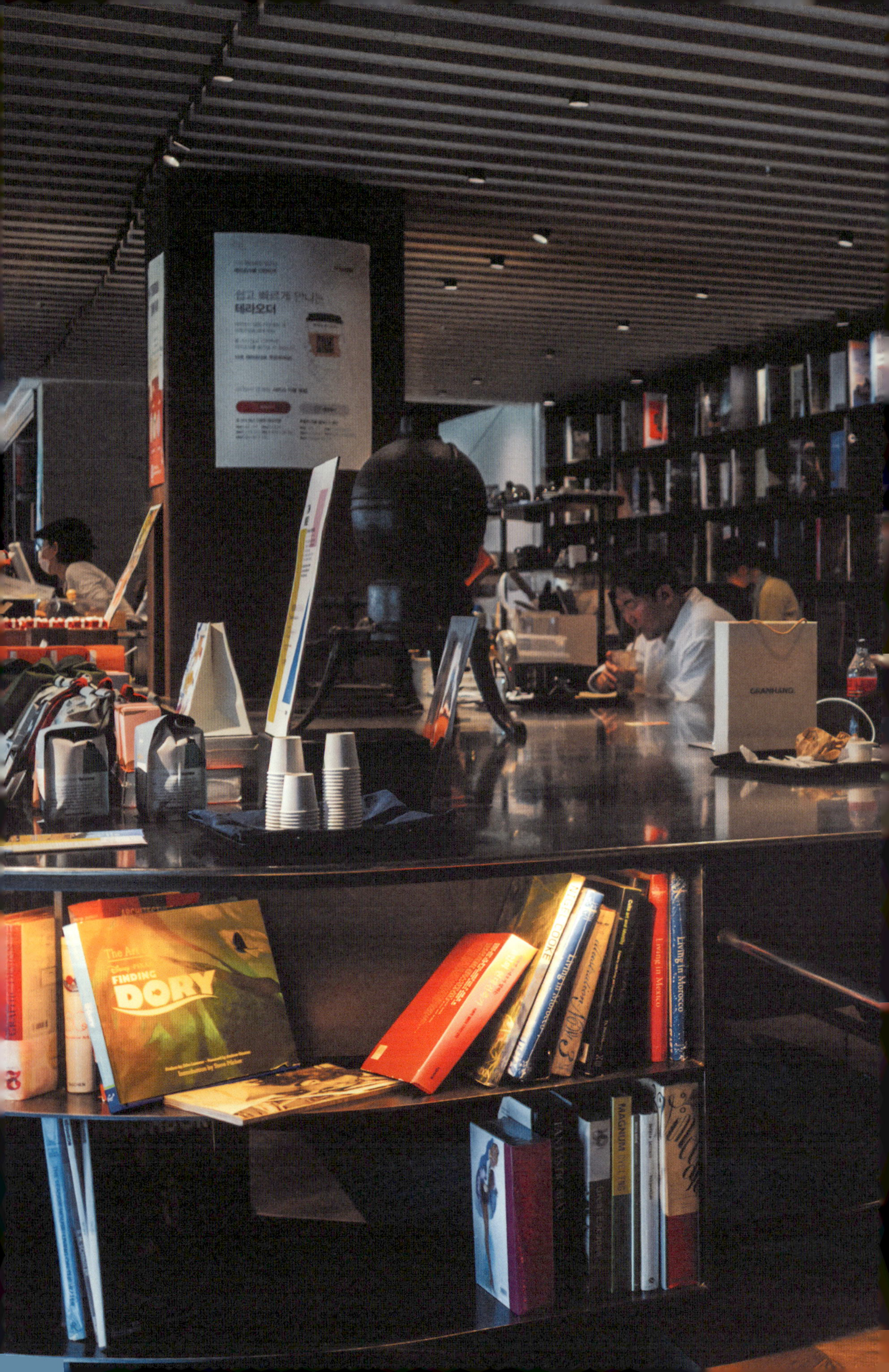
FINDING
DORY
Living in Mexico
Living in Morocco
MAGNUM

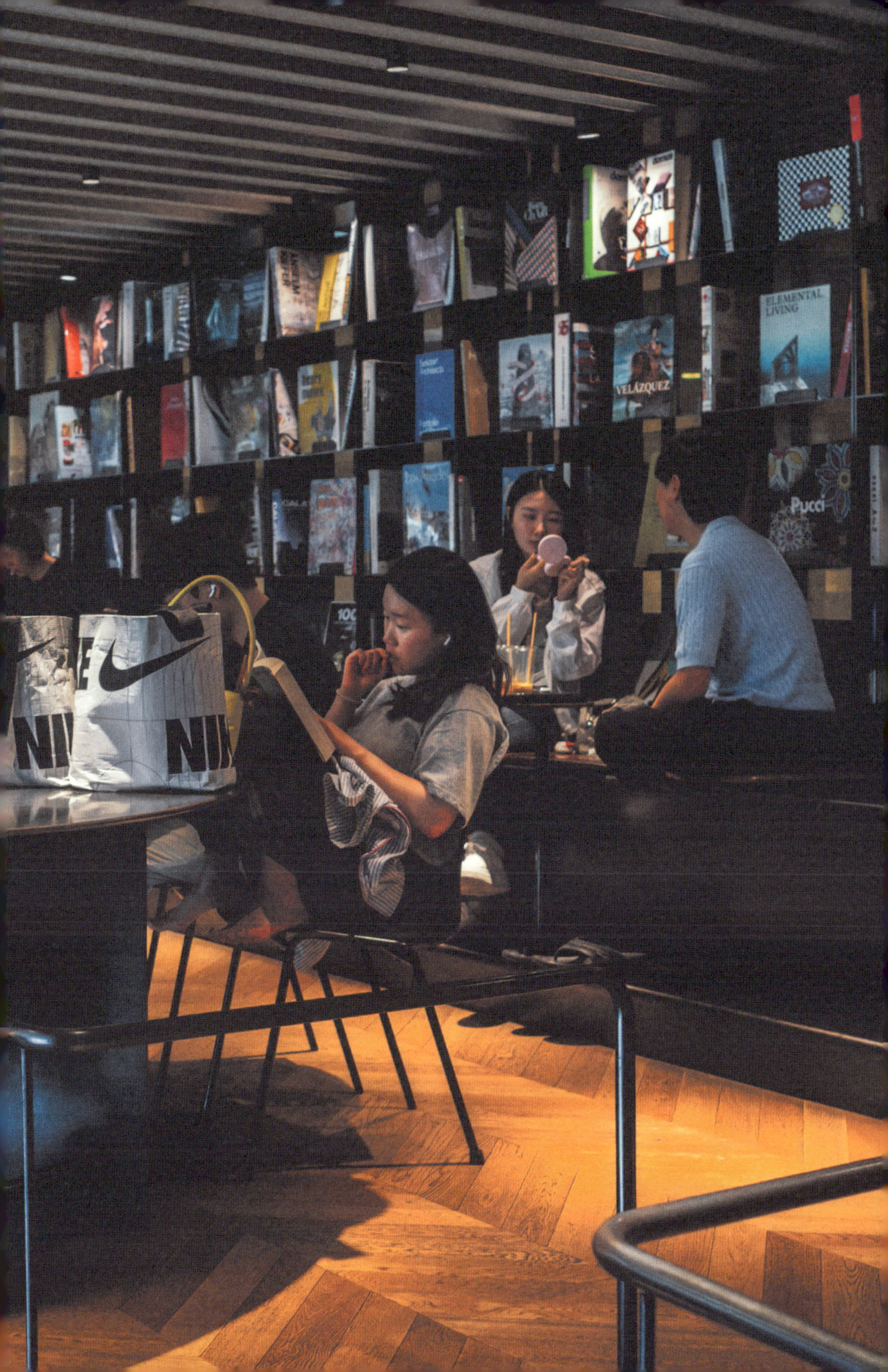
ELEMENTAL
LIVING
VELÁZQUEZ
Pucci

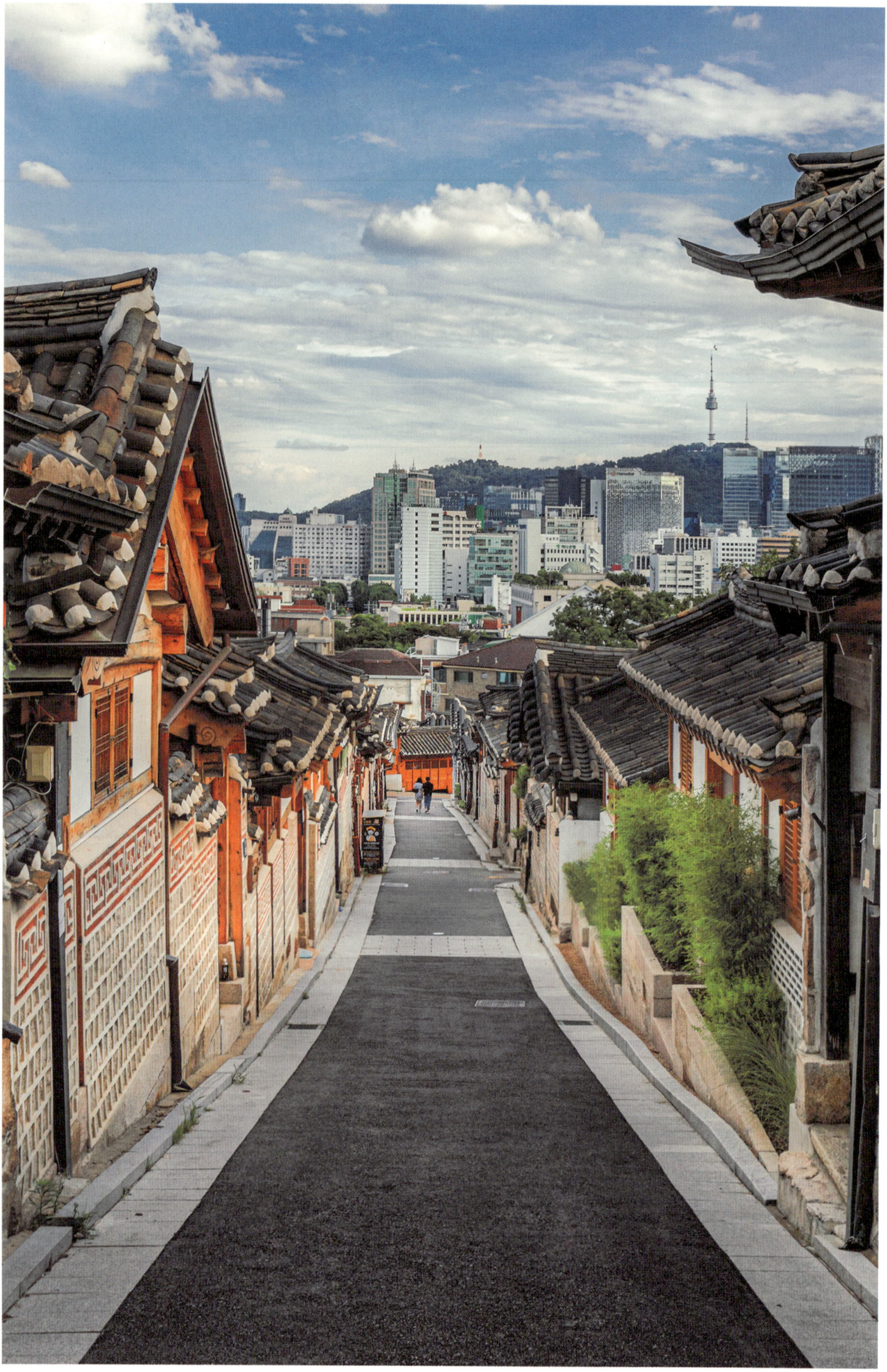

# SEOUL

## 서울

Seoul is a city defined by constant change. Construction, redevelopment, and shifting neighborhoods shape its landscape, while long-standing traditions and daily routines maintain continuity in a city more than 2,000 years old. The scale can be demanding, yet its public transit, commercial corridors, and established residential districts keep daily life moving in a steady, organized way. Within this environment, the city reveals itself through ordinary scenes: commutes, evening gatherings, and everyday exchanges that define life in a large, modern capital.

*Seoul Days & Nights* brings together photographs taken over a ten year period by Sangjun Kim, James Choi, and Sam Landers. Though their backgrounds differ, each approaches the city with an interest in how Seoul balances rapid development with a sense of permanence.

Sangjun Kim worked for a decade as a mechanical engineer at Hyundai, photographing products alongside his full-time engineering role before moving into photography full-time in 2024. His perspective reflects both a technical understanding of the city's built environment and a desire to show Seoul to viewers beyond Korea. As he notes, "In Seoul, the past and present coexist. You can frame older places like Gyeongbokgung or Deoksugung against modern skyscrapers and see both histories in a single image."

James Choi, a Korean filmmaker based in Chicago, returned to Seoul in 2024 for the first time since emigrating in 1974. During a six-month sabbatical, he photographed daily while working on a film, reconnecting with a city that had changed significantly since his childhood.

Korean-born Sam Landers, publisher at Trope, has photographed Seoul during multiple extended visits since 2016. His approach is largely observational, shaped by a street photographer's interest in ordinary details and the quiet movements that define daily life in the city.

Joe McPherson, a Seoul-based food and travel writer, moved to the city in 2004, inspired by his interest in Korean history. His ongoing indepth exploration has led to a focus on Seoul's food culture as the creator of Korea's first food blog, ZenKimchi.

Global interest in South Korea continues to expand. Film, streaming content, and music have introduced international audiences to contemporary Korean culture, but these exports capture only part of Seoul's appeal. When James Choi returned after four decades, he described the city as "an atmosphere—electric, a mix of contradictions that somehow made sense." His observation reflects what the photographers captured: a place where change is constant. As new construction rises beside older districts, a connection to the past remains.

Seoul offers a wide range of material for photographers: dense commercial areas, quieter residential streets, and landmarks that signify the history of this metropolis. Much of *Seoul Days & Nights* focuses on these quiet, in-between scenes, while also including large-scale views—particularly Sangjun Kim's images taken from above—that show the scale and complexity of the city. Together, these perspectives create a portrait of Seoul as it is lived rather than staged.

Seoul holds many qualities at once—organized yet unpredictable, modern yet shaped by tradition, fast-moving but grounded in routine. Through these images, readers can experience the city as the photographers encountered it: evolving, layered, and defined as much by everyday moments as by its continued growth.

JIHYUN KIM

Editor

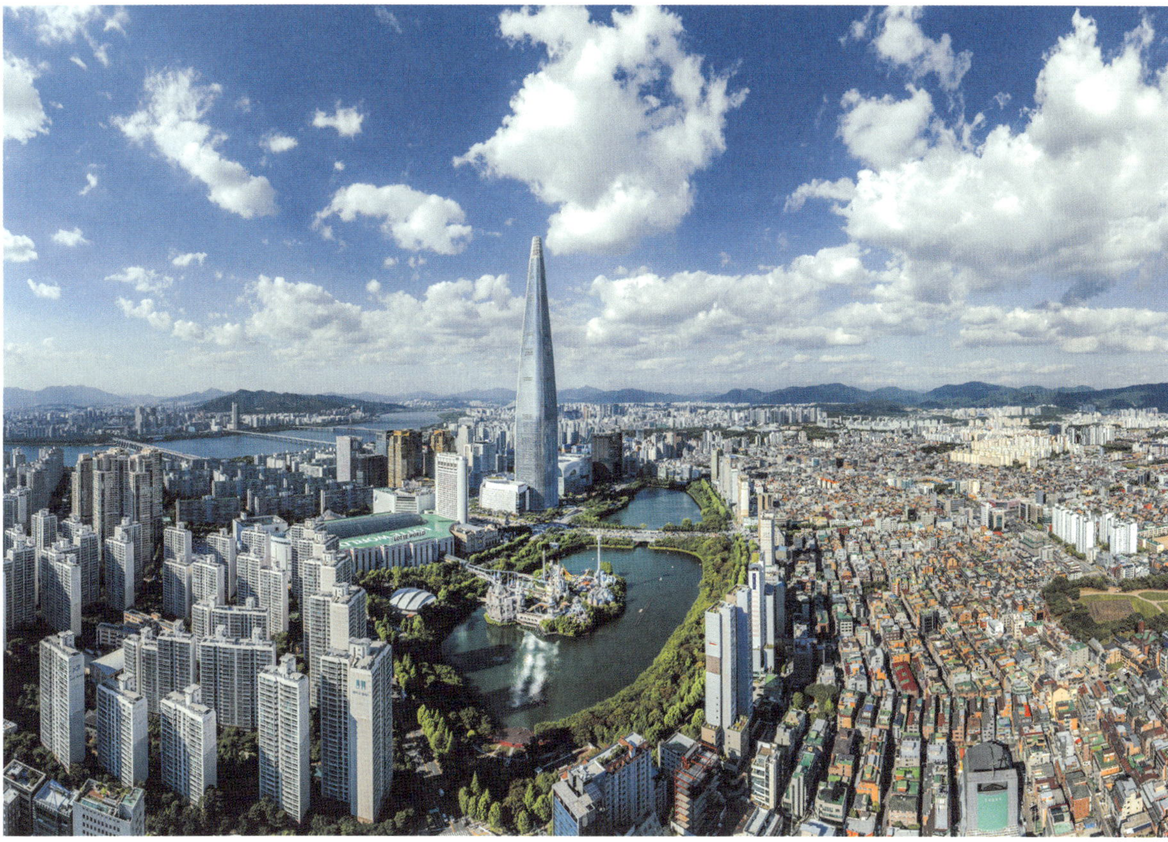

above: Lotte World Tower, Jamsil-dong, Songpa District

+ previous page: Bukchon Hanok Village, Jongno District

+ following page: Statue of King Sejong, Gwanghwamun Square, Jongno District

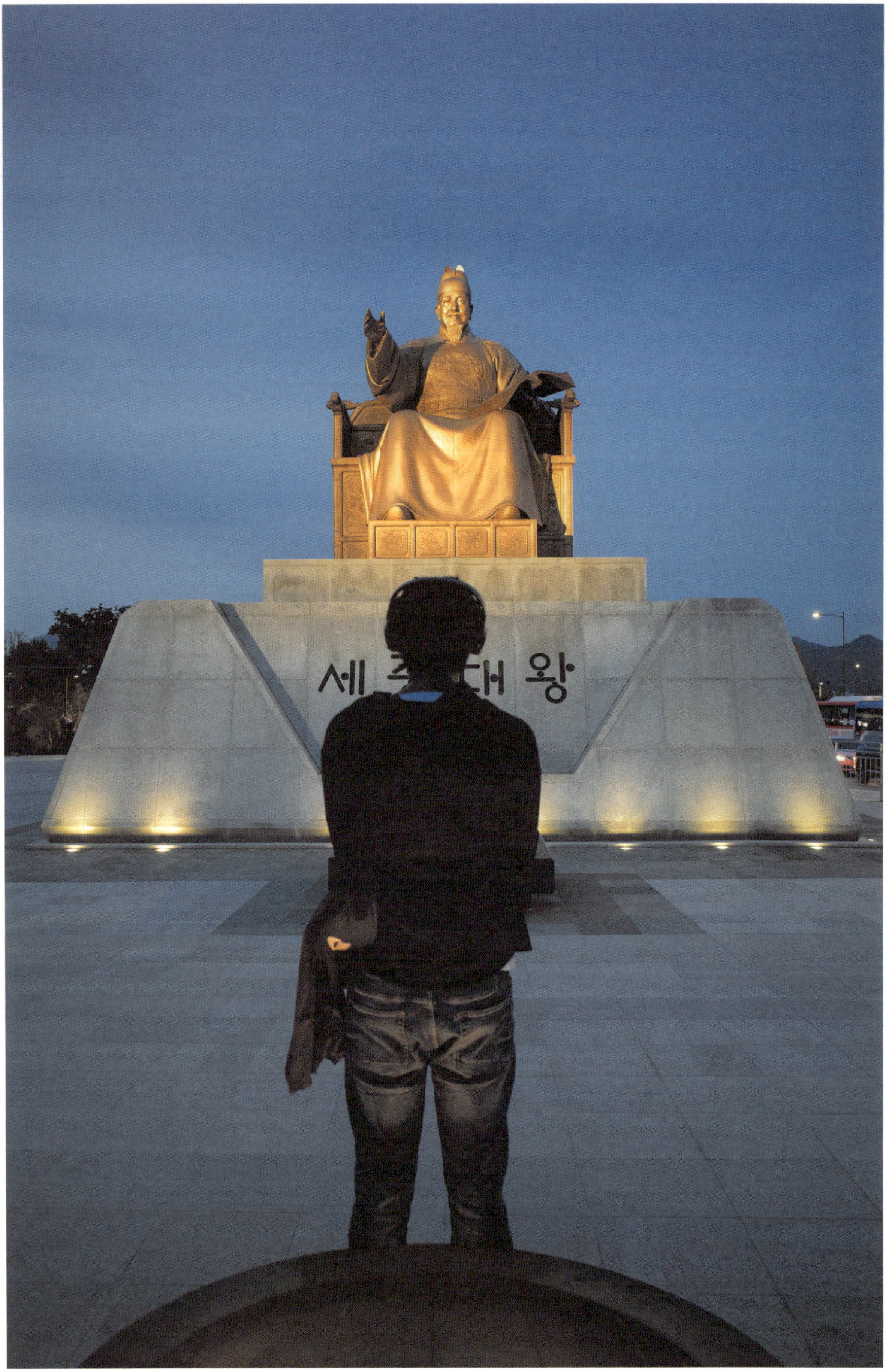

# HWAITING

## 한글

I first heard what I thought was "fighting" while watching K-dramas during the Covid pandemic. I found it amusing at first—actors shouting the word with enthusiasm, sometimes punctuated by a single or even a double fist pump for more emphasis, whenever they wished each other good luck or encouragement before facing a challenge. It seemed strange that they were literally telling someone to fight.

After asking a few Korean friends and doing a bit more research, I discovered the word was actually *hwaiting* (홧팅), borrowed from English and used to express "fighting spirit." It gained greater popularity during the 2002 World Cup as fans cheered on their national team. Today, *hwaiting*, pronounced *pai-ting*, is ubiquitous in contemporary Korean culture, a quick and cheerful way to say "you've got this."

Other forms of "Konglish" include *keopi* (coffee), *pokeu* (fork), *juseu* (juice), *bitamin* (vitamin), *saendeuwichi* (sandwich), *chokollit* (chocolate), *paenti* (underwear), and, amusingly, *opeunka* (convertible).

The Korean alphabet, by linguistic standards, is relatively new. In the 15th century, King Sejong created Hangul to promote literacy among commoners. Logical and beautifully simple, Hangul's 14 consonants were inspired by the shape of the mouth during pronunciation, and its ten vowels by the Confucian principles of heaven, earth, and humanity. Letters are combined into syllabic blocks, making the written language both elegant and efficient.

Over time, Hangul became one of the most important symbols of Korean identity and helped the nation achieve near-universal literacy. Each year, Korea celebrates Hangul Day on October 9, marking the proclamation of the alphabet in 1446. It is a national holiday filled with writing and calligraphy contests, public ceremonies, and visits to monuments, including the statue of King Sejong in Gwanghwamun Square, near the statue of Admiral Yi Sun-Sin.

Working on *Seoul Days & Nights* has brought me back to the city for several extended visits, two of which coincided with Hangul Day celebrations. It's ironic that I can no longer read Hangul or speak Korean, a language I once knew fluently. Time can do that. Leaving Seoul as a child and later adopting English as my main language, while studying French and Urdu, left little room to retain my early Korean. While it's relatively easy to navigate Seoul today without knowing the language, the nuances of communication are still wonderfully complex.

To truly understand Korean culture, it helps to learn even a little Hangul. Korean, I've learned, is a language of economy and empathy. It often omits subjects or verbs, trusting context to fill the gaps. That can make it sound formal or curt to outsiders, but it's actually an expression of cultural sensitivity, leaving space for understanding rather than confrontation. It's also deeply hierarchical, structured around age, rank, and social context. The honorific system, through titles, suffixes, and grammar, reflects the culture's respect for elders and social harmony. You see it play out vividly in K-dramas as subtle shifts in speech show respect, familiarity, or authority.

Returning to Seoul to take photographs allowed me to see the city in a new way, but observing its people reminded me that language is more than speech; it's built on bonds. The city communicates through gestures, expressions, and tones that often say as much as the words themselves. In conversation, inflection carries emotion. A drawn-out vowel can signal sympathy; a sharp ending can imply certainty; and a soft exhale can speak volumes without a single phrase. These unspoken cues are part of how Koreans connect.

Rediscovering Seoul through my camera has been both a return and a revelation. People often say Seoul can't be described, only felt, and they're right. Seoul today stands as one of the most technologically advanced and densely populated cities in the world, a metropolis that rebuilt itself within a single generation. Its skyline rises and resets every few years; old neighborhoods adapt or vanish. It's a city that looks planned from above but improvised from the street, yet somehow, Seoul makes perfect sense. Observing Seoul through the lens offers perspective on how deliberate and somehow organic its transformation has been. The still images provide a moment of reflection and allow imagination to fill the gaps.

The photographs in this book capture Seoul's contradictions: the past and future intertwined, creativity balanced by practicality. I walked the city's districts and climbed Inwangsan Mountain to see its full expanse. While Seoul proper covers about 234 square miles, the metro area spans more than 4,800 square miles with a population near 26 million people. Most of the images in this book focus on central Seoul, where fashion, architecture, and culture overlap most vividly, showing that progress here is not just economic or architectural, but cultural.

Seoul will undoubtedly continue to change; it will look different each time I return. Yet knowing that its language will always bind its people to their past gives me a quiet reassurance, that no matter how much the skyline shifts, I'll always be visiting a Seoul that feels, in some way, familiar. To the people of Seoul—*hwaiting!*

SAM LANDERS

Trope Publishing Co.

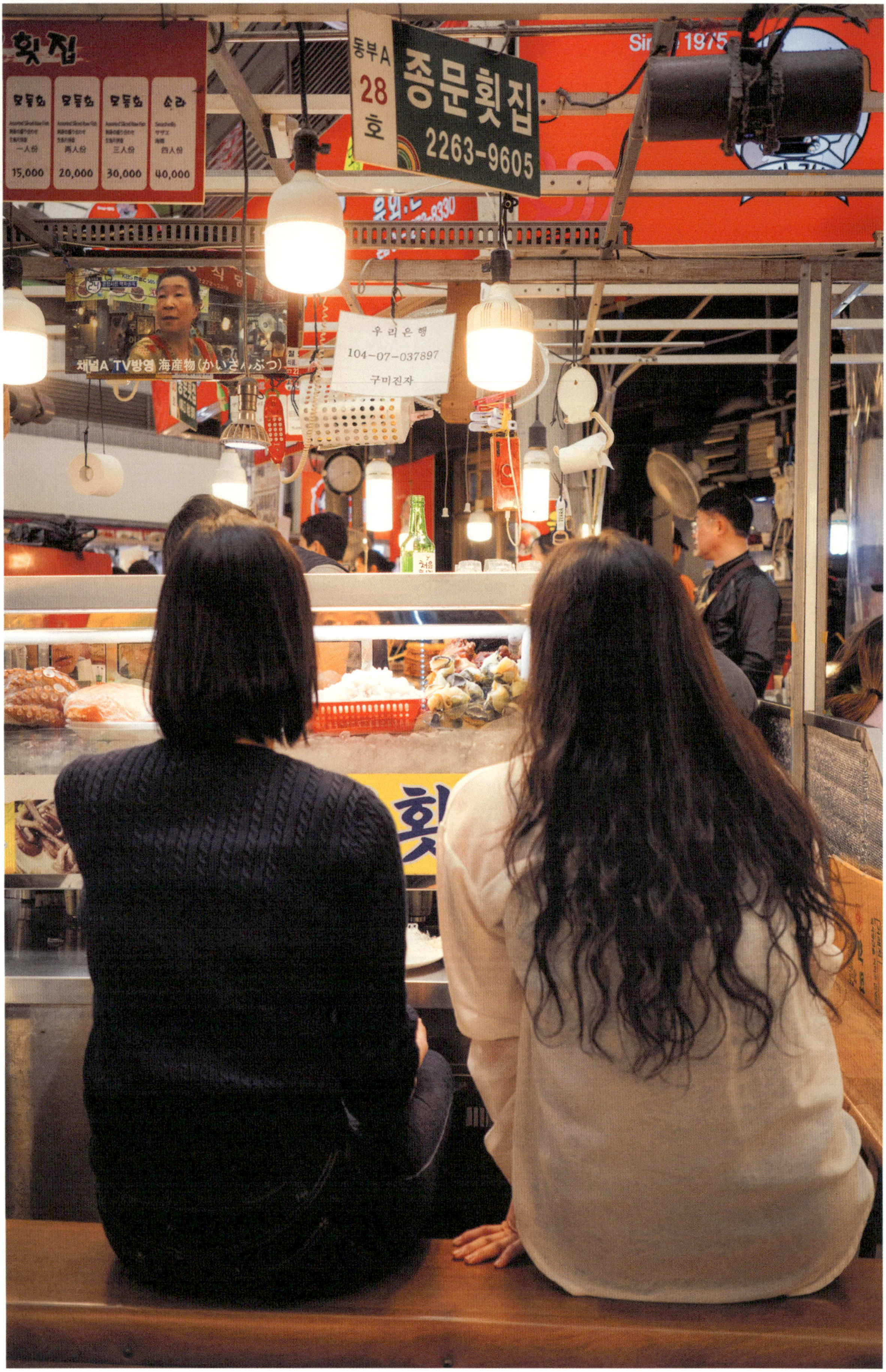
횟집
모둠회 모둠회 모둠회 소라
一人份 兩人份 三人份 四人份
15,000 20,000 30,000 40,000
동부A 28 호
종문횟집
2263-9605
우리은행
104-07-037897
구미진자
채널A TV방영 海産物(かいさんぶつ)

# BAP

밥

(bap) Beyond a simple word for food, "bap" is deeply embedded in Korean culture, symbolizing sustenance, happiness, strength, and a communal spirit that emphasizes sharing meals as a form of social connection.

## HOW KOREANS BUILD BONDS, ONE TABLE AT A TIME.

Meals in Korea are rarely solo affairs. They are communal events. During most meals, everything is shared except the rice and personal bowls of soup. The social aspect of Korean dining is so ingrained that some restaurants refuse to seat single diners. In K-dramas, when a character is eating or drinking by themselves, it's shorthand that they have hit rock bottom.

Since modern big city Koreans live in small apartments and many young adults live with their parents, friends rarely socialize within the home. They go out. Because of this, Korean cities teem with restaurants, pubs, and cafés. A TV food and travel show host I worked with observed that Seoul had more restaurants per capita than any city he'd ever visited.

Most every article and book on Korea marvels at how quickly it modernized, or even futurized. With this came a jolt in eating habits that still have strings tied to tradition. Japanese invaders in the 16th century were surprised by how much rice Joseon-era Koreans ate. Early photos of Korean tables showed the familiar banchan side dishes accompanied with what looks like a giant mixing bowl of rice—for one person!

People are surprised to learn that most popular Korean dishes are not that old. The average Korean knows that dak galbi (grilled chicken), budae-jjigae (army base stew), and Korean fried chicken came about in the second half of the 20th century. Yet many don't know that andong jjimdalk (soy braised chicken), kimbap (seaweed wrapped rice), and even the ubiquitous cabbage kimchi are also fairly new. In fact, cabbage kimchi, invented in the mid-19th century, didn't become popular until the 1950s. Post-war rice shortages forced the 1960s authoritarian government to impose standardized steel bowls to hold around a half cup of rice, which is standard today. Even though the world thinks of grilled meats when they hear of Korean food, meat itself was a luxury until the post-industrial economy. When someone suggests going out for Korean BBQ, they don't use that word. Instead, they suggest going out for "meat."

Young people have vacated their hometowns for the big cities in droves. More singles are living, and eating, alone. In Korea, this has become an issue serious enough for media attention. Restaurants, websites, social media accounts, and books have popped up catering to *honbap* — single dining. A little over ten years ago, single diners streamed live videos of mukbang celebrities gorging on feasts so they wouldn't feel like they were eating alone.

Another communal aspect of Korean dining is that when people go out to eat, they usually don't ask what particular restaurant or what type of cuisine everyone would like. Instead, they ask what specific dish they want to eat because everyone will be sharing that same dish. Even though rituals are more relaxed these days, certain hierarchies are observed. The elder, be it the grandfather, the boss, or just the "older brother" in a university group, orders the food. Their glass is the first poured. Yet it's also considered good form that the elder pays for at least the first meal.

The best places to eat are small mom-and-pops, where the proprietor treats you like a member of their family. If they feel a connection — *jeong* — you will likely get some extra treats. Yet these homey spaces are dying out. 20 years ago, one could easily walk into a baekban house, sit on the cozy heated floor, and just get served whatever the cook made that day. Fly-by-night franchises with touchscreen table tablets have pushed them out. Instagrammy dishes have replaced flavor and warmth.

A typical Korean night out goes in the sequence of 1-cha, 2-cha, 3-cha. The first cha is the main meal. The second cha is more of a pub. The third cha is more drinking or entertainment, like a private noraebang karaoke room. In groups of friends with lower social distance hierarchies, the polite thing to do is not to split the check. One person pays for one cha while another pays for another cha. It all evens out. Situations occur when diners argue over who gets the privilege to pay the check. One tactic is to pay the check while the other person is in the bathroom.

Korea's intense work culture has fueled the restaurant scene. Restaurants near business districts already have the banchan laid out on tables before the one-hour lunch rush. The places that serve food the quickest win the most customers. After lunch, workers line up for coffee to power them through the rest of the afternoon.

As the day starts to wind down, workers fear that their boss will announce an impromptu *hwesik*— a company-sponsored team dinner after work. Usually, these after-work dinners are announced ahead of time, but some bosses still expect everyone to cancel their plans to join him for dinner and drinks even when a gathering is last-minute. Attendance is technically not required, but it is. The goal is to create camaraderie in the workplace.

The ritual of who gets to pour to whom can get intense during these outings. Speeches are made with applause. Drinking games are played. Those who don't want to get drunk wisely make sure not to empty their glasses, so they don't get refilled. Hwesiks typically follow the 1-cha,

2-cha, 3-cha tradition. Yet many somehow "get lost" during the trek to the second location. Those who can stick with it get rewarded with hangovers and closer ties with their boss.

These days, the hwesik doesn't have the stranglehold it used to, yet it still frames how meals in Korea are communal experiences. They build ties. From the extended family celebrating a birthday to university pals going out for chicken and beer to the boss at a large multinational announcing a hwesik, Korea's dining scene is central to modern society.

JOE MCPHERSON

ZenKimchi

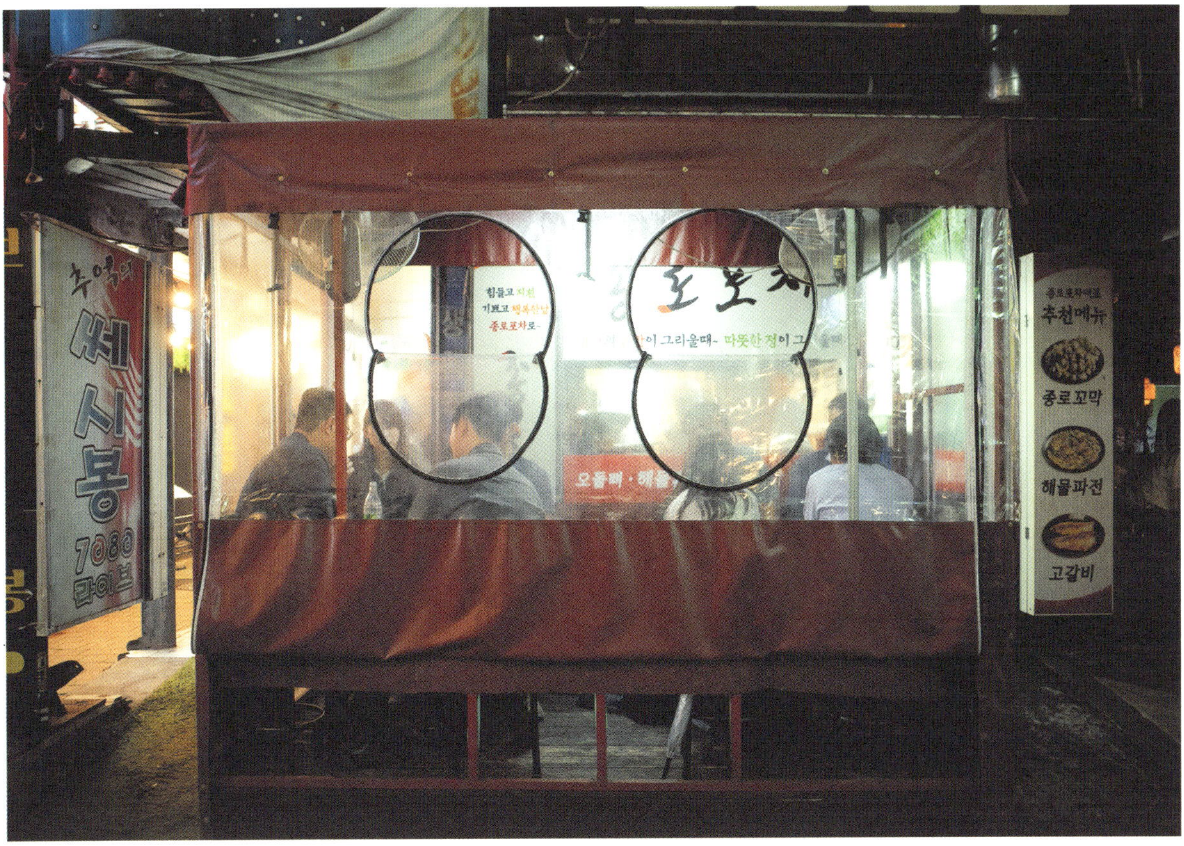


above: Pocha Street, Jongno 3-ga, Jongno District

+ page 20: Gwangjang Market, Jongno District

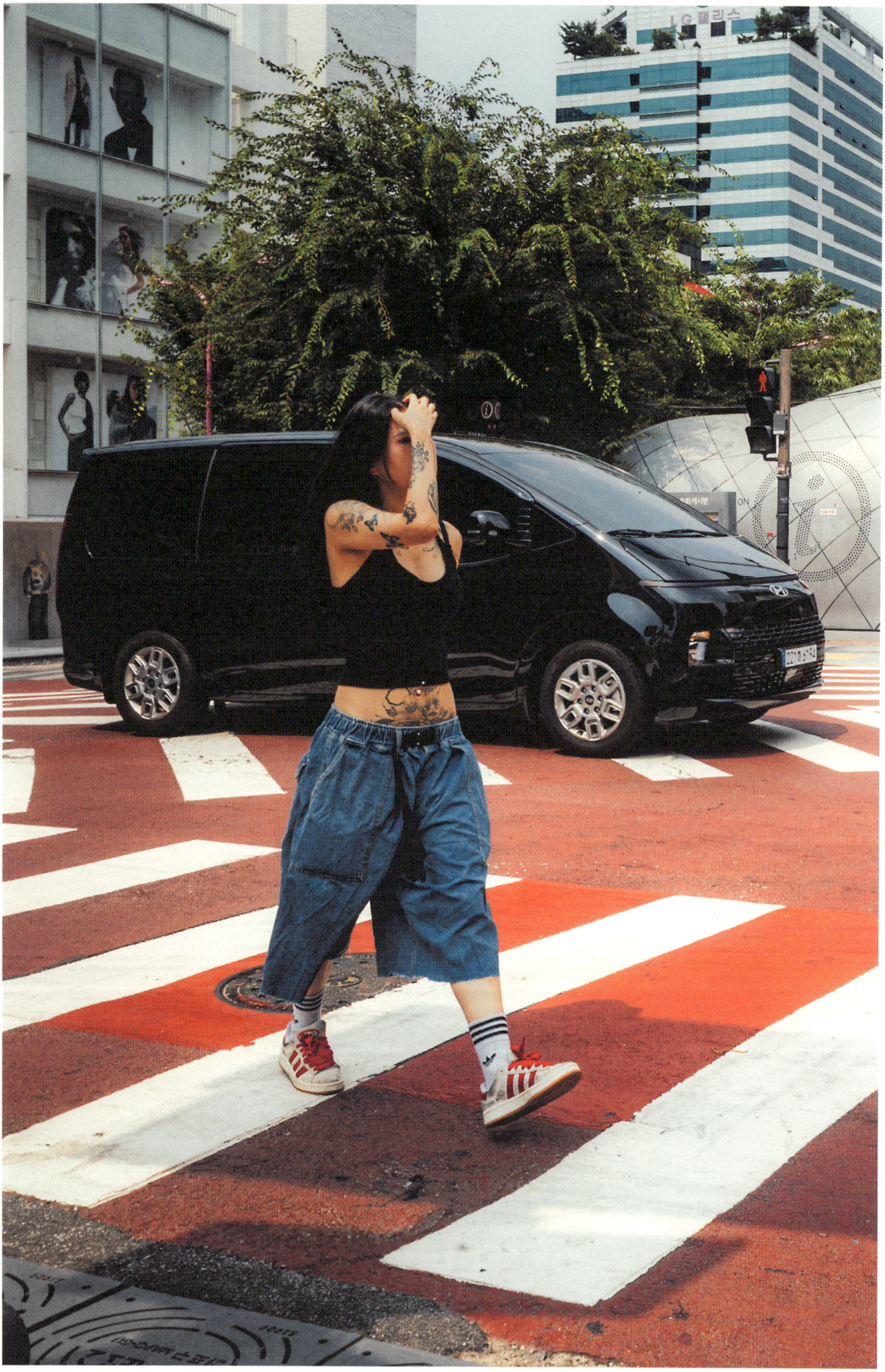

# RETURN TO SEOUL IN 24 FRAMES

서울

I hadn't been back to Seoul since I was seven years old, a wide-eyed boy in a children's choir, returning briefly to a country I had already begun to forget. My family left Korea when I was six. We immigrated to the U.S., like many families did in the 1980s, chasing opportunity, or perhaps running from the weight of history. I didn't have a say in it, of course. One day I was in Seoul, with the scent of doenjang-jjigae drifting from neighbors' windows, and the next I was in suburban America, speaking a language that didn't yet fit my mouth, eating cheeseburgers.

I don't remember much from that time. Trying to cut out a Ppopgi cookie, now made famous in *Squid Game*; looking out at the flooded Jamsu Bridge over the Han River; the feel of my grandfather's hand as he pulled me through a crowded market; and playing in the backyard of my grandparent's rural house which is now Gangnam. Memory is unreliable; it warps, hides, rewrites.

Coming back was like returning to a dream you're not sure was ever yours. Stepping off the plane, the air itself felt familiar. It wasn't a specific smell I could name, but just a comforting scent that settled deep in my bones. It was the first sign of what would become an onslaught of rediscovery.

Seoul didn't feel like a city; it felt like an atmosphere that was electric. A rush of contradictions that somehow made perfect sense. The old folded itself into the new with no apology. Ancient palaces like Deoksugung stood proudly amidst towering skyscrapers. In neighborhoods like Bukchon and Seochon (West Village), traditional hanok houses, with their curved tiled roofs, nestled comfortably beside trendy cafes and boutique shops.

A testament to a culture that reveres its past while hurtling into the future.

The old and new weren't just reflected in the architecture but in the people. I kept noticing the old people.

Maybe it's because mine worked into their 70s behind a cloud of steam and chemicals in the dry cleaning shop we owned in Chicago. Back then, I thought that's just what you did: you worked until your body said, "Stop." But in Seoul, there was something different. This place, for all its hyper-modern speed, never fully let go of the past. The people moved with a purposeful grace, a collective rhythm that was both efficient and deeply human.

At Sewoon Plaza in Jongno, I felt it most. Repairmen hunched over analog machines. Rows of VCR parts. Typewriters next to motherboards. Kids vaping on the street below, just a few steps from old men who looked like they'd stepped out of the 1970s, slacks, hats, cigarettes dangling from their fingers. There's a resilience in these pockets of Seoul. A refusal to disappear. The whole plaza felt like a metaphor: a relic of industry and noise, still breathing, still relevant. Like the city is saying, "You don't have to erase the old to make space for the new."

And the city doesn't.

You can step into a diner that feels frozen in time with linoleum floors, metal trays, and metal chopsticks and then watch a couple next to you livestream their lunch to a thousand followers. It's my childhood, except everyone has an iPhone. It's a drama set, except no one is acting. Or maybe everyone is.

One afternoon I sat on a bench at the National Museum of Modern and Contemporary Art, observing a father watching his son play across the museum's stone courtyard. Rain lingered on the ground. It felt like something out of an Ozu film, static, contemplative, suspended in time. That's how the whole trip felt. Like standing inside an old photograph and watching the people move.

Another time, my family wandered a quiet street in Bukchon, where we came upon a wall mural of two elderly lovers kissing. The text beside it read: "We Are Young." As my daughter zoomed past on her balance bike, she stopped, her tiny frame eclipsed by the figures on the wall. The scene felt impossibly cinematic, too perfect, too staged, and yet it was real. Life imitating art. Or maybe the other way around.

Memorable moments were countless. Wandering through the labyrinthine alleys of Namdaemun Market, I felt a tangible connection to generations of merchants and shoppers. The quiet reverence at a Buddhist temple, the lively chatter in a local restaurant. The many, daily protests around City Hall. Loudspeakers, signs, an old man shouting into a mic about justice or housing or reunification. I'd forgotten that in Korea, protest is a right, not a disruption. Freedom isn't whispered here. It's sung. Each experience chipped away at the layers of forgetting, revealing a deeper sense of belonging. Even the pools felt old-school in 2024 with plain signage, no frills. Just water and time. It reminded me of the public pools from my youth in the U.S. But there was something gentler in the light, more tender in its simplicity. Like the city knew I needed one last breath before going home.

But where is home?

That question followed me everywhere through the buzzing markets of Myeong-dong, through the mist on Inwangsan Mountain, through the soft lull of a subway car at 11 p.m. filled with sleeping students and ajummas hauling groceries. Home wasn't a place. It was a frequency. And for the first time in decades, I had tuned into it again. Seoul was no longer a childhood ghost. It was alive, flawed, fast, full of contradictions. But it held me. Just enough. Long enough.

So, I started taking photos, not to capture Seoul, because you can't, not really. But to see what my body remembered before my mind could catch up. Just to remember that I was there. That once, after 44 years, I came back. And the city in its own quiet, chaotic way welcomed me like a forgotten dream you suddenly realize was real all along.

This trip was more than just a visit; it was a quiet homecoming to a heritage I hadn't realized I'd forgotten. To strangers who looked like family. And to the real family I had been apart from for so long. It reawakened my whole being, forcing me to confront the fundamental question: Who am I? Seoul, with its electric energy, its vibrant colors, and its respectful embrace of both past and future, showed me that the threads of my identity, though stretched across an ocean and decades, were still firmly rooted here. I didn't want to let go of that feeling, that profound sense of connection and understanding. It made me wonder what my life would have looked like had we never left. Would I be one of those men fixing analog machines in Sewoon Plaza, surrounded by half-century-old radios and vacuum tubes? Would I be the dad walking his daughter through the museum, pointing to relics of my own youth? Or would I still be chasing something I couldn't name? The truth is, Seoul didn't give me answers. But it cracked something open. And in that opening, I found space. For memory. For loss. For wonder. For home.

JAMES CHOI

Beachwood Films

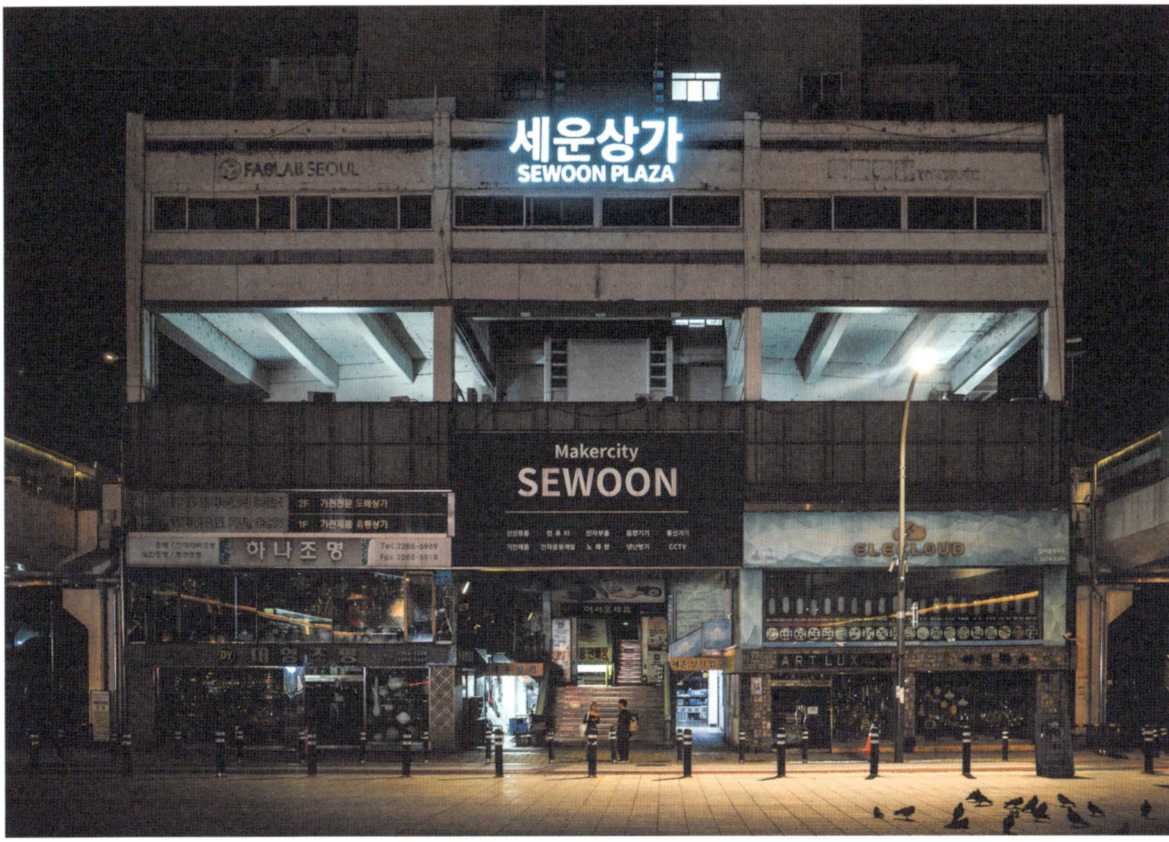


above: Sewoon Plaza, Jongno District

+ page 26: Hongdae, Mapo District

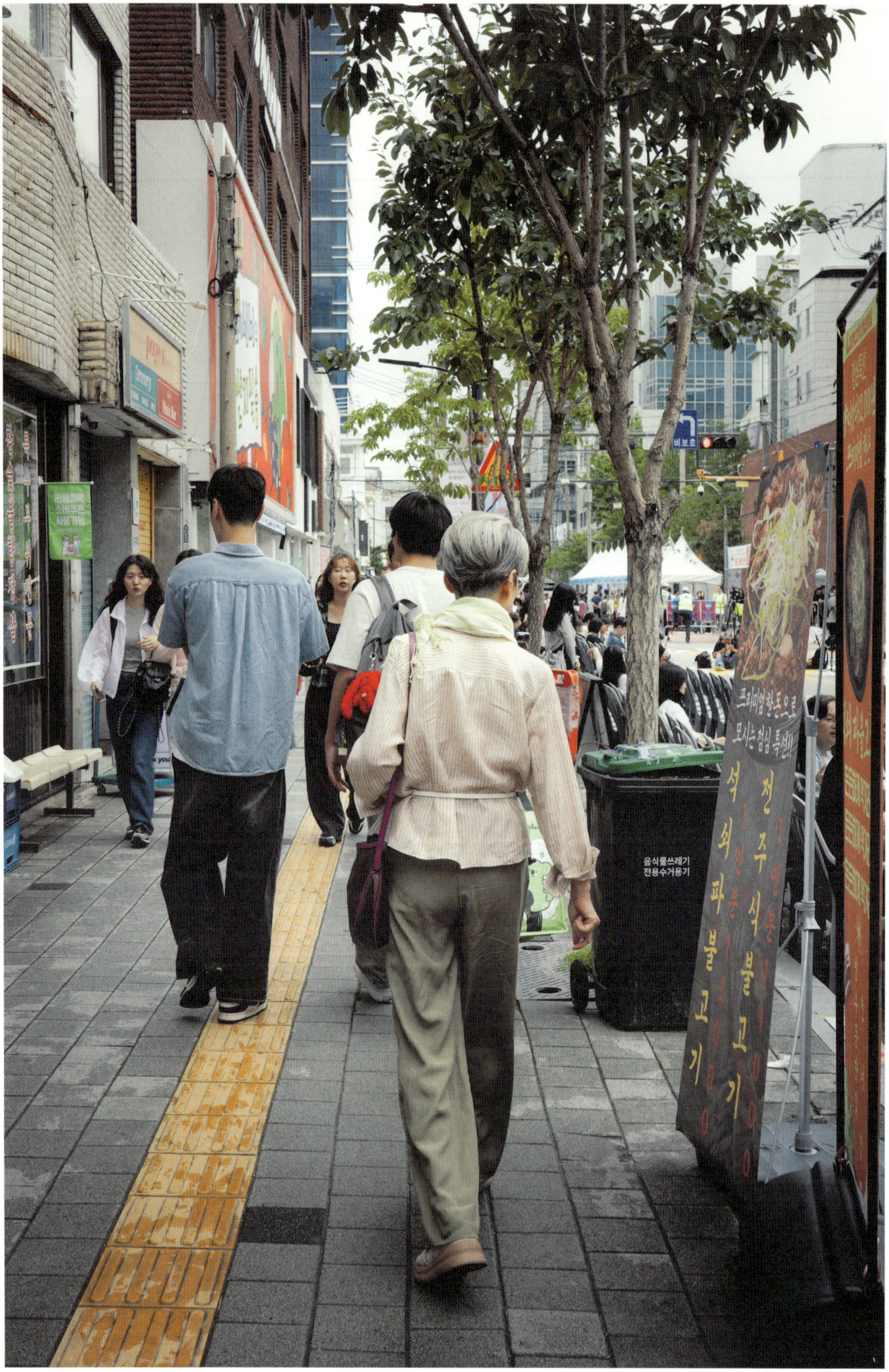
비보호
프리미엄한돈으로
모시는 점심 특선!!
전주식불고기
석쇠파불고기
음식물쓰레기
전용수거용기

# JEONG

정

(juh-ong) is a Korean concept of deep emotional bonds, affection, and attachment that is difficult to translate into English. It encompasses feelings of kindness, warmth, loyalty, and a strong sense of shared connection beyond etiquette or reciprocation in everyday social relationships. Jeong is intrinsically Korean because it represents a deep emotional and psychological bond fundamental to Korean society, emphasizing collective responsibility and interconnectedness.

**Seoul is one of the world's largest and most densely populated capitals, with nearly ten million residents living in a relatively compact basin framed by low mountains. Its scale is visible in the concentration of housing, the reach of its transit network, and the steady flow of people on the streets well into the night. Even as the city expands and redevelops at a rapid pace, long standing social patterns remain evident. Seoul seems to move with a practical, work driven pace shaped by a population accustomed to continual change. Small, routine interactions such as commuters sharing limited space, neighbors offering brief acknowledgments, and the quiet cooperation that guides daily movement reflect a consistency that persists beneath the city's growth. These details are modest, but they help explain how Seoul maintains a sense of continuity amid ongoing modernization.**

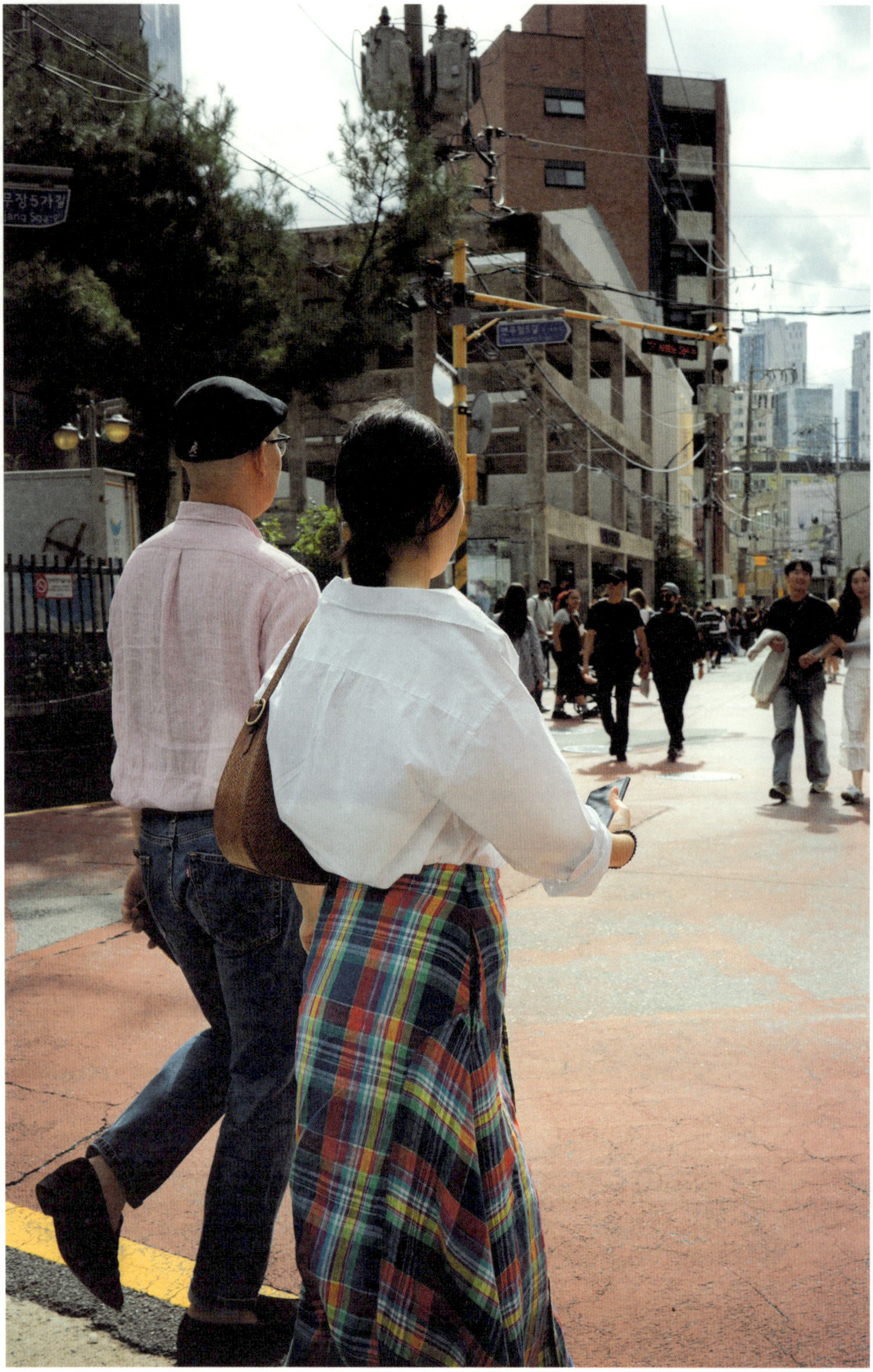

above + previous spread: Seongsu-dong, Seongdong District

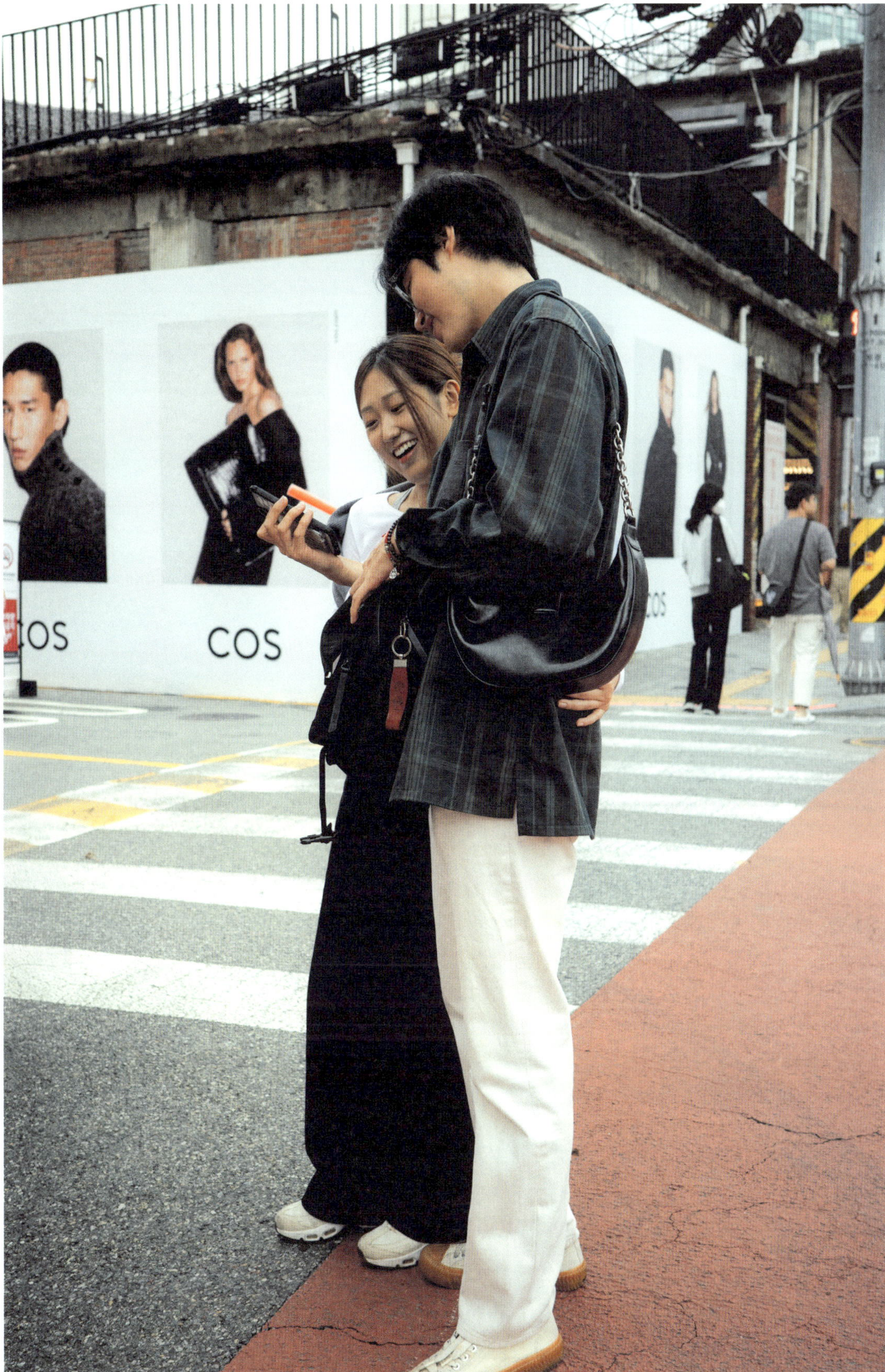

Seongsu-dong, Seongdong District

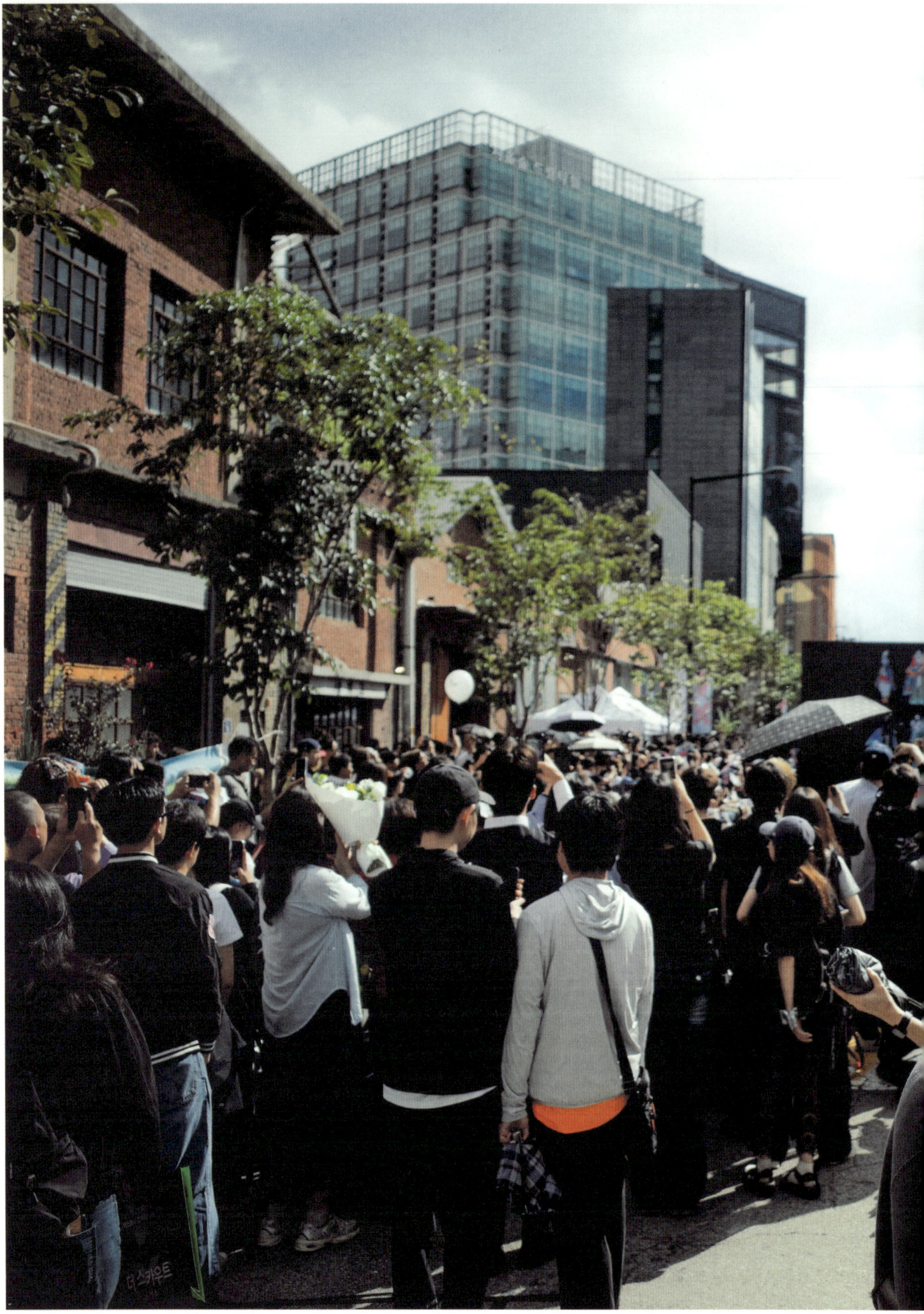

Seongsu-dong, Seongdong District

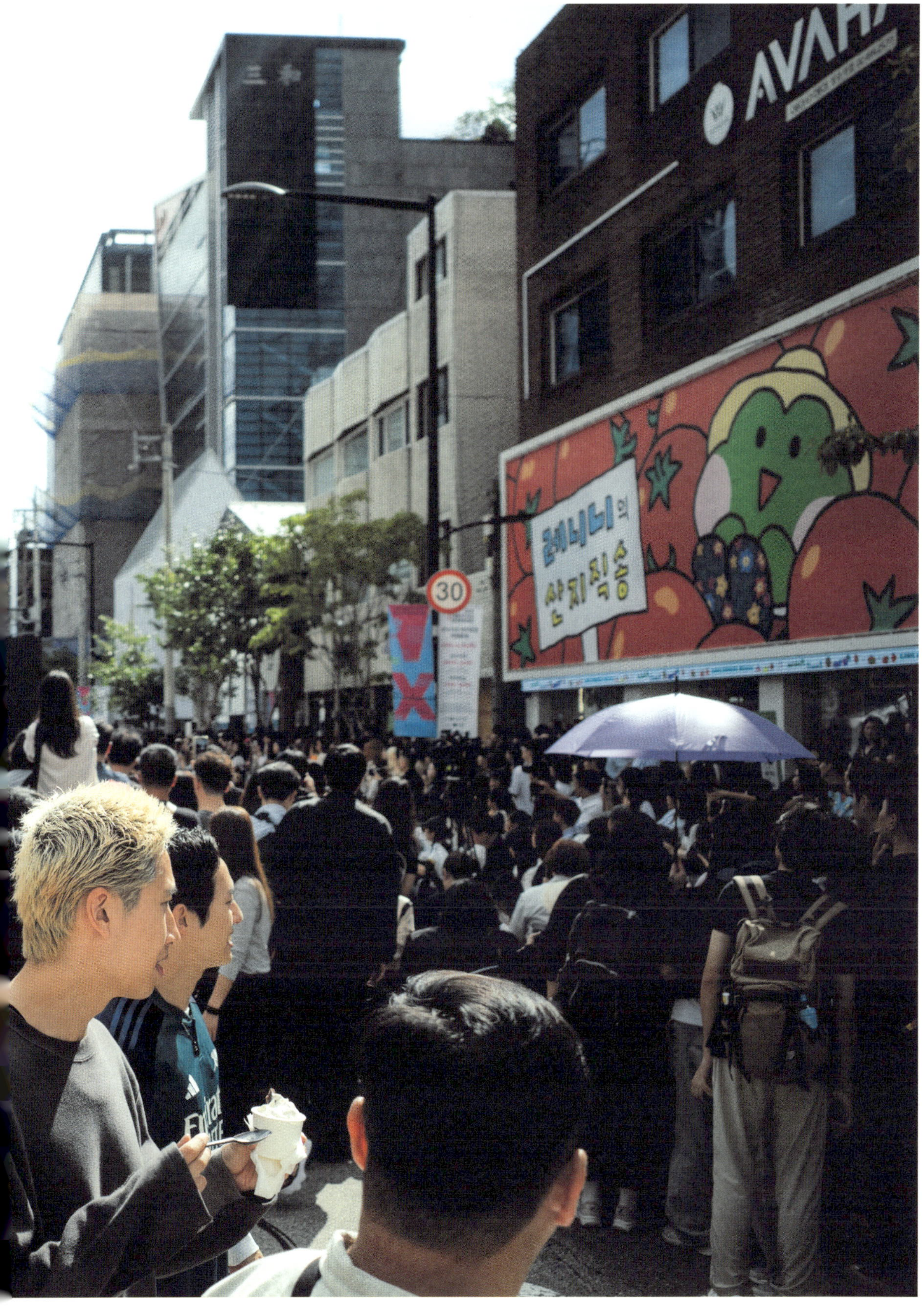
30
레니니의
산지직송

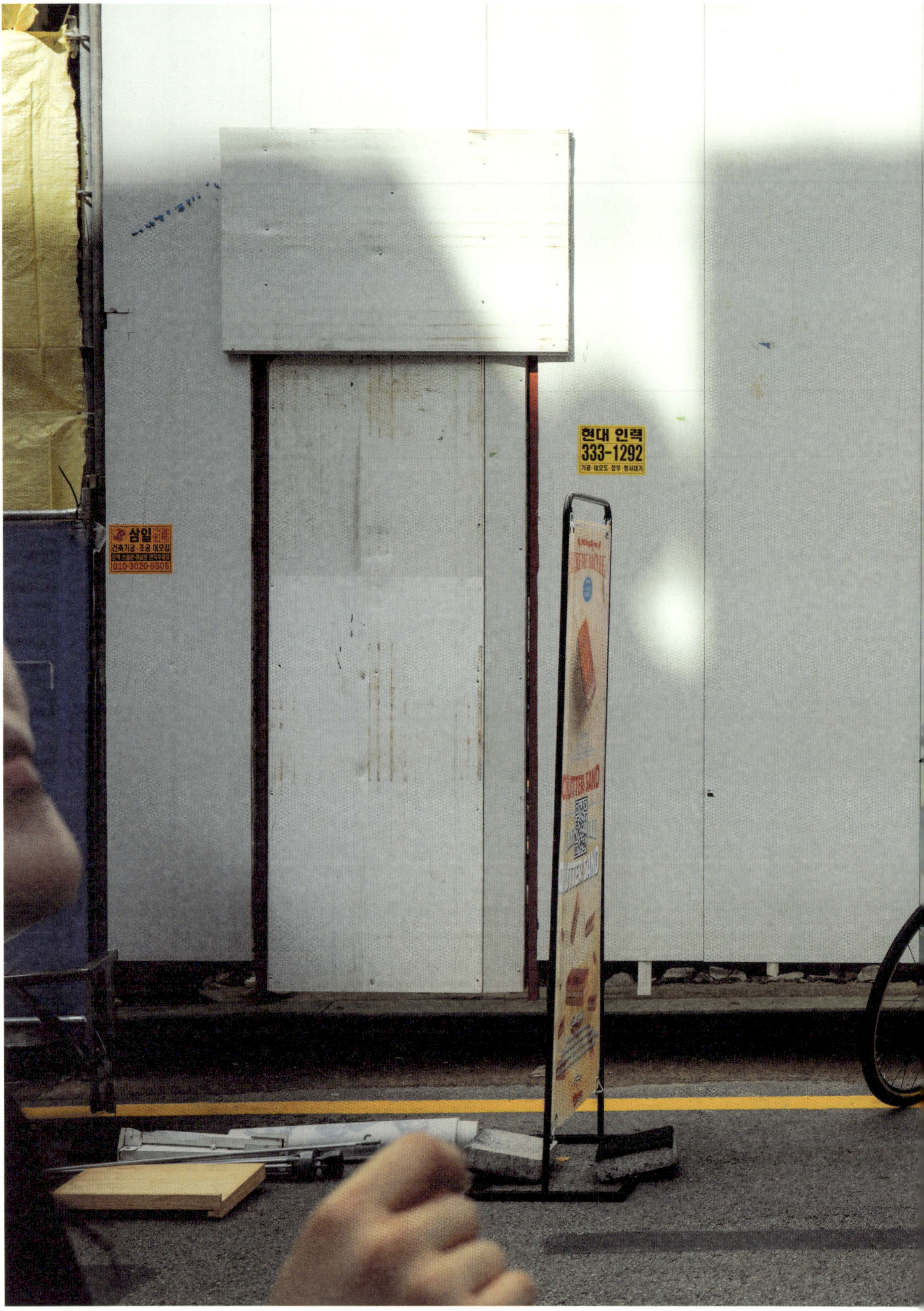


Seongsu-dong, Seongdong District

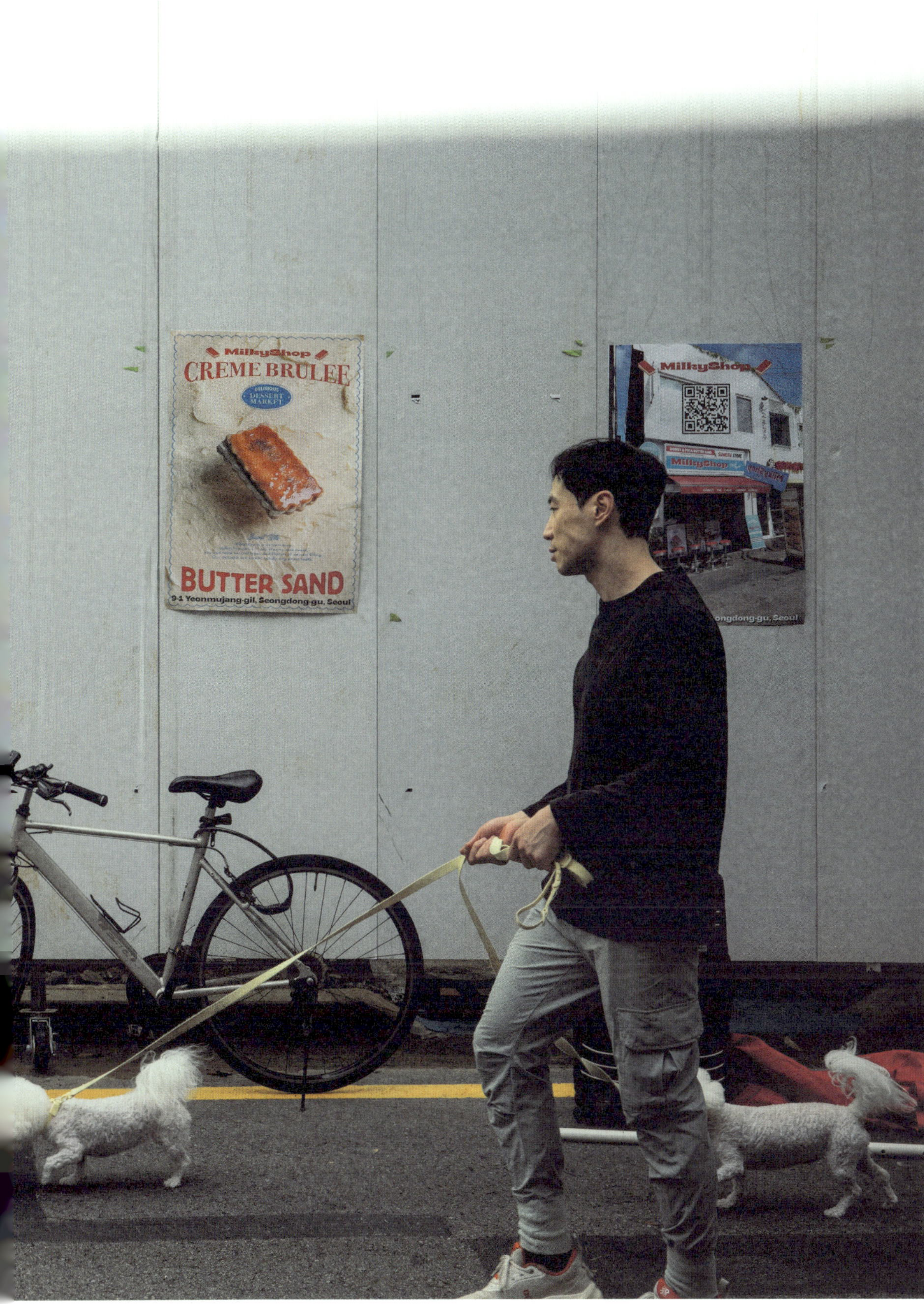
MilkyShop
CREME BRULEE
DELICIOUS
DESSERT
MARKET
BUTTER SAND
9-1 Yeonmujang-gil, Seongdong-gu, Seoul
MilkyShop
MilkyShop
ongdong-gu, Seoul

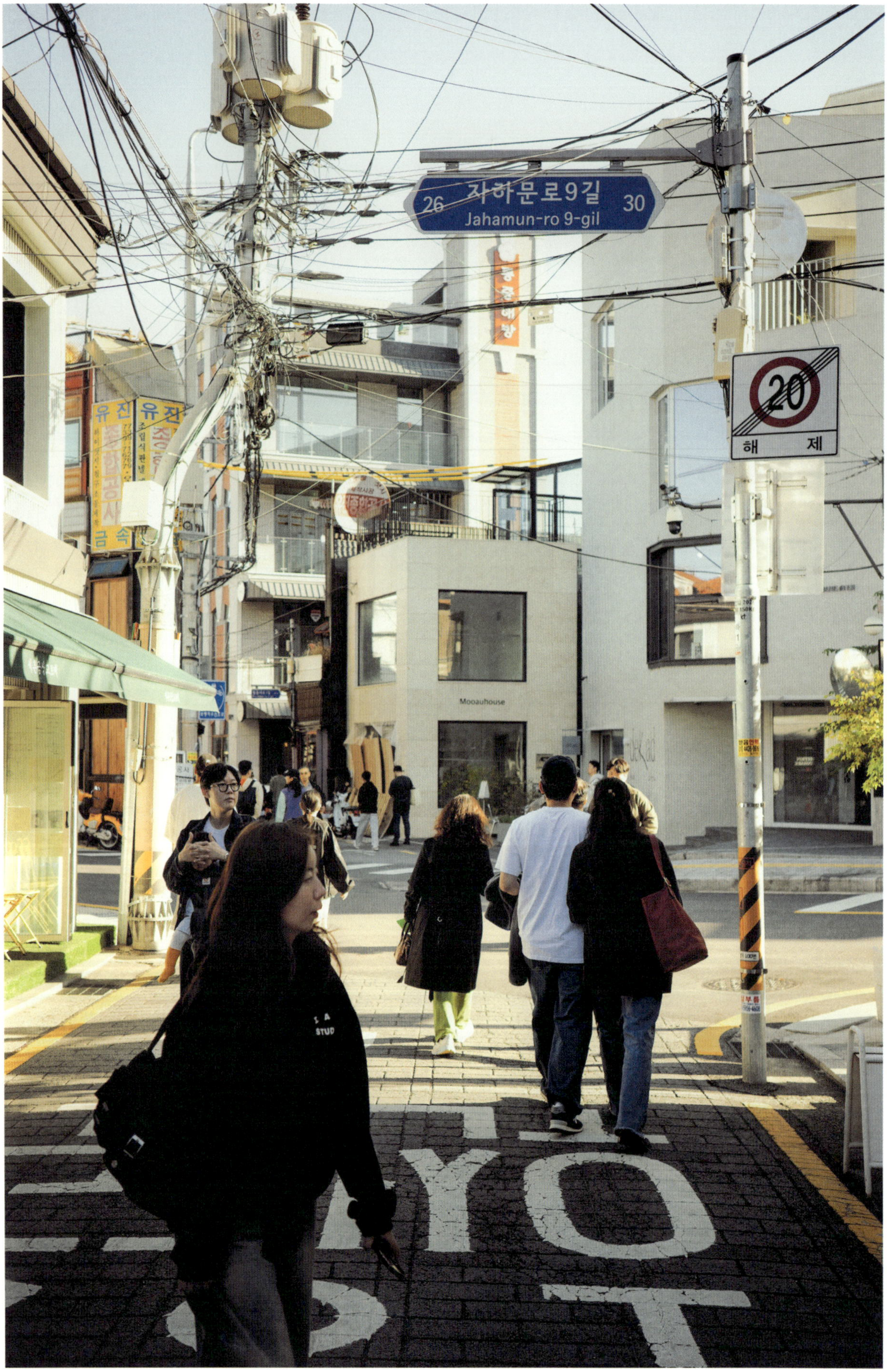
26 자하문로9길 30
Jahamun-ro 9-gil
20
해 제
Mooauhouse

left: Tongin-dong, Jongno District

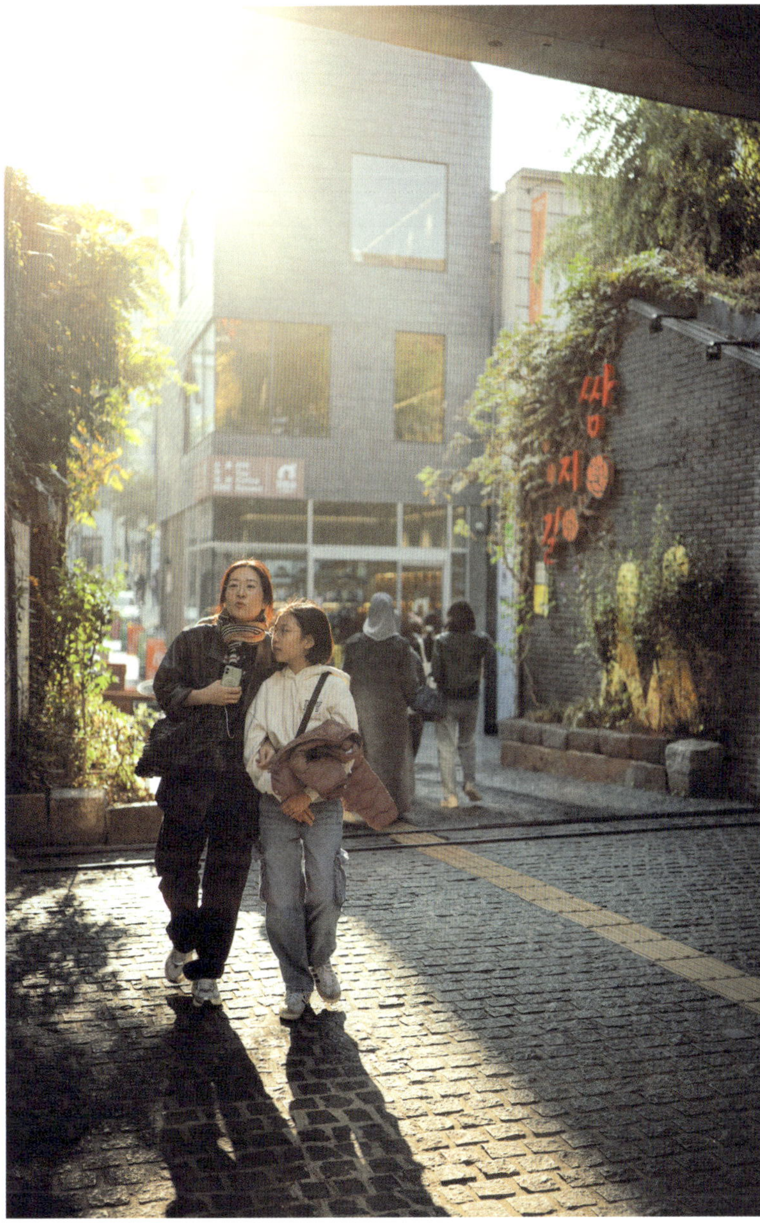


right: Insa-dong, Ssamzigil,
Jongno District

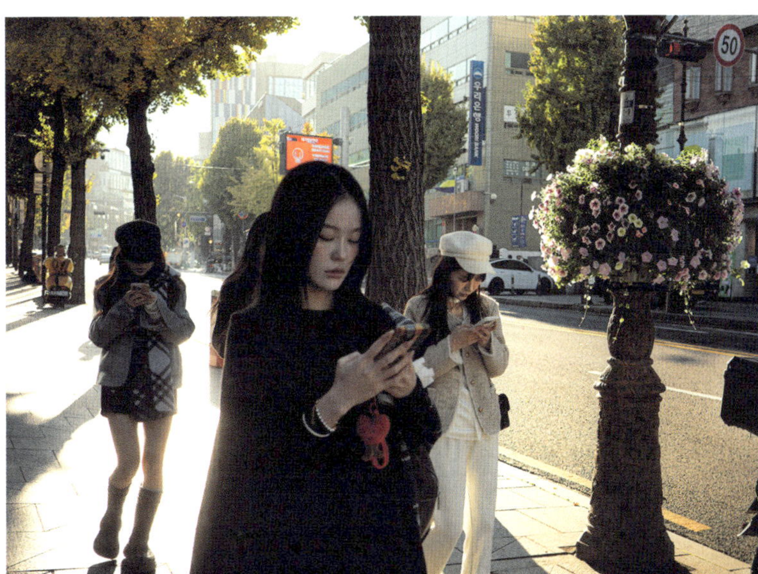


right: Itaewon, Yongsan District

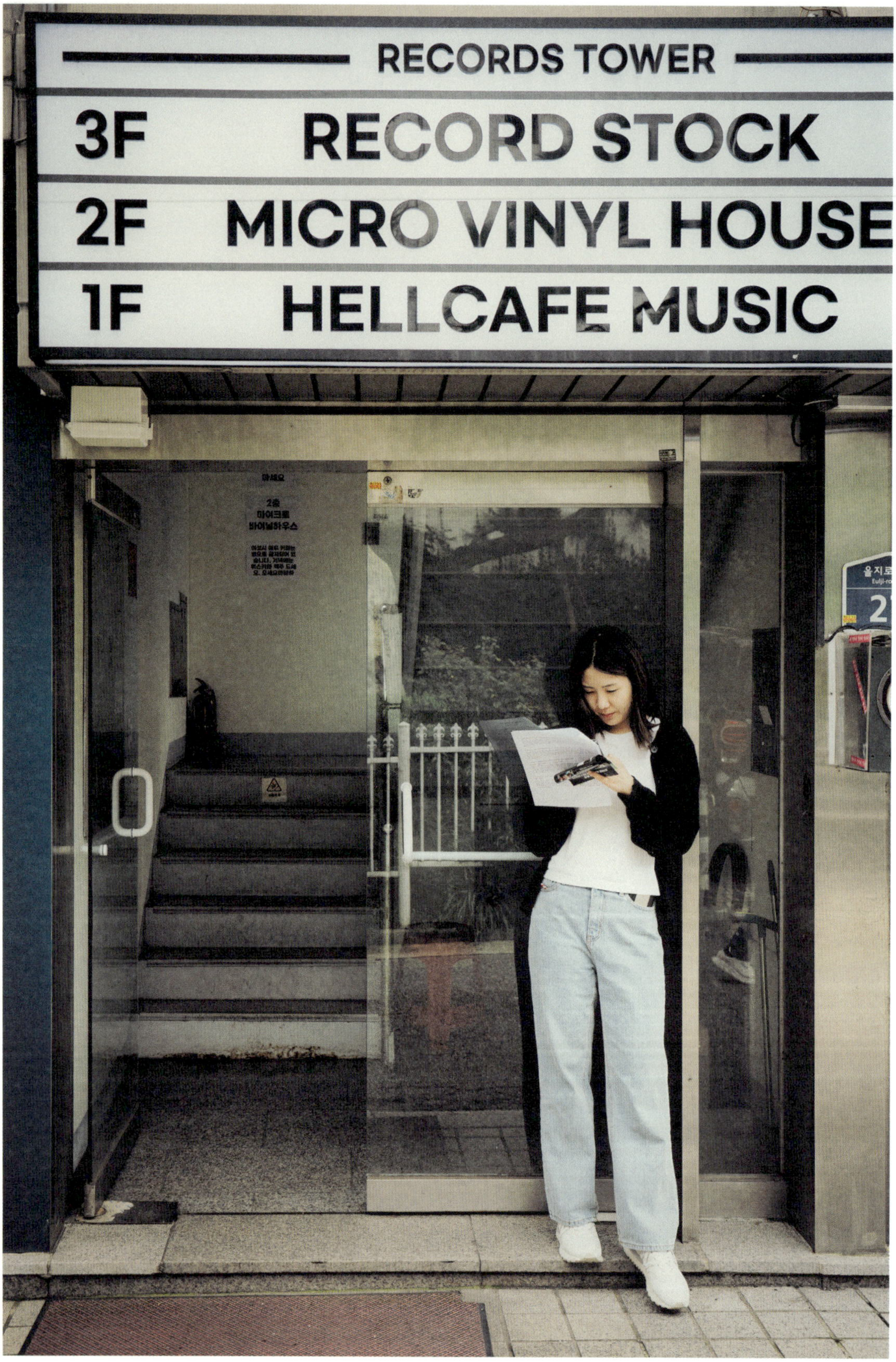


Jugyo-dong, Jung District

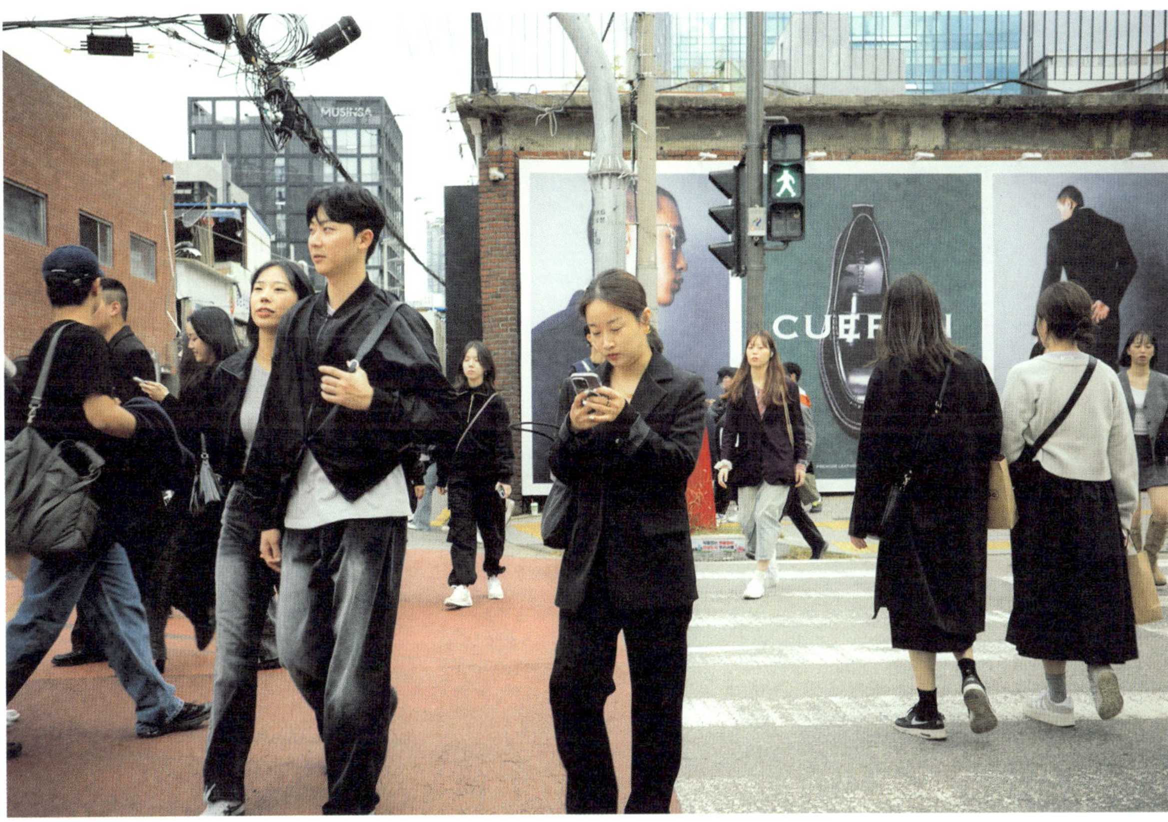


Seongsu-dong, Seongdong District

left: Tongin-dong, Jongno District

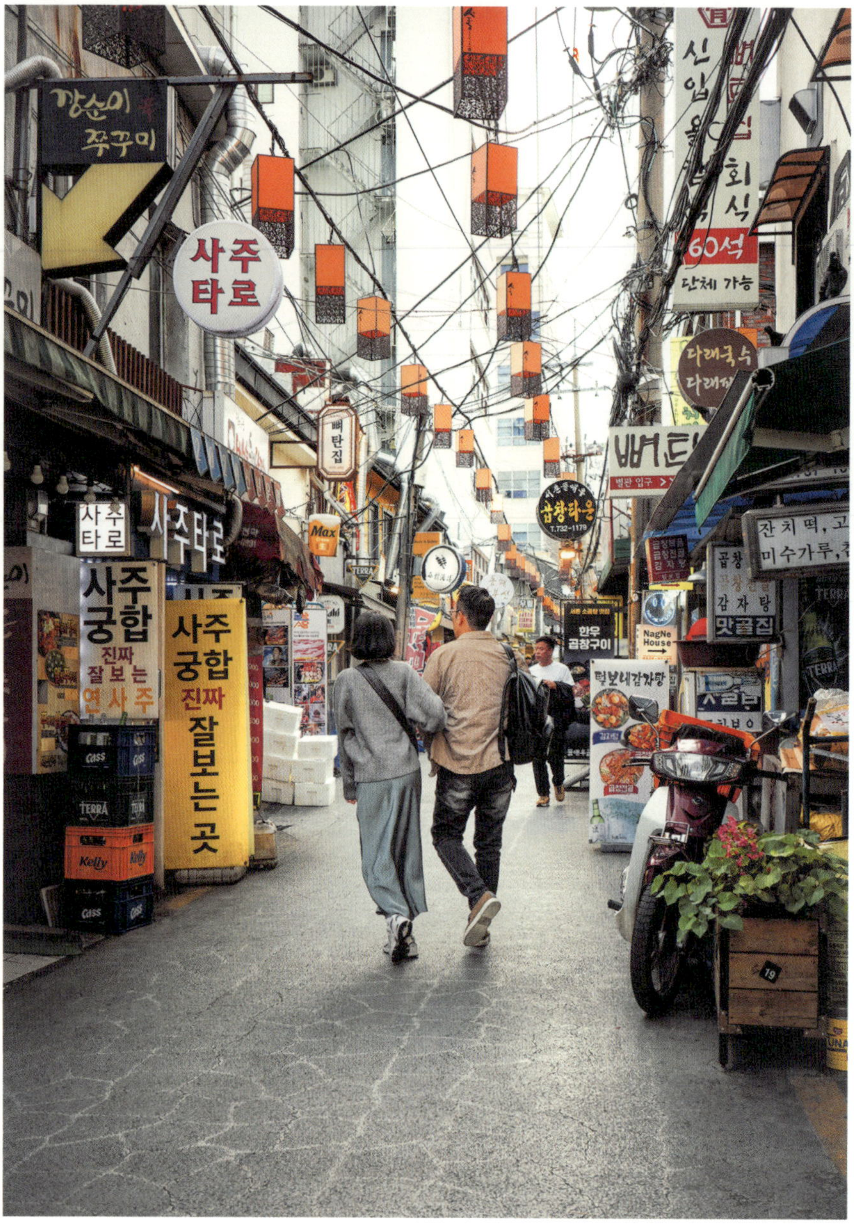


right: Garosu-gil, Gangnam District

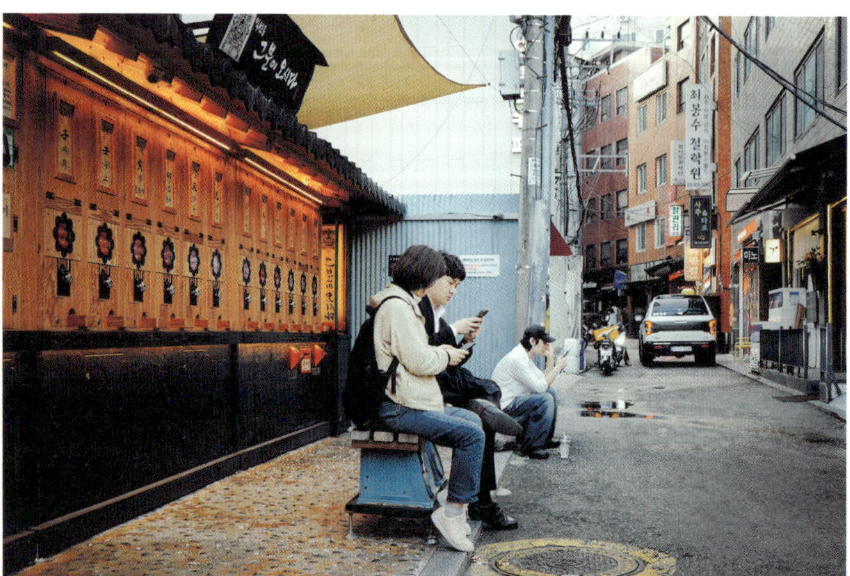


left: Ikseon-dong, Jongno District

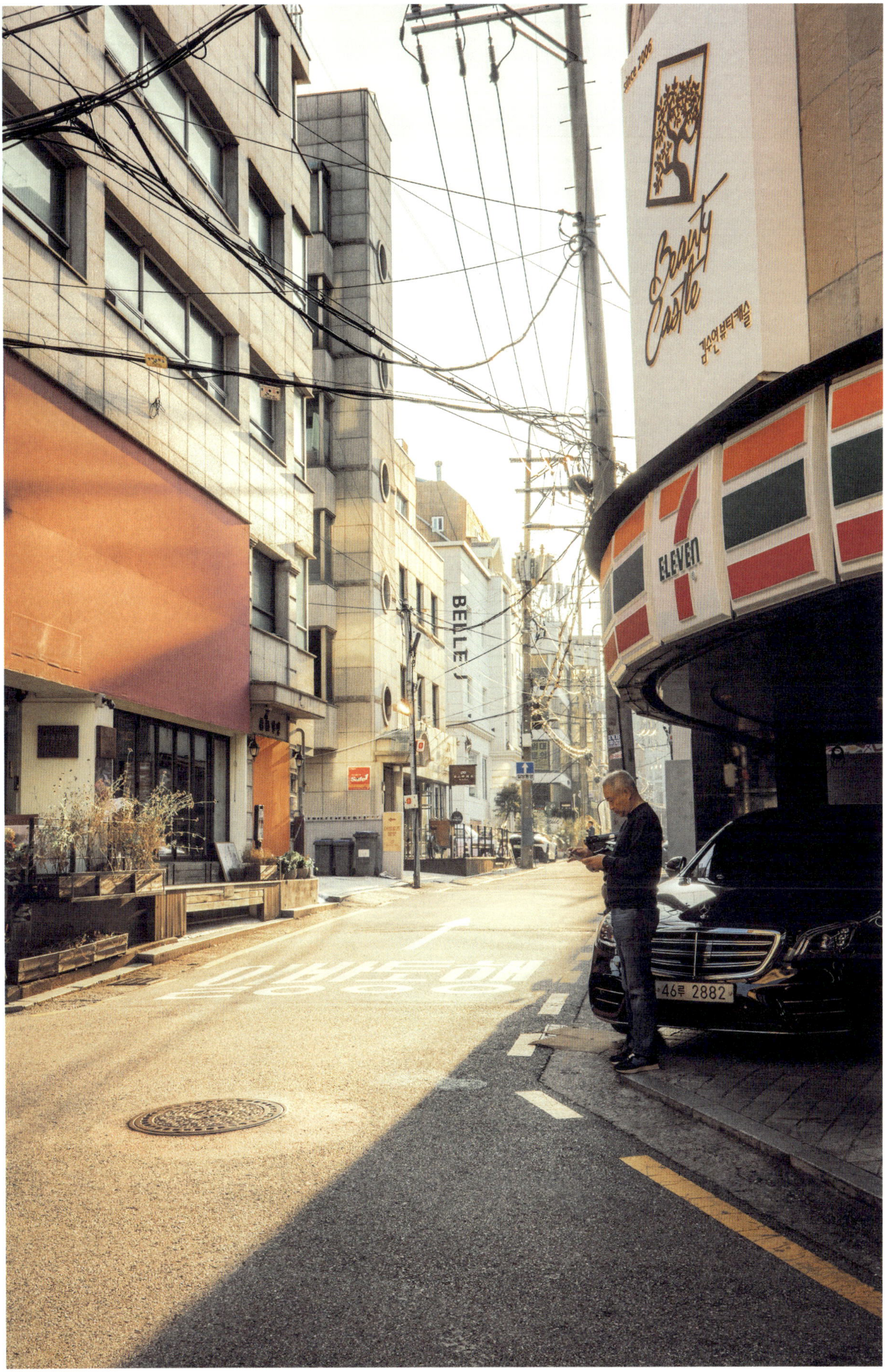
Since 2006
Beauty Castle
김수연뷰티캐슬
ELEVEN
BELLE
46루 2882

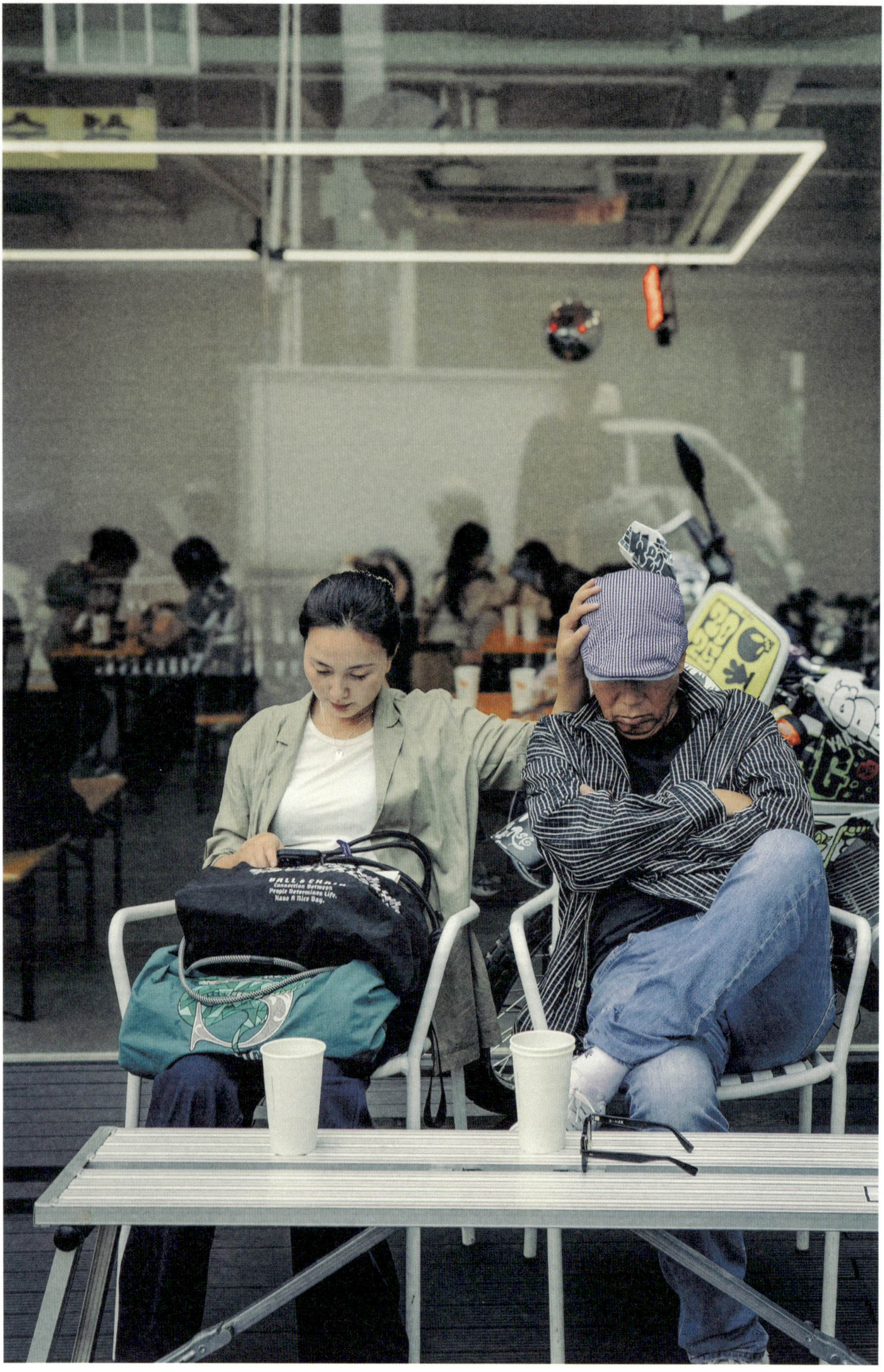
Connection Between
People Determines Life.
Have A Nice Day.

# NUNCHI

눈치

(noon-chi) refers to the ability to read a situation—picking up on unspoken cues, adjusting to others' needs, and sensing the right moment to act or speak. It's a form of social awareness that helps maintain harmony in both everyday interactions and more formal settings.

In Korean society, nunchi functions as an unspoken social skill that shapes how people navigate crowded cities, workplace hierarchies, and group settings. It allows individuals to sense mood and intention without direct conversation, helping interactions flow smoothly in environments where subtlety is valued. Many Koreans take pride in the idea of nunchi, seeing it as a uniquely Korean form of emotional intelligence, something learned through culture, daily life, and shared expectations rather than formal rules. In Seoul's dense and fast-moving pace, nunchi becomes a practical tool for moving through relationships and public spaces with minimal friction, anchoring a distinct aspect of contemporary social behavior.

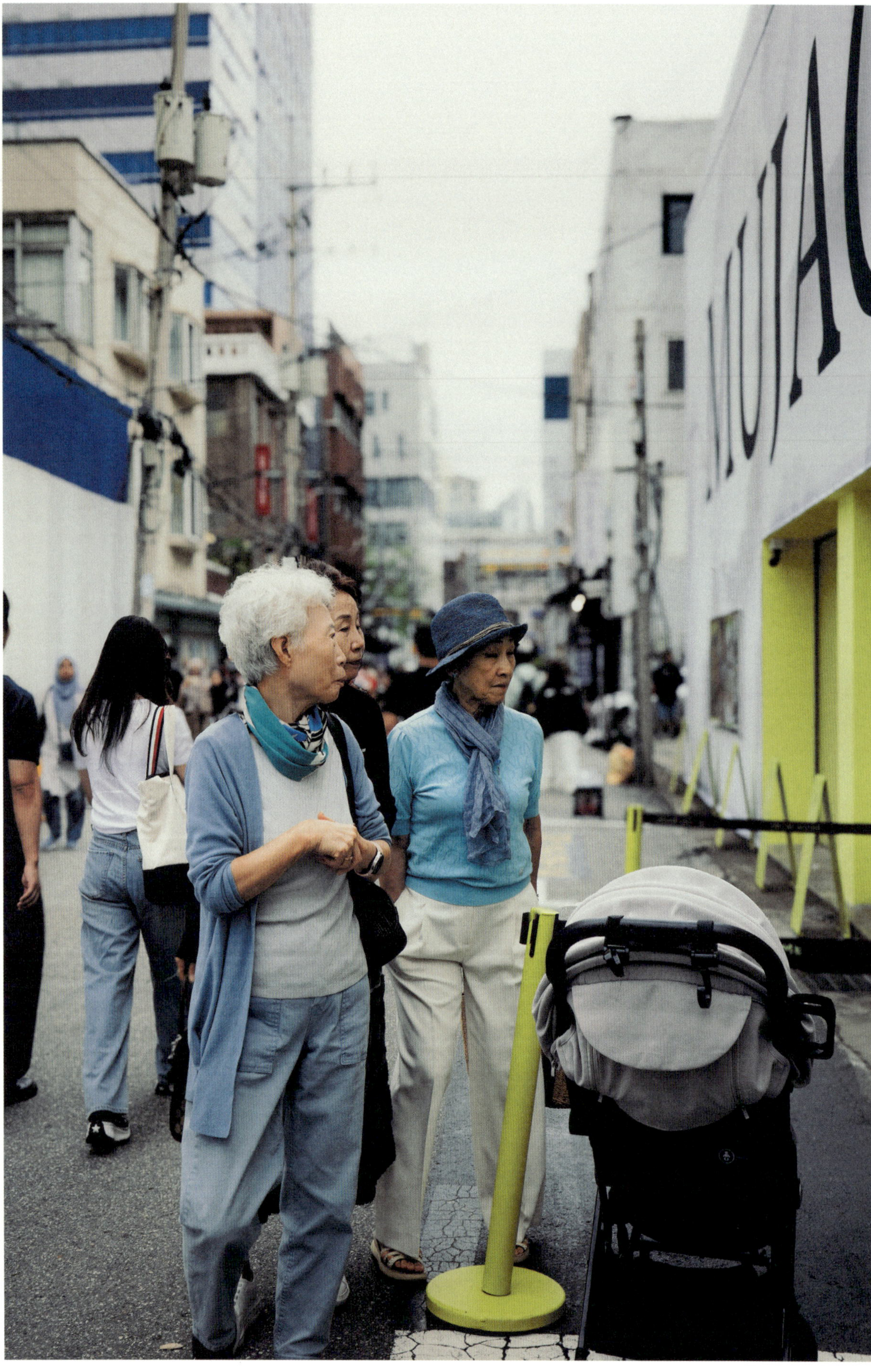

left + previous spread:
Seongsu-dong, Seongdong District

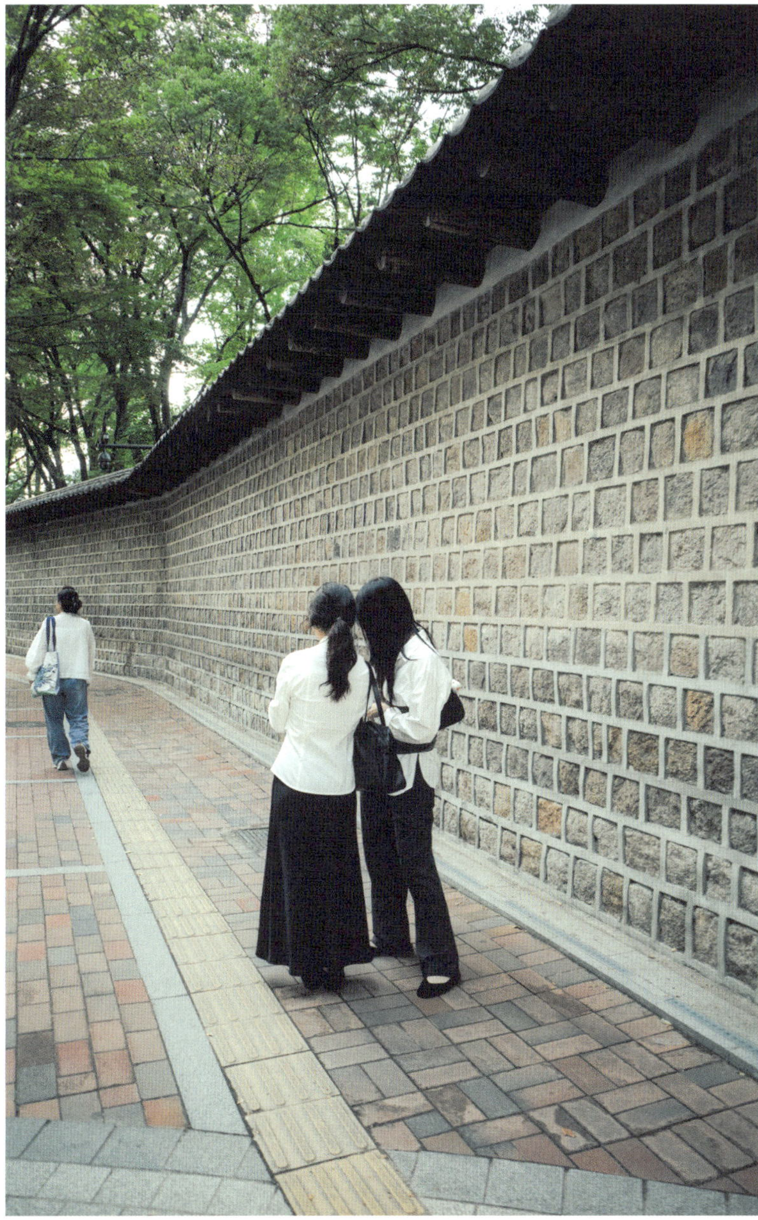

right: Deoksugung-gil, Jung District

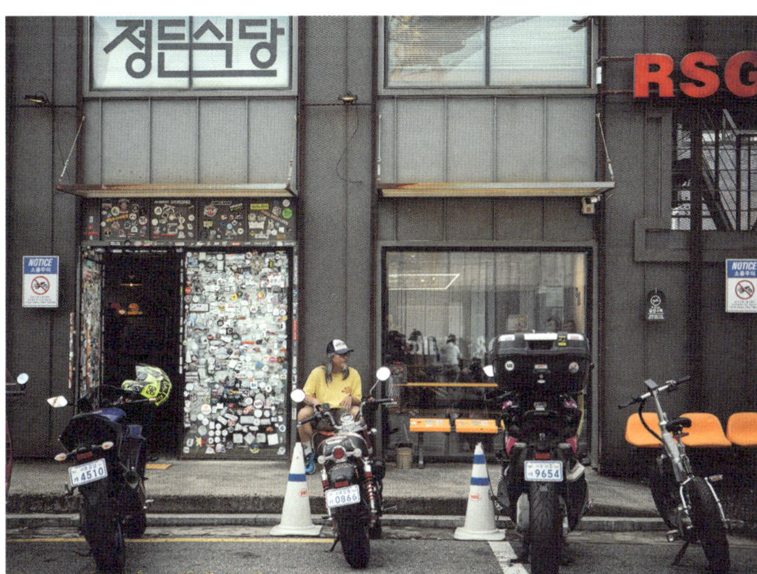


right: Seongsu-dong, Seongdong District

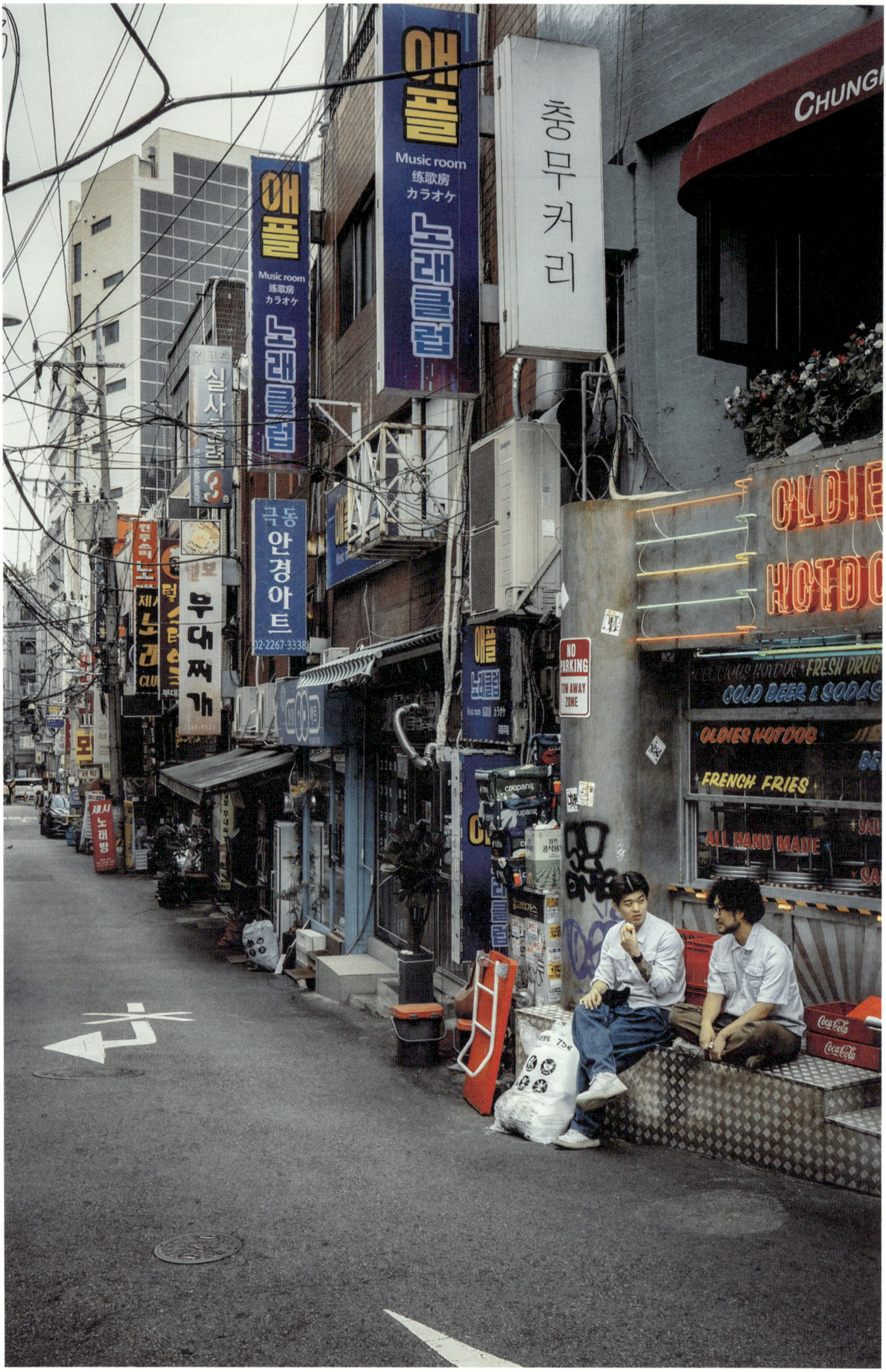

애플
Music room
练歌房
カラオケ
노래클럽
충무커리
극동
안경아트
02-2267-3338
우대찌개
NO PARKING
TOW AWAY ZONE
COLD BEER & SODAS
OLDIES HOTDOG
FRENCH FRIES
ALL HAND MADE
노래방

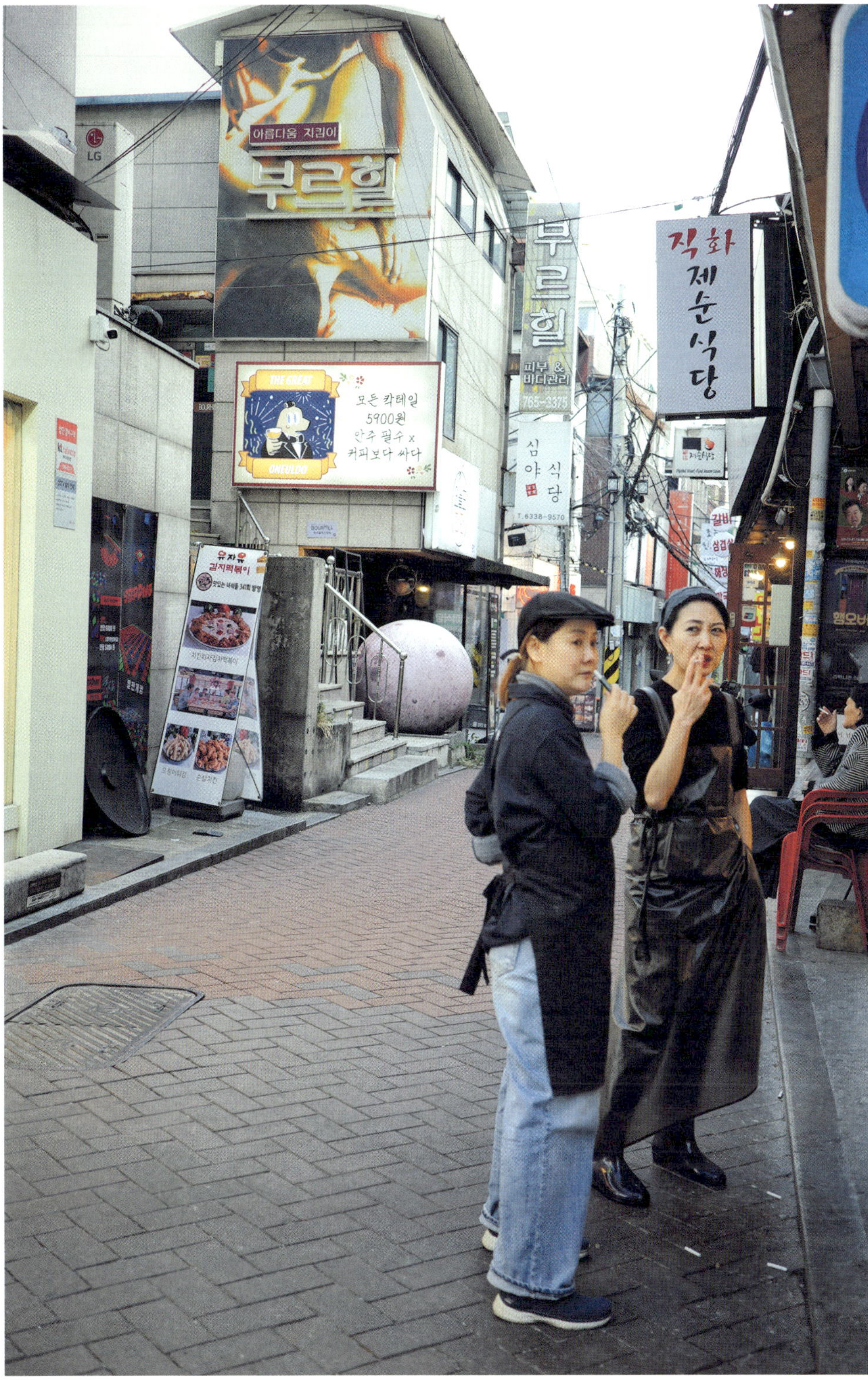


left: Chungmu-ro, Jung District + above: Daehak-ro, Jongno District

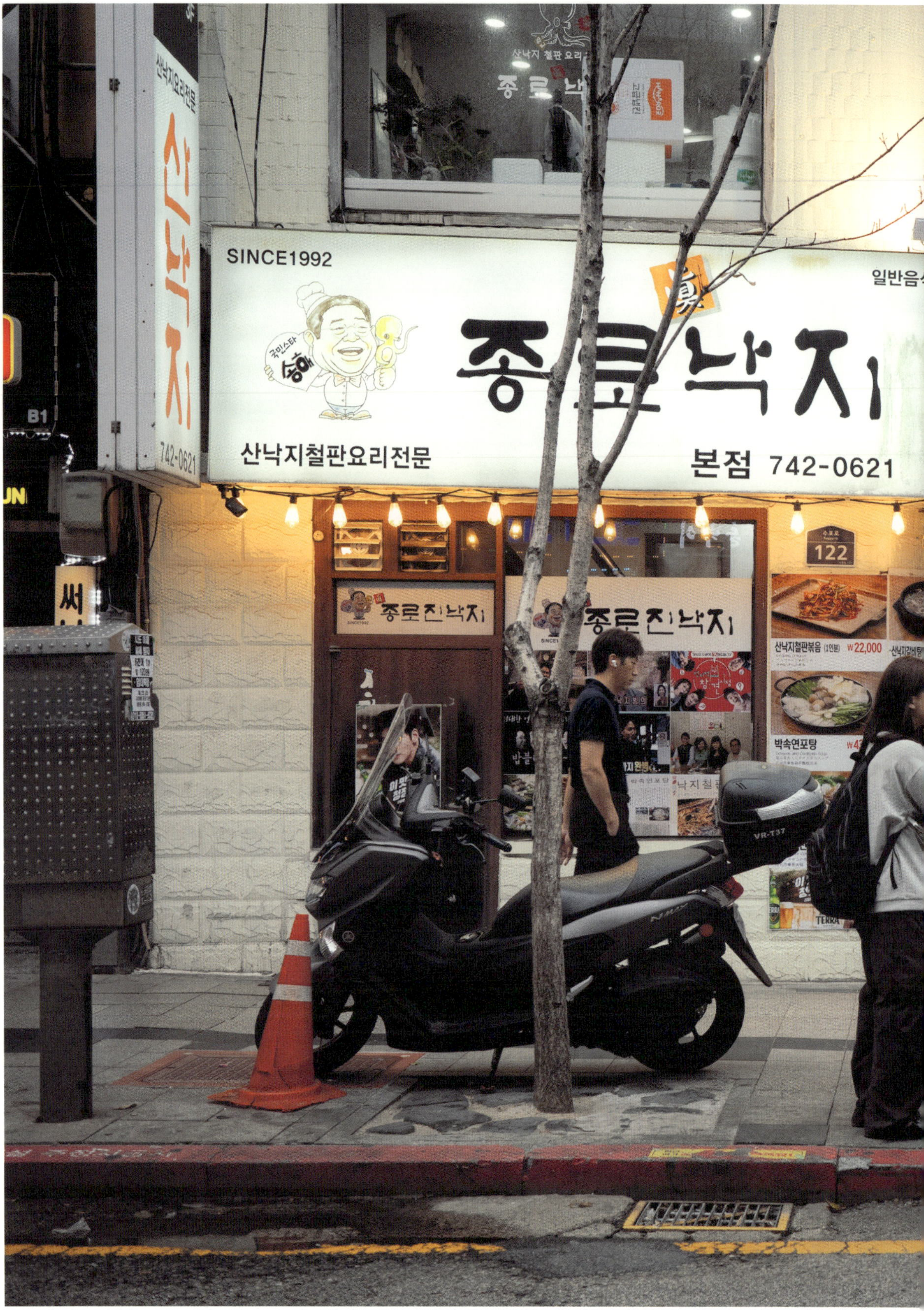


Jongno 3-ga, Jongno District

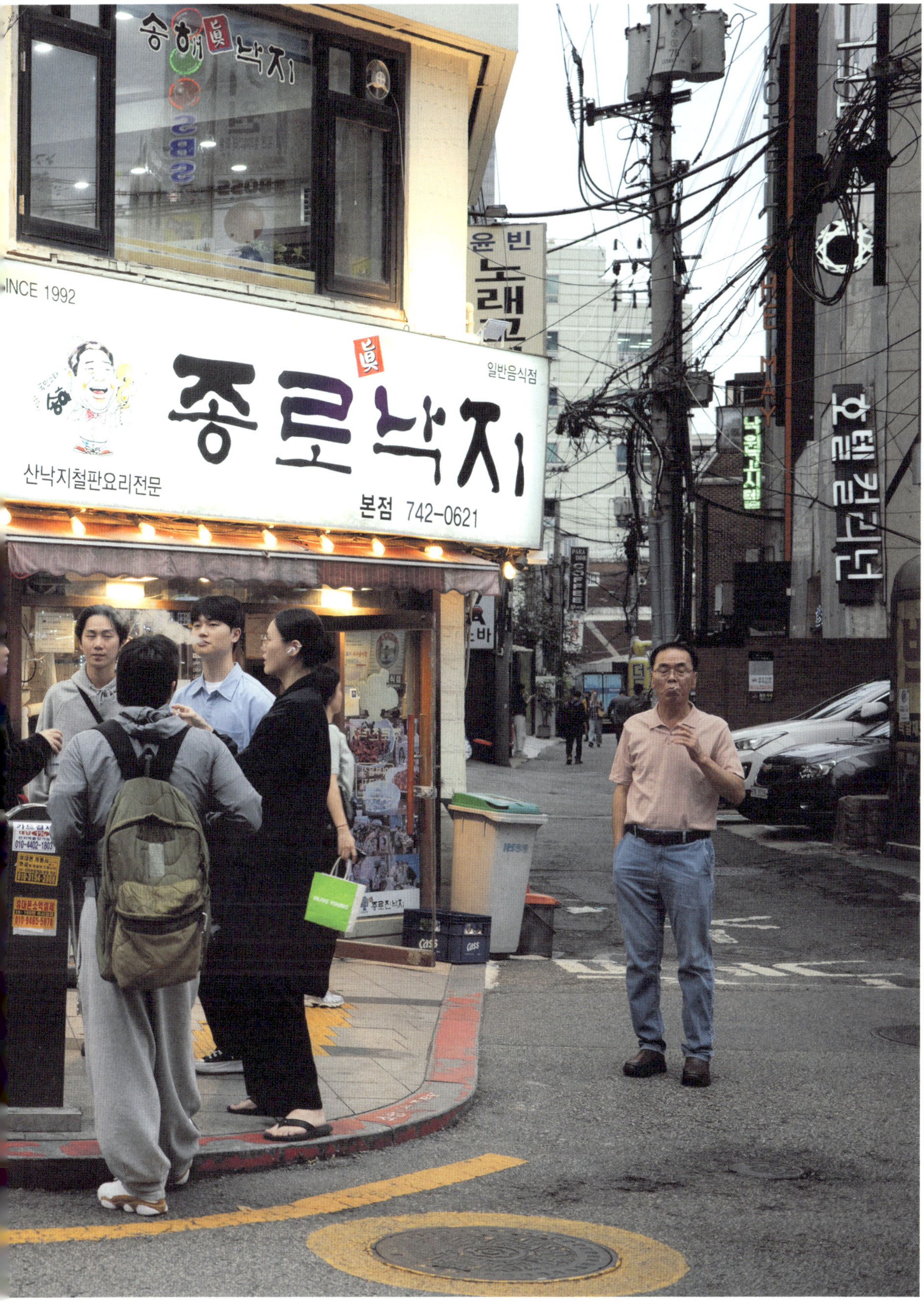
INCE 1992
종로낙지
일반음식점
산낙지철판요리전문
본점 742-0621

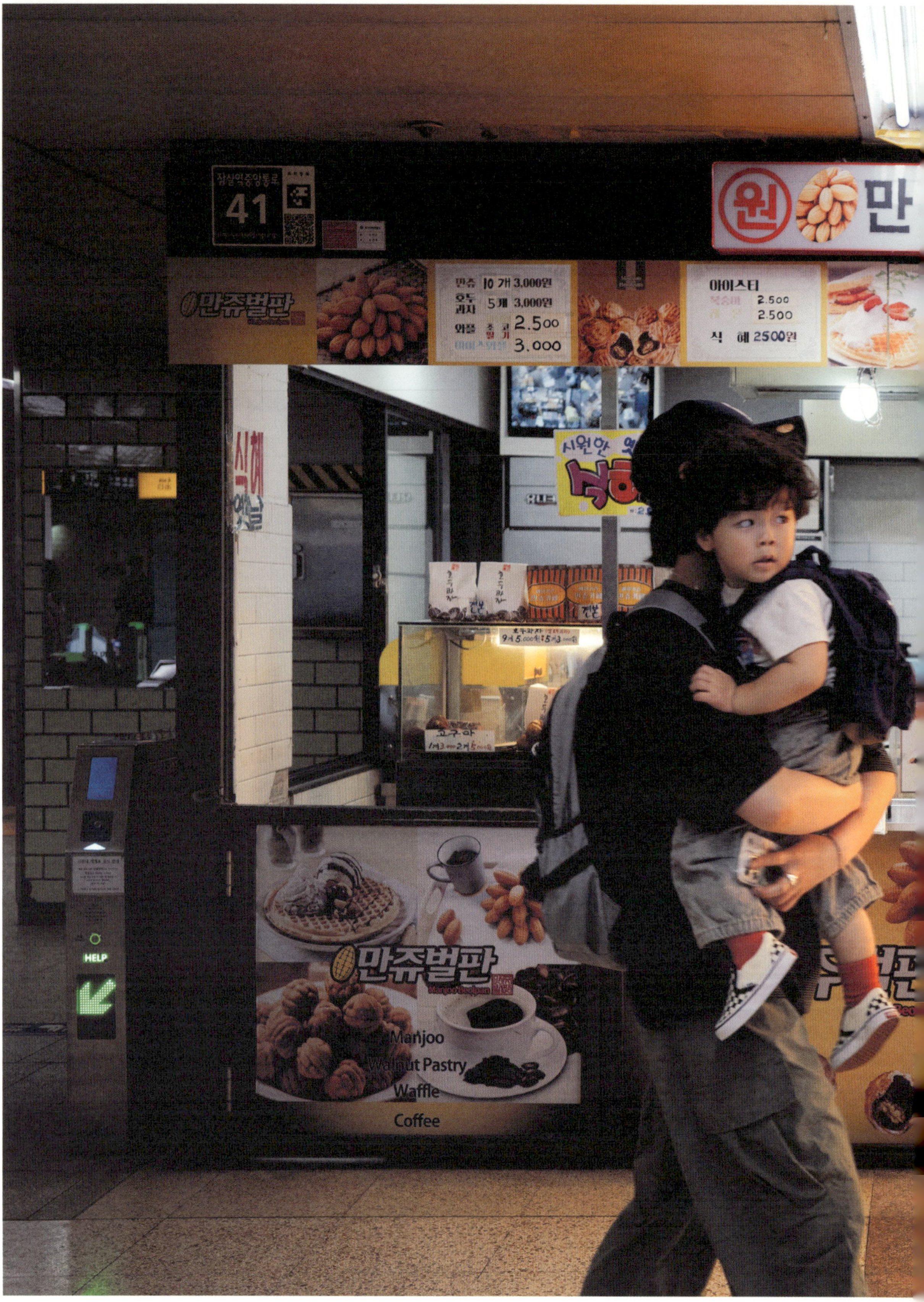


Jamsil-dong, Songpa District

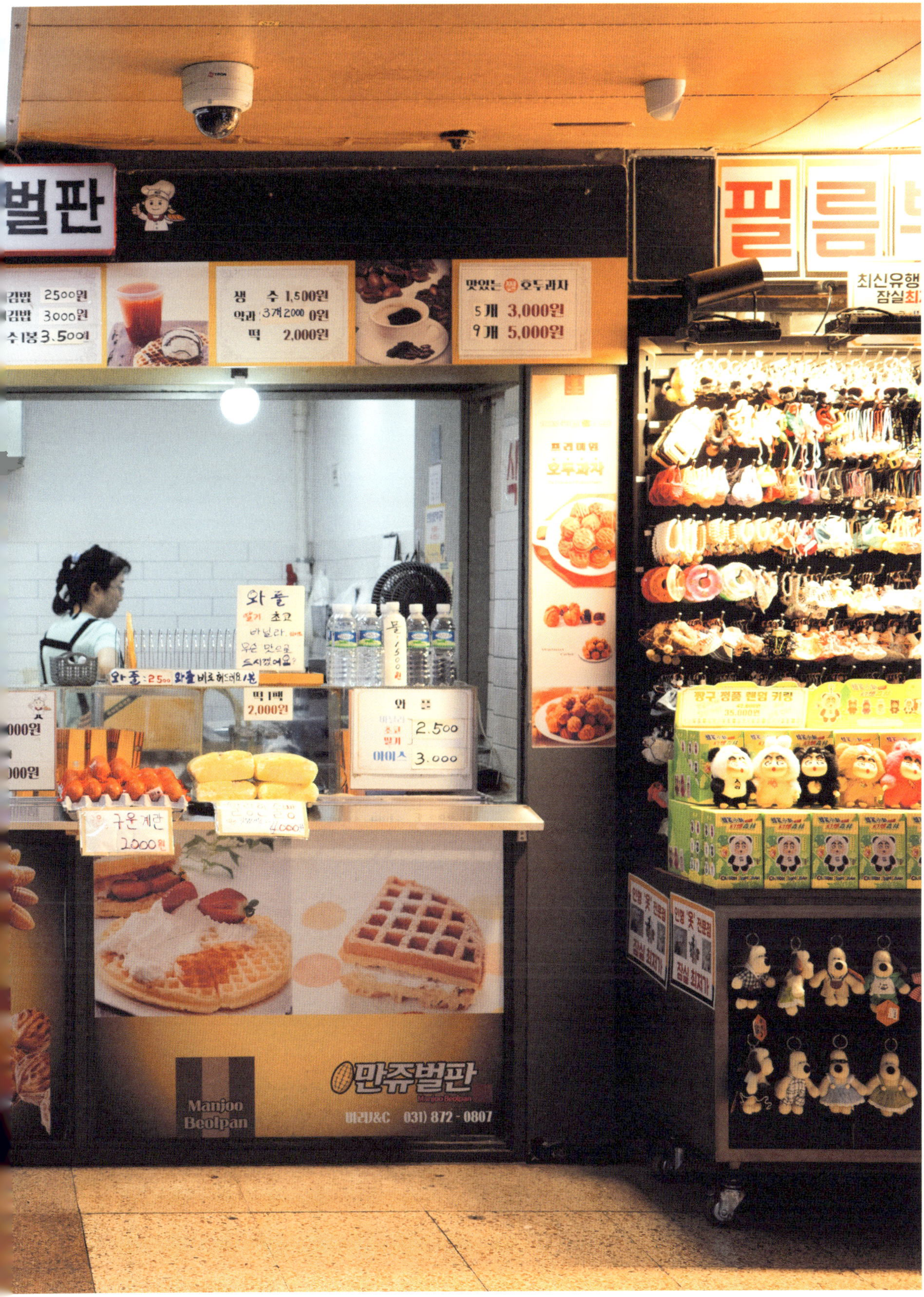
벌판
필름
생 수 1,500원
떡 2,000원
맛있는 호두과자
5개 3,000원
9개 5,000원
떡 1팩
2,000원
구운계란
2,000원
만쥬벌판
Manjoo Beolpan
031) 872 - 0807

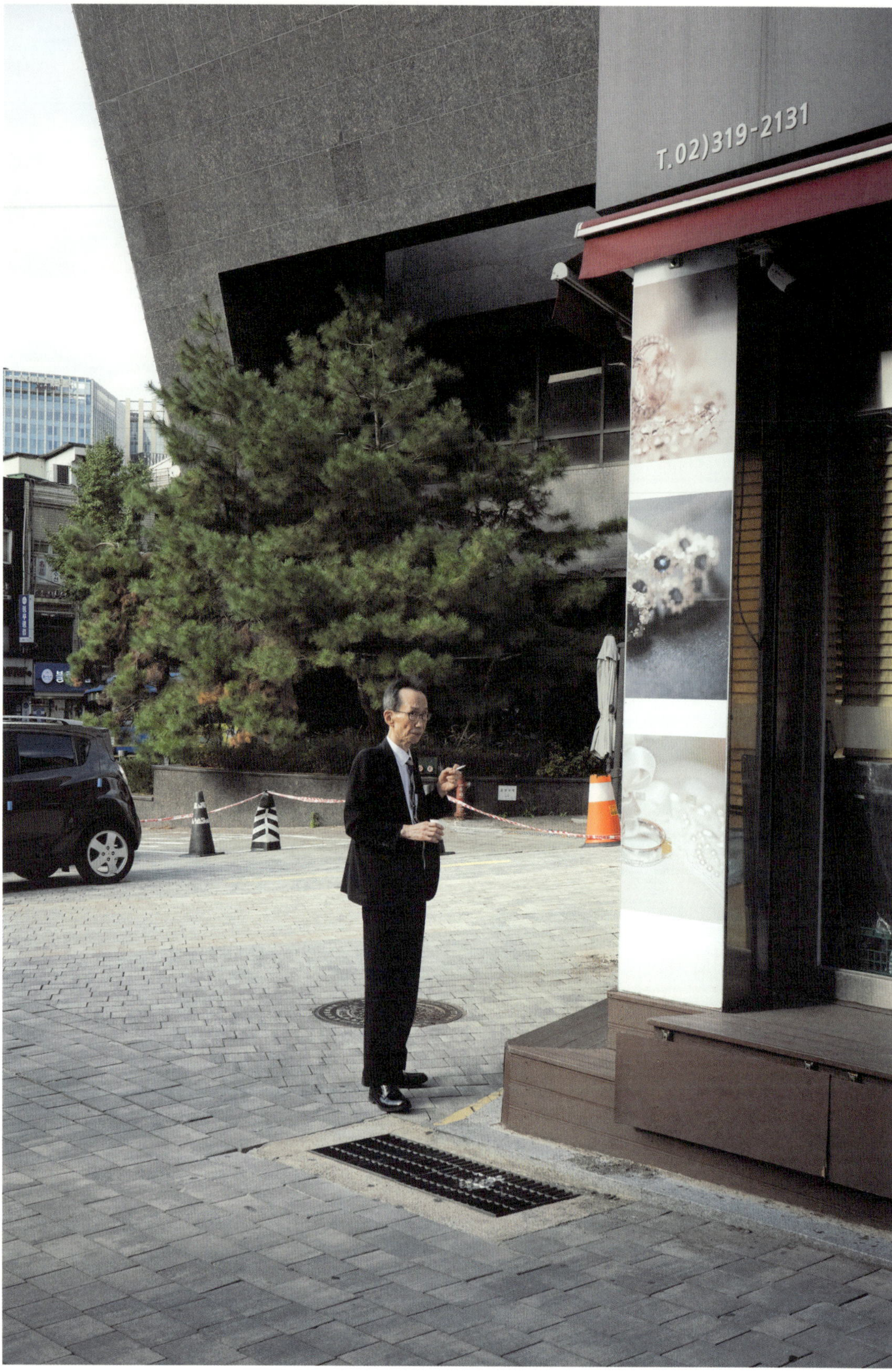


Namchang-dong, Jung District

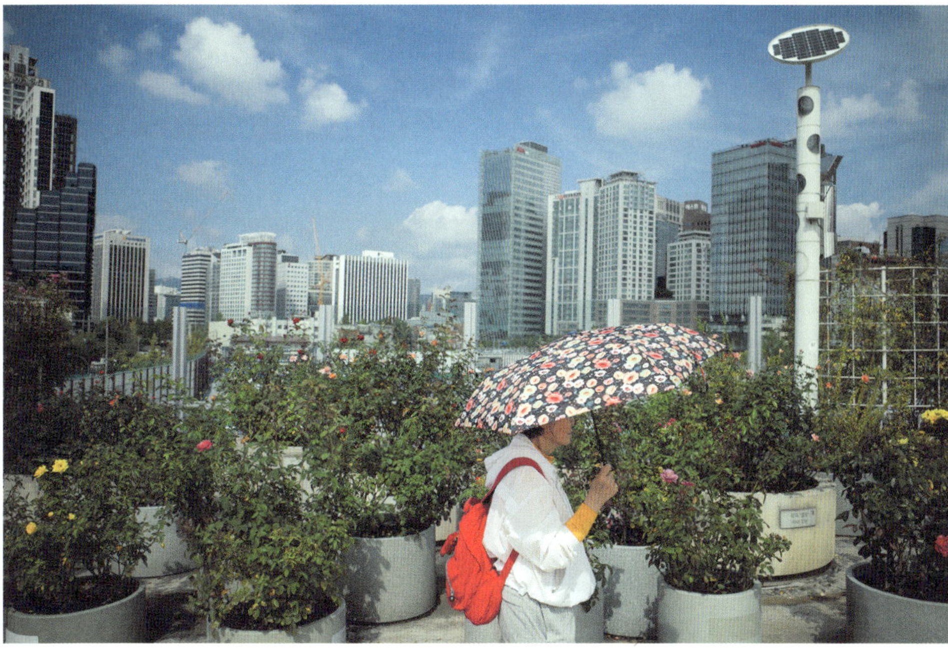

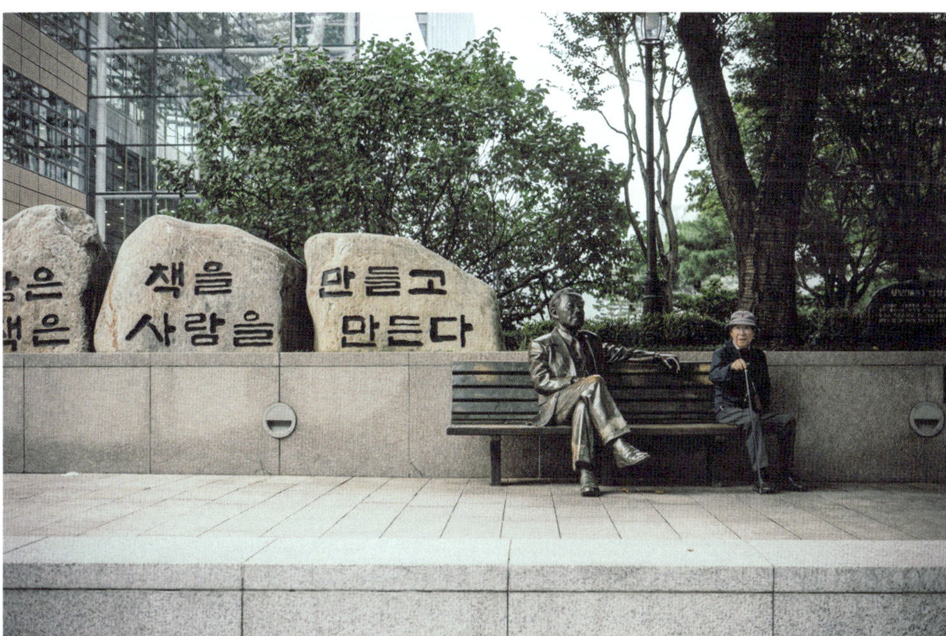


above: Seoul Station, Seoullo 7017, Jung District + below: Jongno 1-ga, Jongno District

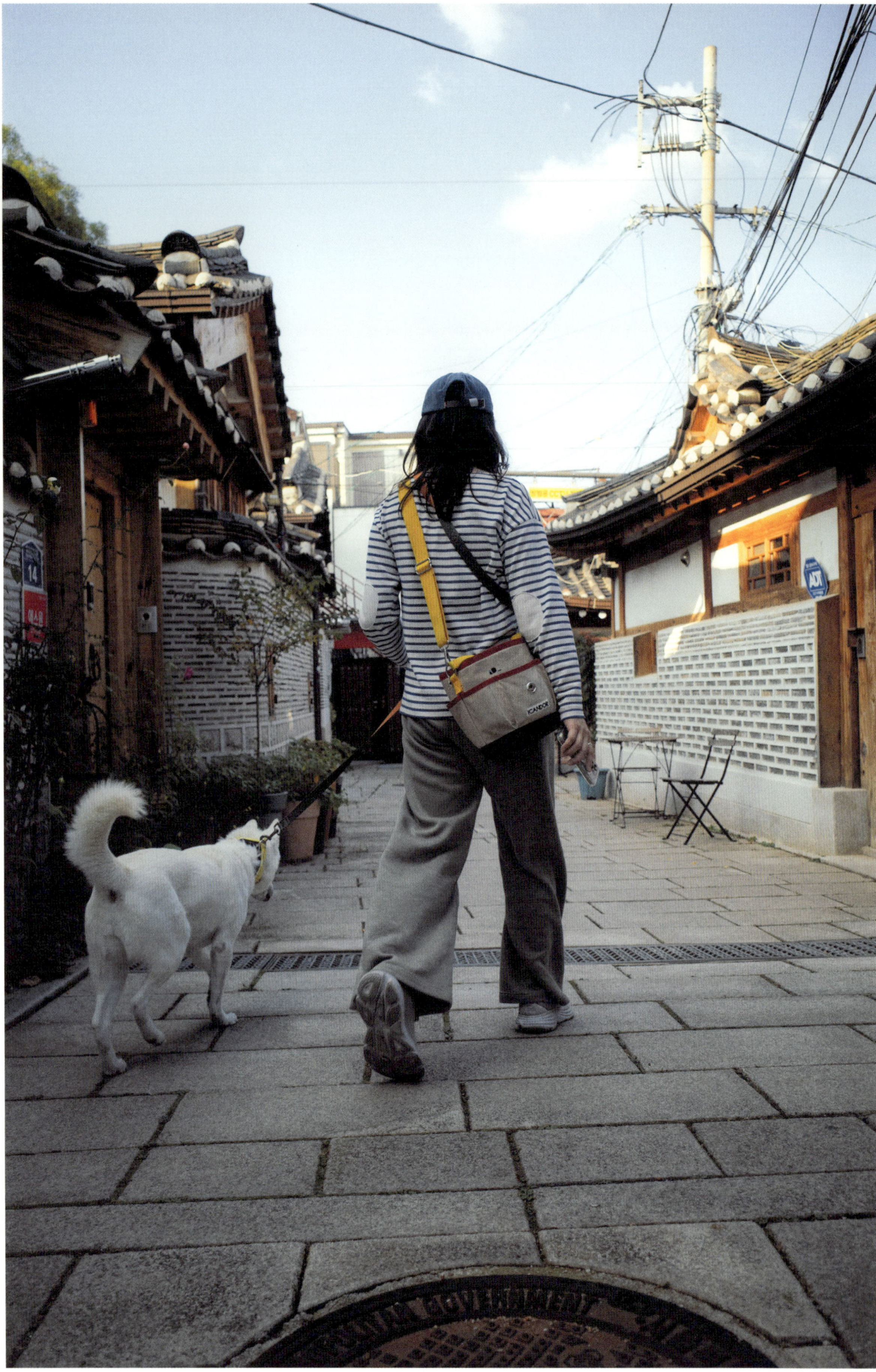
14
ADT

left: Seochon, Jongno District

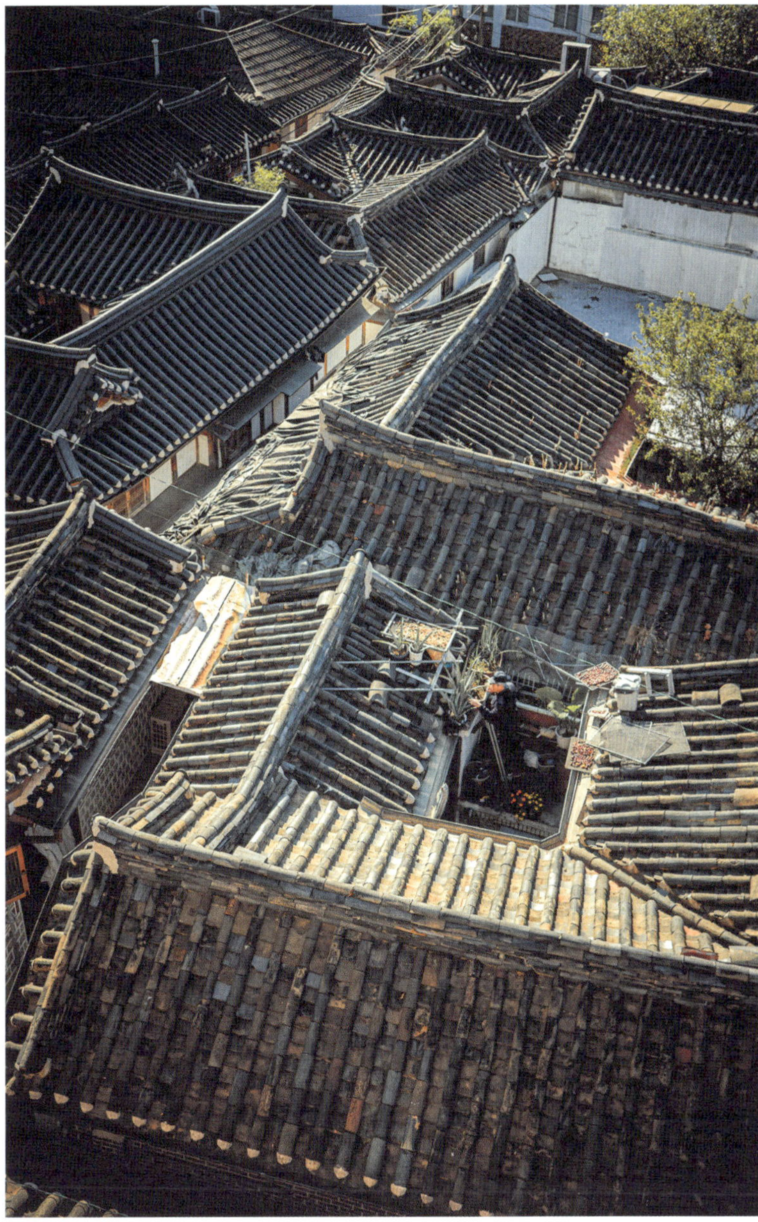

right: Anguk-dong, Jongno District

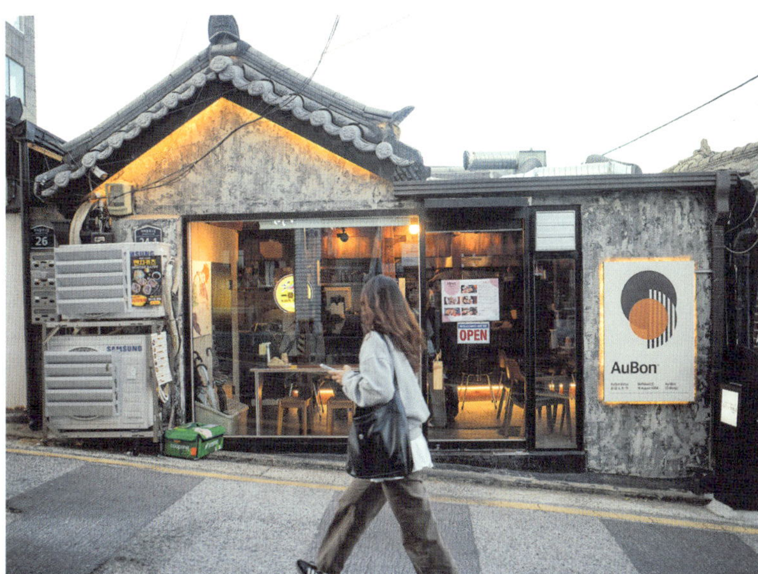


right: Seochon, Jongno District

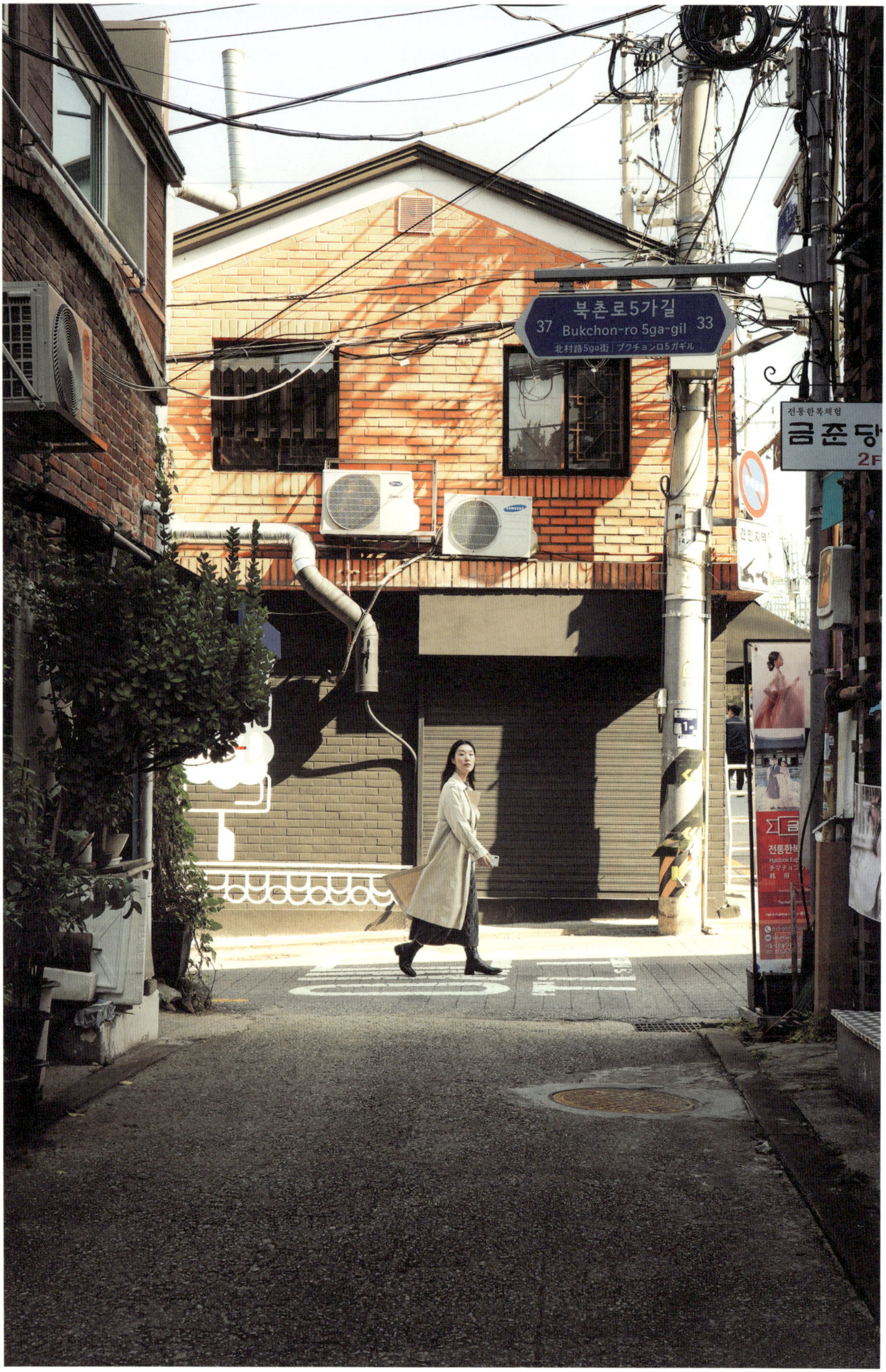
북촌로5가길
37 Bukchon-ro 5ga-gil 33
北村路5ga街 | プクチョンロ5ガギル
전통한복체험
금준당
2F

left: Bukchon, Jongno District

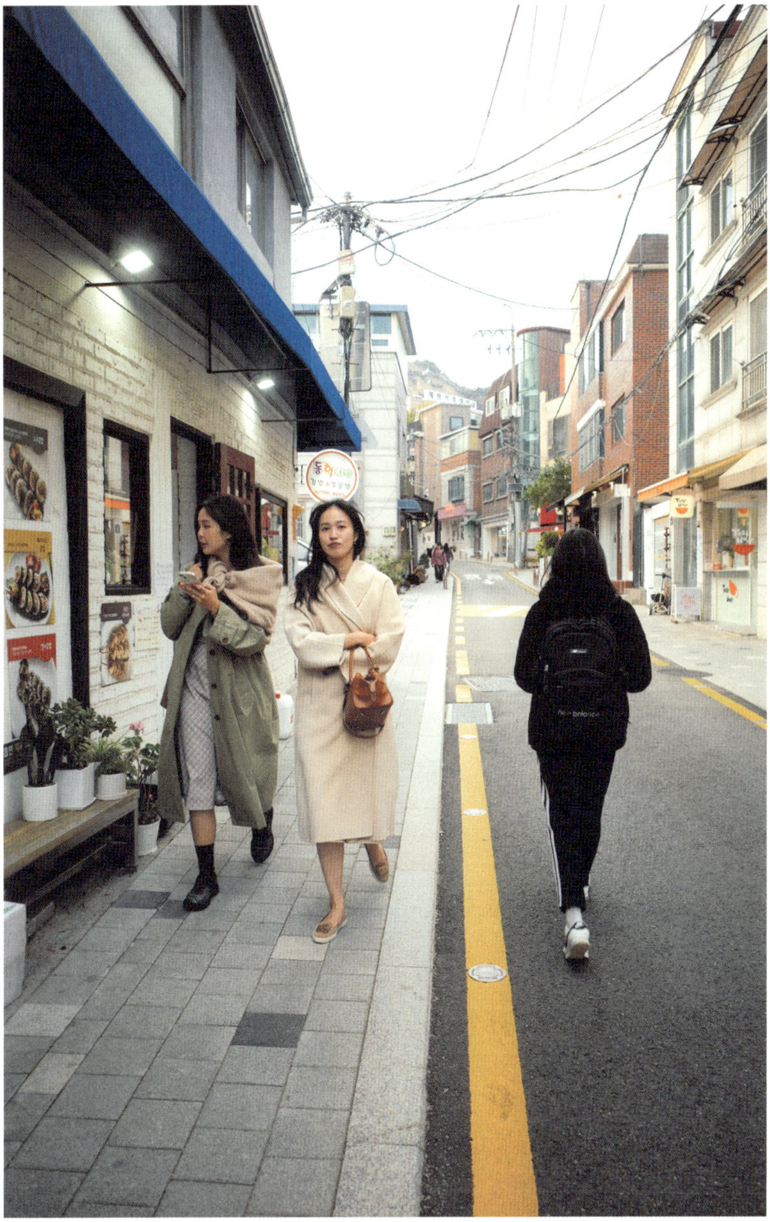

right: Seochon, Jongno District

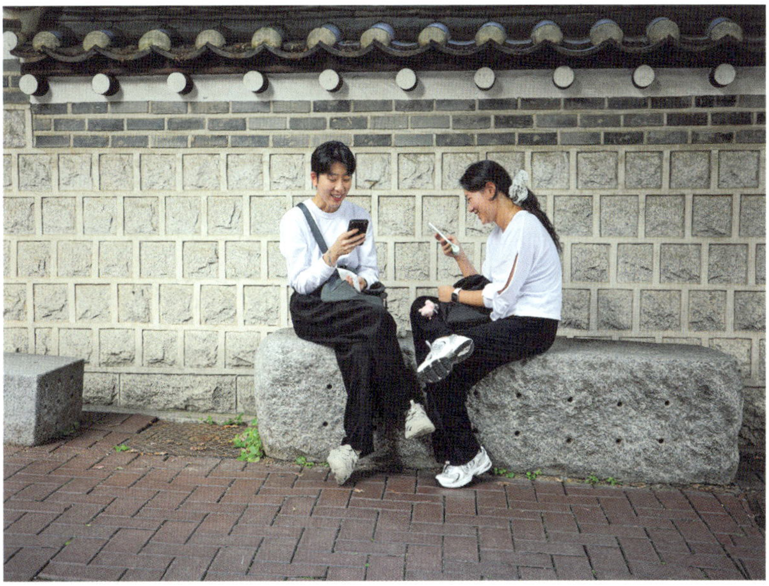

right: Seochon, Jongno District

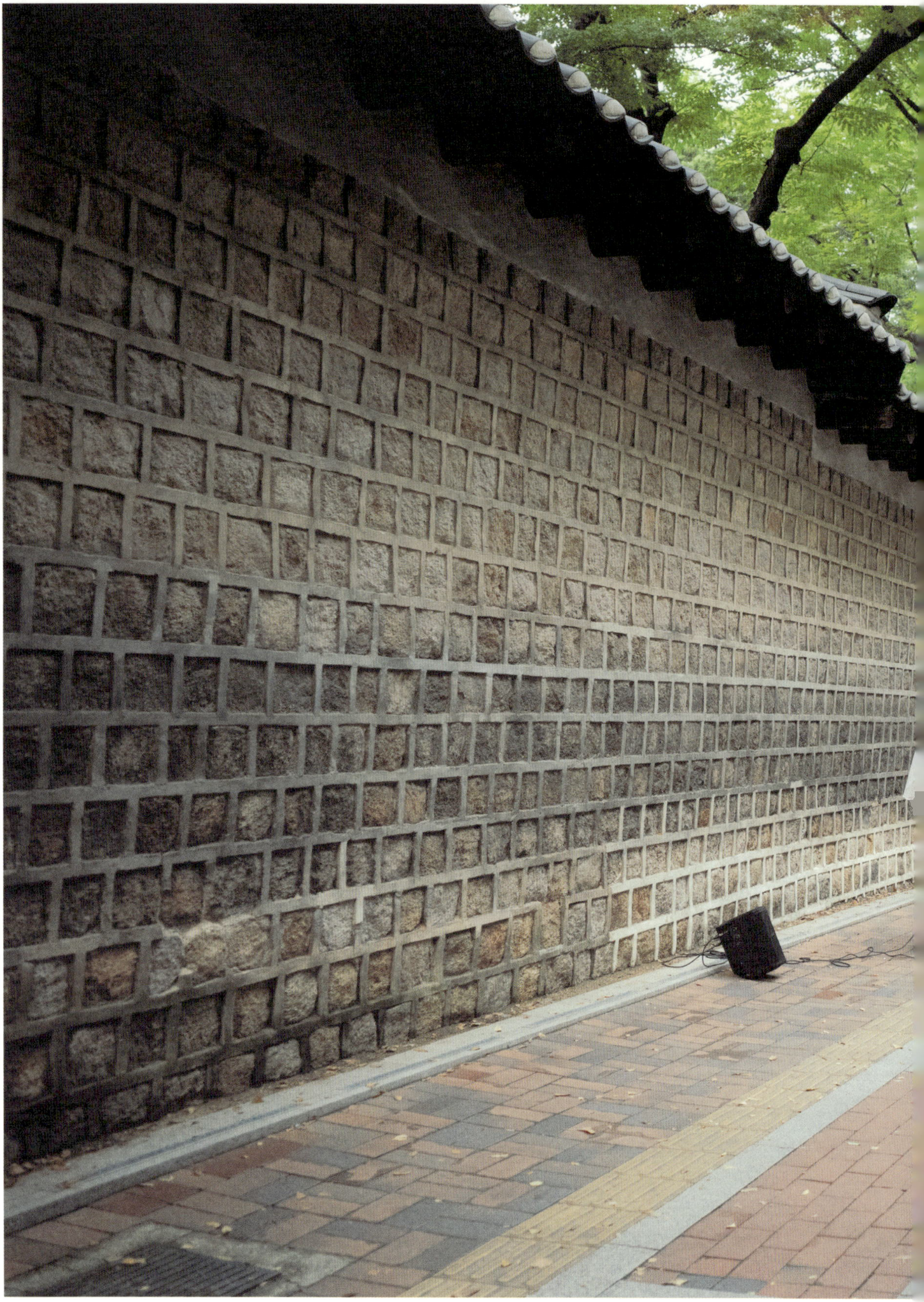

Deoksugung-gil, Jung District

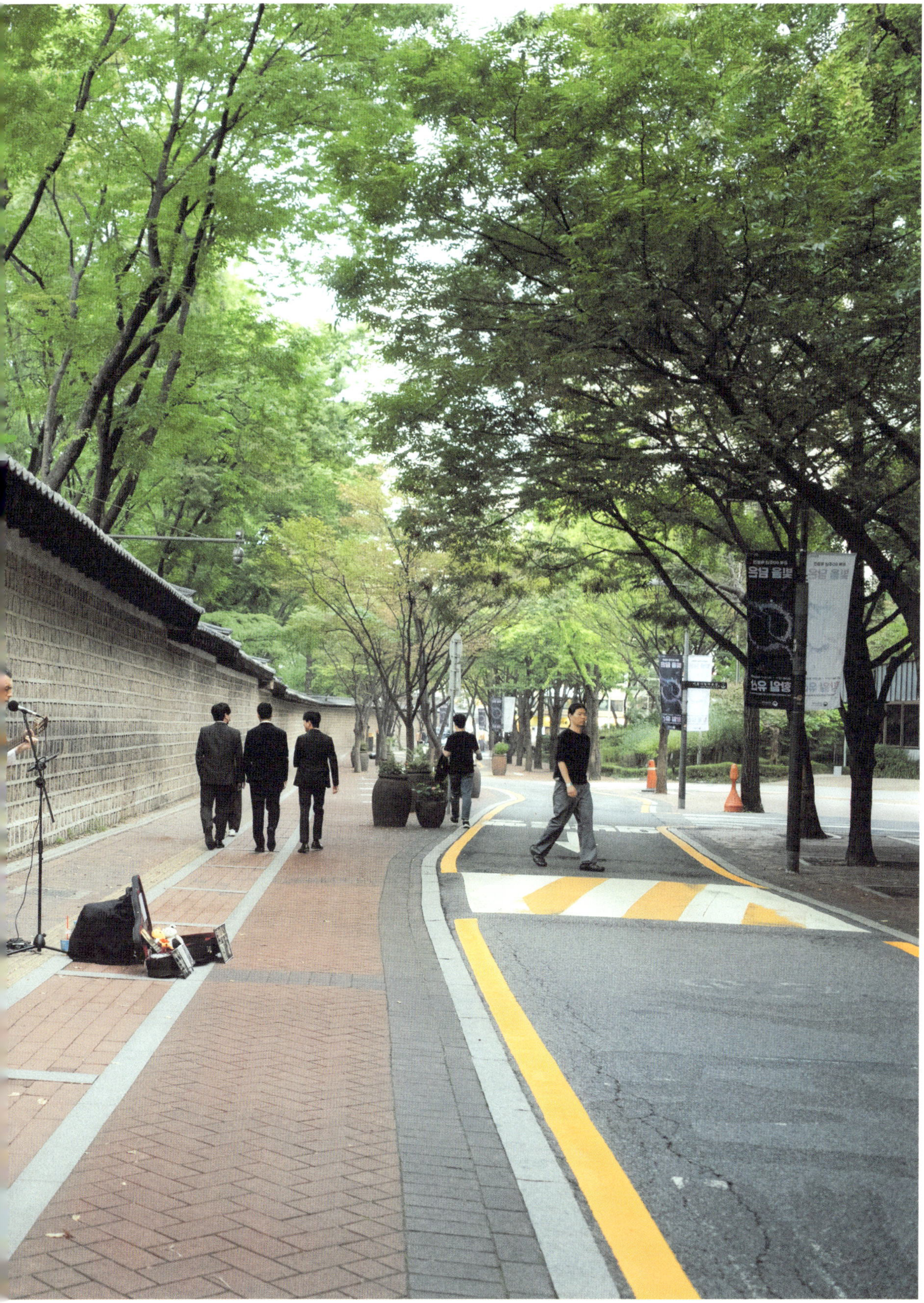

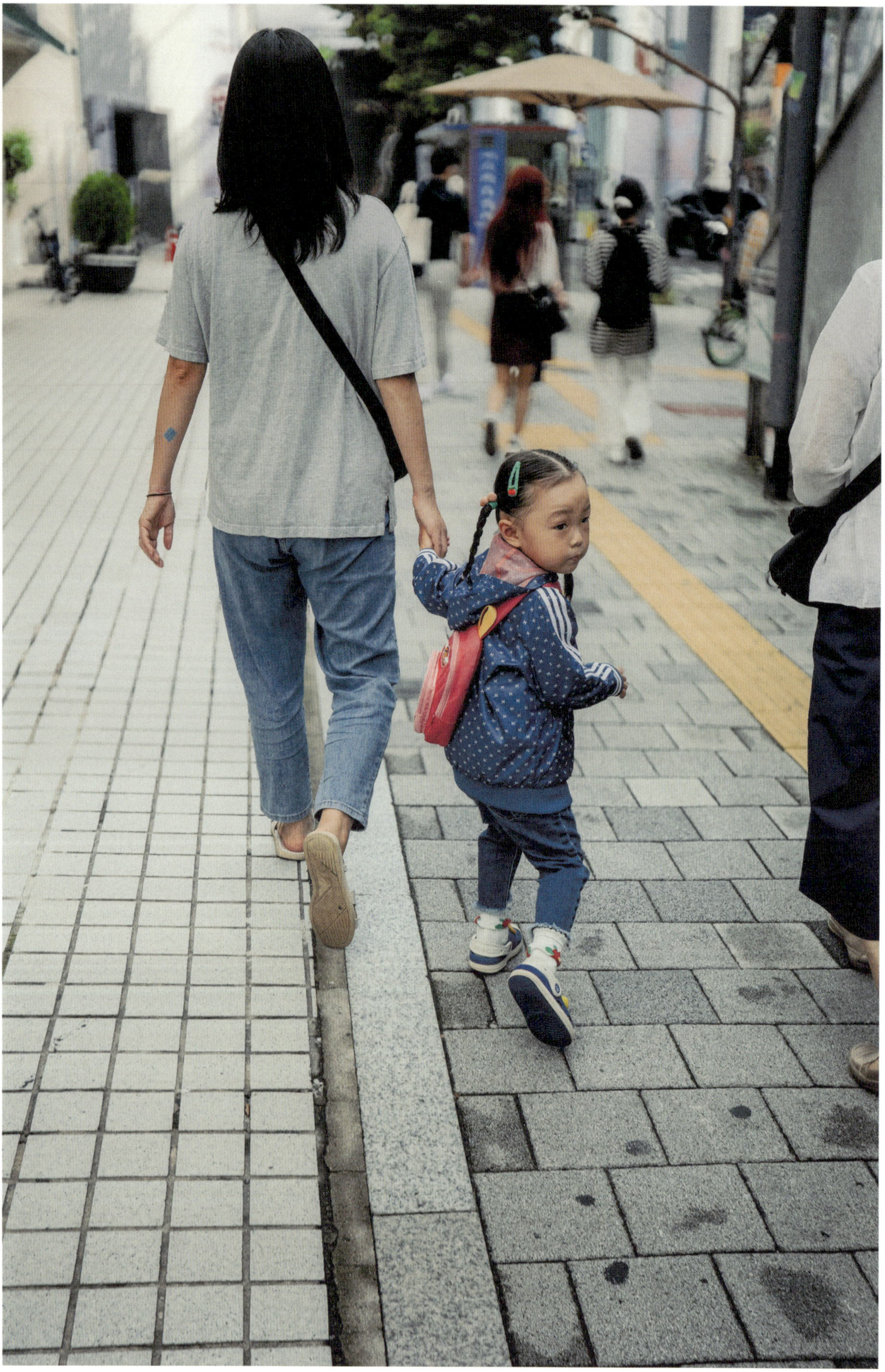

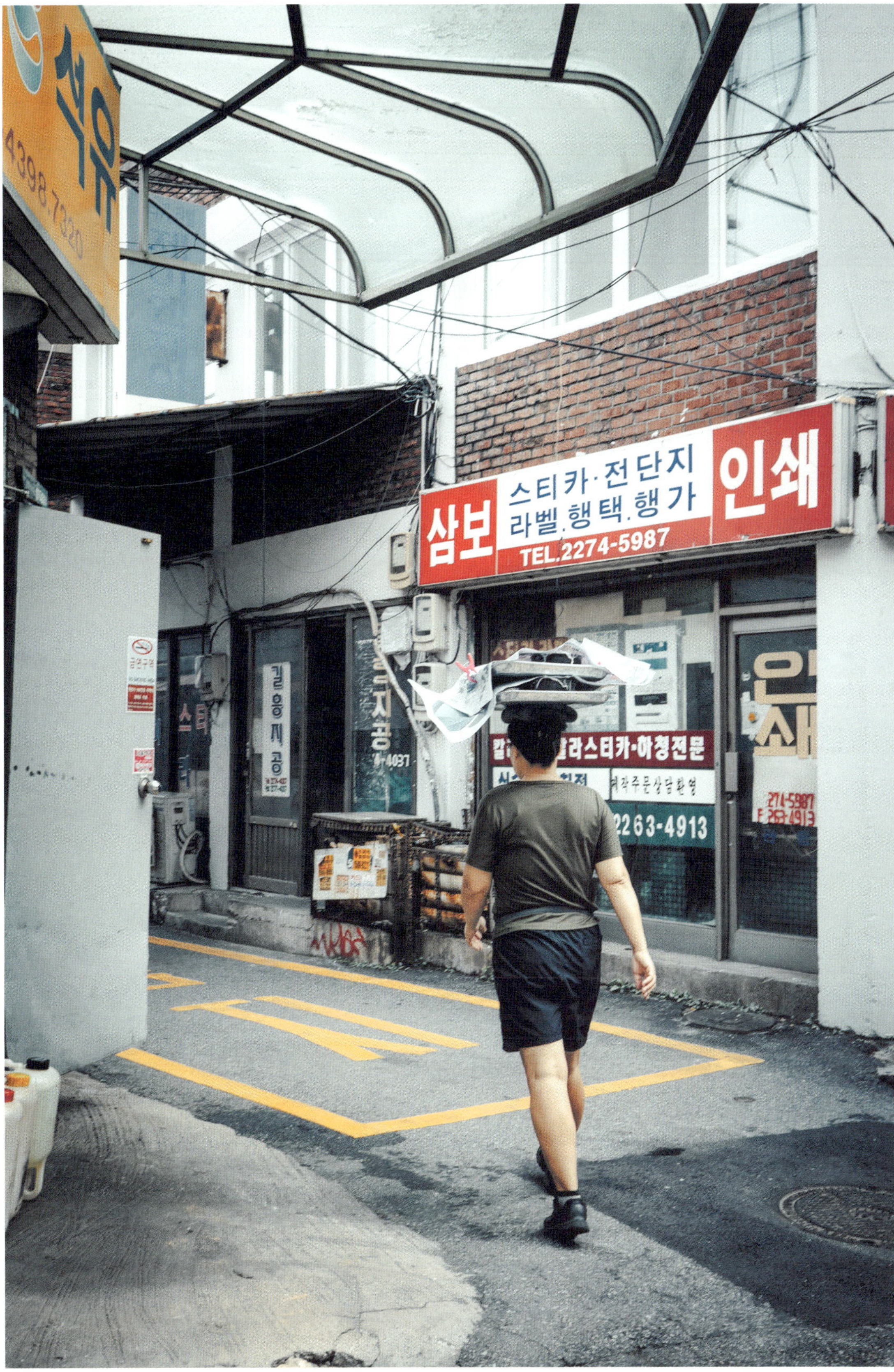


left: Seongsu-dong, Seongdong District + above: Euljiro 4-ga, Jung District

# BYEONHWA

## 변화

(byun-hwa) is a word that translates to “change” or “transform” but carries a broader sense of transition and adjustment that Koreans recognize in everyday life.

Seoul has changed dramatically in a single generation, shifting from a post-industrial city into a modern, globally connected capital. New transit lines, public spaces, and redevelopment projects have reshaped how people live and experience the city. Much of its art and design has evolved as well, with traditional forms being reinterpreted with cleaner lines, updated materials, and contemporary architecture. Hanok districts, traditional markets, and long-standing craft influence still thread through this continued transformation, offering contrast rather than nostalgia.

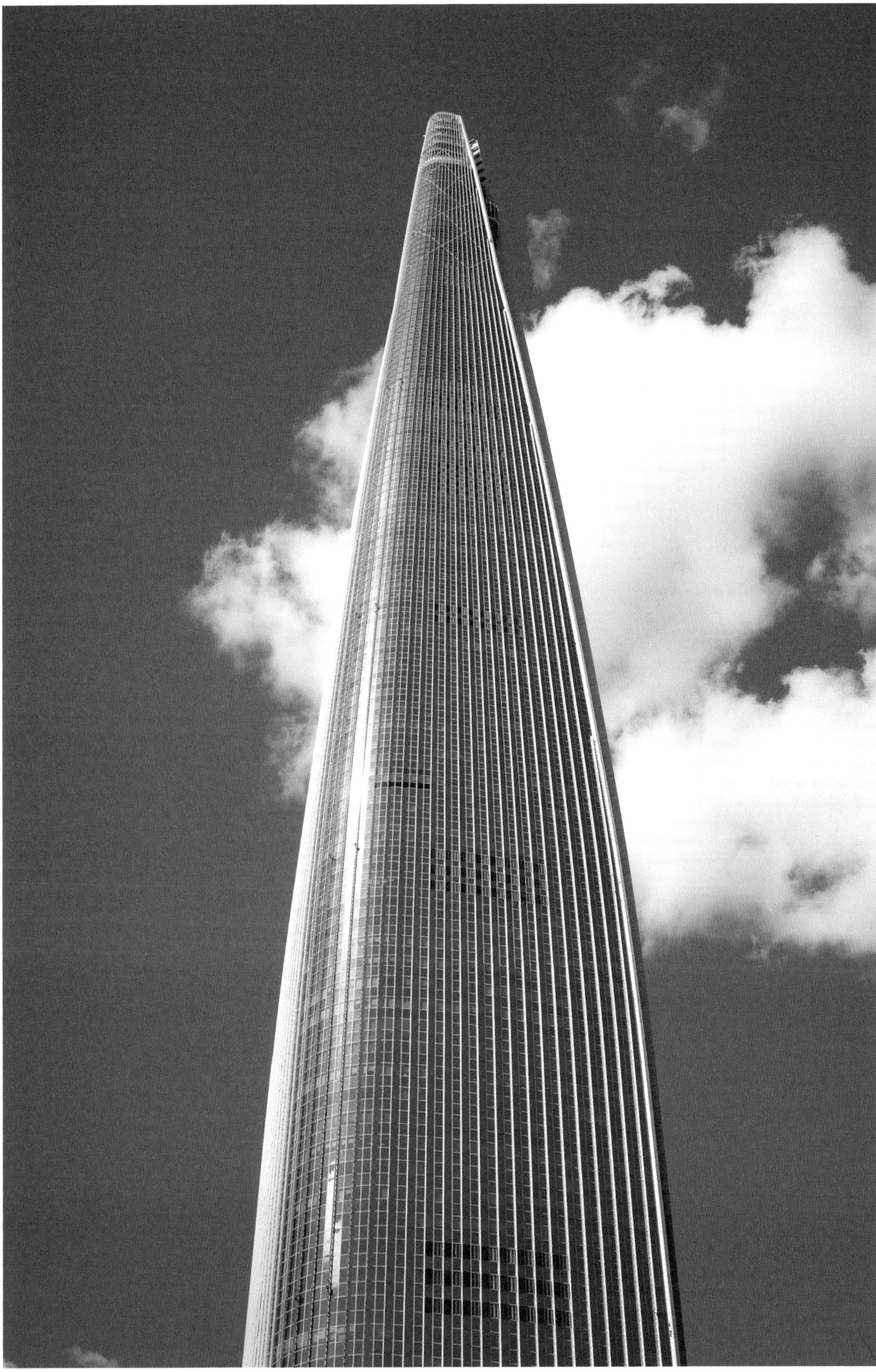

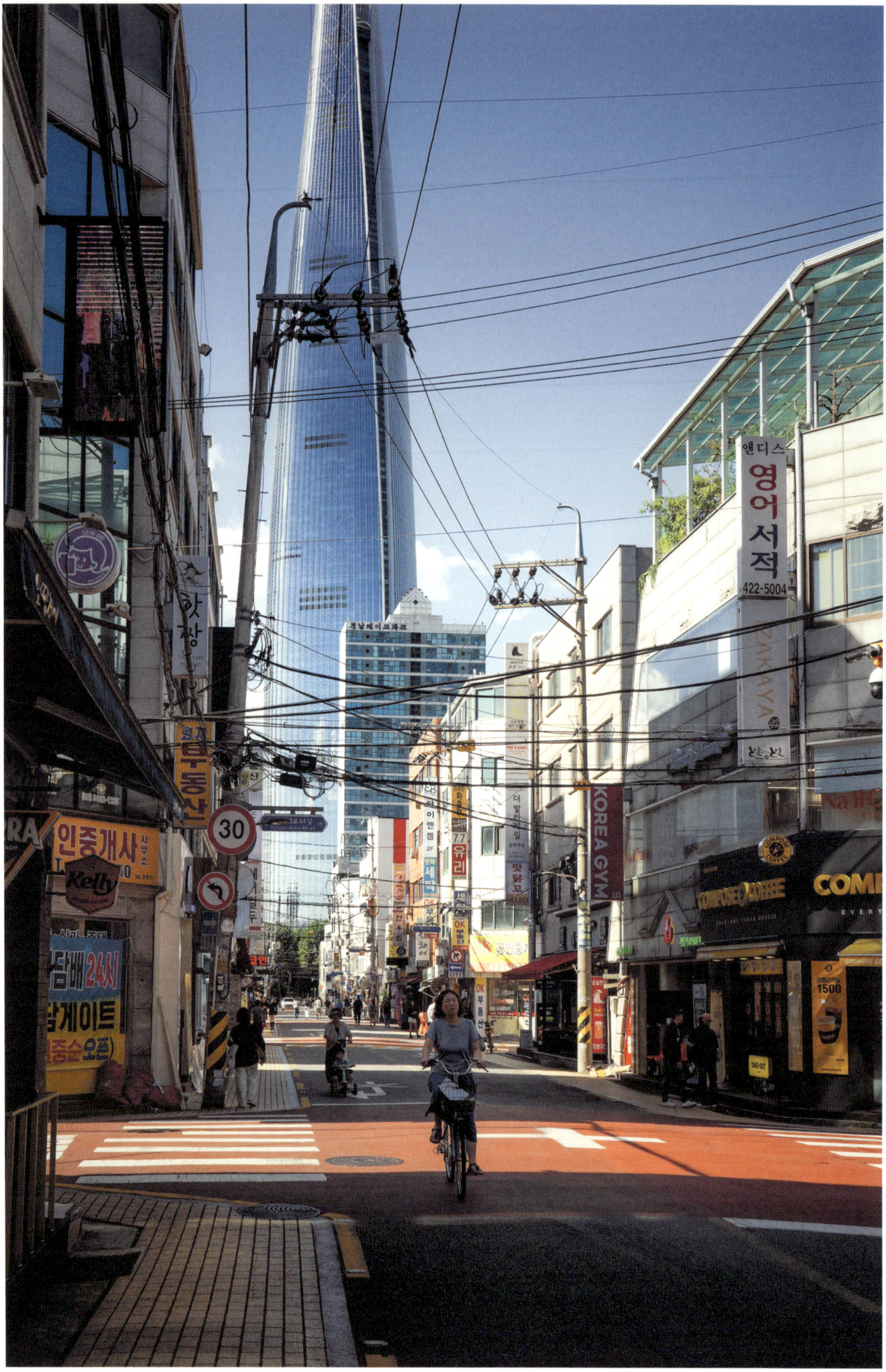

앤디스
영어서적
422-5004
KOREA GYM
COMPOSE COFFEE
30
부동산
Kelly
담배24시

left: Songpa-dong, Songpa District + previous spread: Lotte World Tower, Jamsil-dong, Songpa District
below: Jayang-dong, Gwangjin District

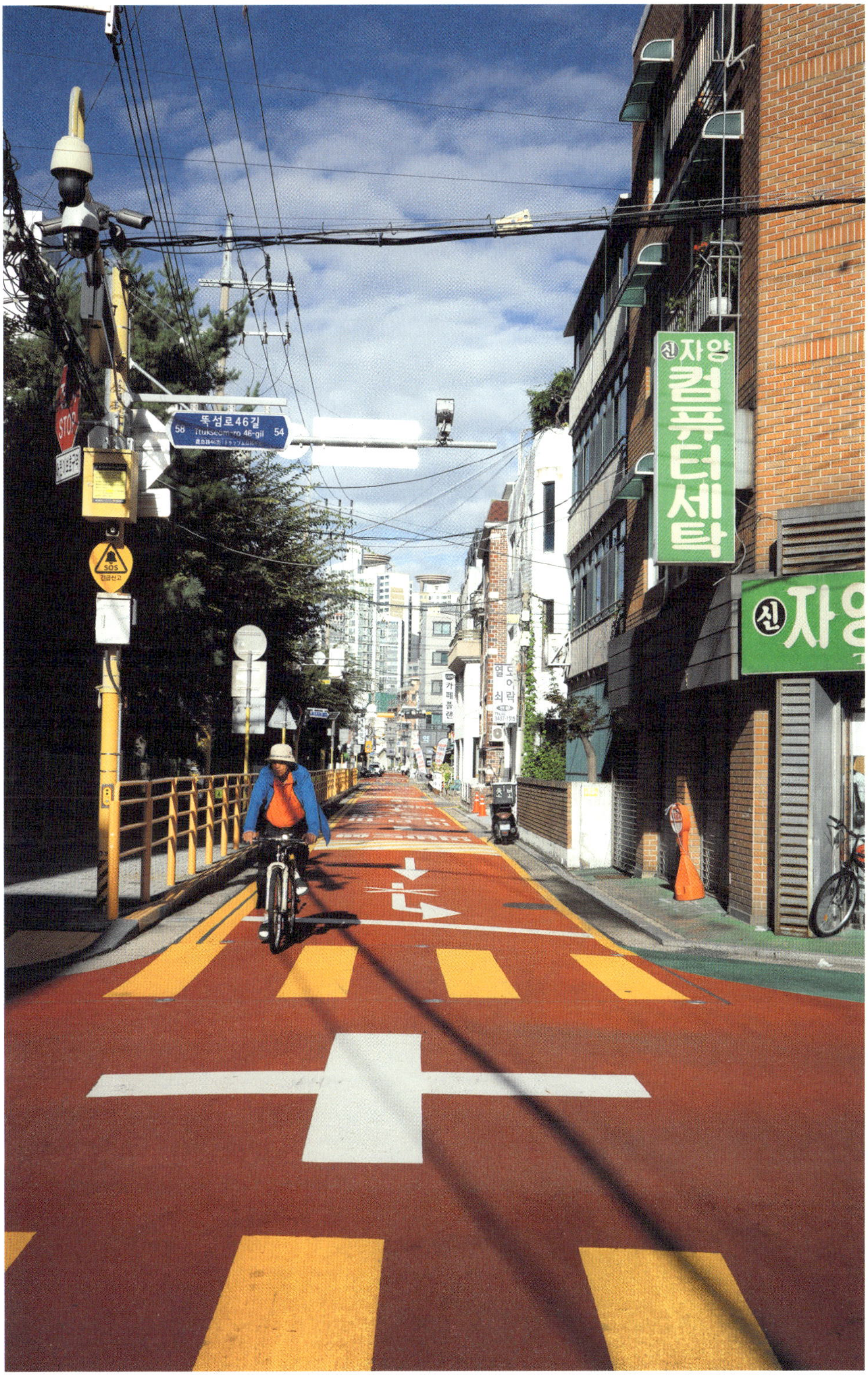

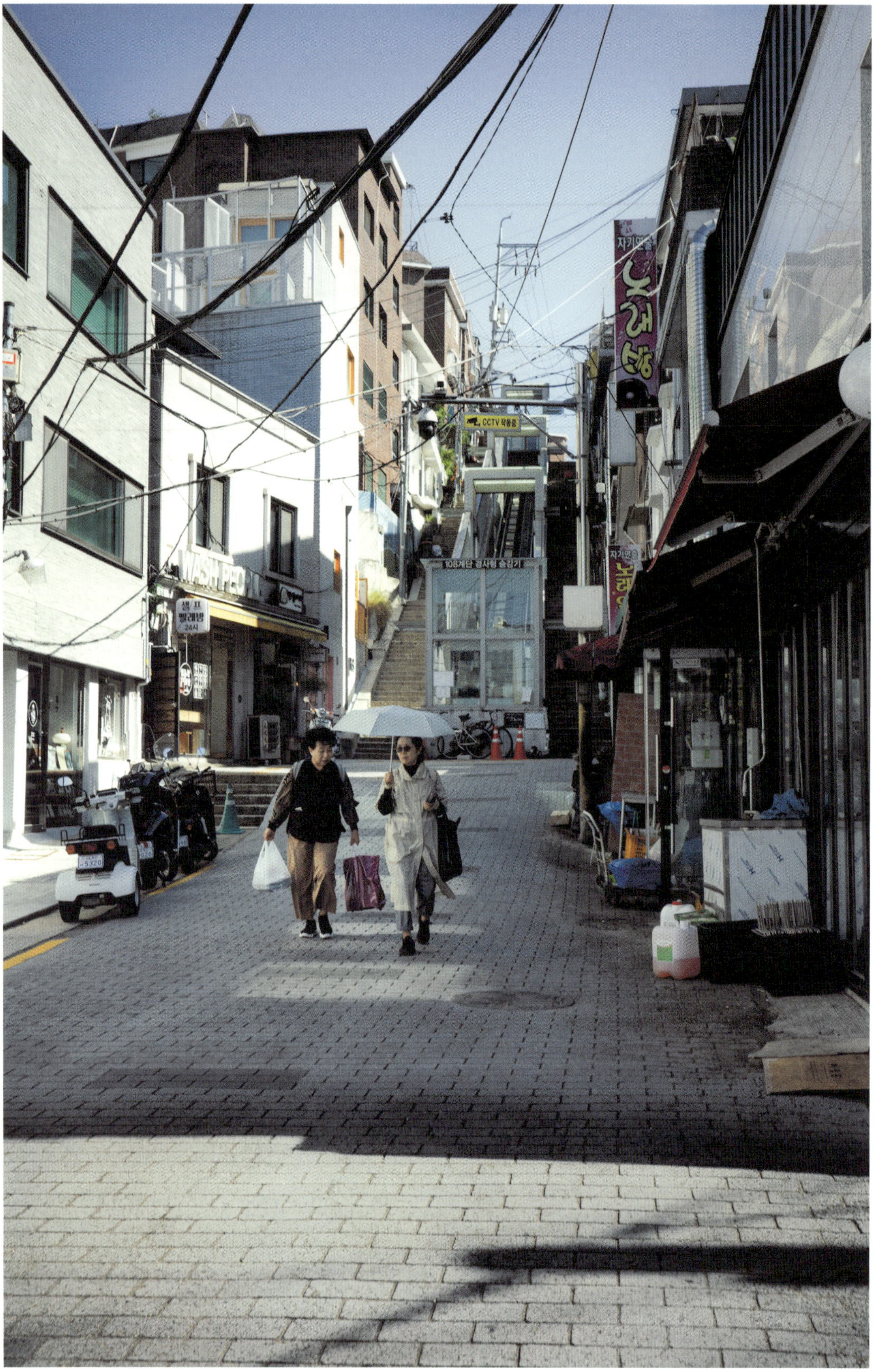


Haebangchon, Yongsan District

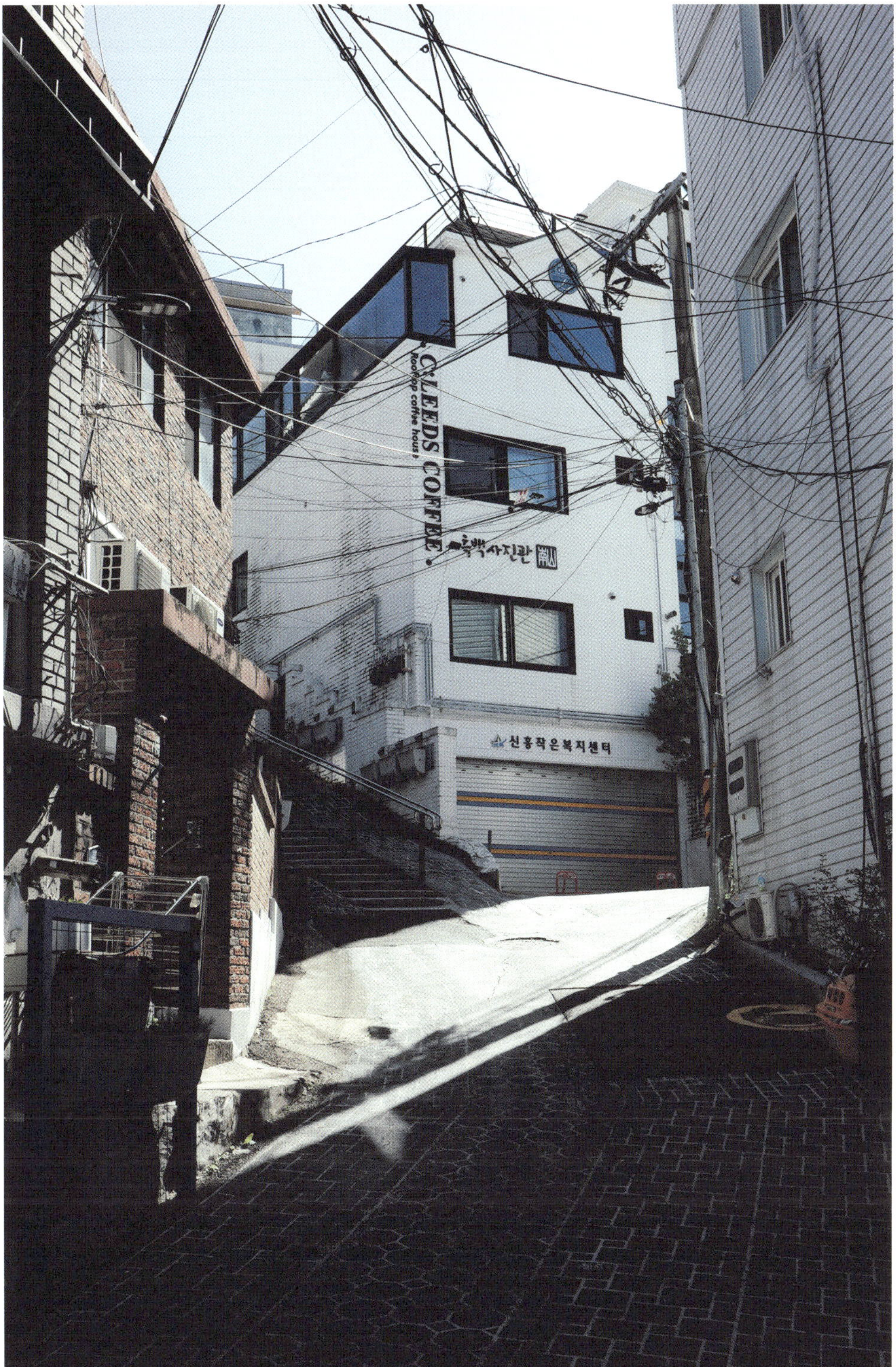


Haebangchon, Yongsan District

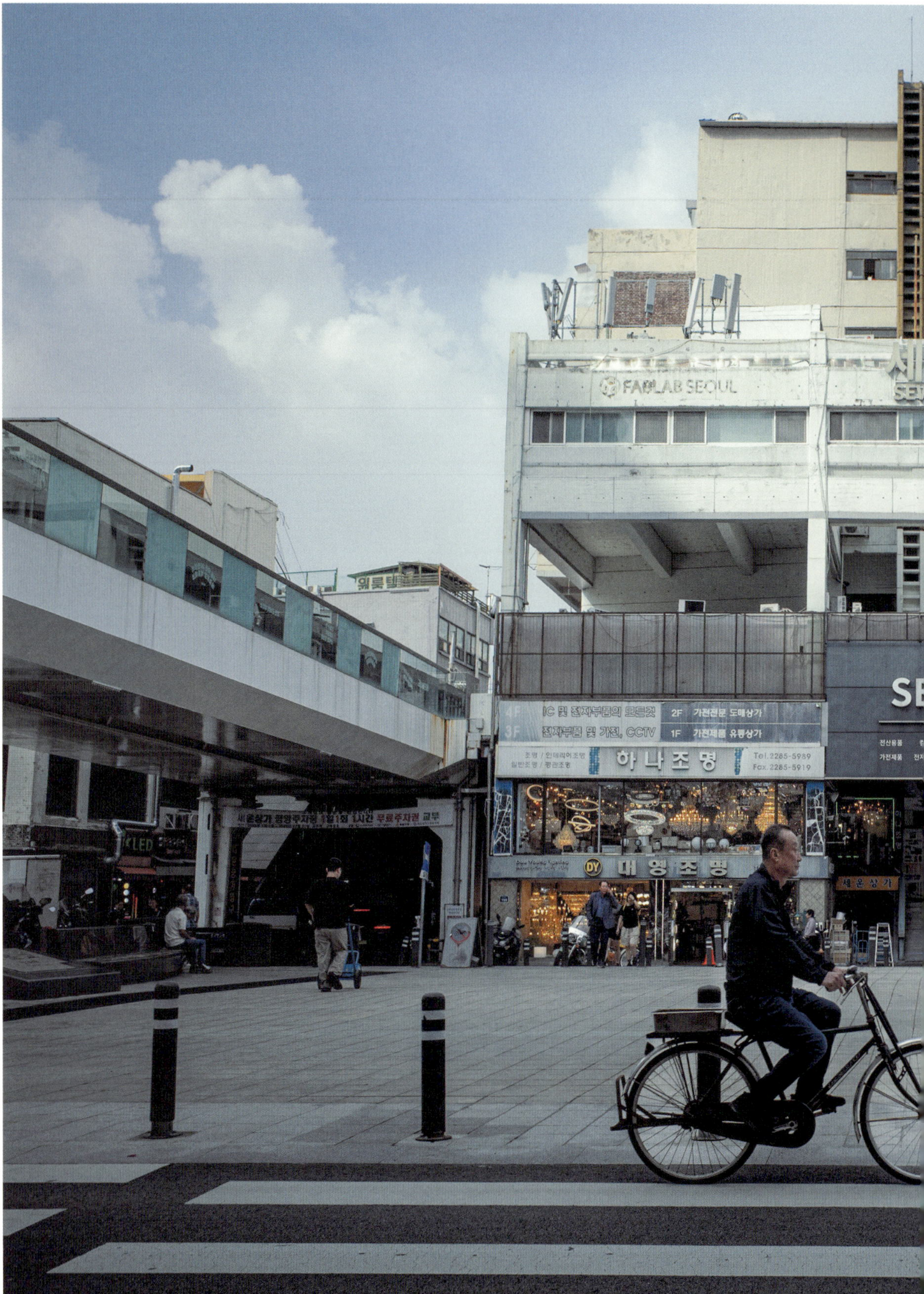


Sewoon Plaza, Jongno District > Sewoon Plaza is Korea's first comprehensive electronics market, established in 1968

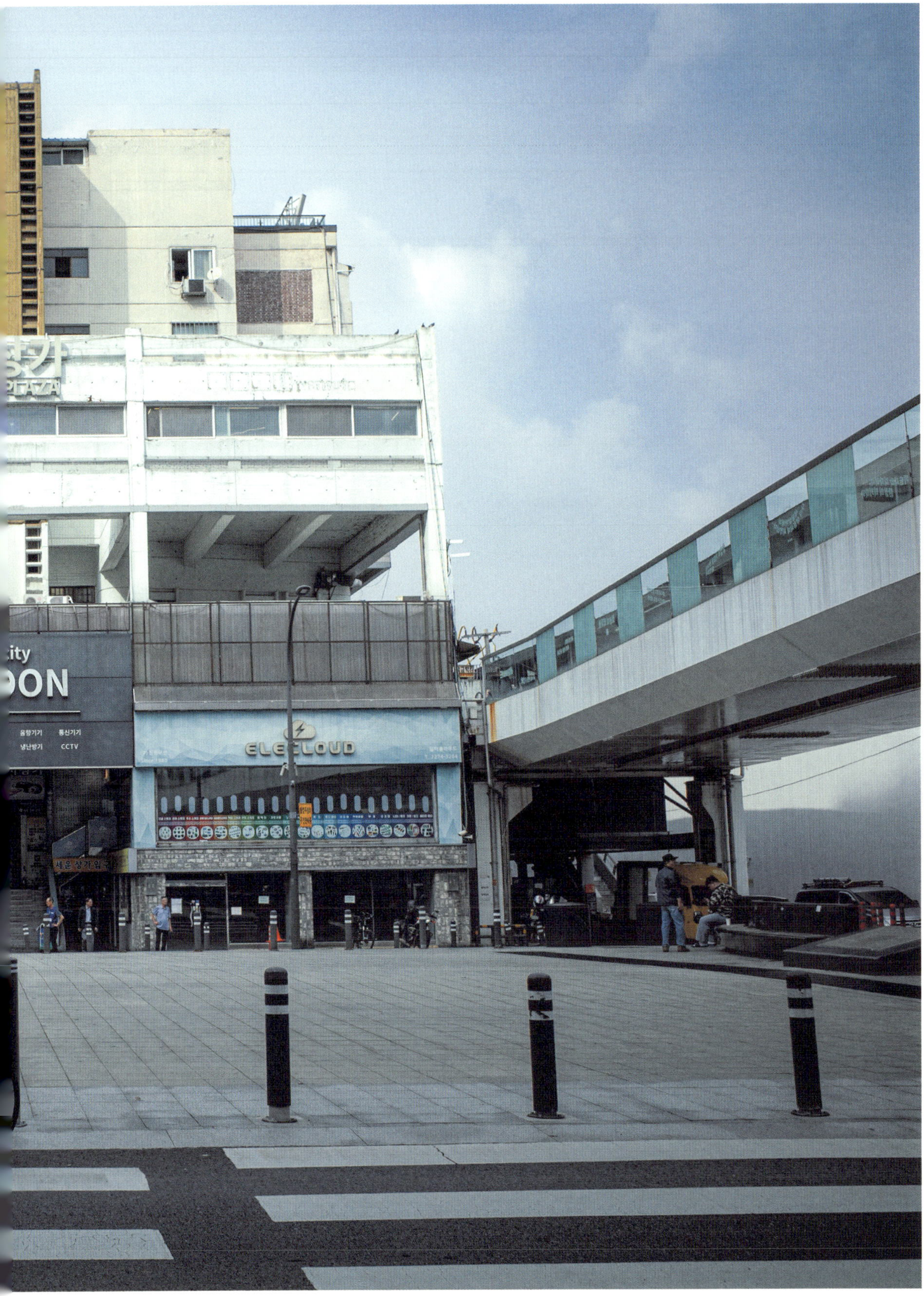
ity
DON
음향기기 통신기기
냉난방기 CCTV
ELECLOUD

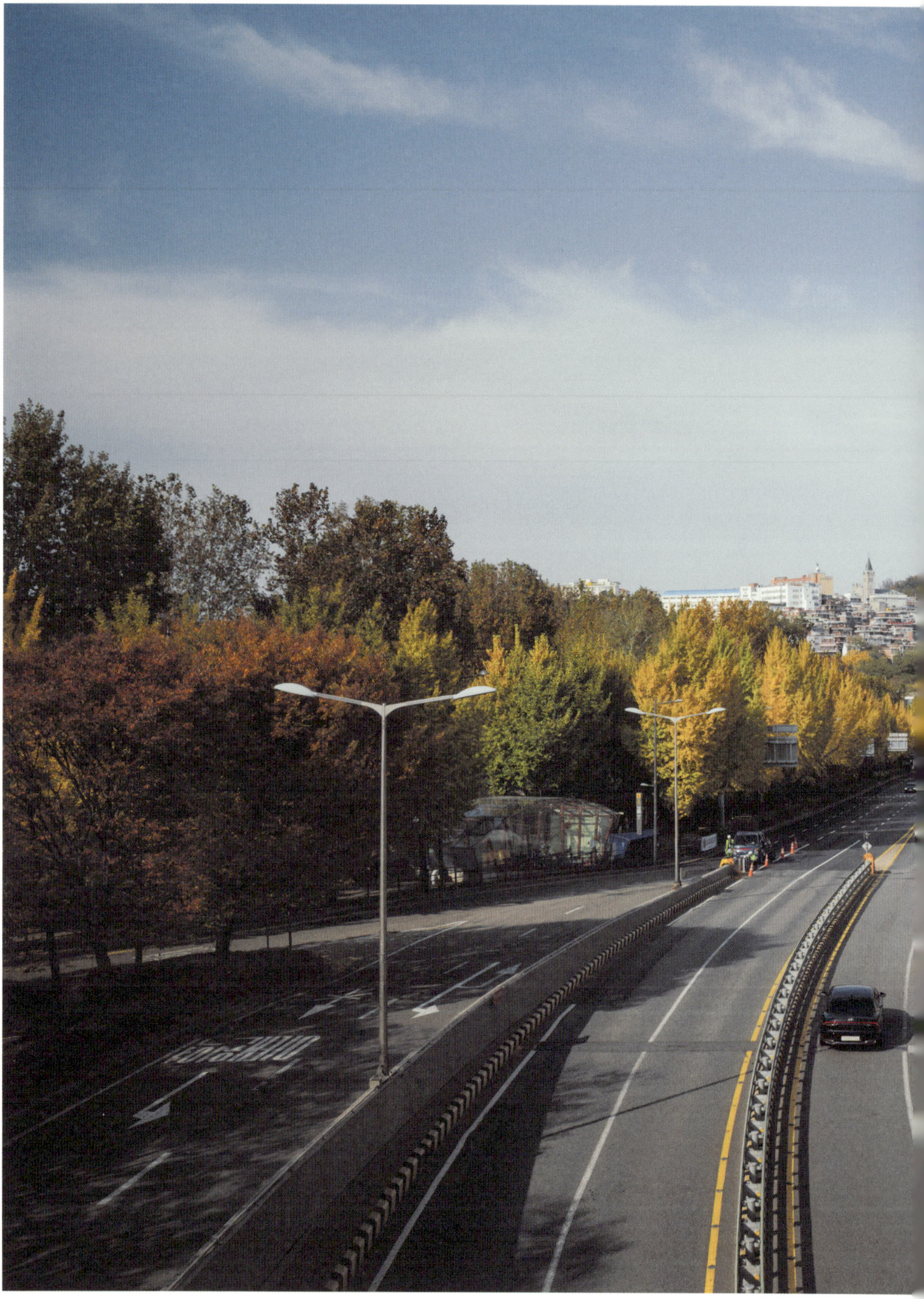

Itaewon, Yongsan District

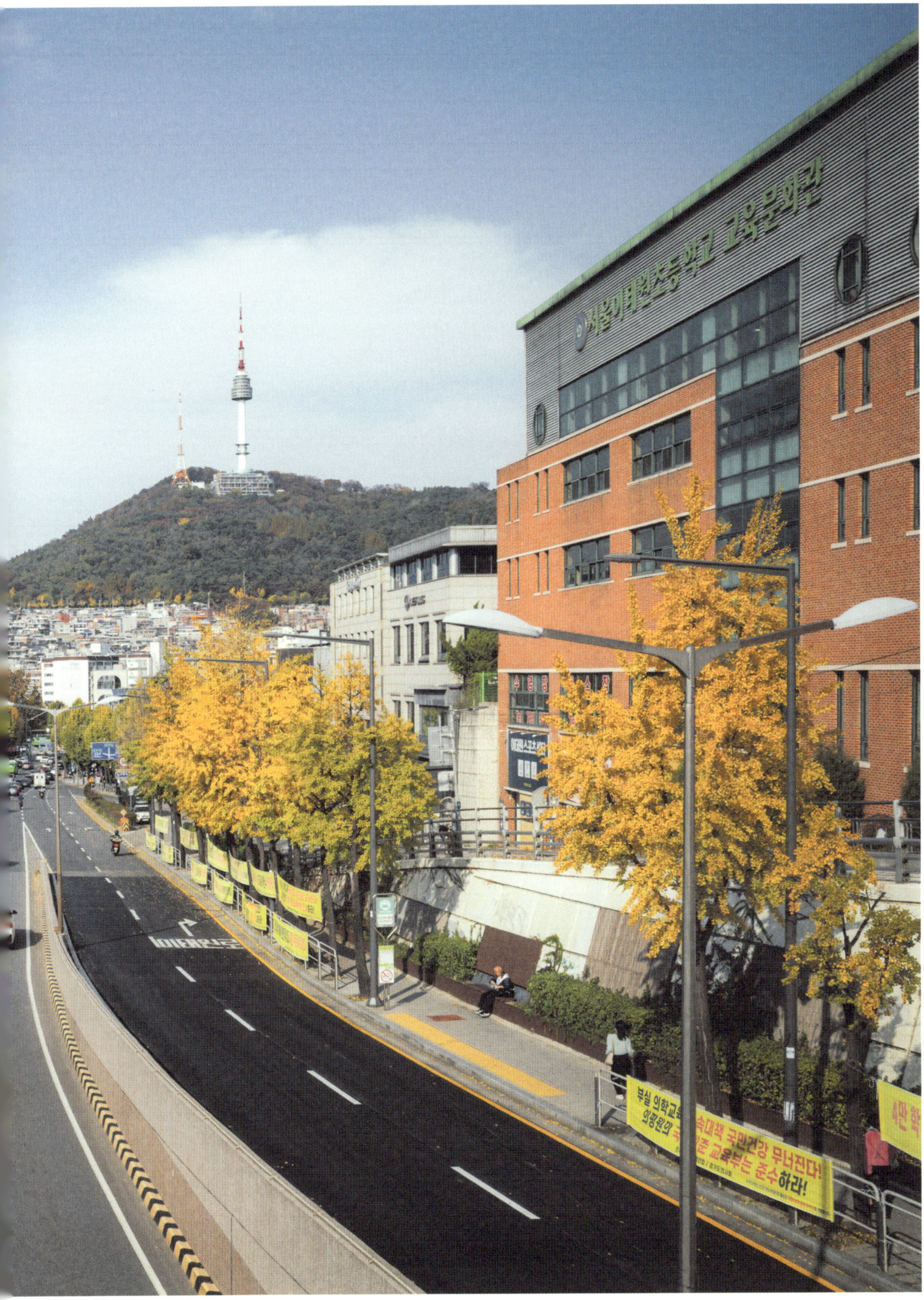
서울이태원초등학교 교육문화관
부실 의학교
속대책 국민건강 무너진다!
의평원의
준 교육부는 준수하라!

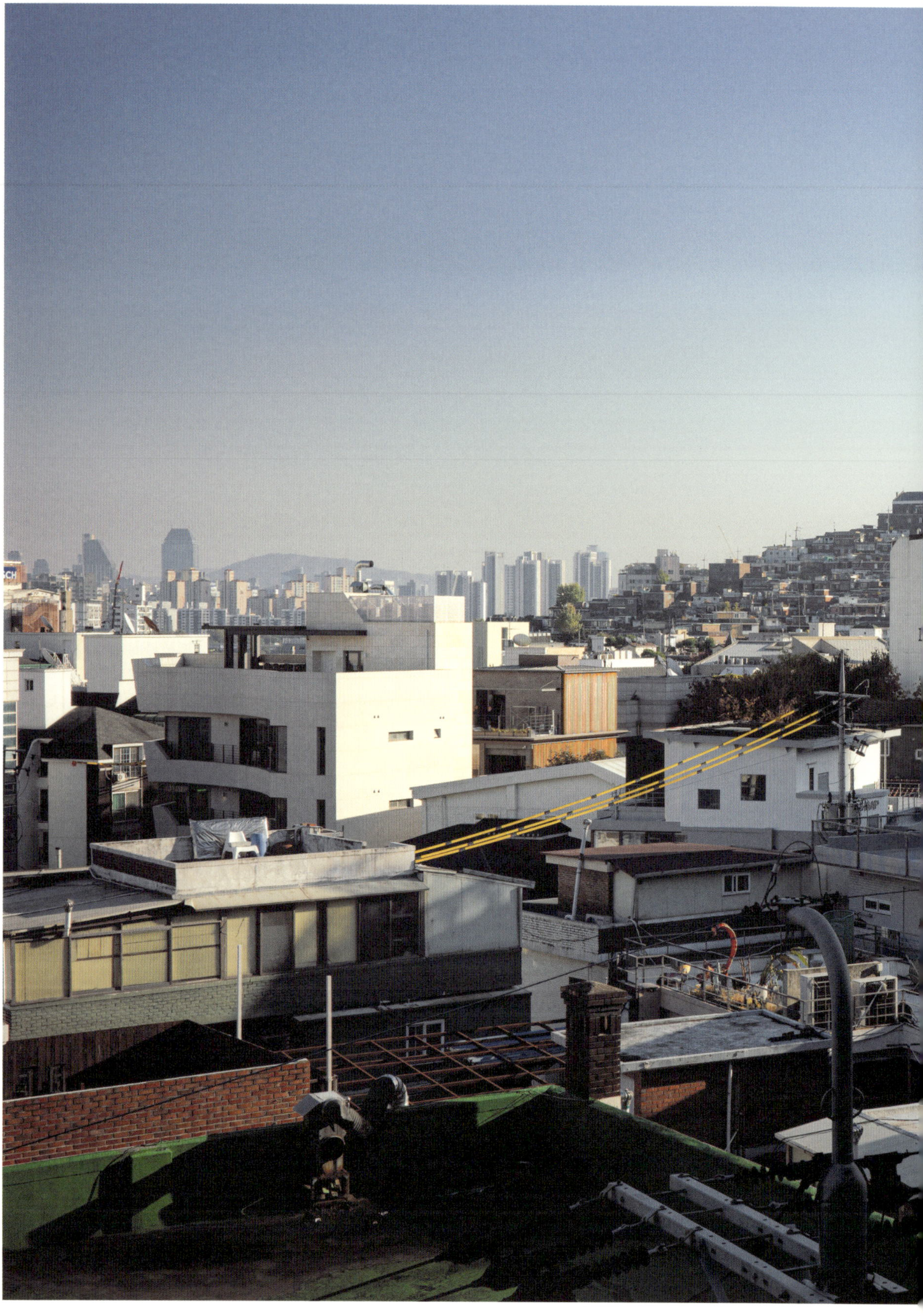

Itaewon, Yongsan District

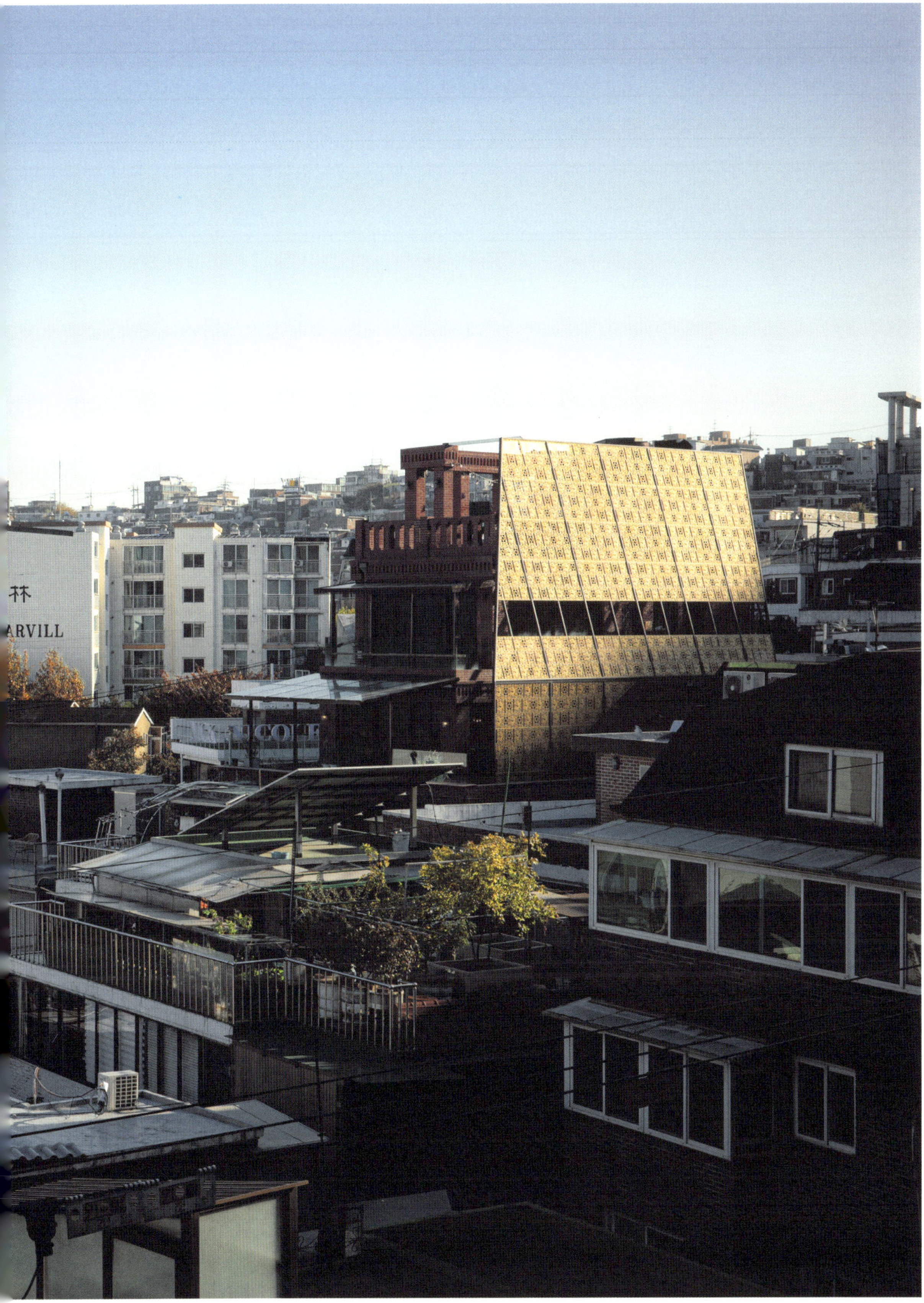
林
ARVILL

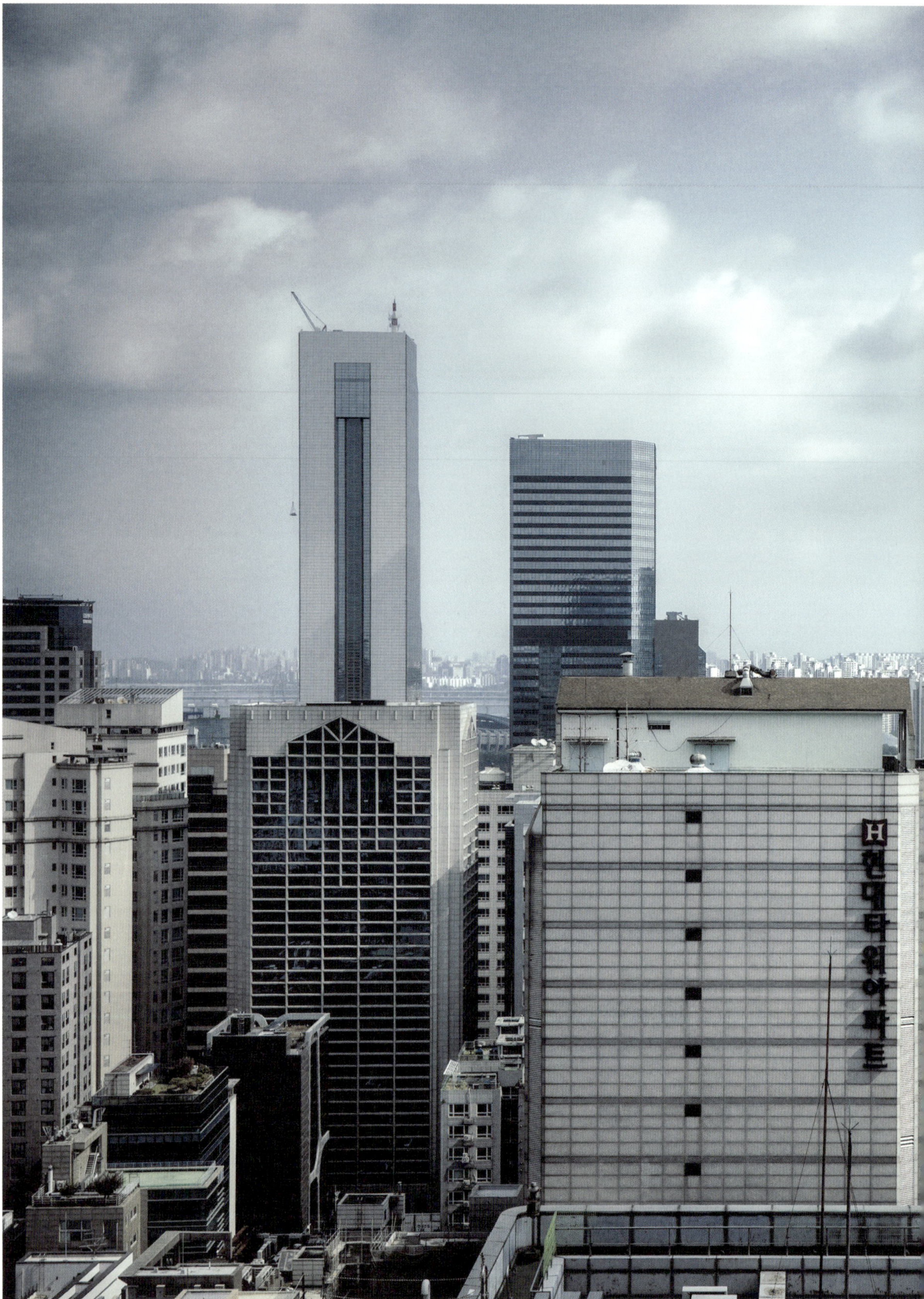


Seolleung, Gangnam District

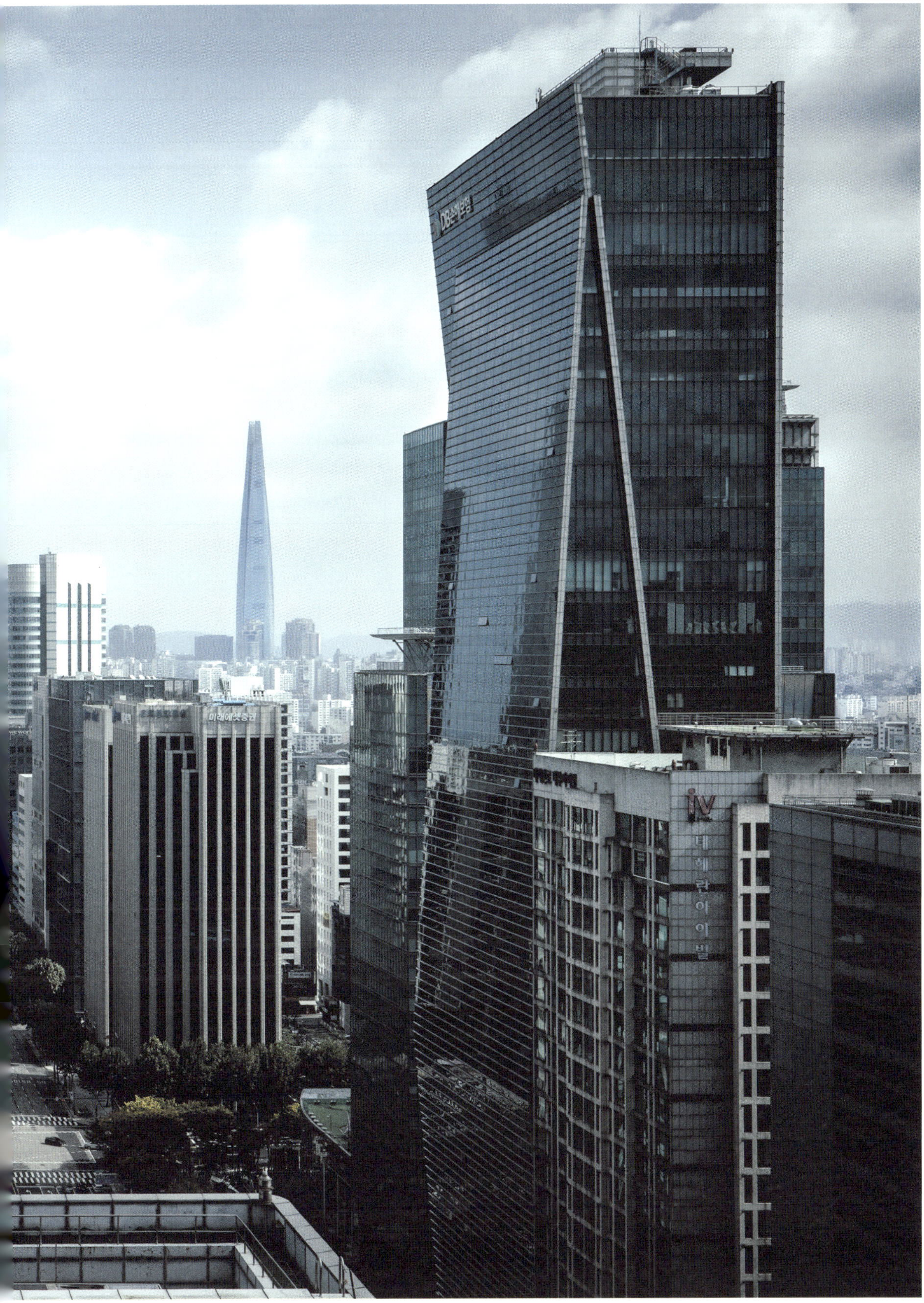
미래에셋증권
iv
테헤란아이빌

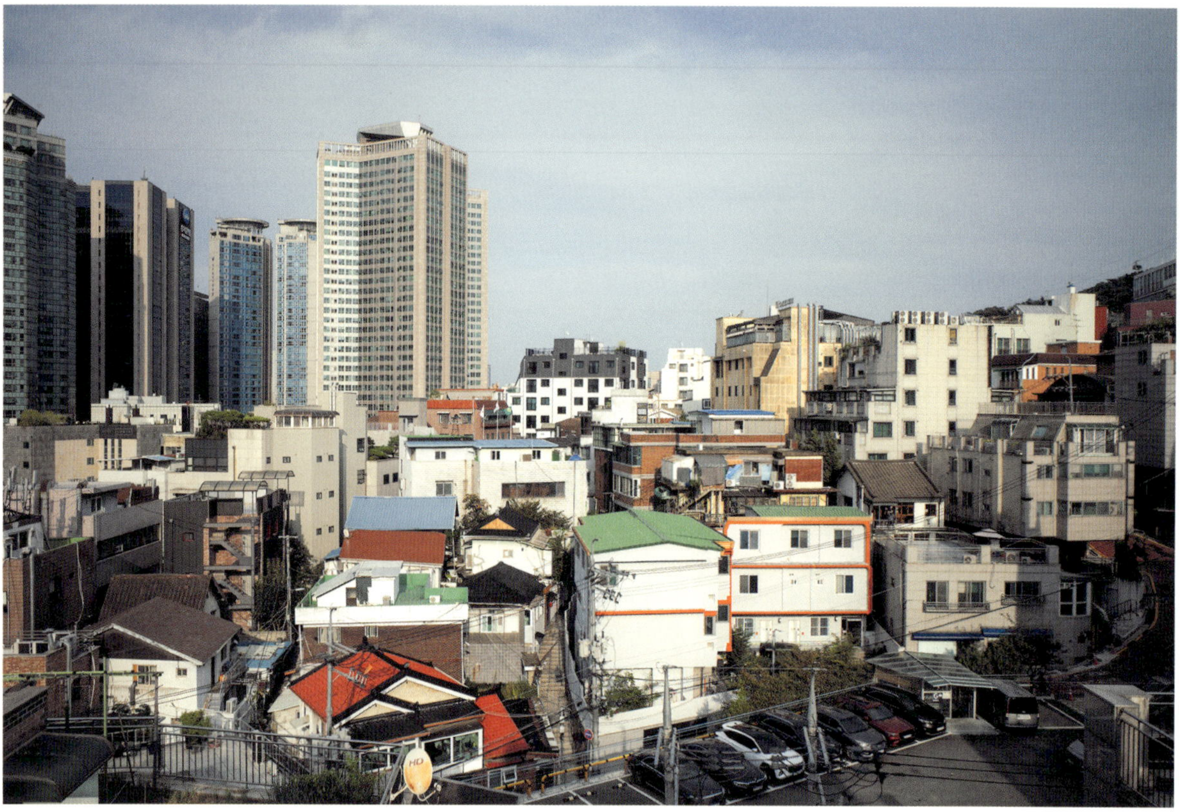

above: Hoehyeon-dong, Jung District + right: Olympic Park, Bangi-dong, Songpa District

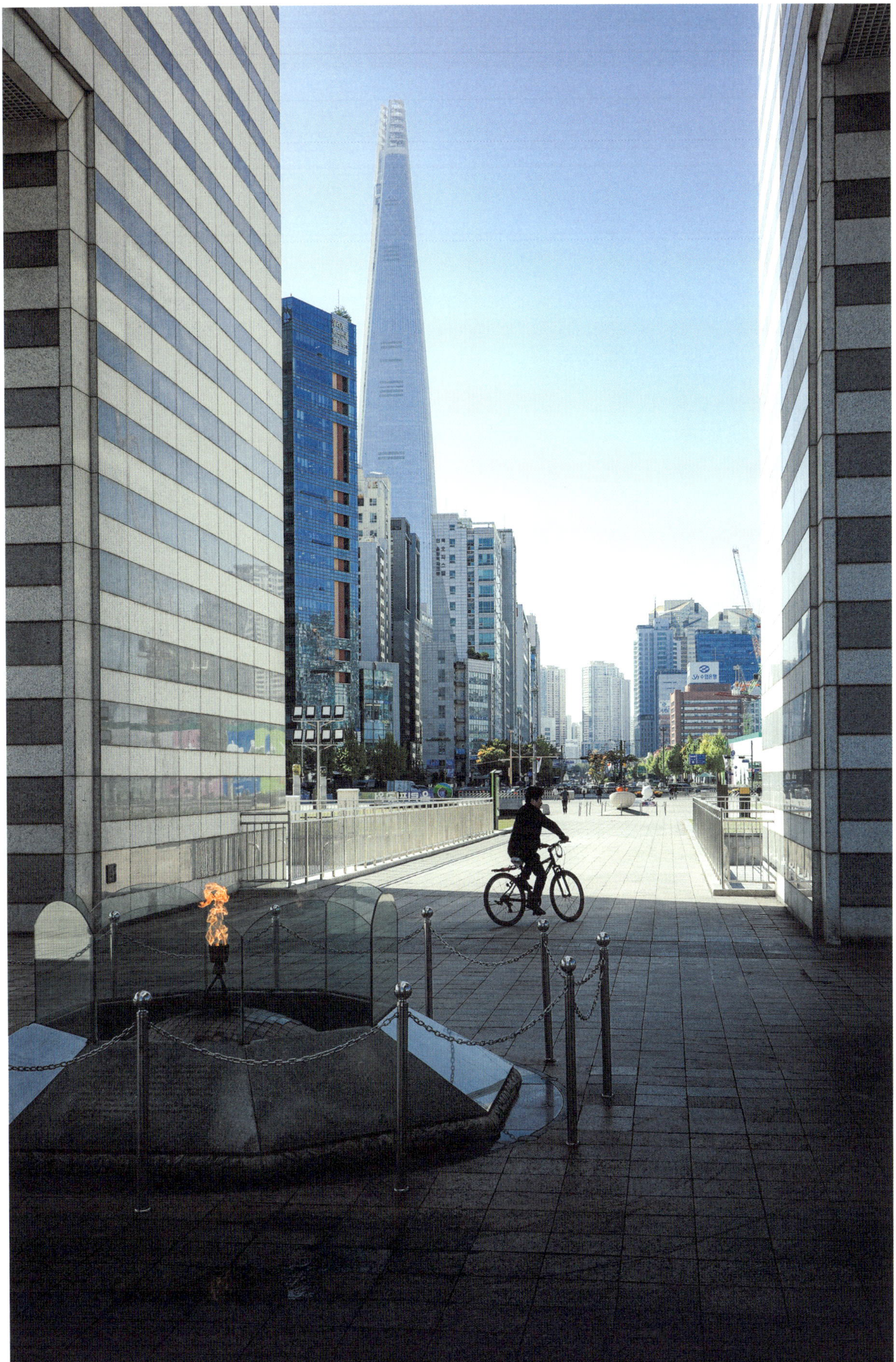

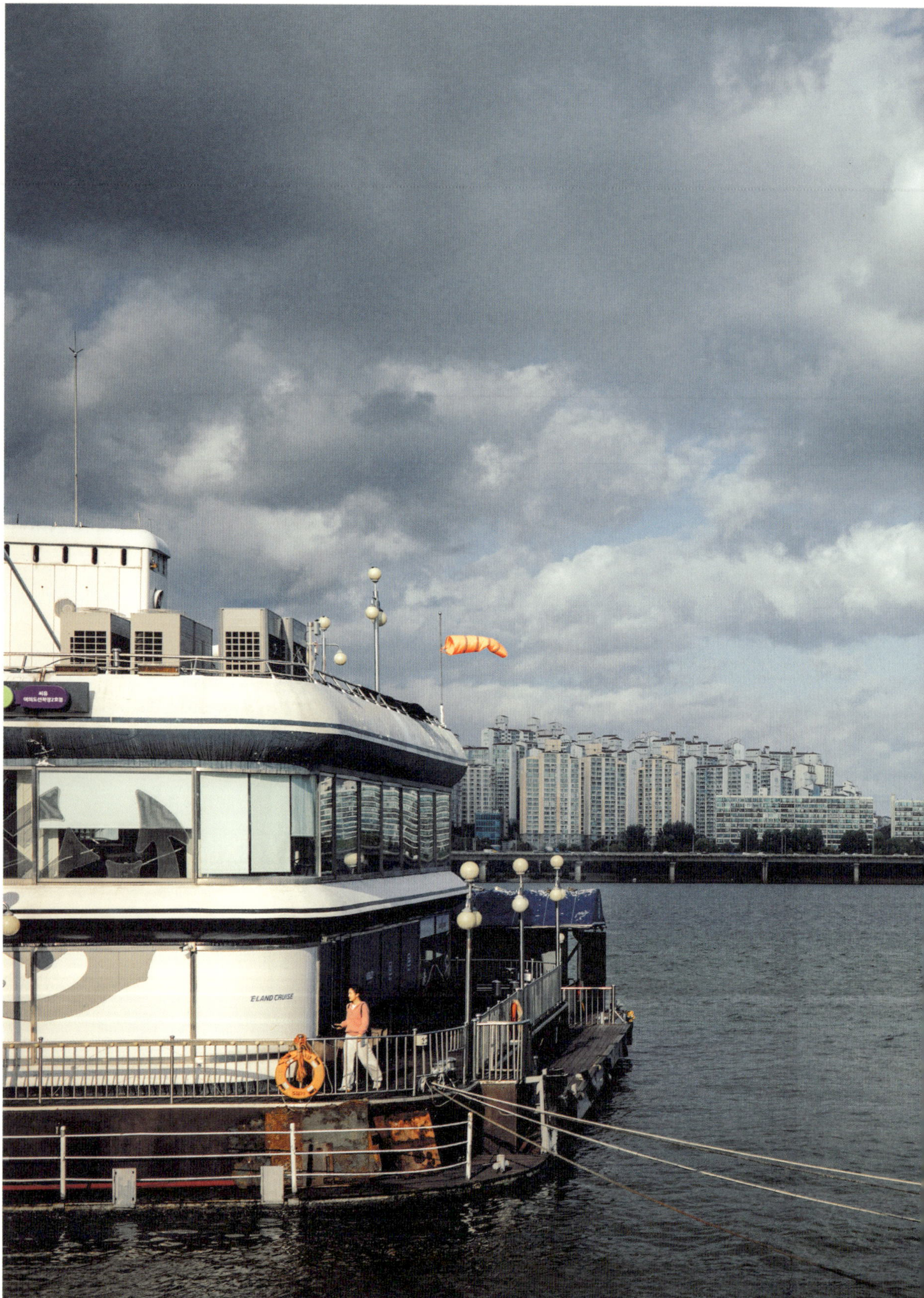


Wonhyo Bridge, Yeouido, Yeongdeungpo District

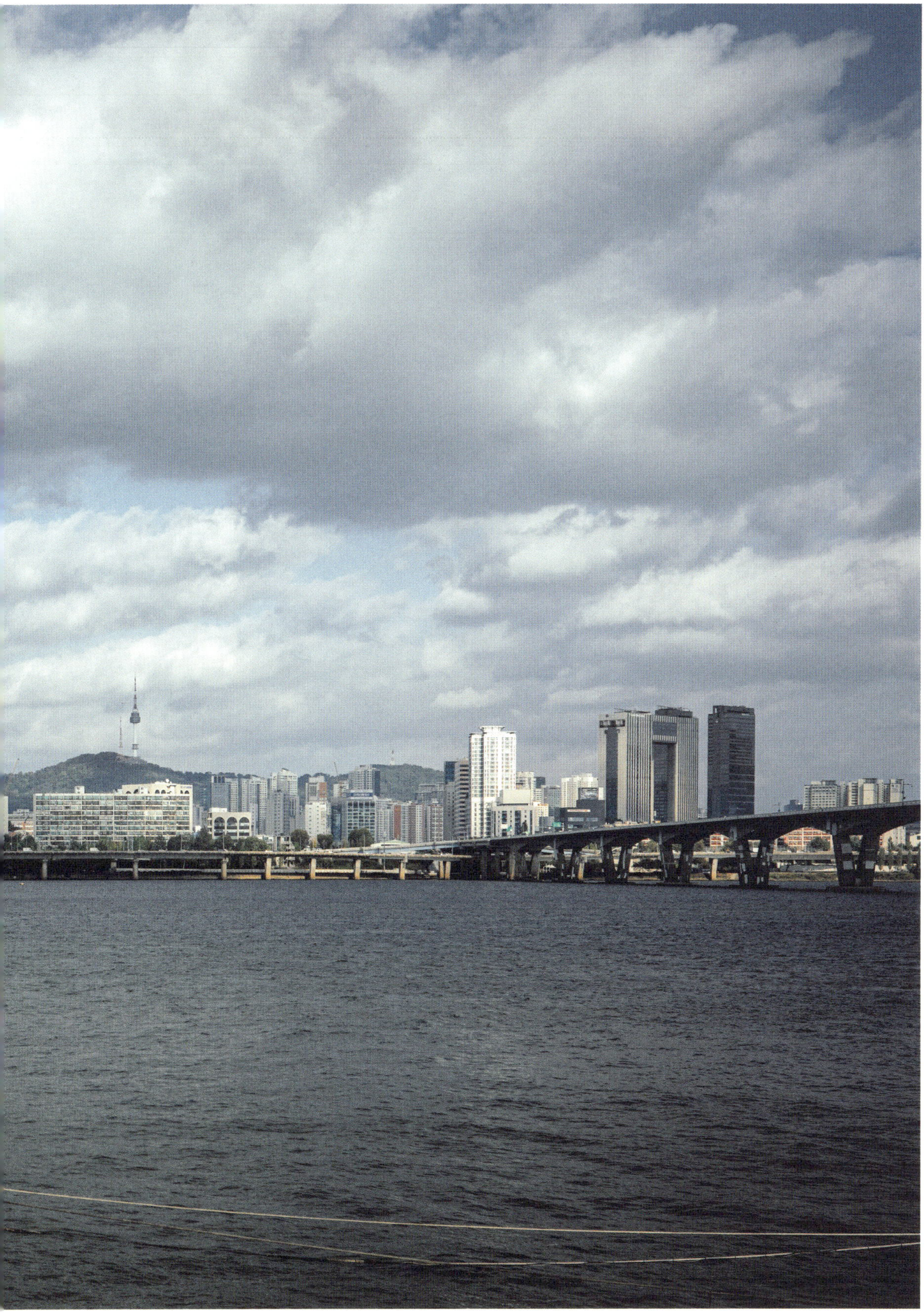

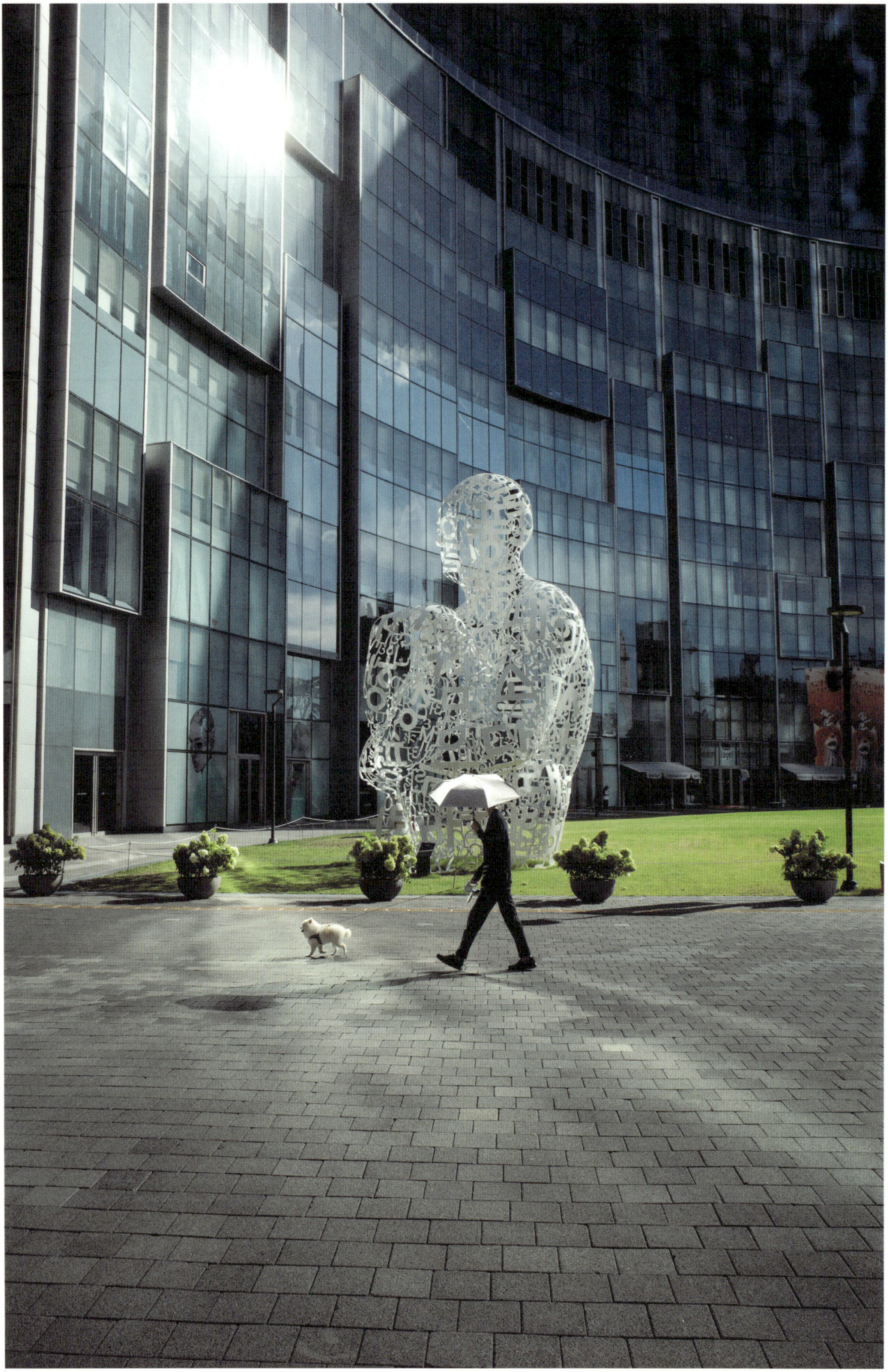

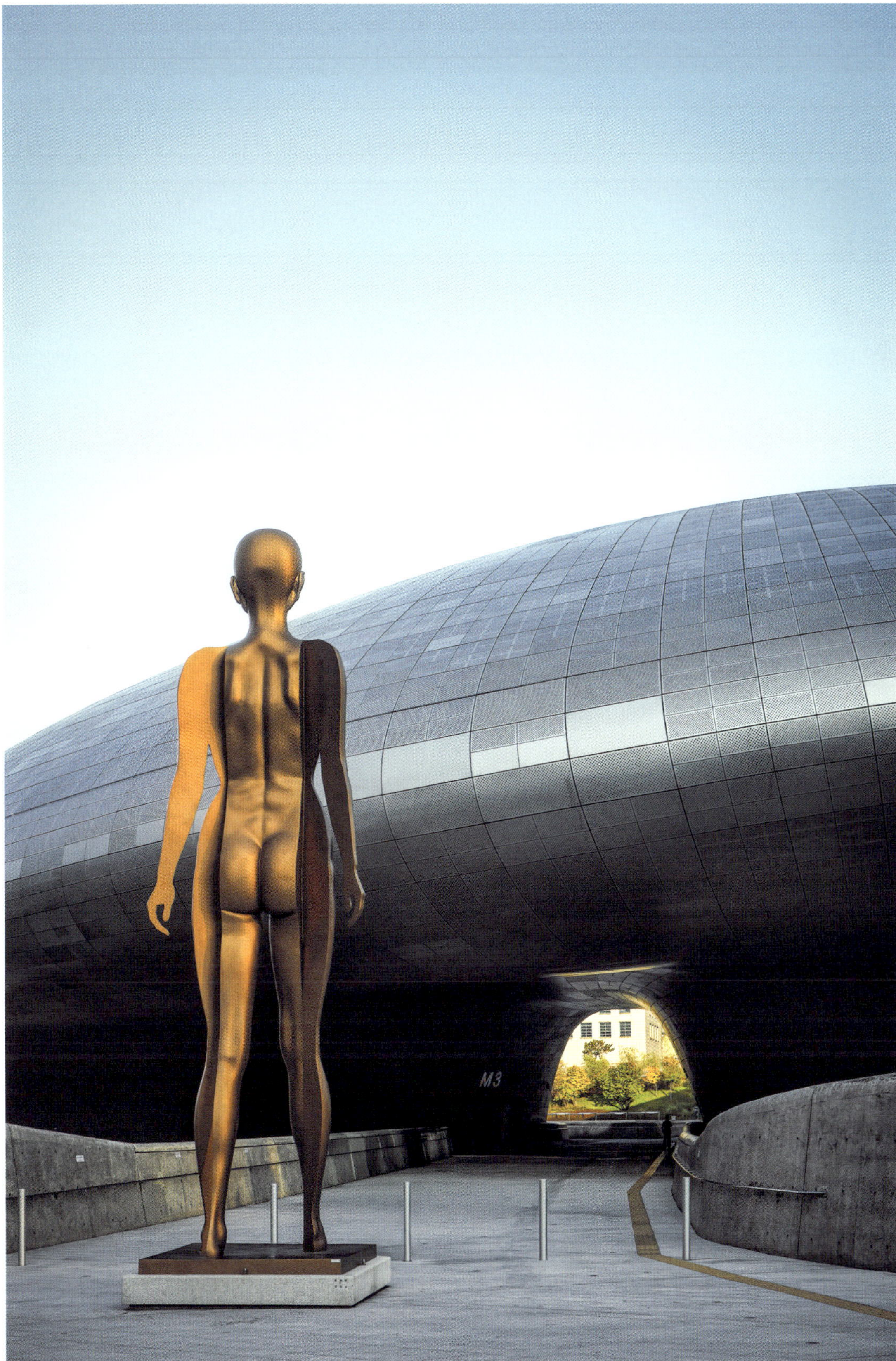


left: Jamsil-dong, Songpa District + above: Dongdaemun Design Plaza (DDP), Jung District

> Designed by British-Iraqi architect Zaha Hadid

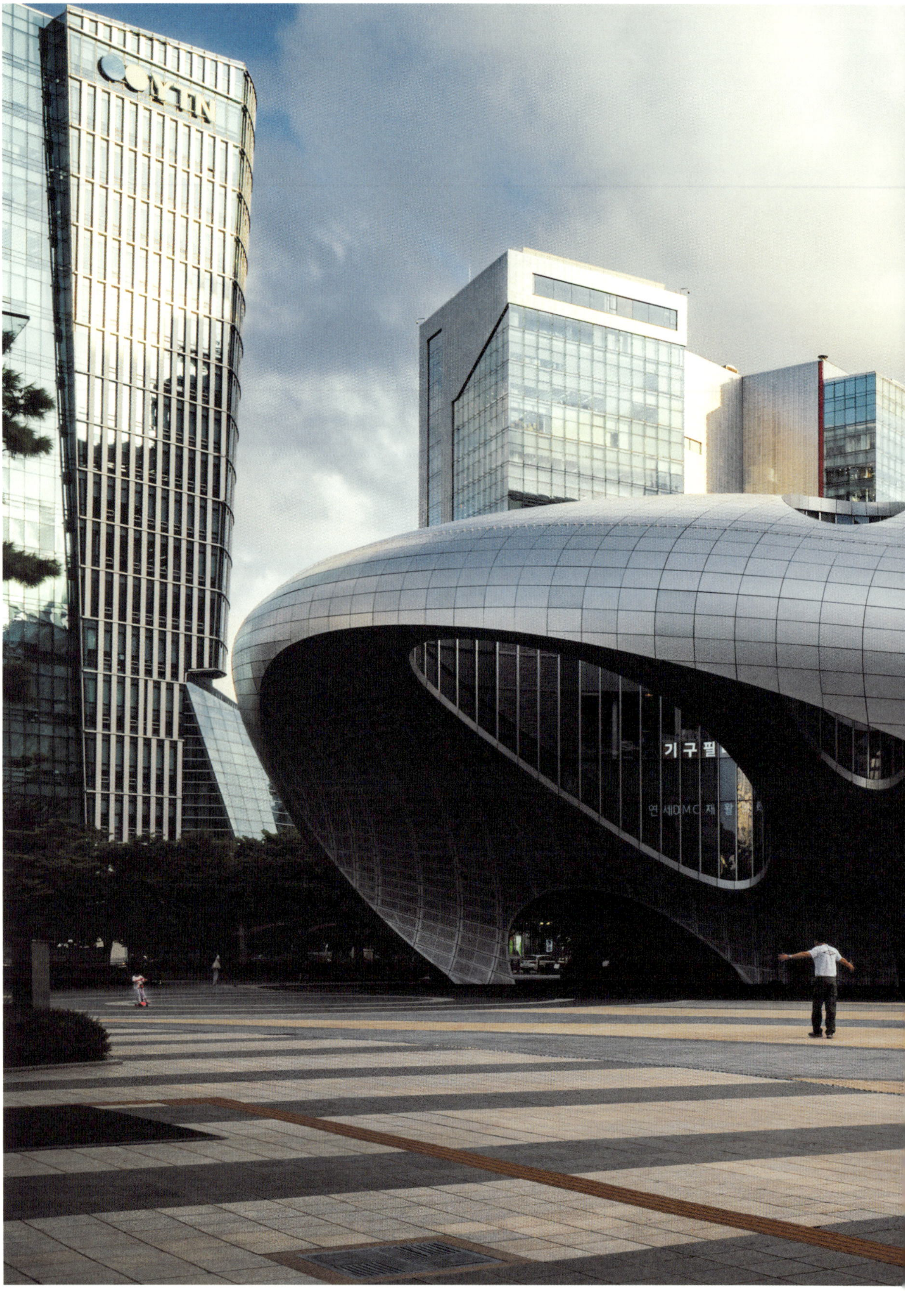


Sangam-dong, Mapo District > Munhwa Broadcasting Corporation (MBC) Headquarters and Media Center

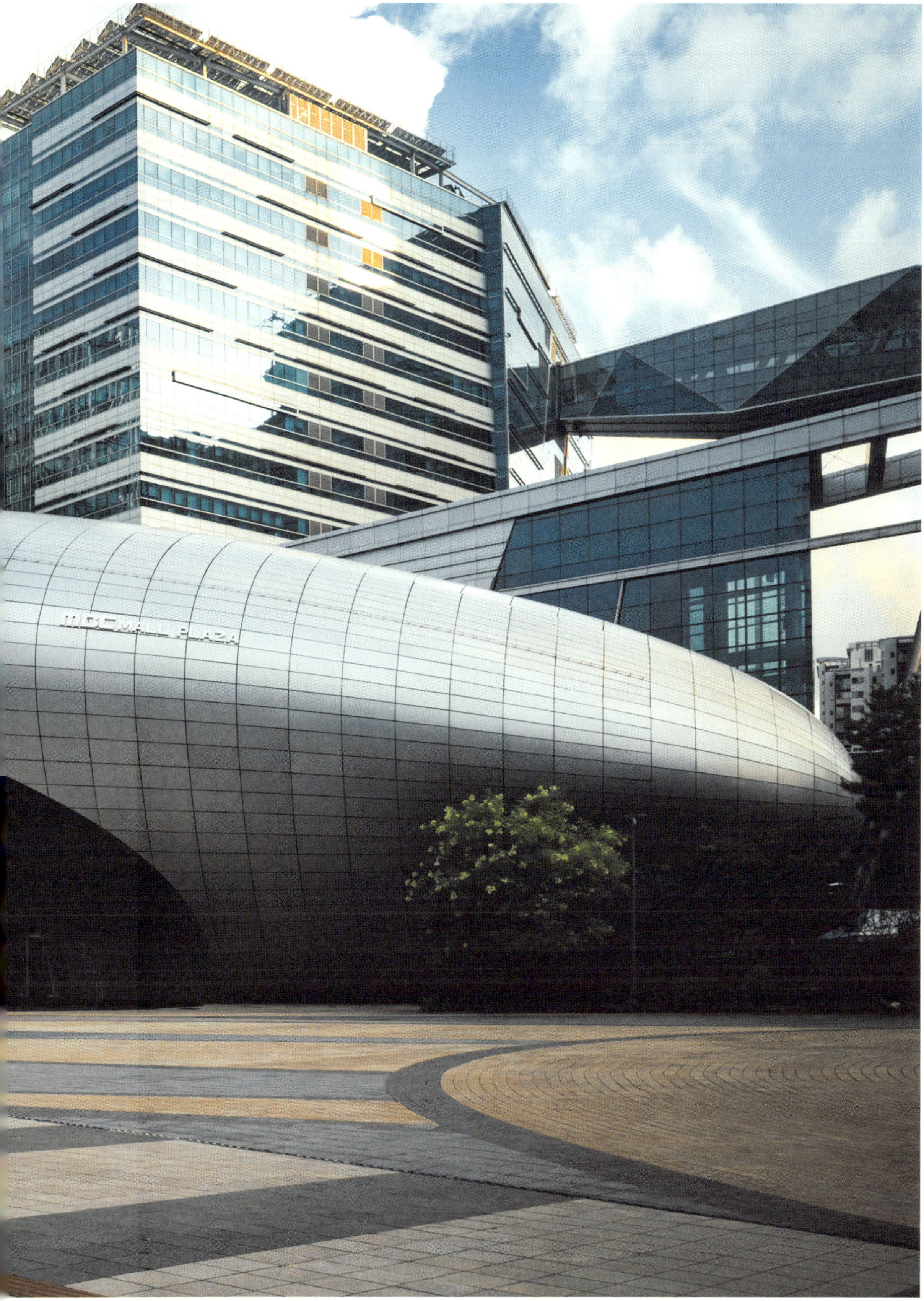
MBC MALL PLAZA

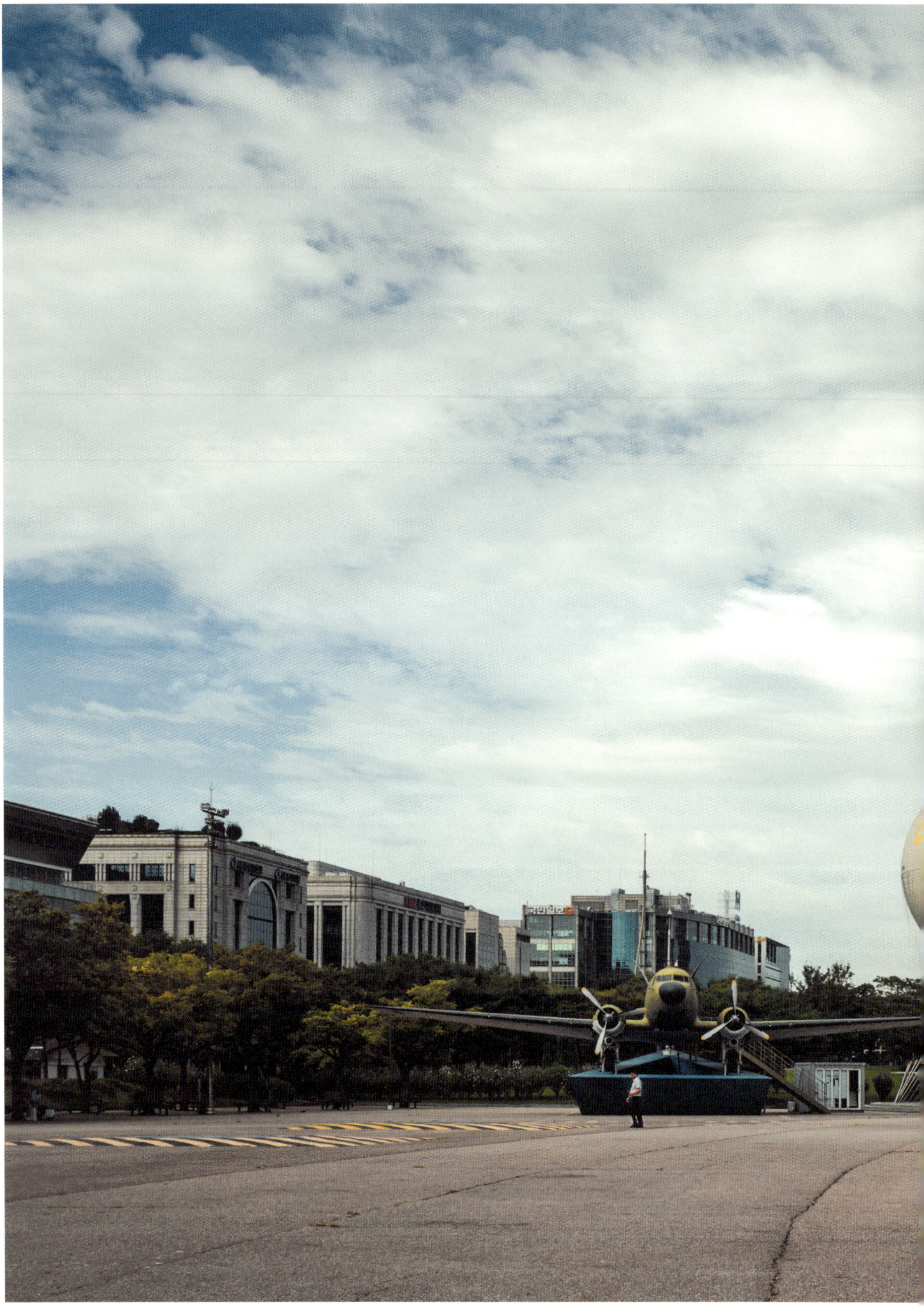

Yeouido Park, Yeouido, Yeongdeungpo District > C-47 Aircraft Exhibition hall and former airfield

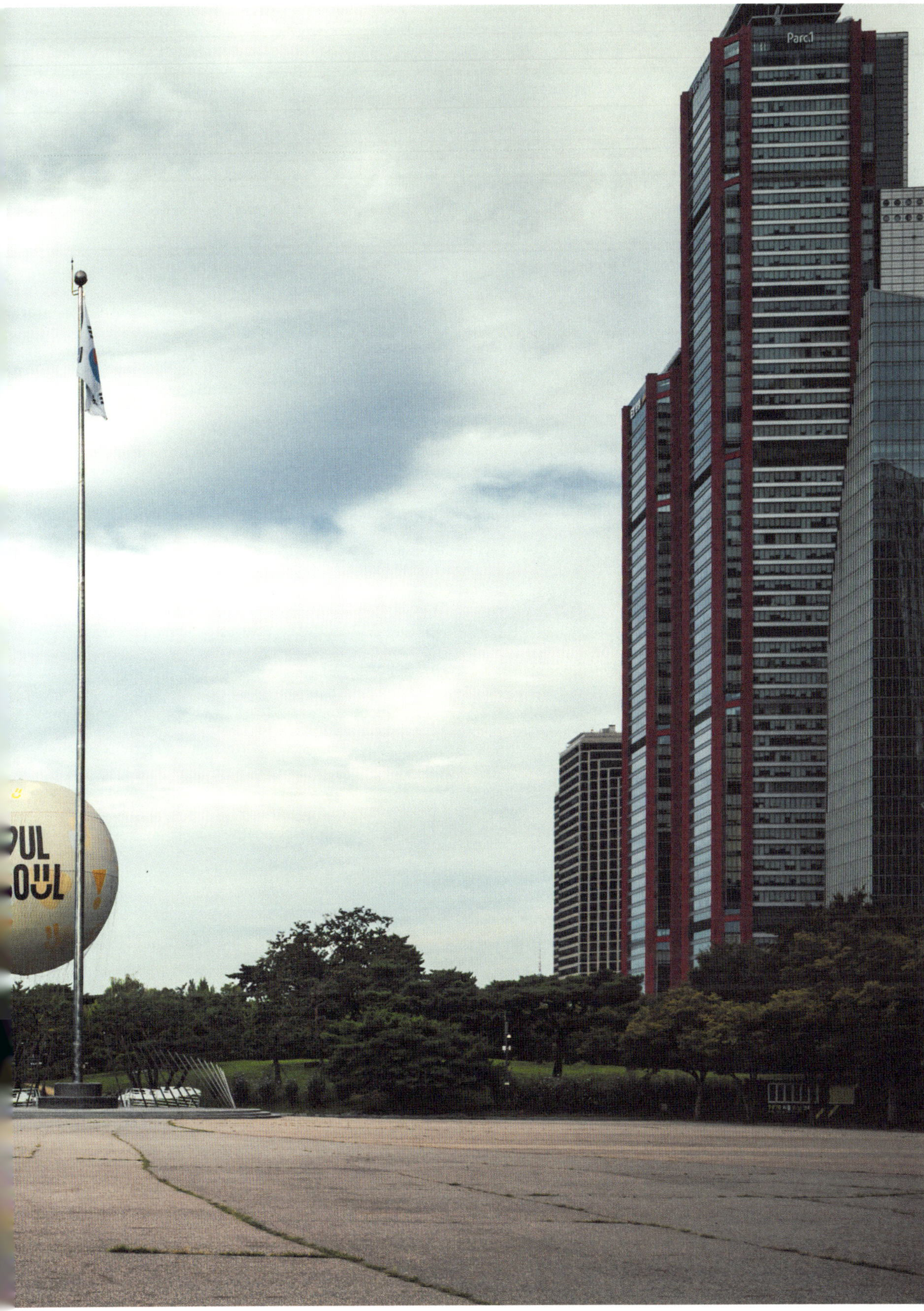
Parc.1

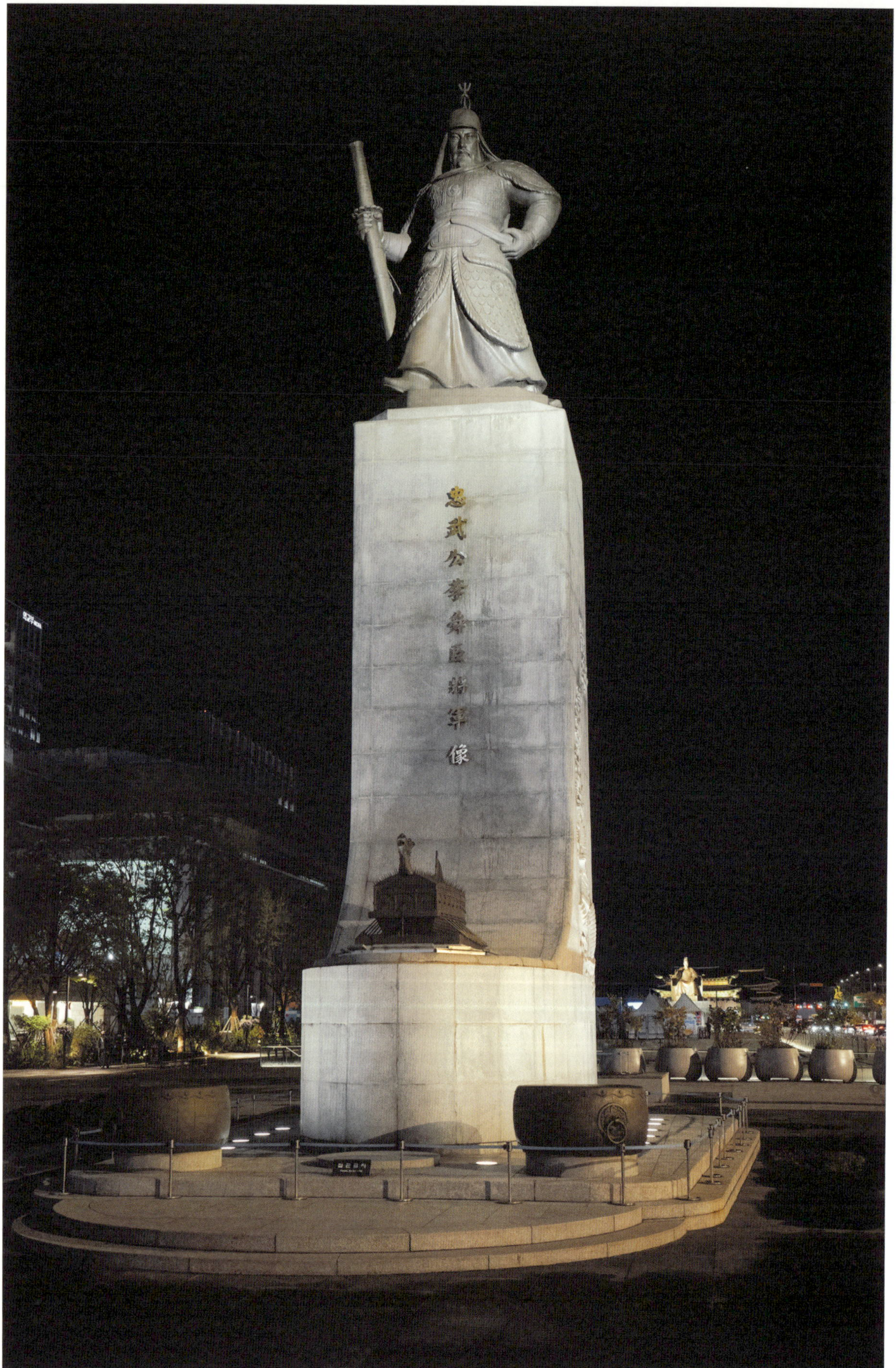
忠武公李舜臣將軍像

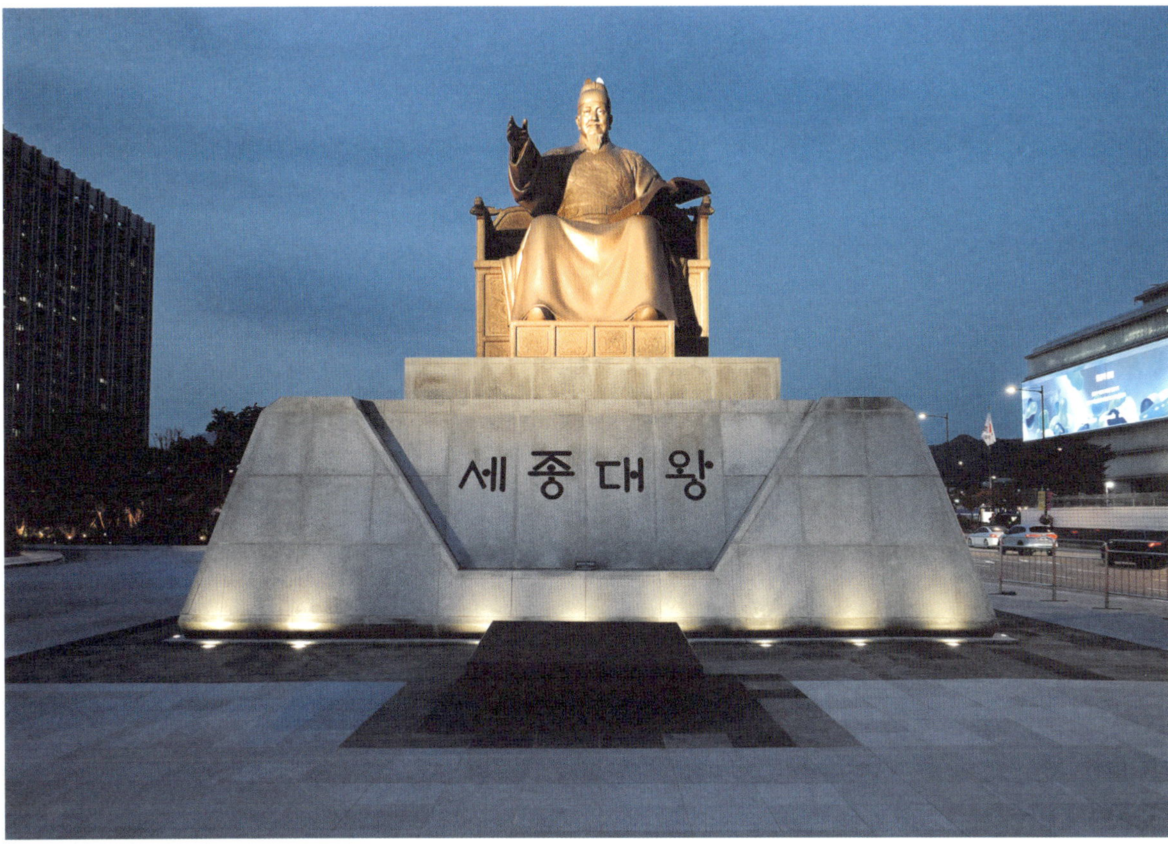


left: Statue of Admiral Yi Sun-Sin + above: Statue of King Sejong, Gwanghwamun Square, Jongno District

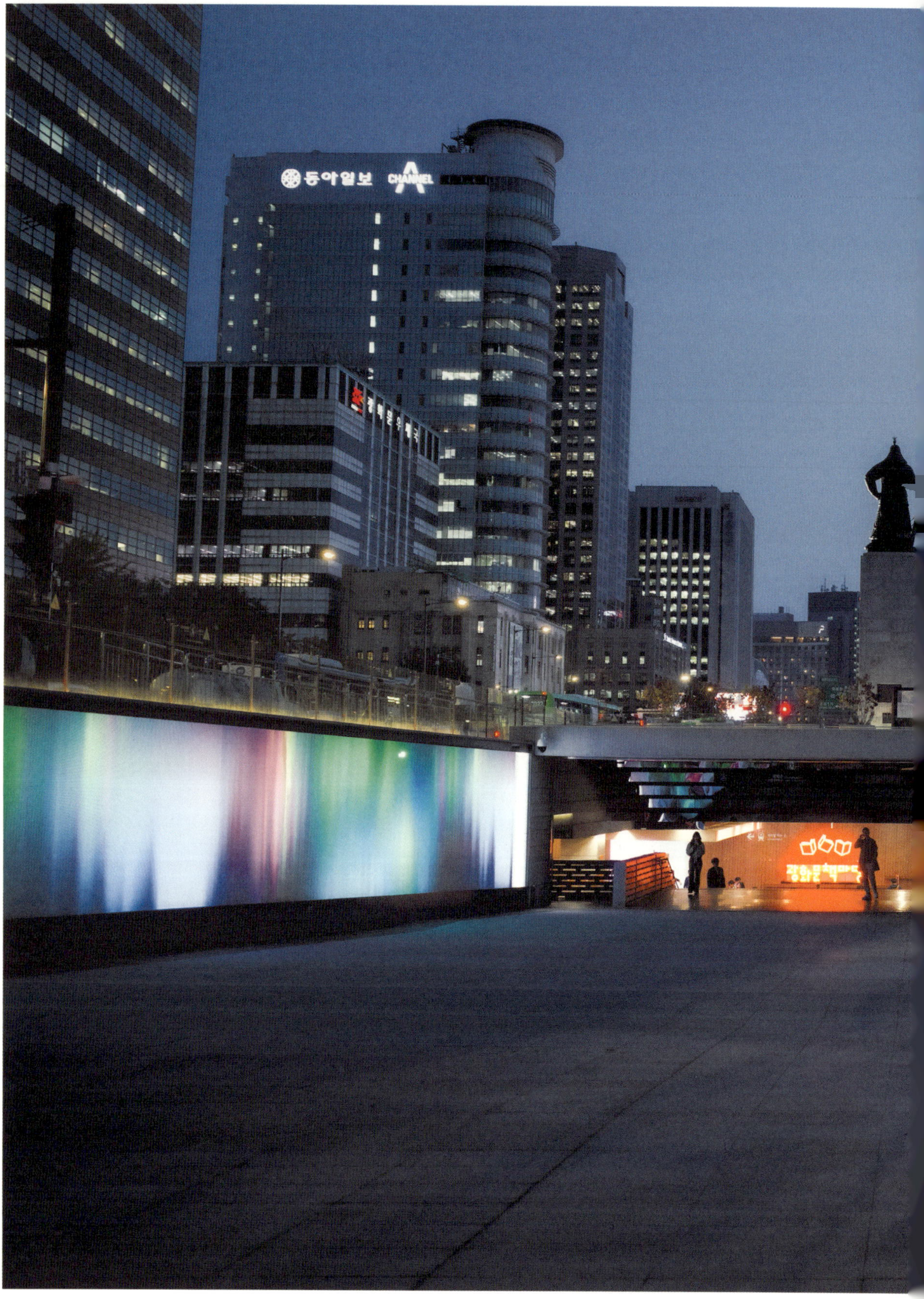


Gwanghwamun Square, Jongno District > Rear view of the Admiral Yi Sun-Sin statue

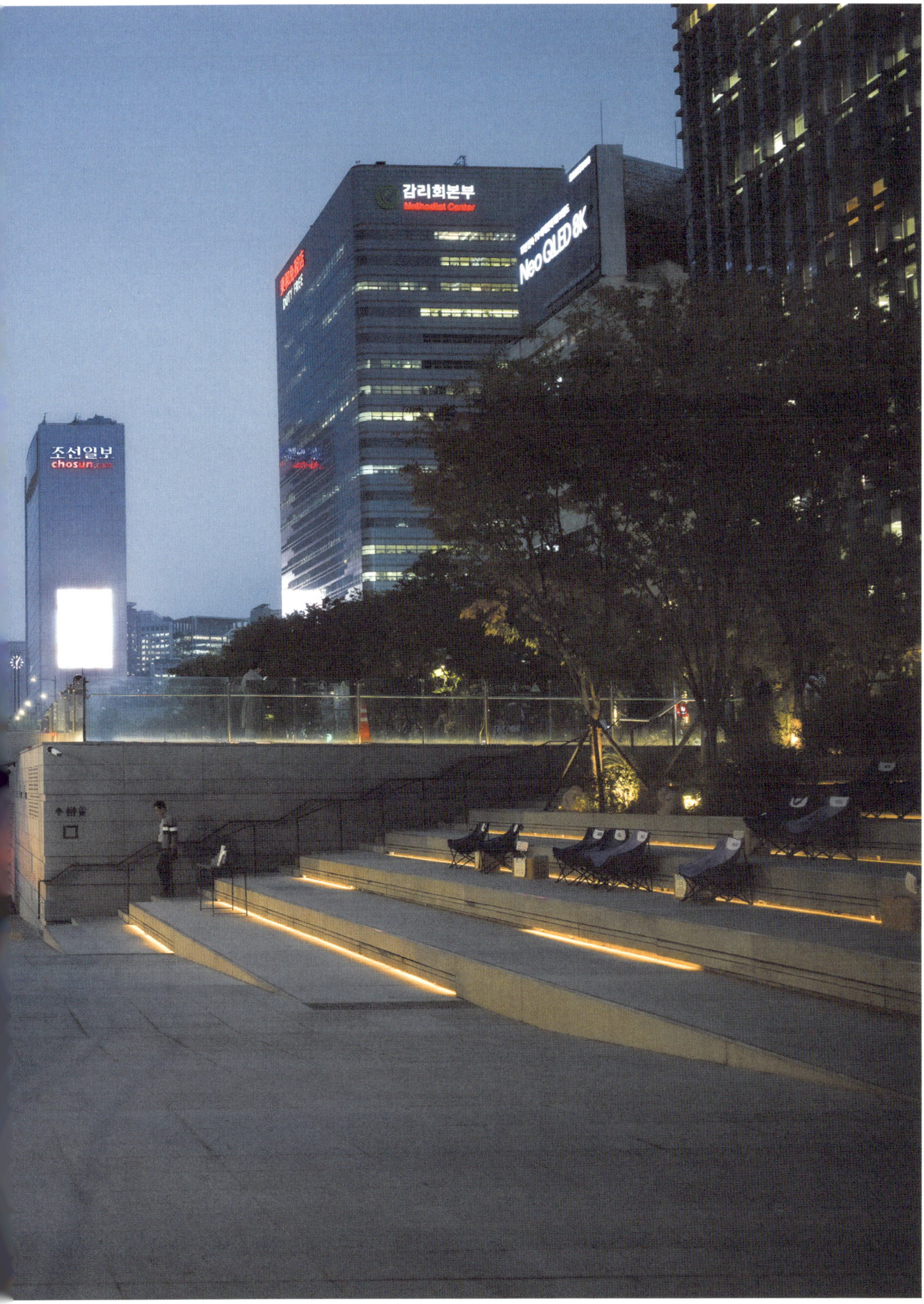
조선일보
감리회본부
Methodist Center
Neo QLED 8K

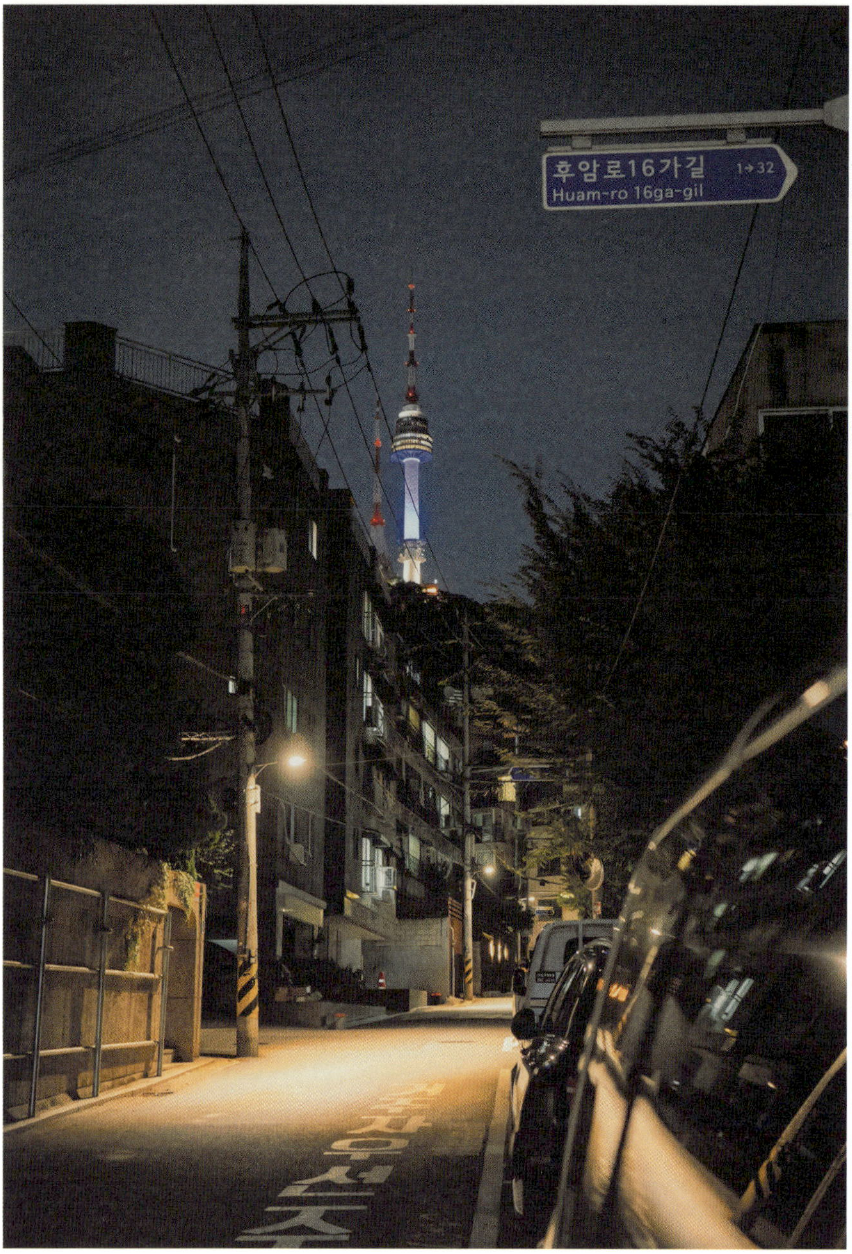


Huam-dong, Yongsan District

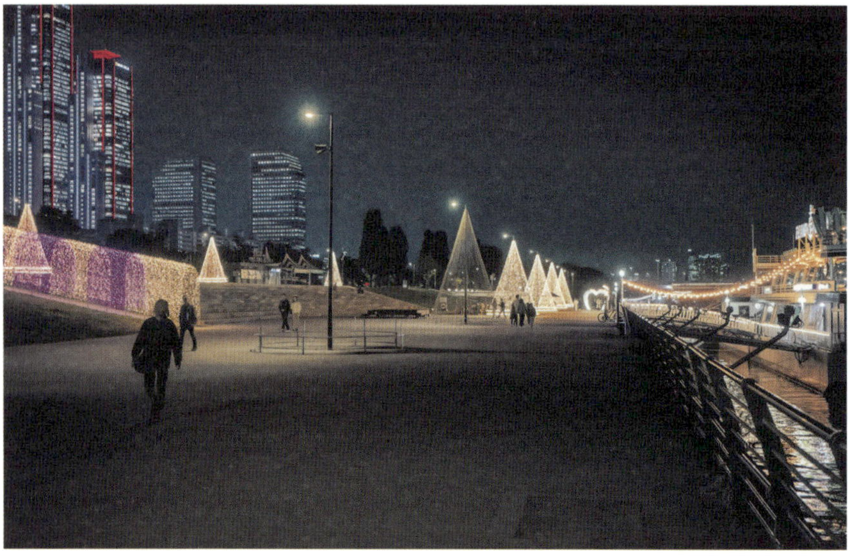

Yeouido Hangang Park,
Yeongdeungpo District

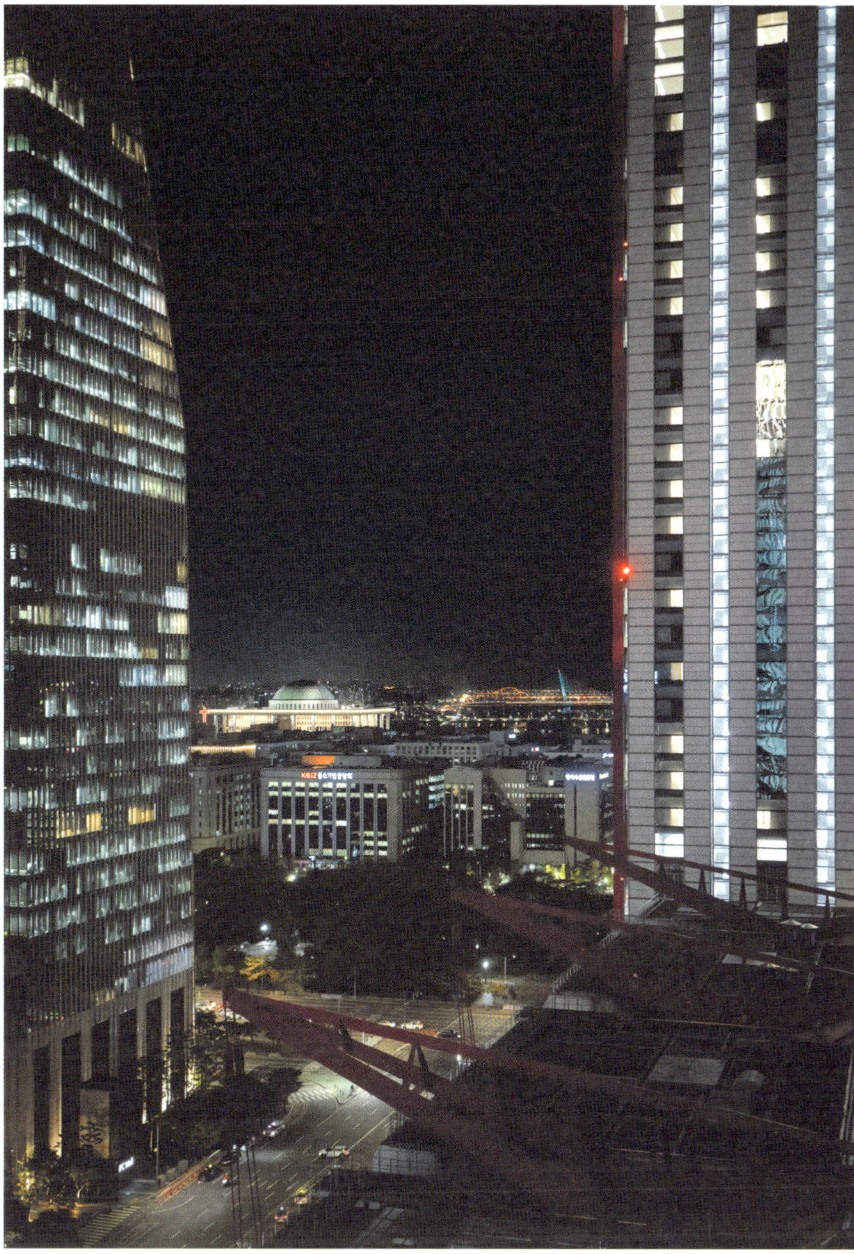

National Assembly Building, Yeouido, Yeongdeungpo District

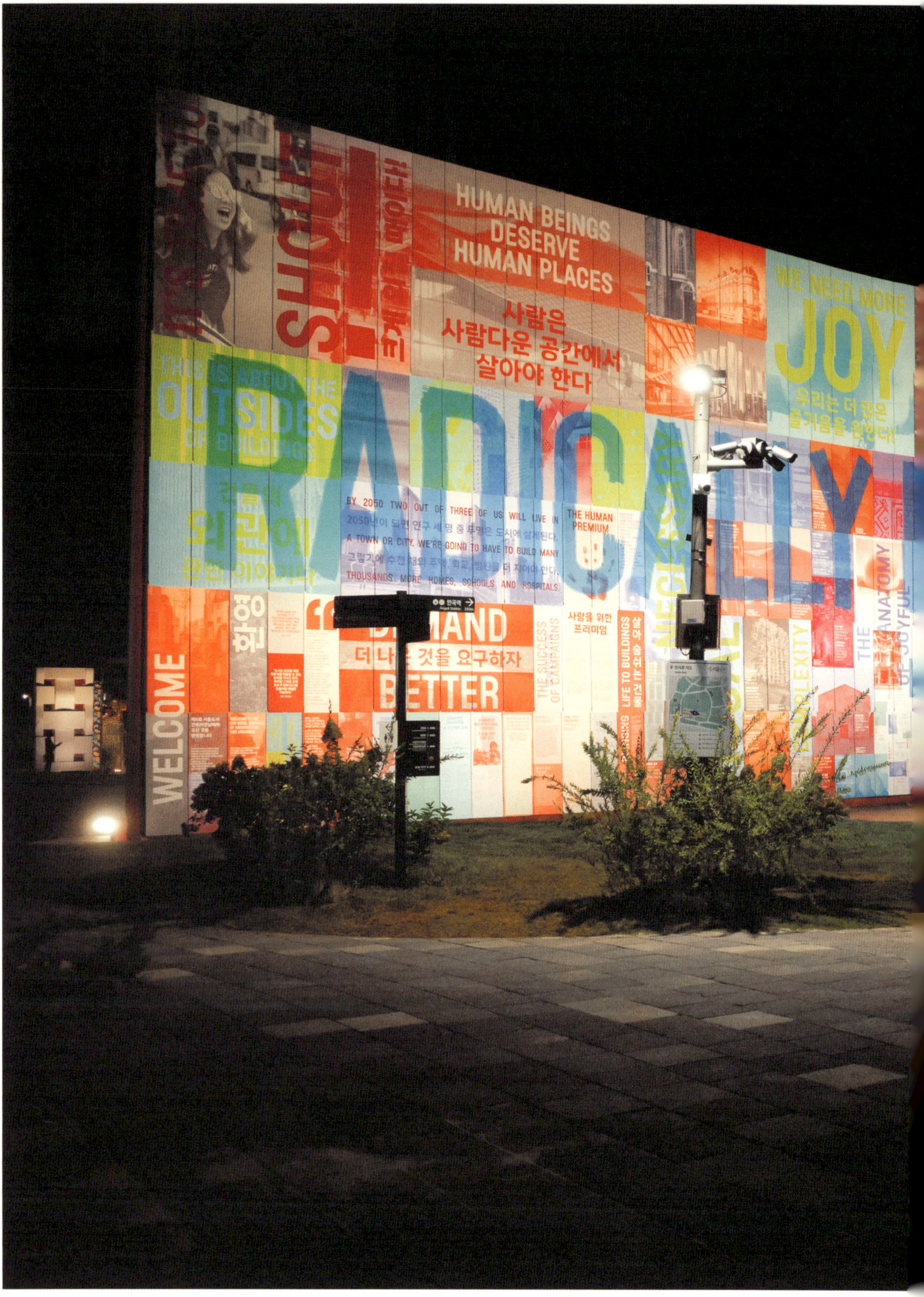


Songhyeon Green Plaza, Songhyeon-dong, Jongno District

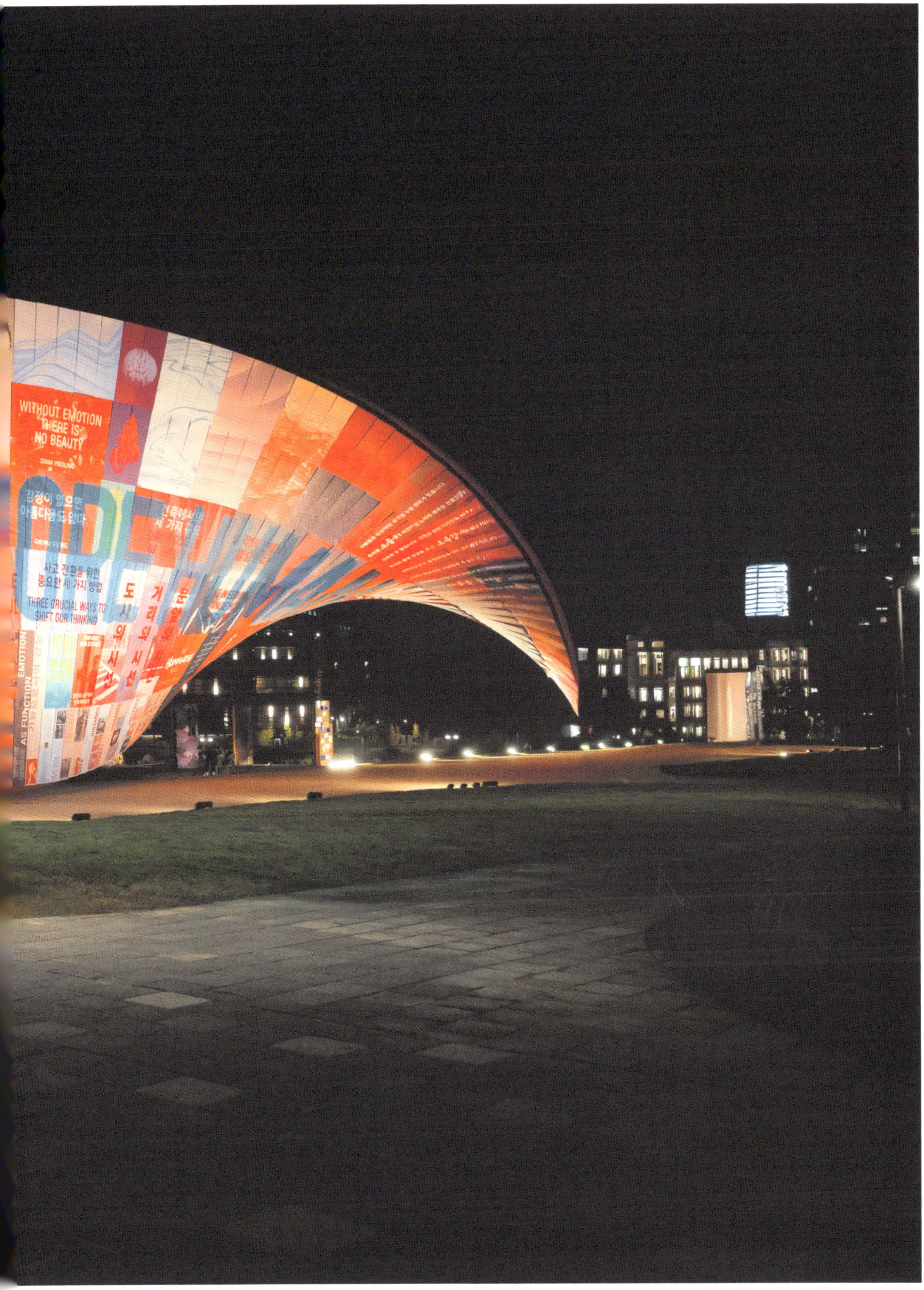
WITHOUT EMOTION THERE IS NO BEAUTY
DIANA VREELAND
감정이 없으면 아름다움도 없다
사고 전환을 위한 중요한 세 가지 방법
THREE CRUCIAL WAYS TO SHIFT OUR THINKING
도시의 시선
거리의 시선
AS FUNCTION EMOTION

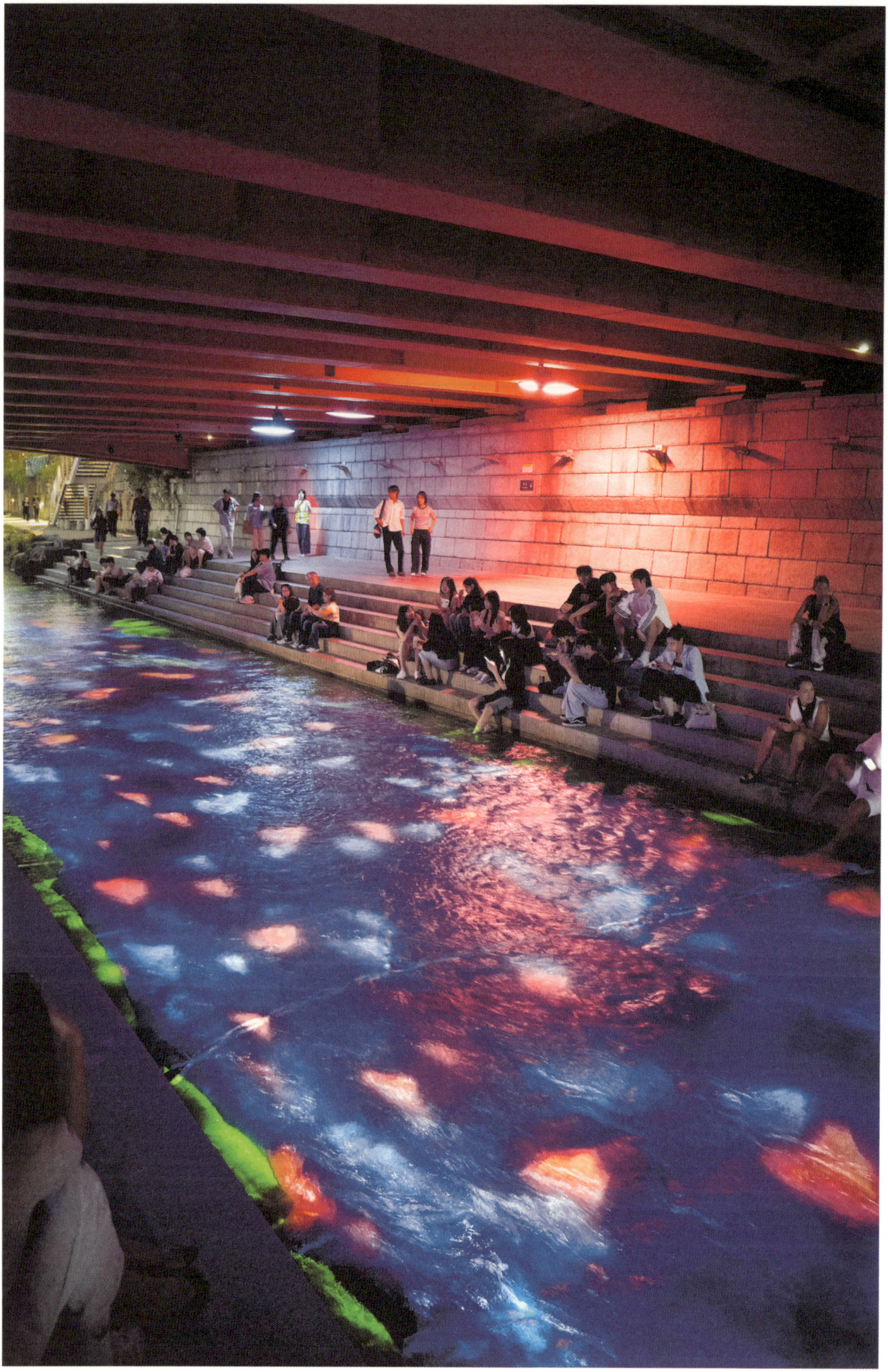

# EOL

얼

(uhl) is a term for the Korean spirit, emphasizing its energetic, joyful, and dynamic aspects. It's described as being the energy that turns dreams into reality and is integral to what it means to be Korean.

Cheonggyecheon is a seven mile restored stream running through central Seoul, from Gwanghwamun and the Jongno Districts down to the Hangang River. Its origins date back to the 14th century Joseon dynasty, when it flowed naturally through Hanyang, the dynasty's capital, serving residents in daily life and drainage. As Seoul modernized, the stream became polluted and was covered with concrete in the 1950s and later buried under an elevated highway. In 2005, Cheonggyecheon was uncovered and transformed into a park lined with linear walkways, bridges, and art installations. The project reintroduced natural water flow, improved air quality, and quickly became one of the city's most popular public spaces. It reflects the city's ability to reinvent itself while restoring balance between people, nature, and its historical roots.

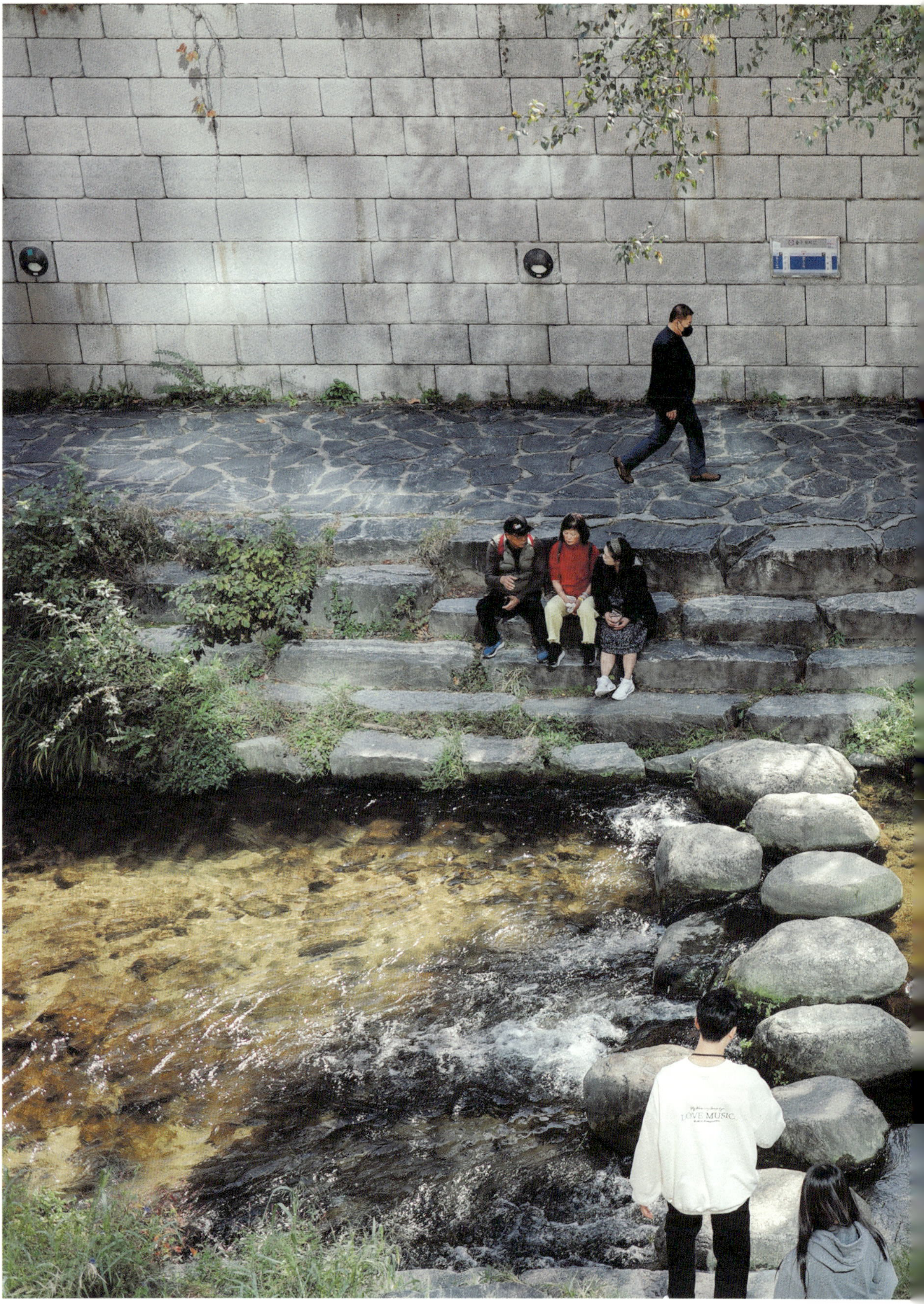


above + previous spread: Cheonggyecheon, Jongno District

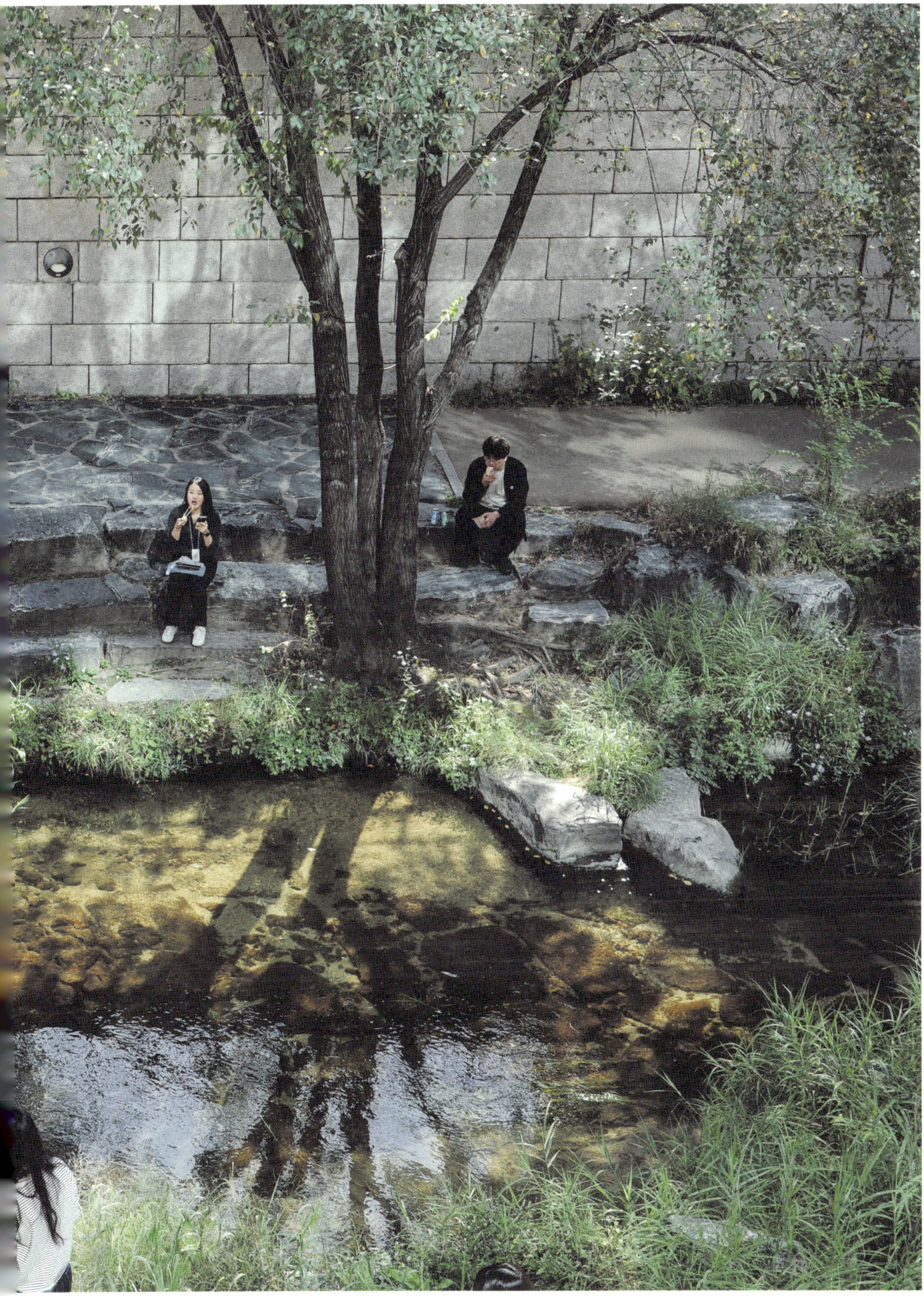

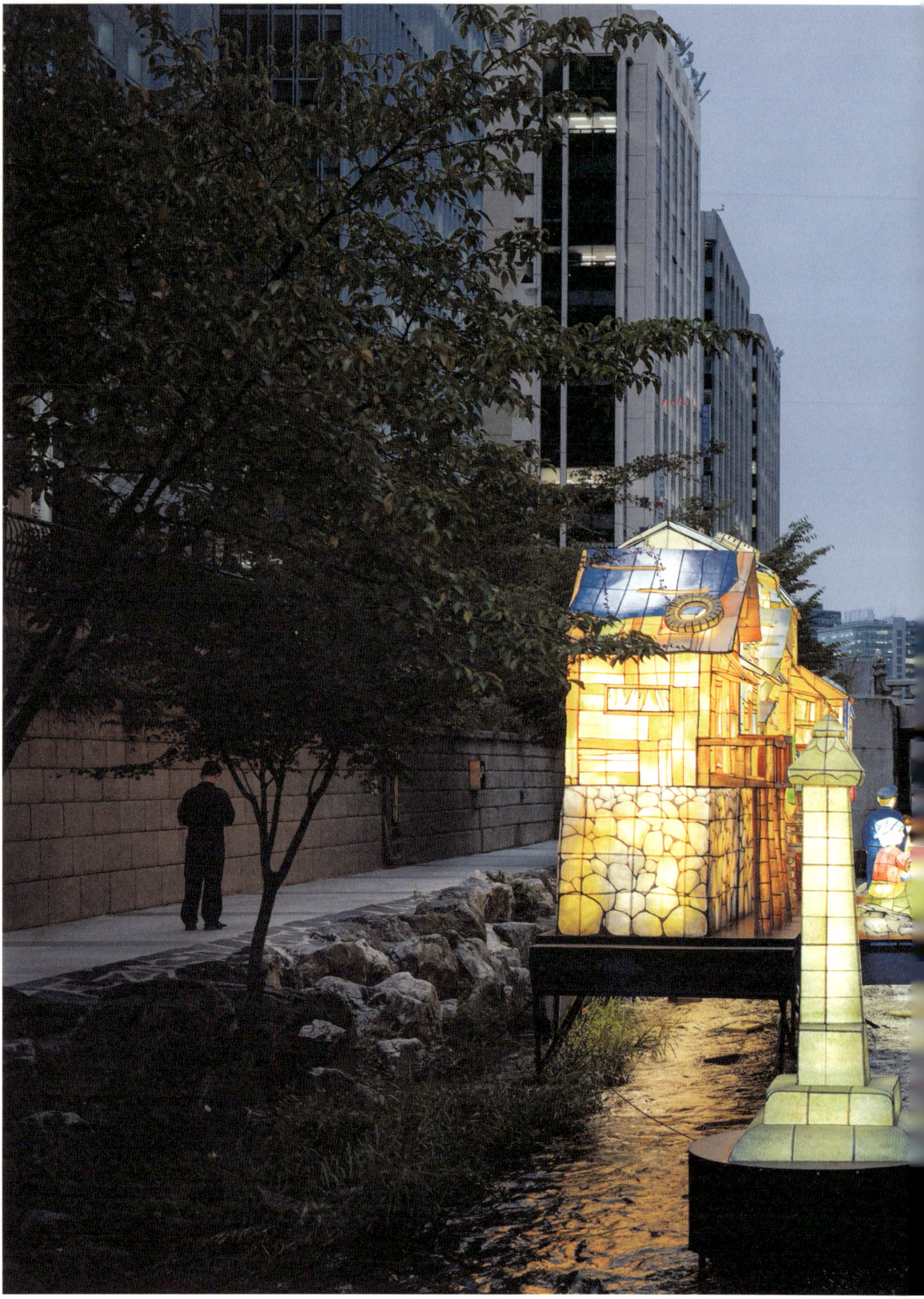

Cheonggyecheon, Jongno District

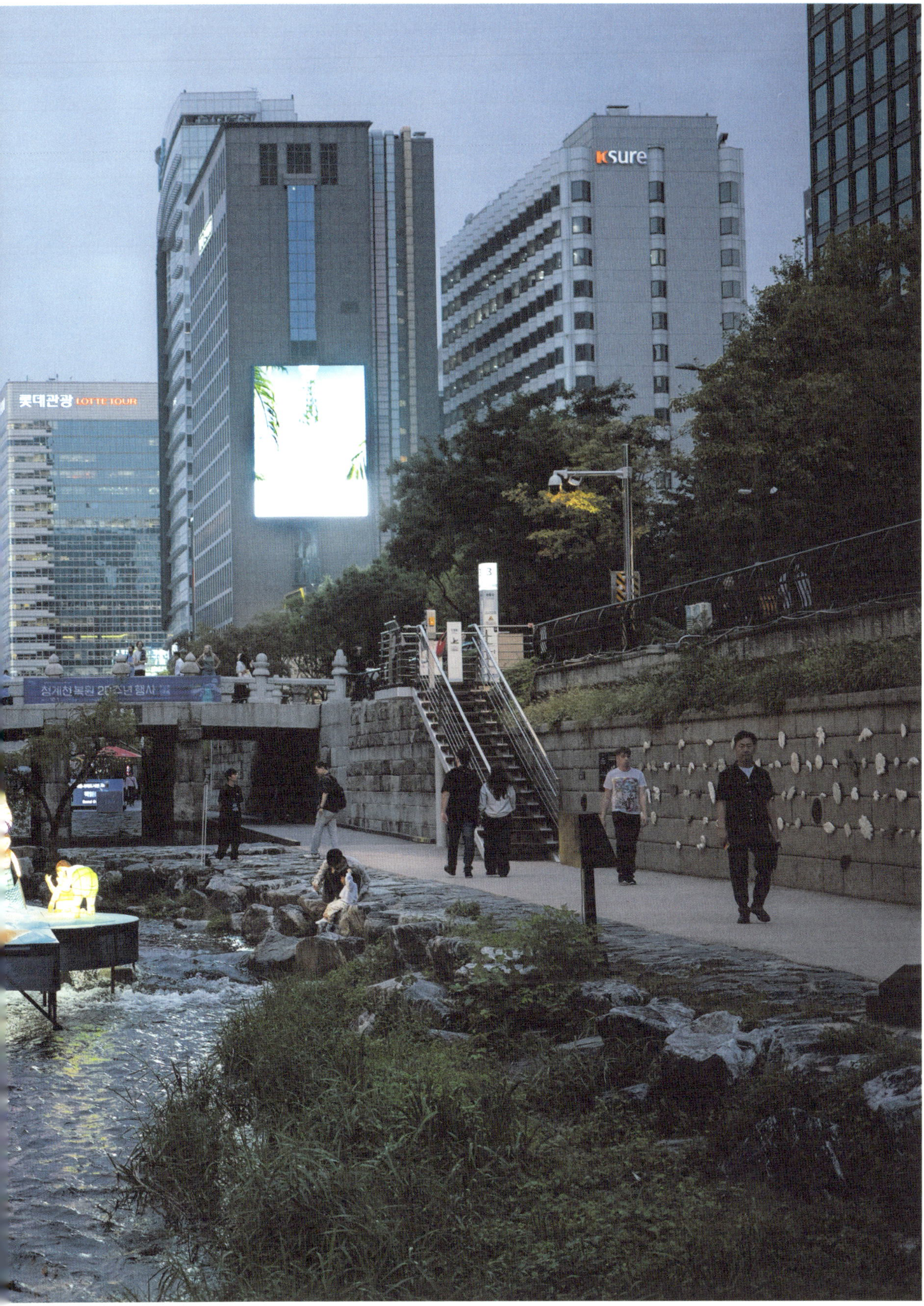
롯데관광 LOTTE TOUR
Ksure

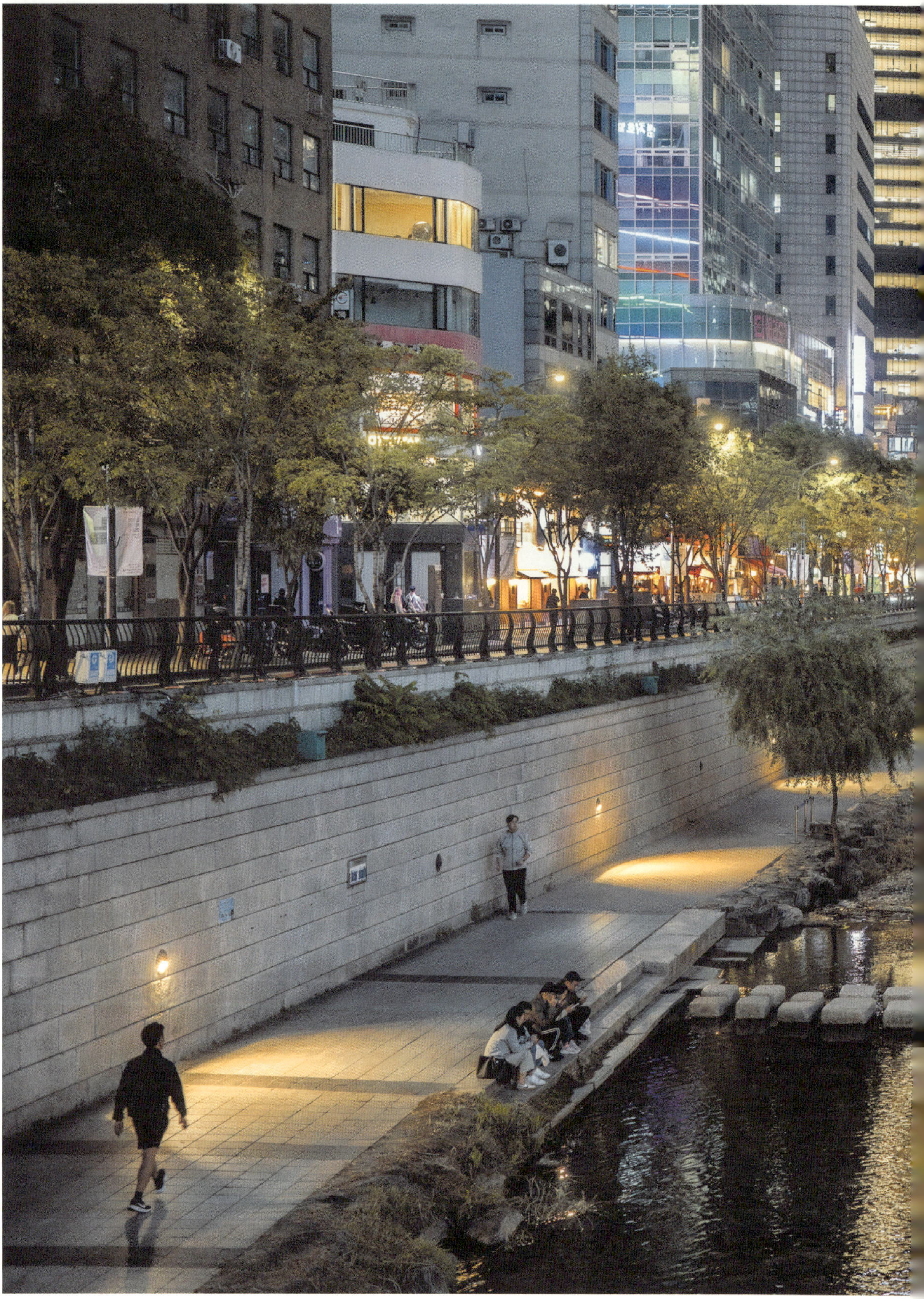

Cheonggyecheon, Jongno District

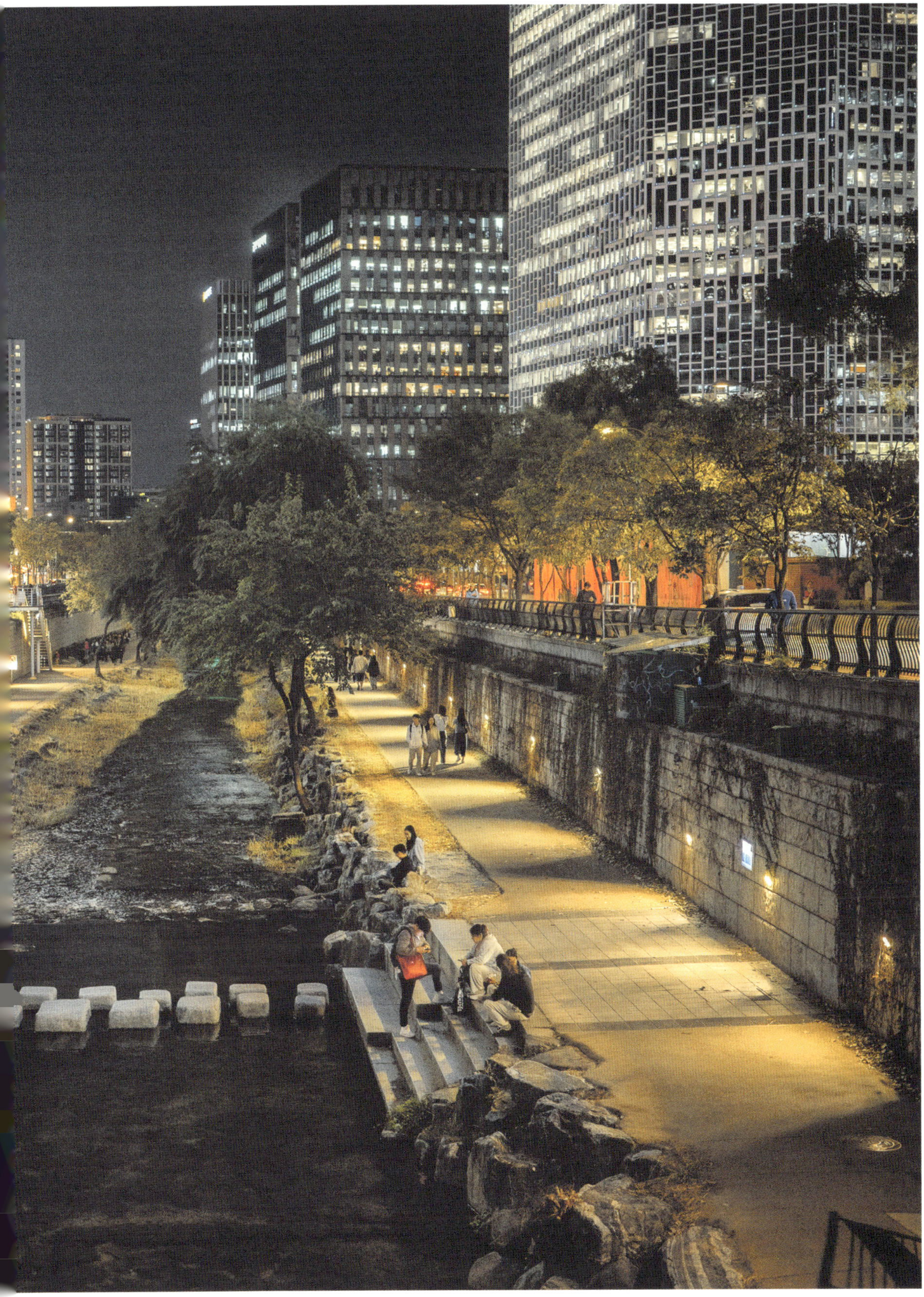

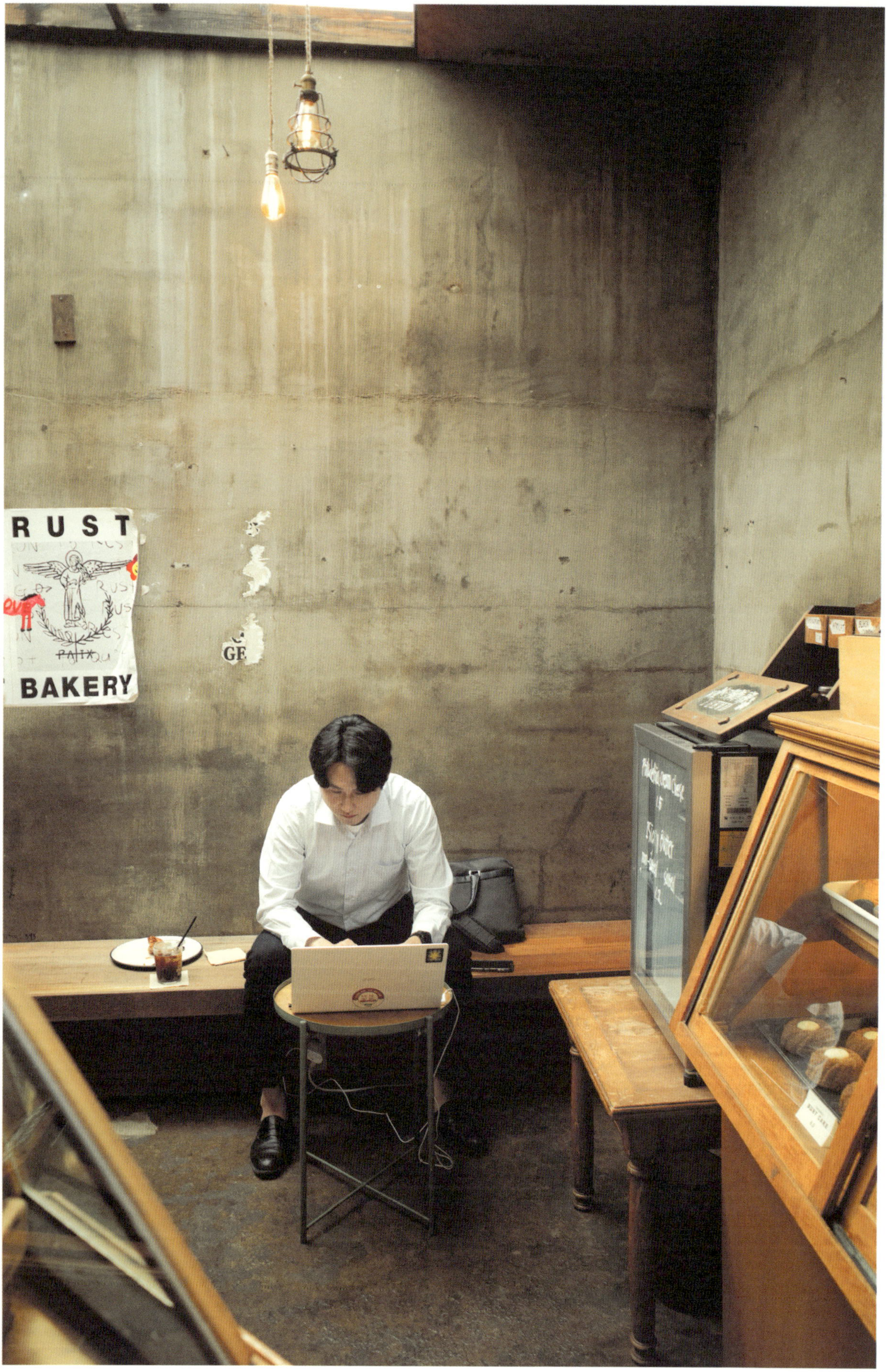
RUST
BAKERY

# KAPE

## 카페

(kah-peh) refers to modern coffee shops, spaces designed for espresso, ambience, and social gathering. Over the past decade, Seoul has experienced an explosive rise in cafés, growing to more than 15,000 coffee shops across the city, from global chains to tiny neighborhood roasters. Nationwide, South Korea counts over 100,000 cafés, nearly double the number of convenience stores, with South Koreans drinking an average of over 400 cups of coffee a year. This boom has turned café culture into a defining part of Seoul's urban life.

Cafés in Seoul serve as "third spaces"—not just for coffee, but for studying, dating, working remotely, and social signaling. Many cafés are independently owned and design-driven, often doubling as concept stores, galleries, or studios. Café culture reflects Seoul's social pace and aesthetics: a blend of modern design, technology, and community.

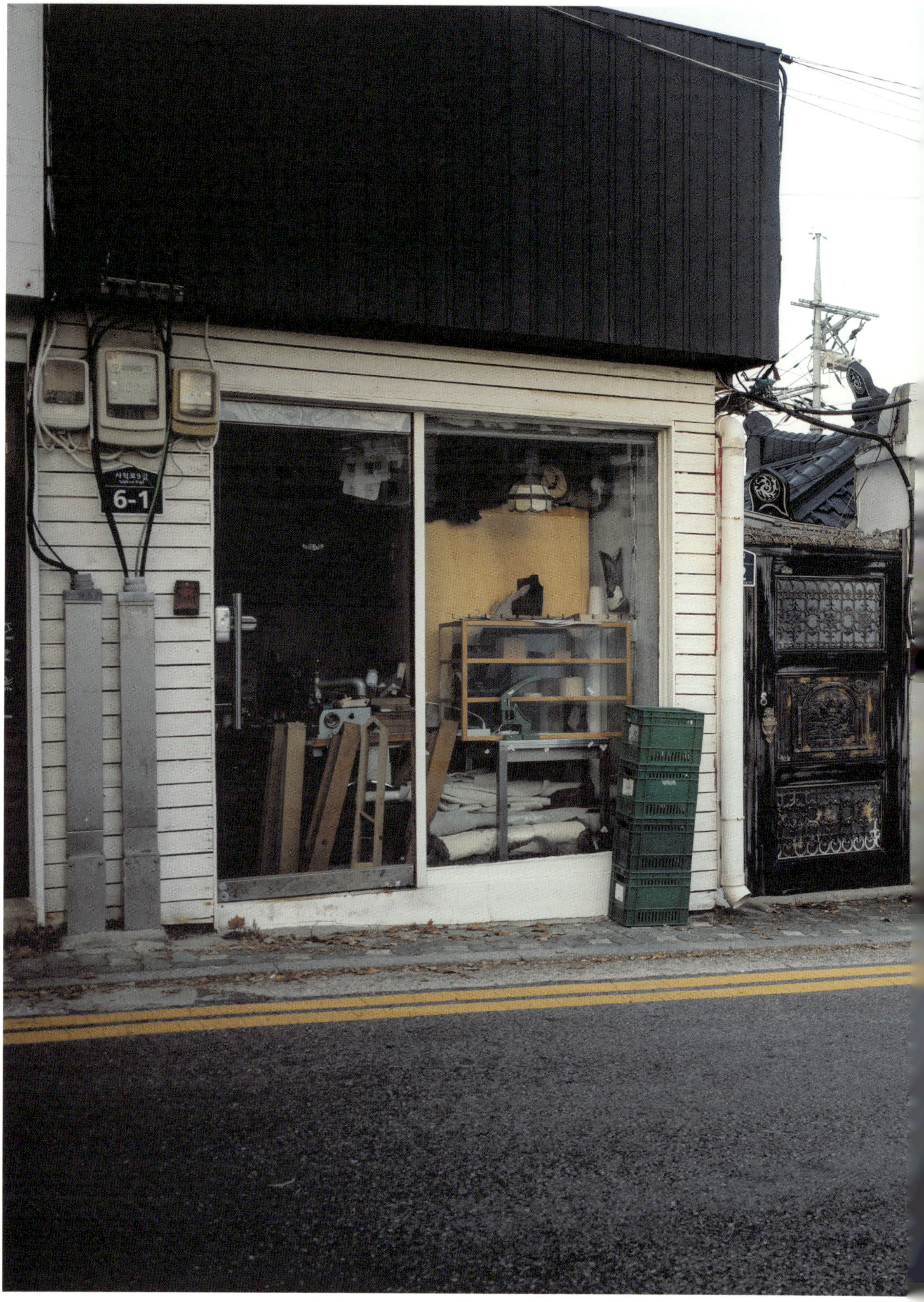


above: Sajik-dong, Jongno District + previous spread: Mullae-dong, Yeongdeungpo District

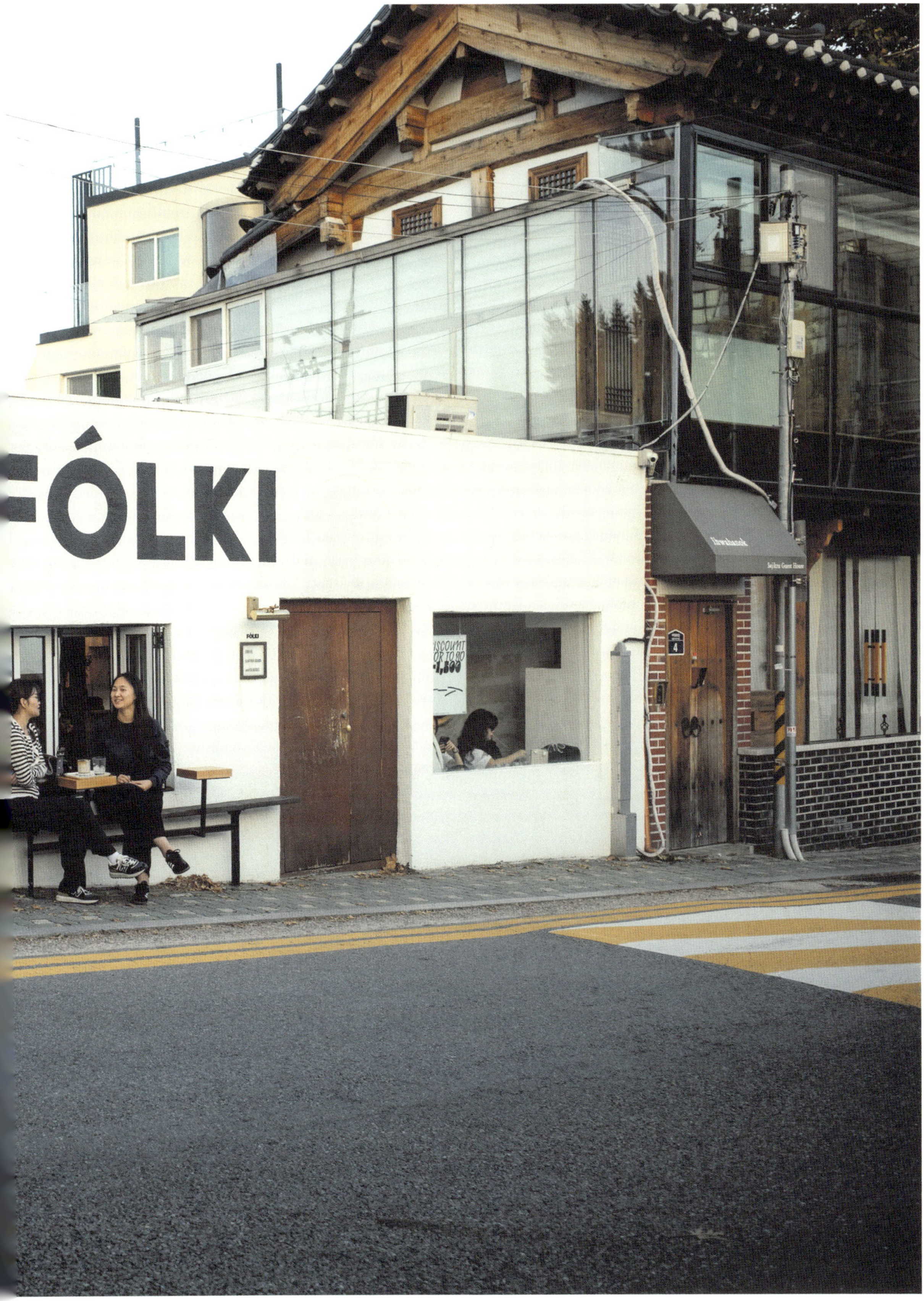
FÓLKI

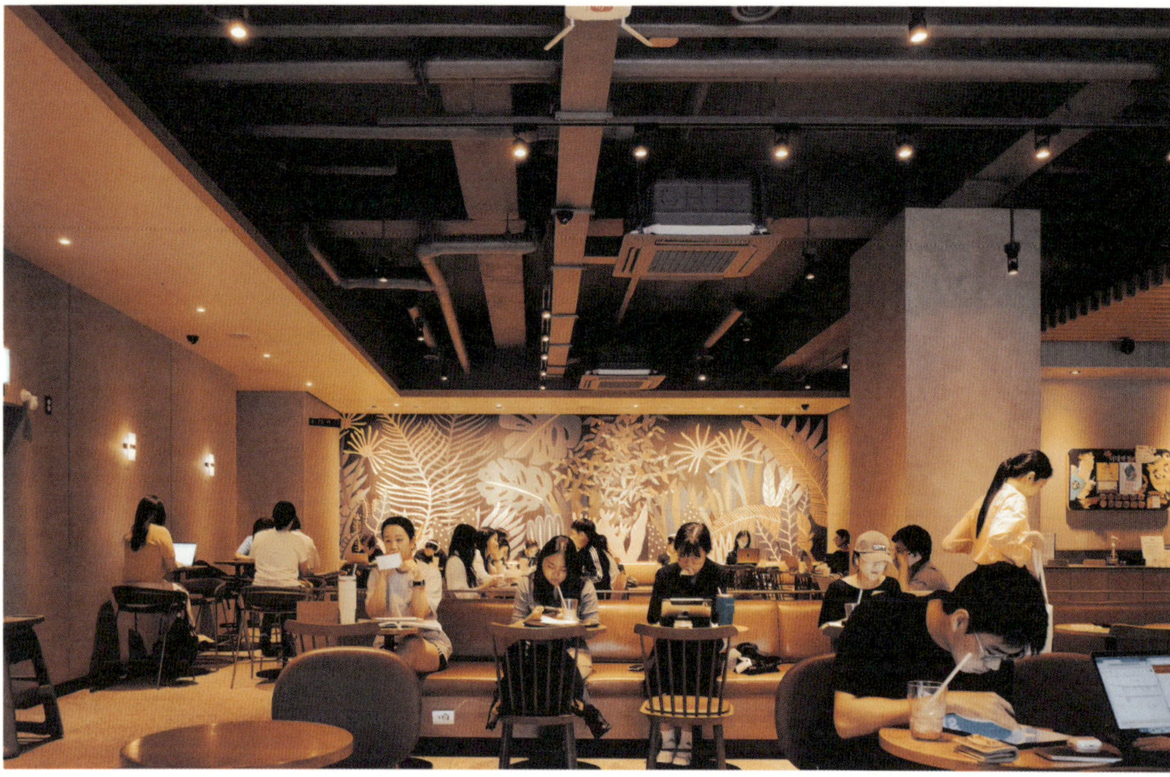

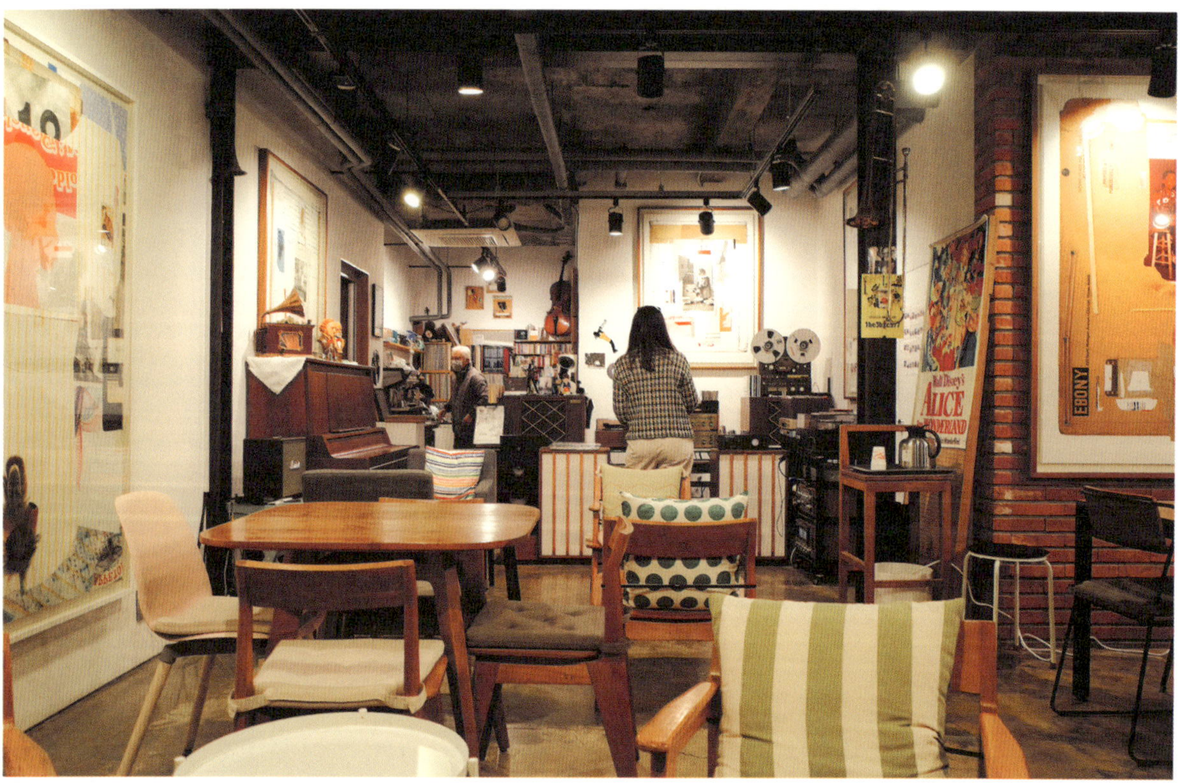


above: Ewhayeodae, Seodaemun District + below: Bukchon, Jongno District

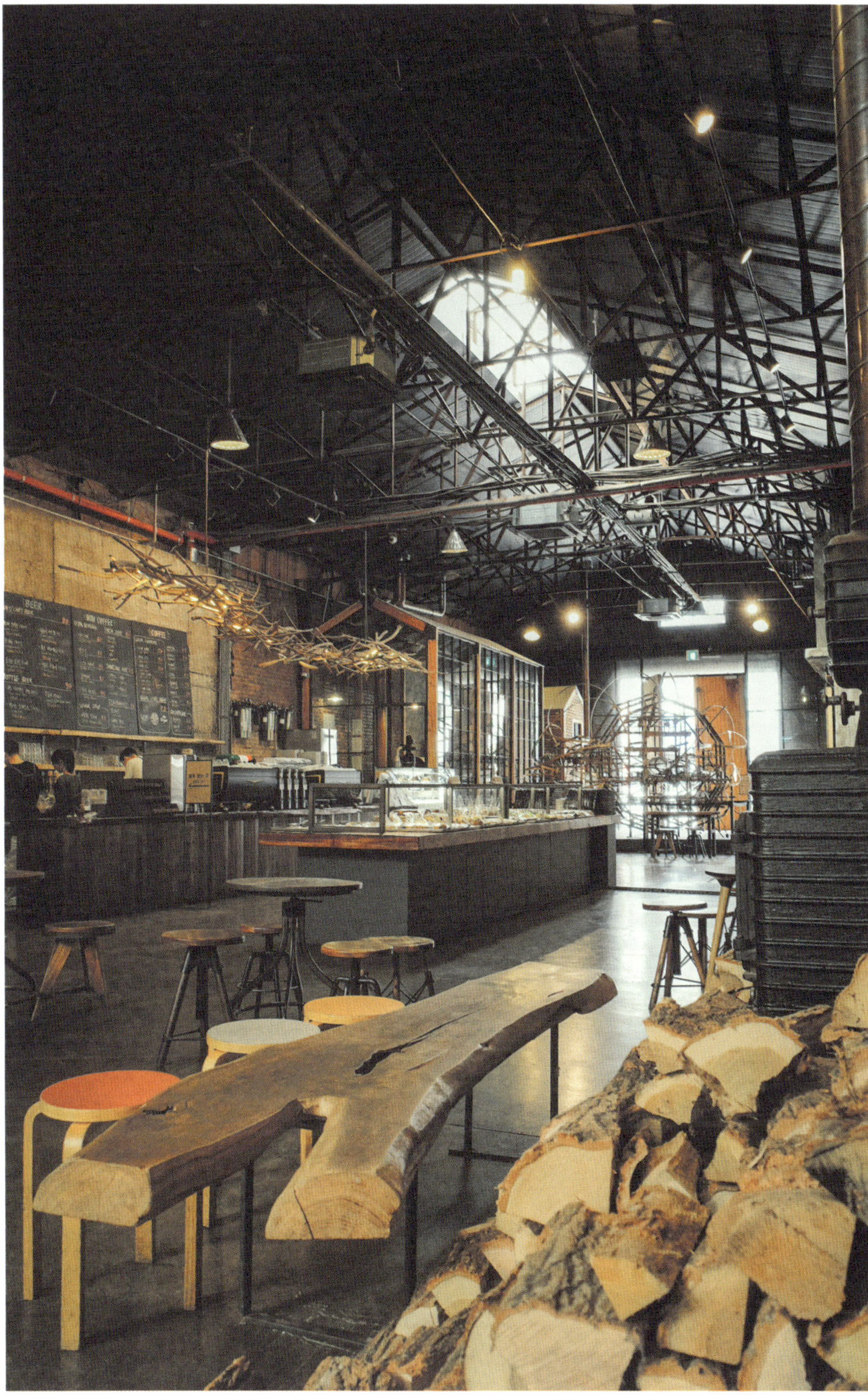

Seongsu-dong, Seongdong District

Anguk-dong, Jongno District

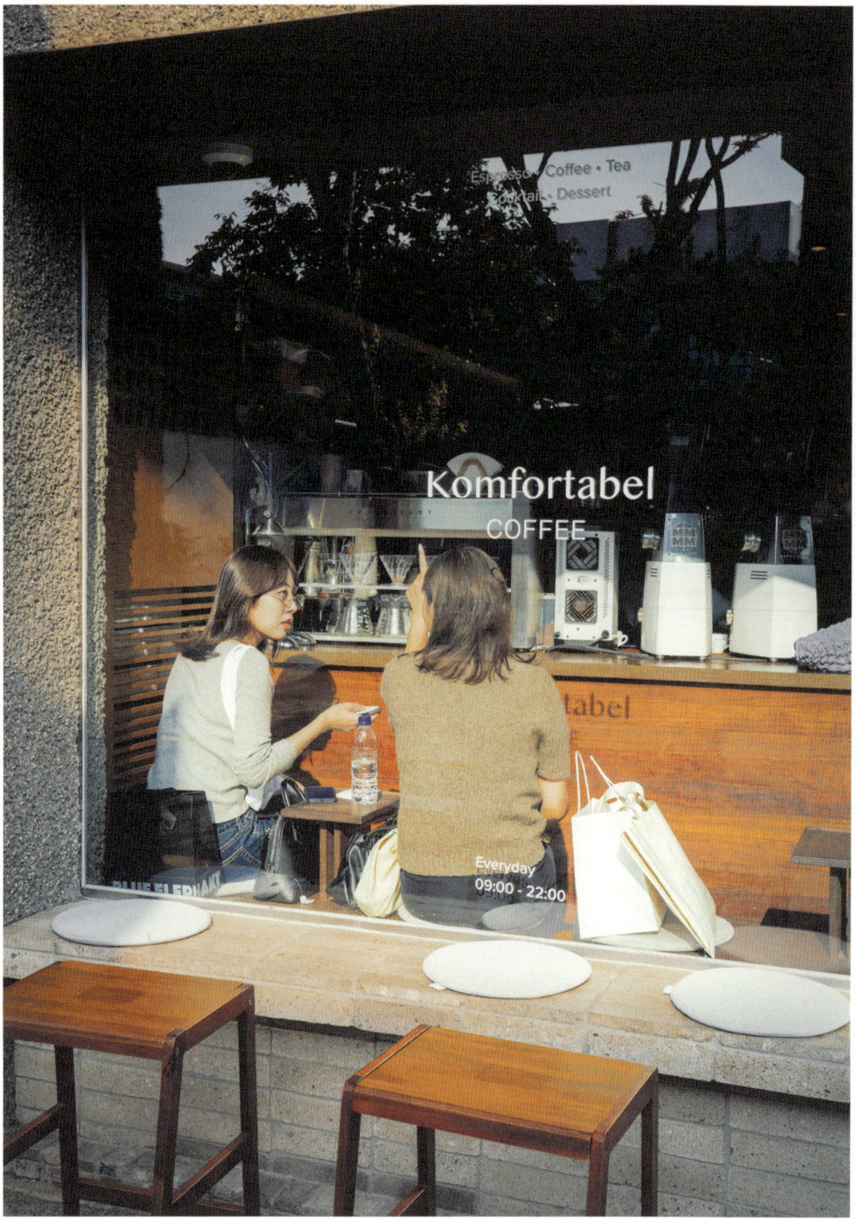


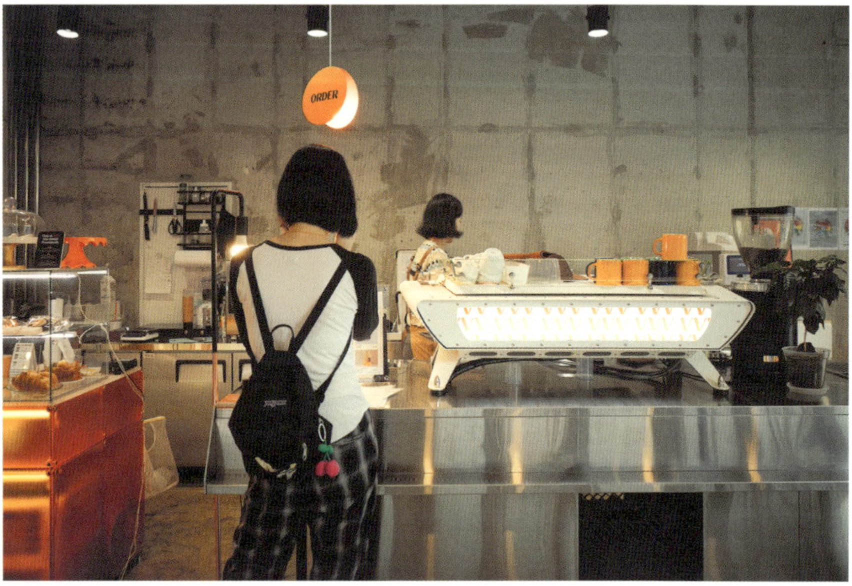


Ikseon-dong, Jongno District

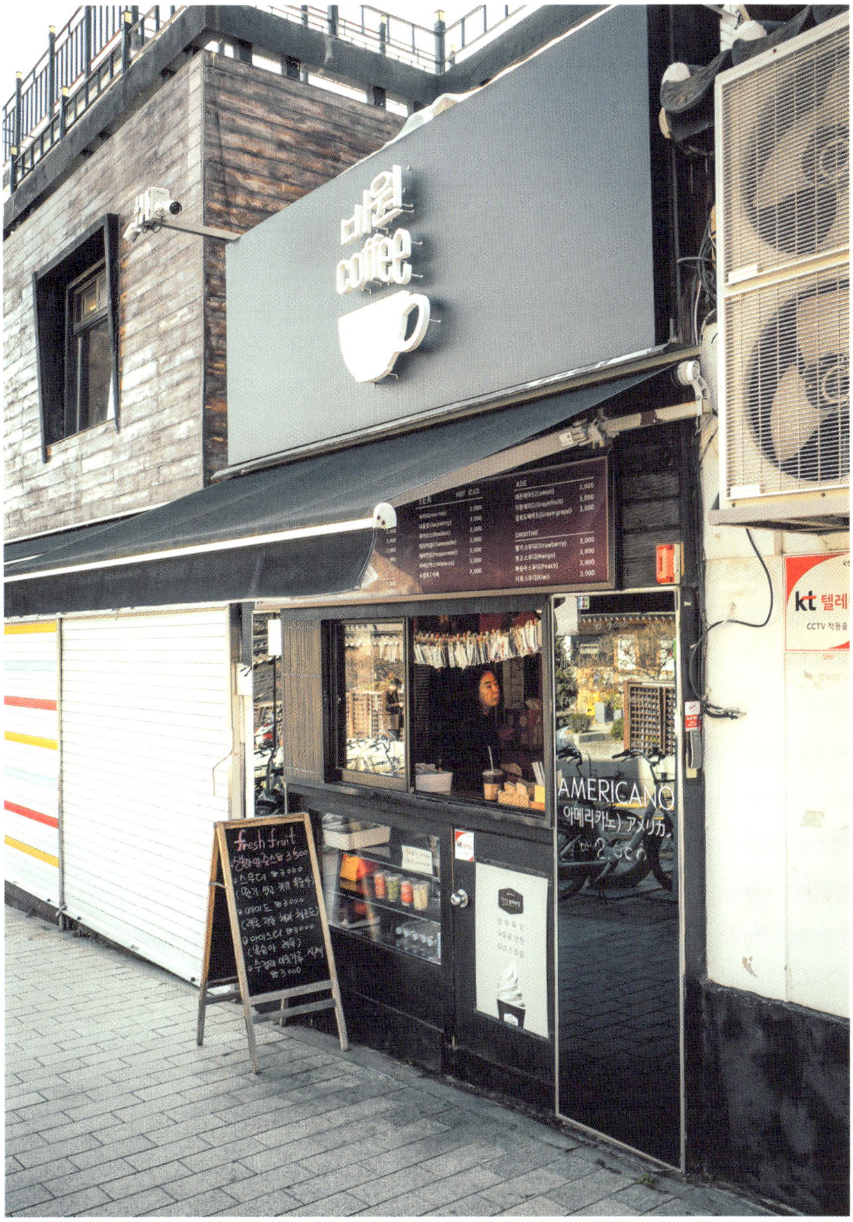


Anguk-dong, Jongno District

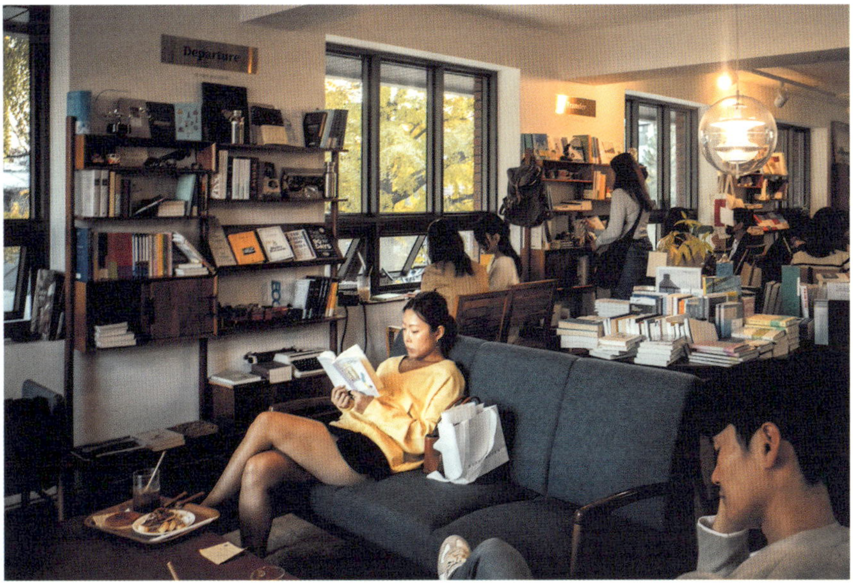


Tongin-dong, Jongno District

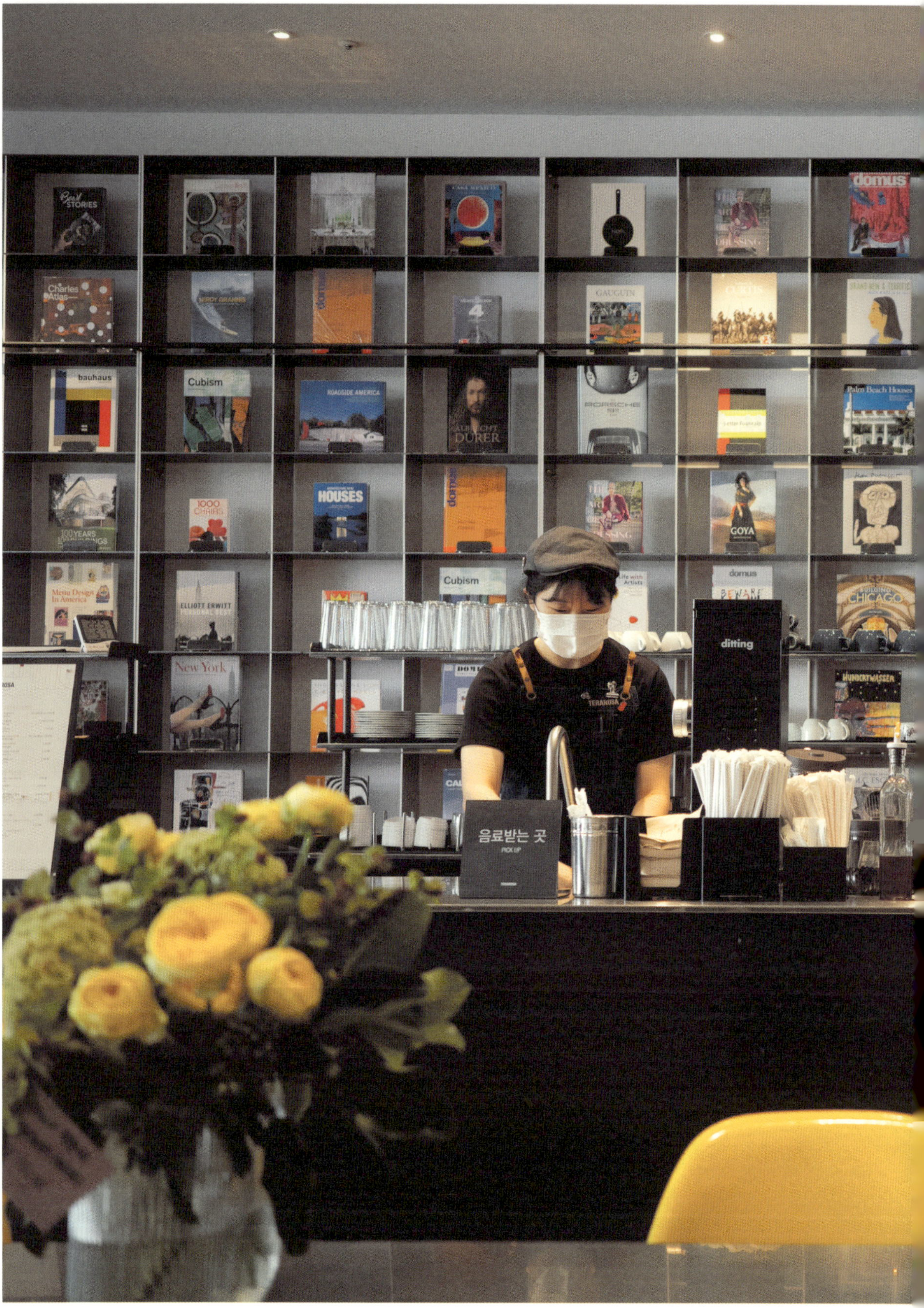


Jongno 1-ga, Jongno District

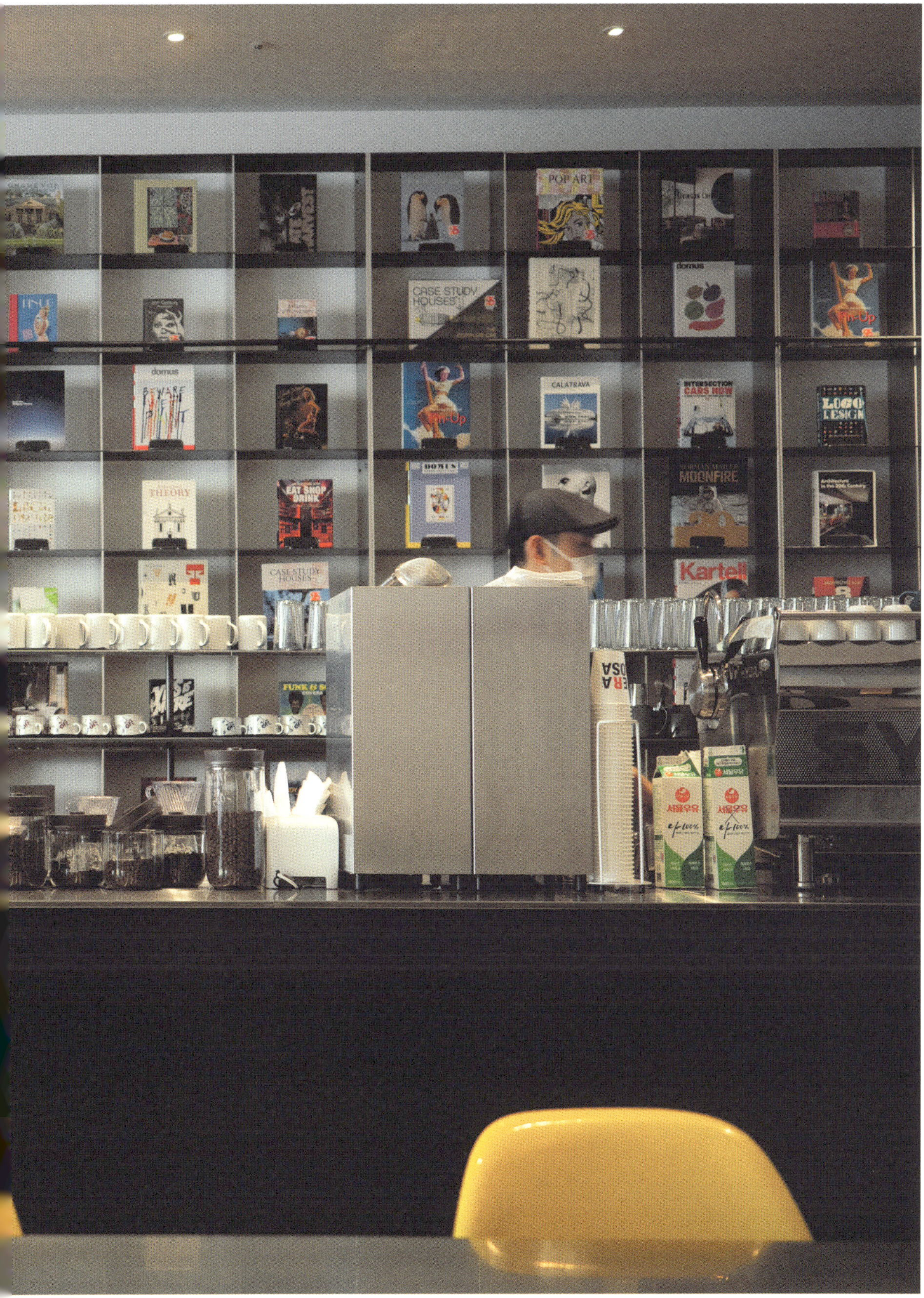
POP ART
CASE STUDY HOUSES
domus
CALATRAVA
INTERSECTION CARS NOW
MOONFIRE
THEORY
EAT SHOP DRINK
Kartell
CASE STUDY HOUSES
서울우유

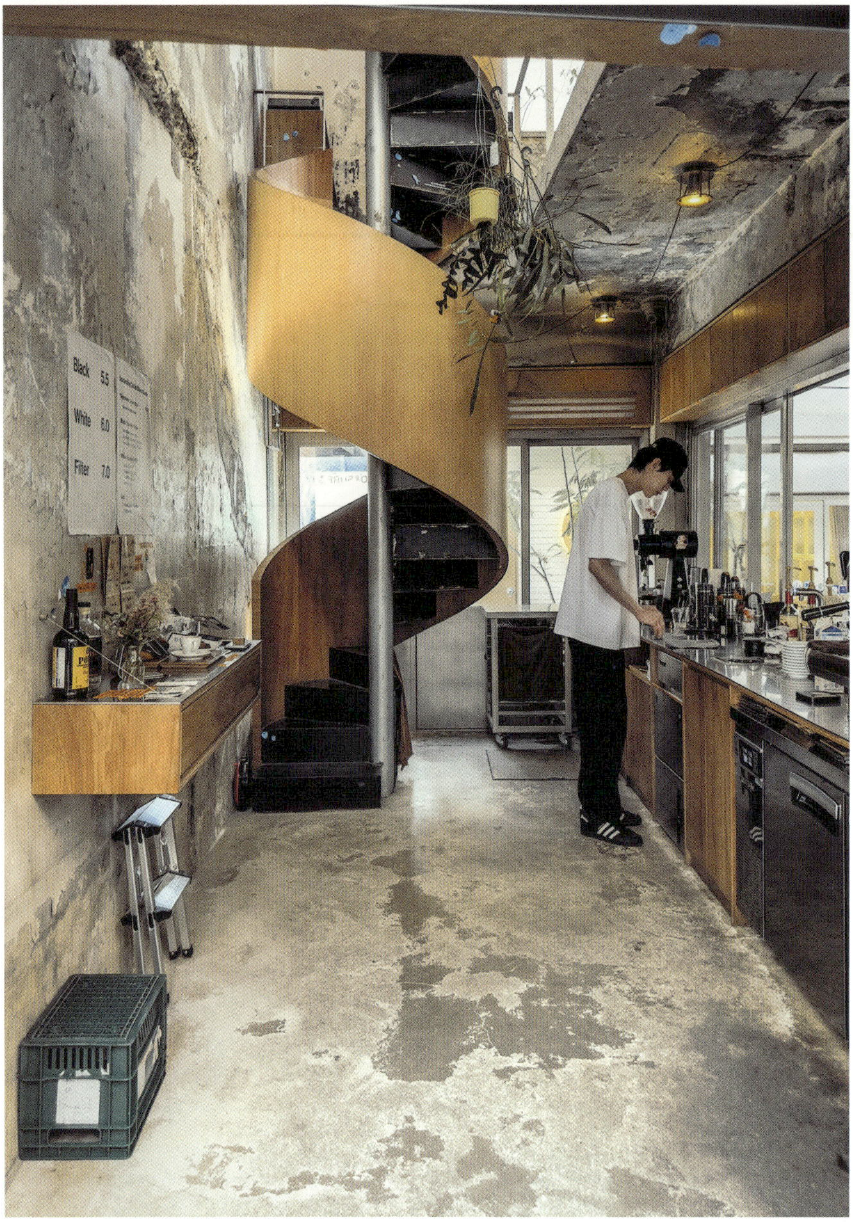


left: Haebangchon, Yongsan District

right: Bukchon, Jongno District

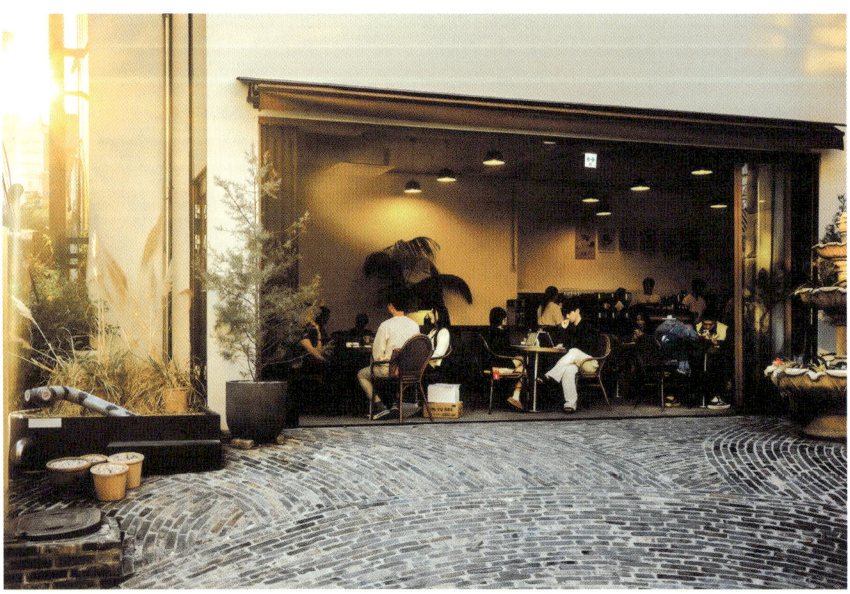

left: Garosu-gil, Gangnam District

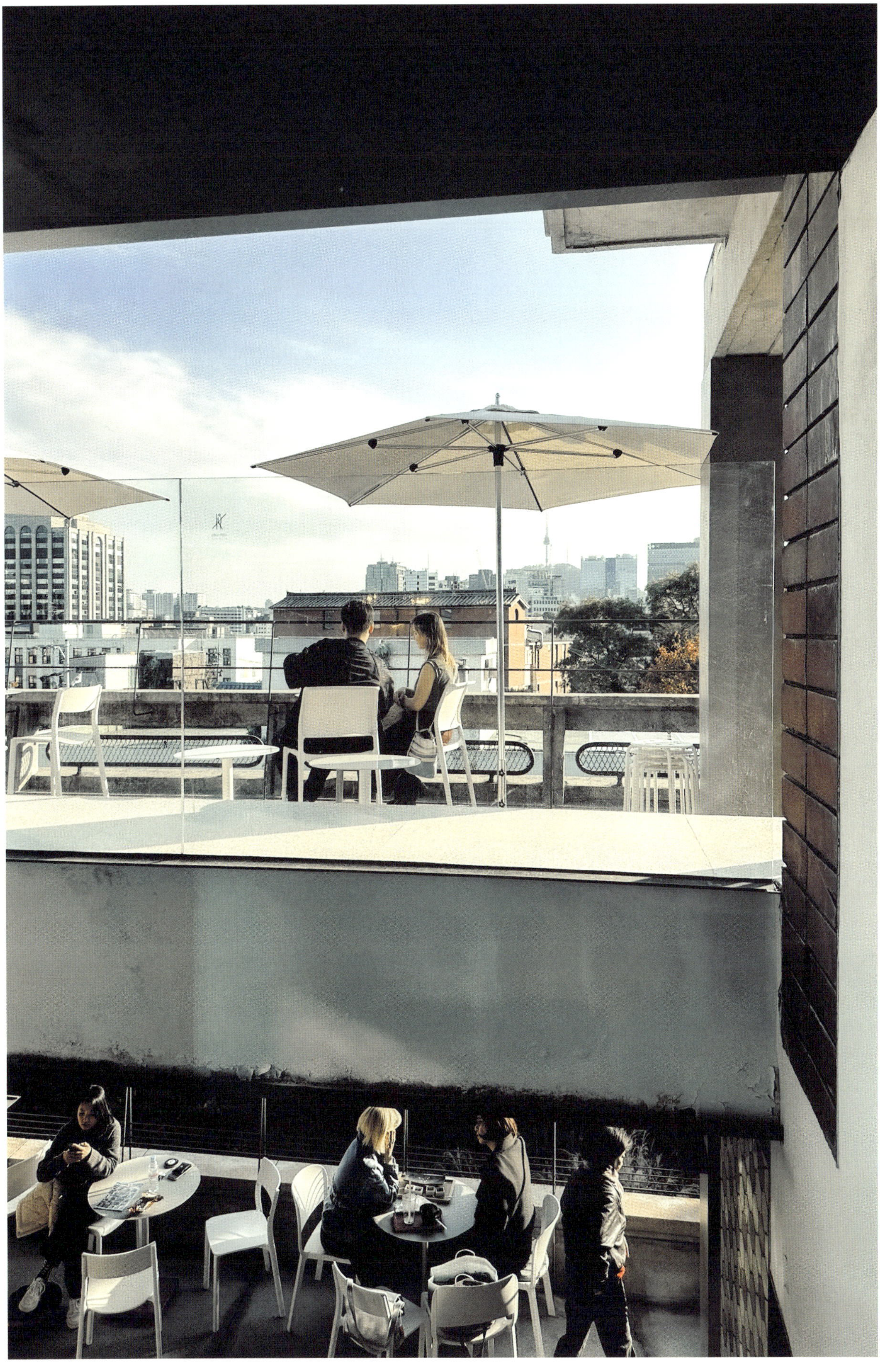

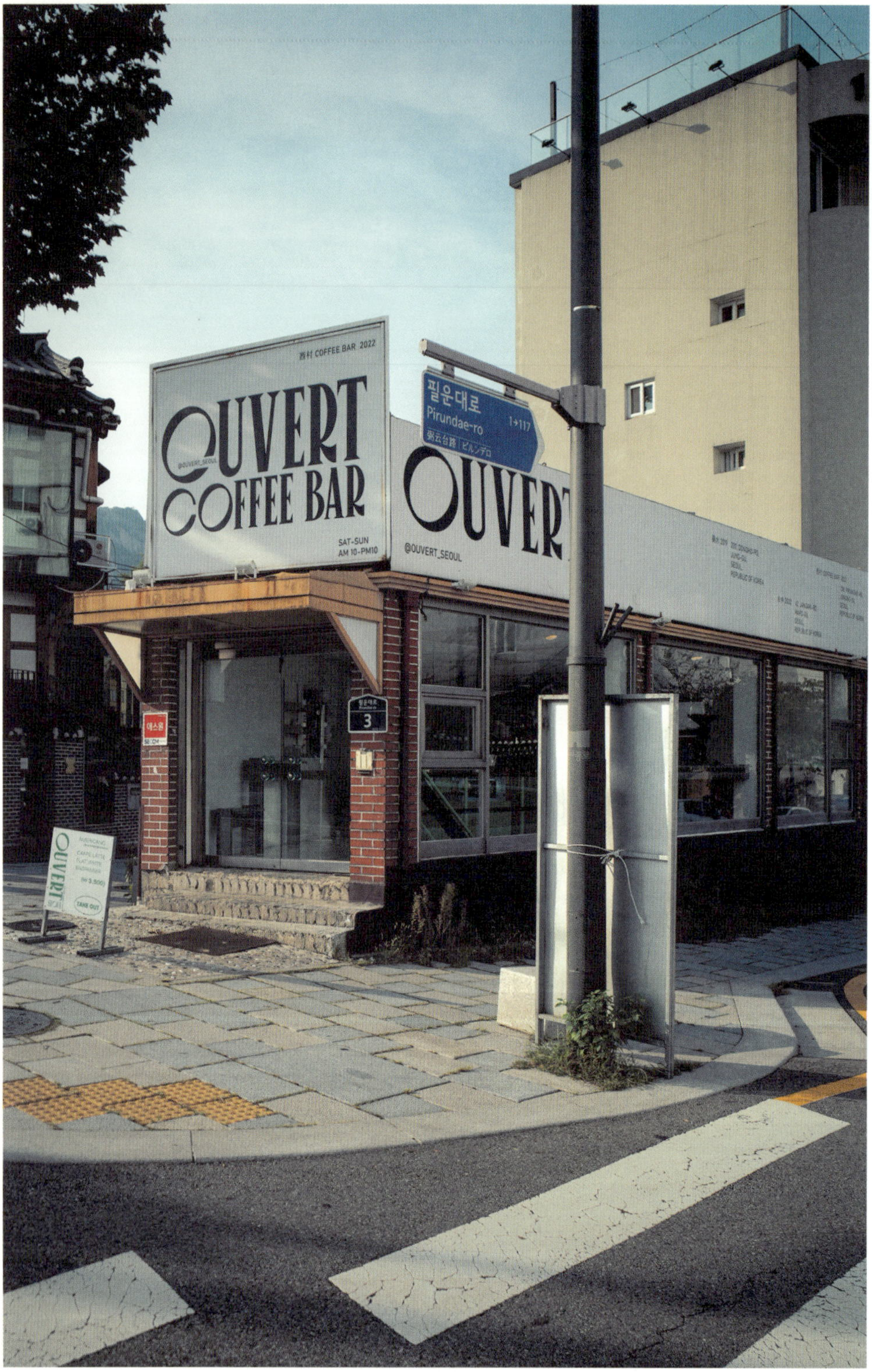
西村 COFFEE BAR 2022
OUVERT
COFFEE BAR
@OUVERT_SEOUL
SAT-SUN
AM 10-PM10
필운대로
Pirundae-ro
1→117
OUVERT
@OUVERT_SEOUL
3
TAKE OUT

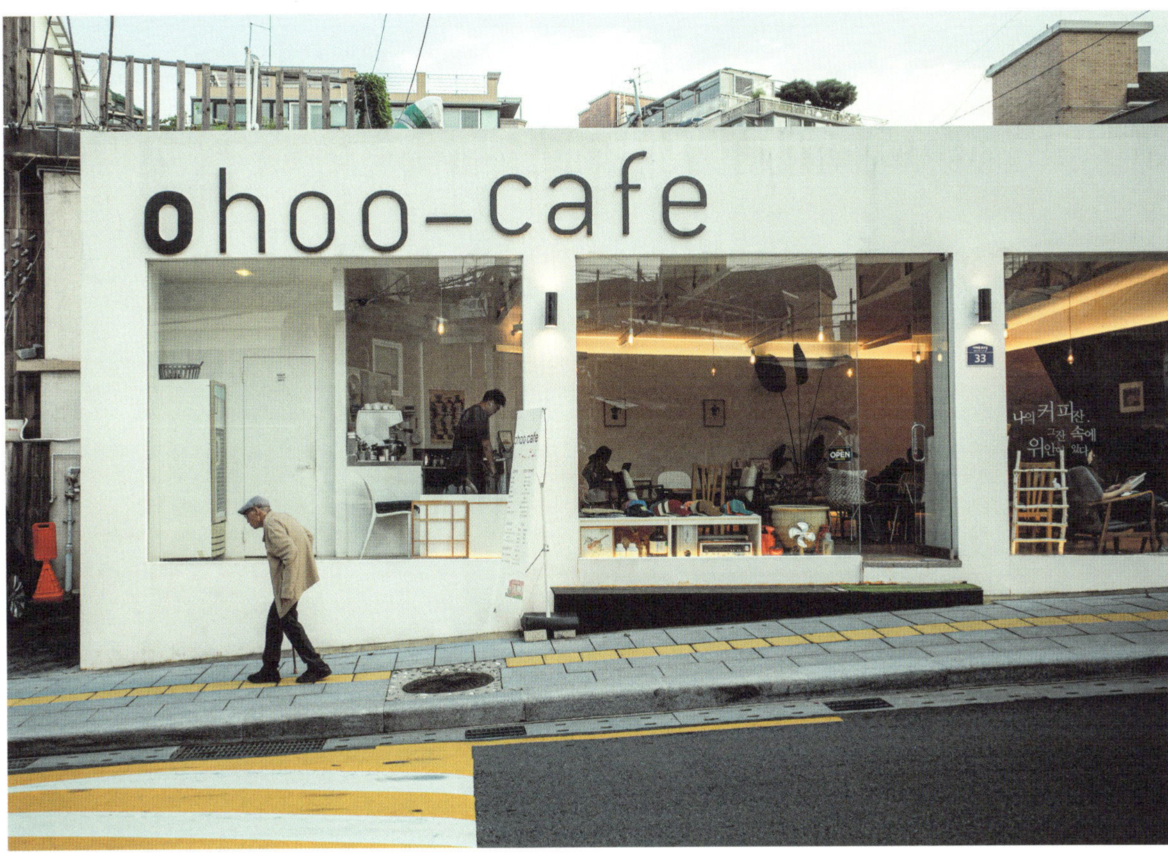


left + above: Seochon, Jongno District

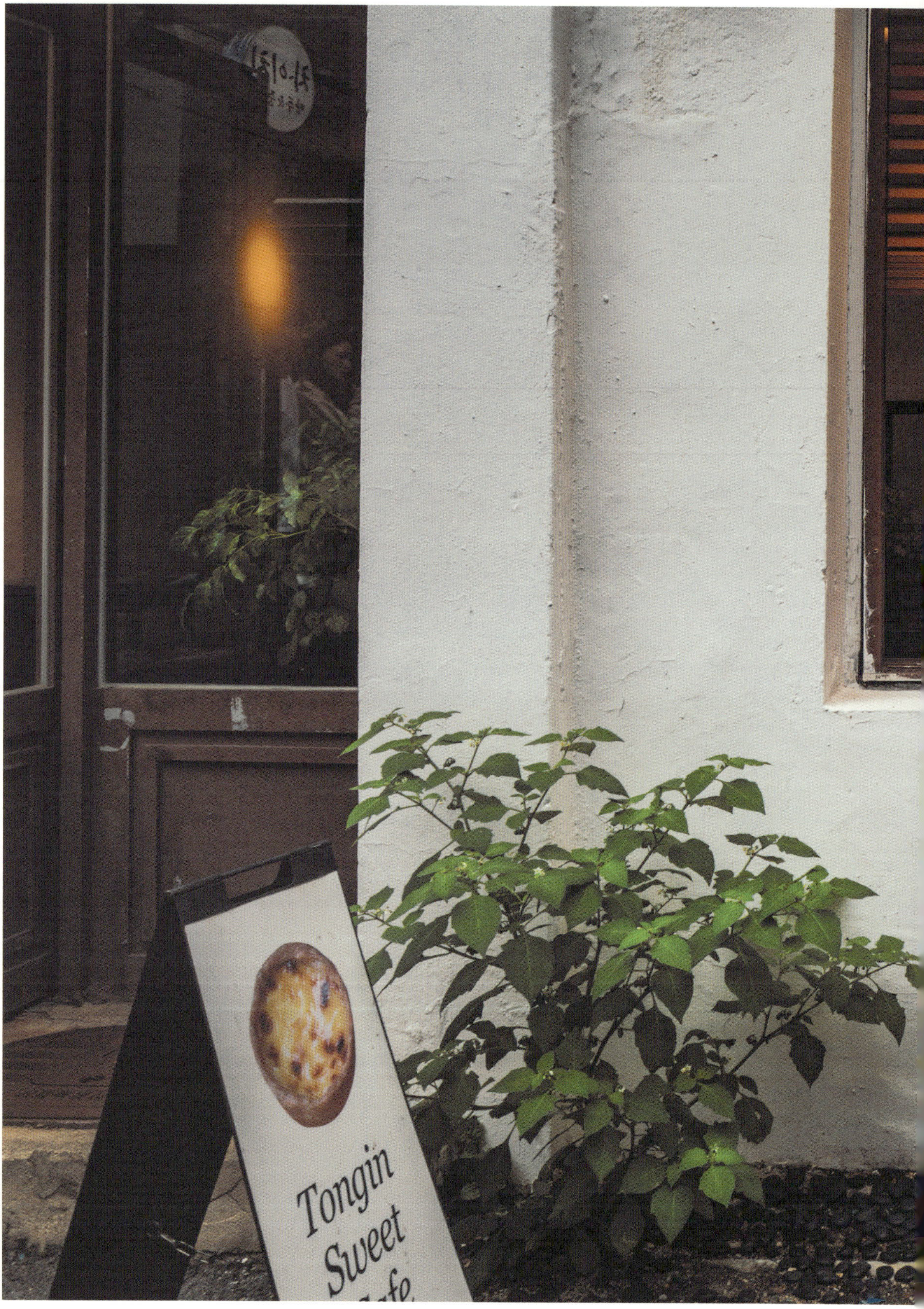


Tongin-dong, Jongno District

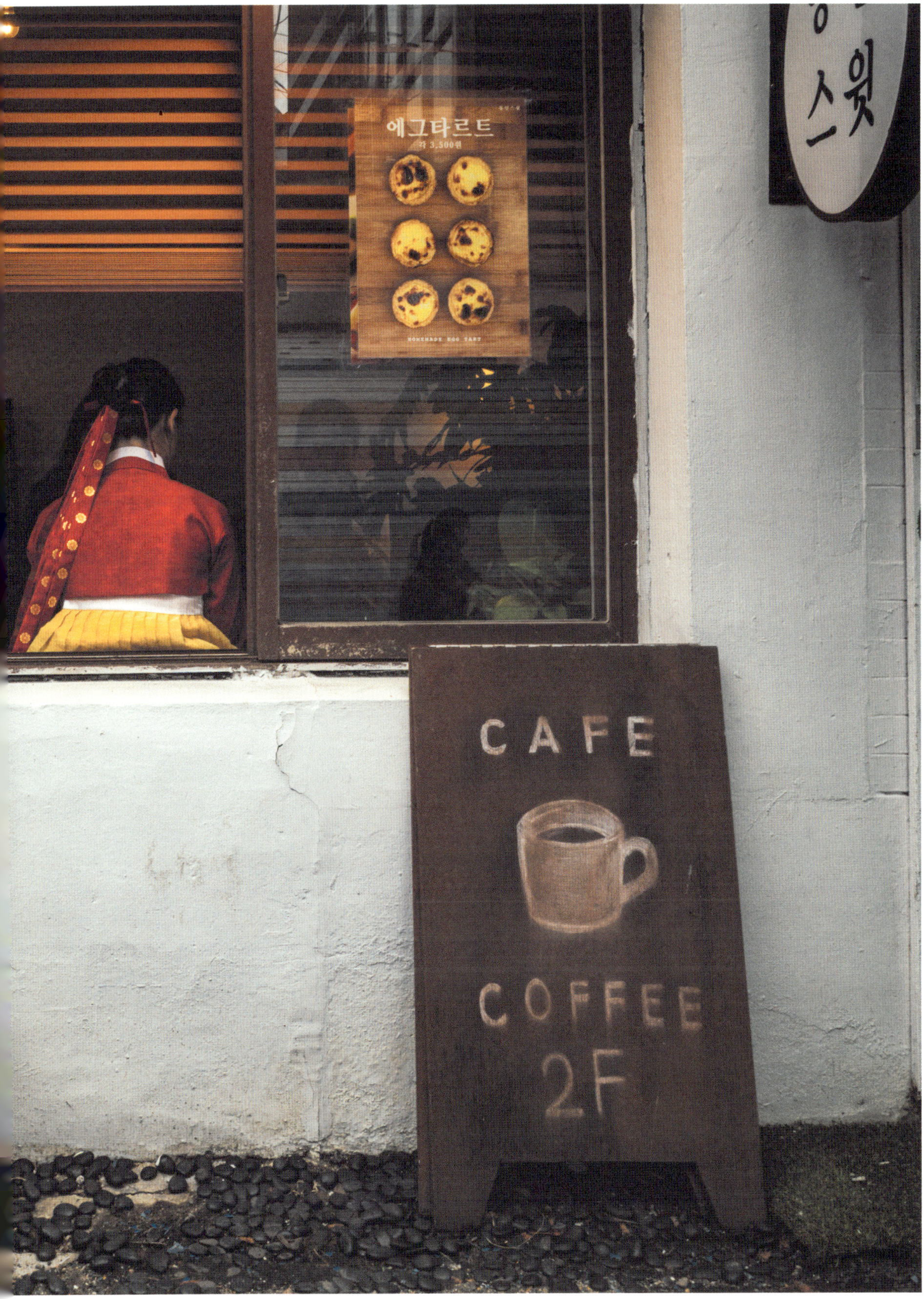
에그타르트
각 3,500원
HOMEMADE EGG TART
스윗
CAFE
COFFEE
2F

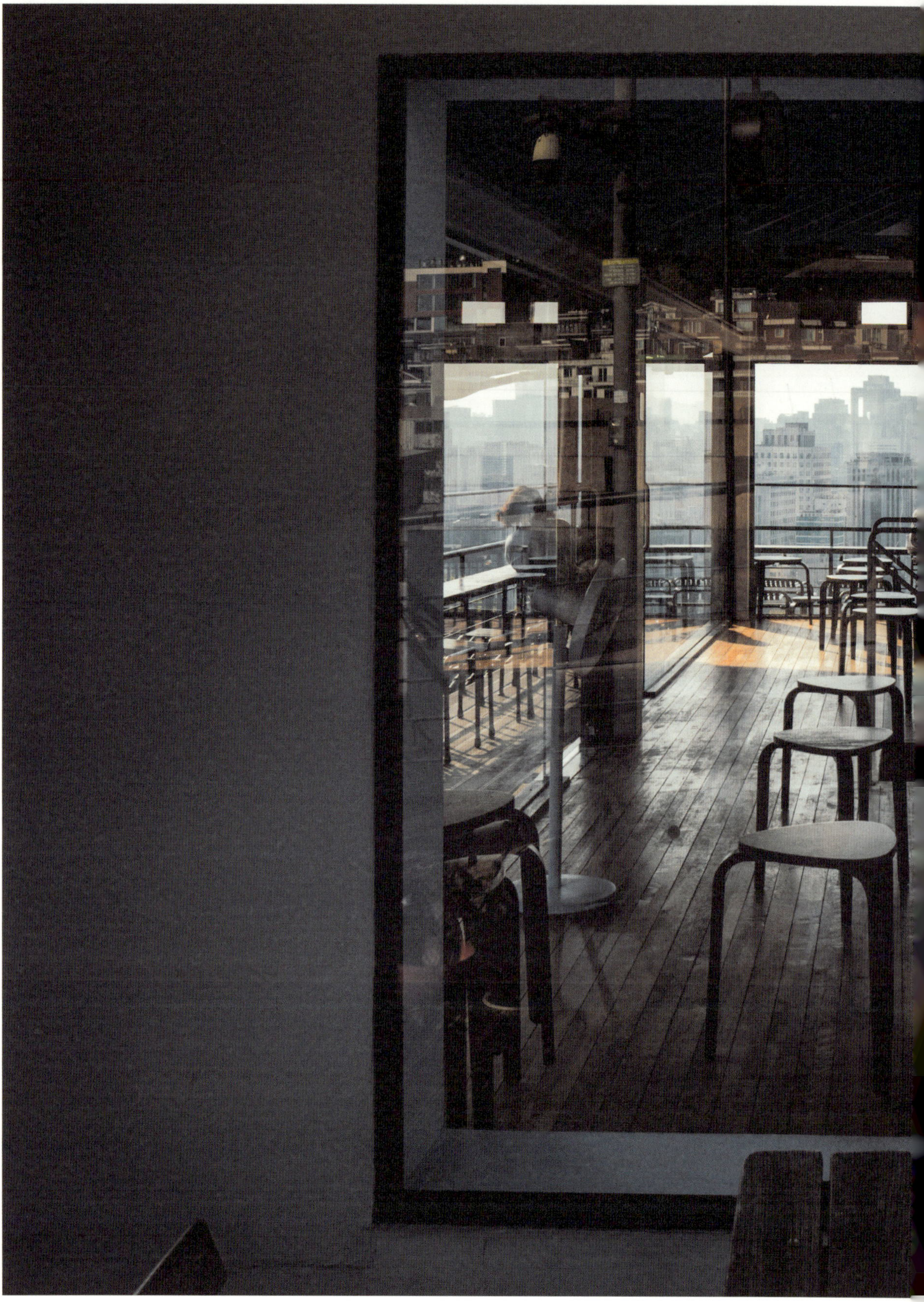

Naksan Park, Jongno District

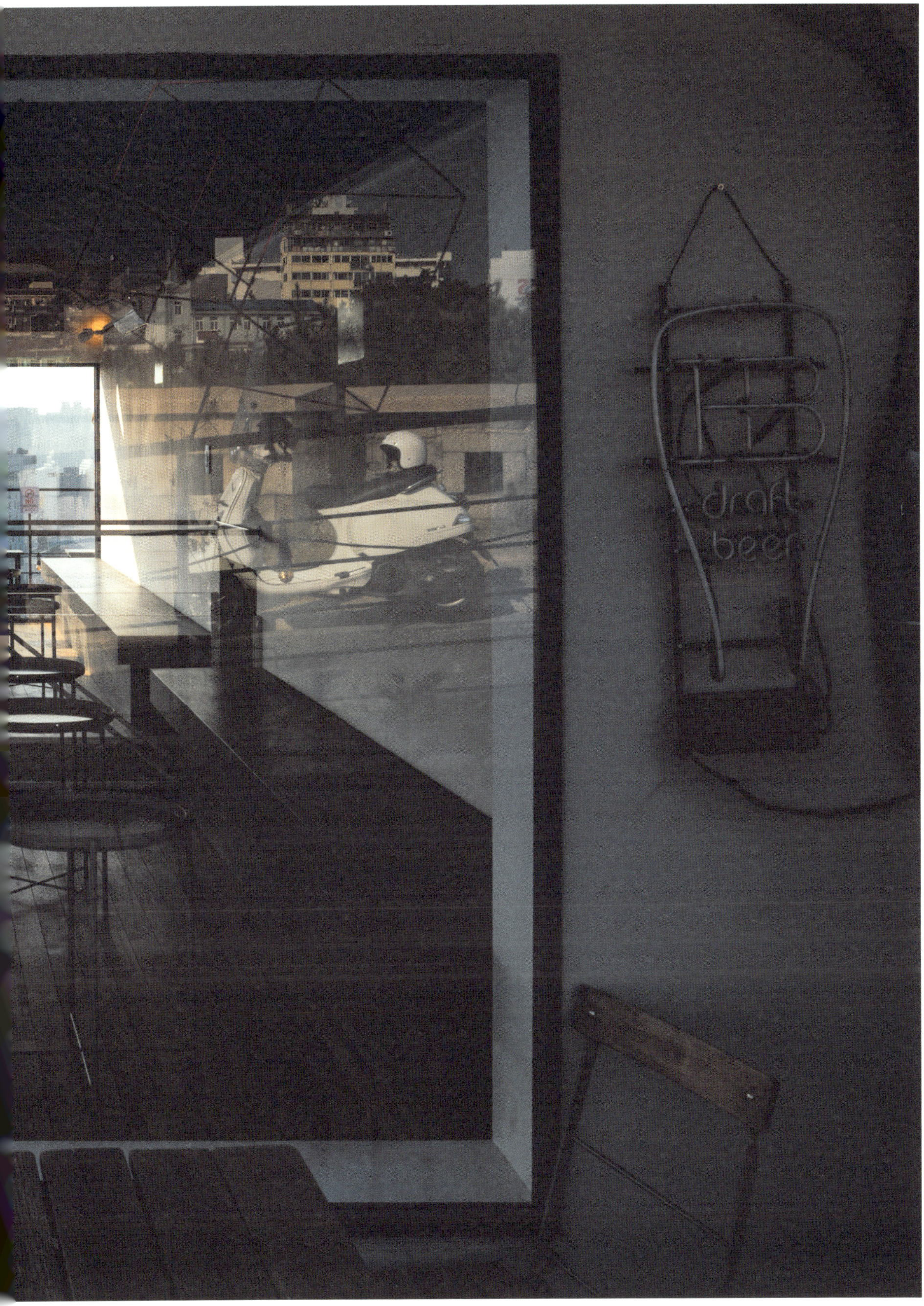
draft
beer

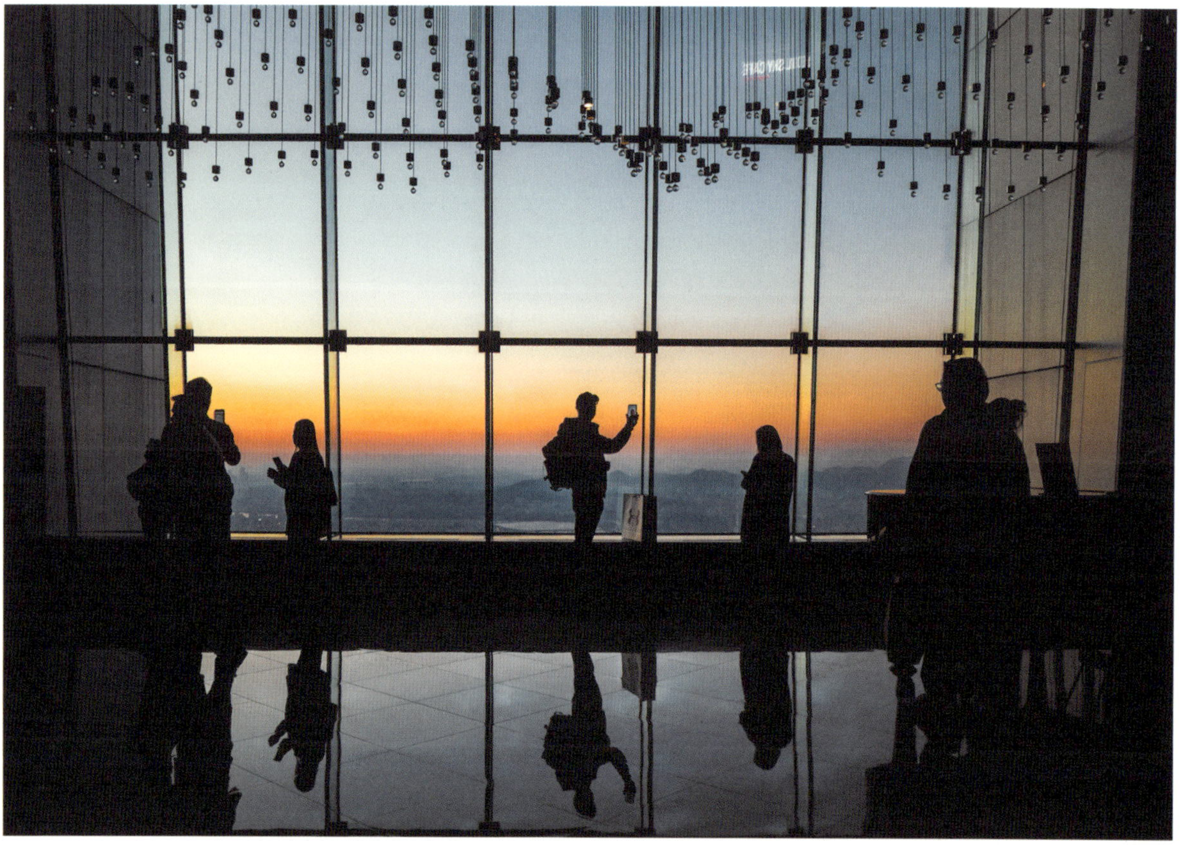

Lotte World Tower, Jamsil-dong, Songpa District

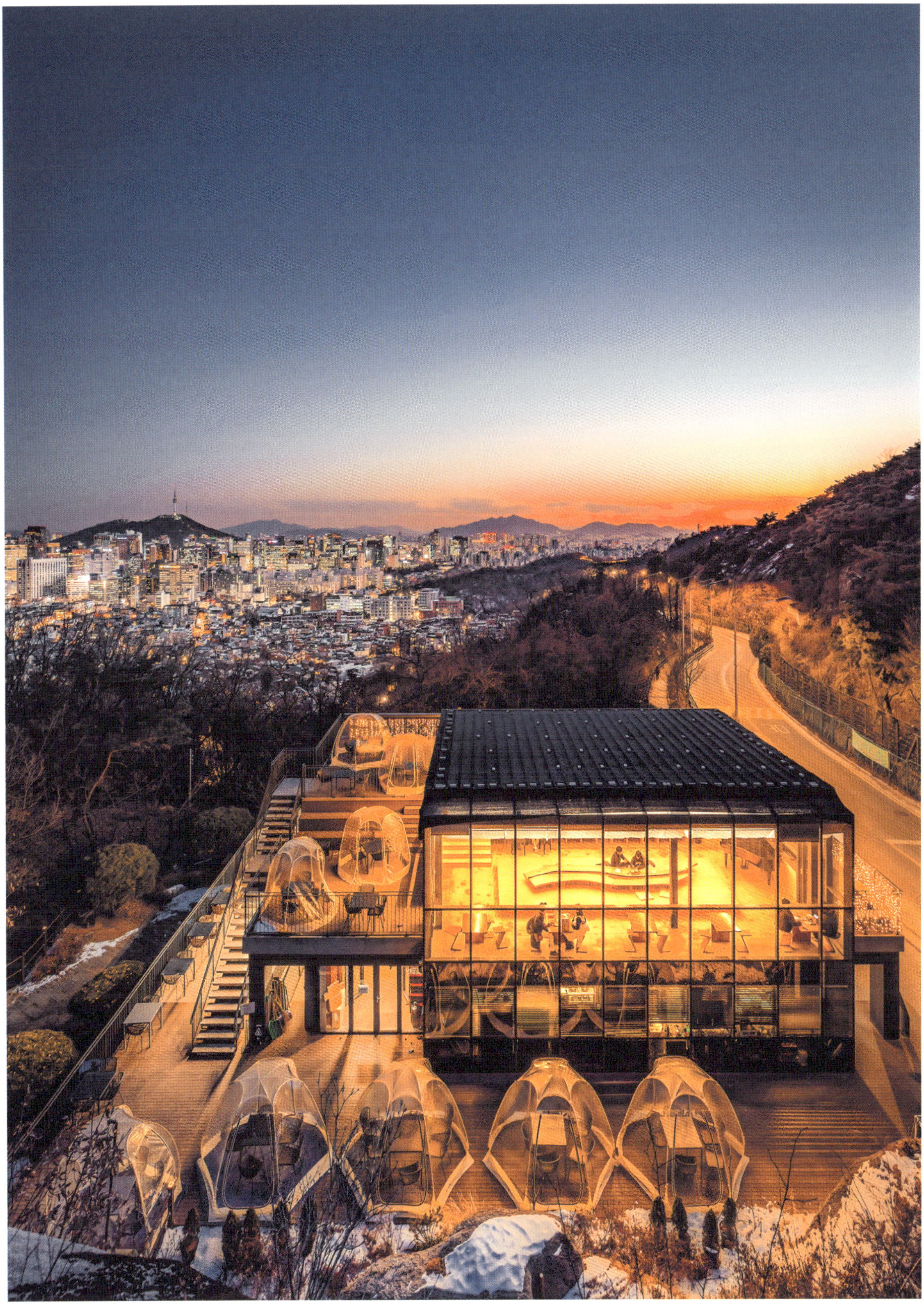

Inwangsan Mountain, Jongno District

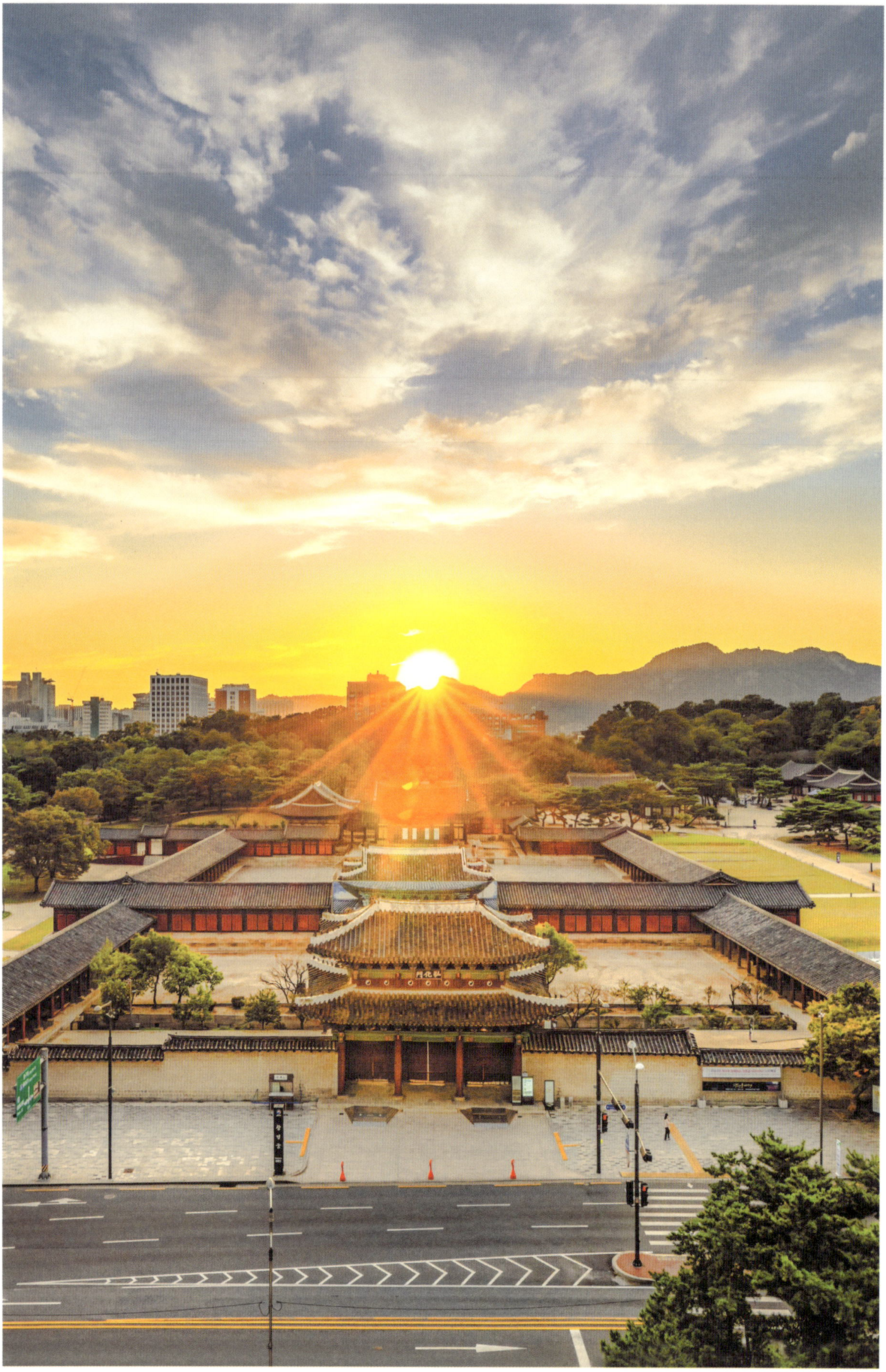

## JOSEON

조선

(jow-see-uhn) means "Land of the Morning Calm." When King Taejo founded the Joseon dynasty in 1392, he chose the name Joseon to symbolize a new beginning—a nation reborn with moral clarity, discipline, and harmony after the turbulent Goryeo era. The name also connects to an even older kingdom called Gojoseon (Old Joseon), said to be Korea's first ancient state, thereby linking the new dynasty to Korea's legendary origins. Today, "Joseon" carries both historical and emotional weight. It represents the foundation of Korea's traditional culture—its Confucian values, aesthetics, and identity—that still echo in modern Korean life, design, and etiquette.

Seoul's royal palaces offer a glimpse into Korea's 600-year-old Joseon Dynasty, each blending traditional architecture with the city's modern skyline. The grand Gyeongbokgung Palace, built in 1395, stands as the main royal seat with vast courtyards, majestic gates, and mountain backdrops. Nearby, Changdeokgung Palace, a UNESCO World Heritage site, is celebrated for its harmony with nature and its tranquil Secret Garden, an oasis of calm in the heart of the city.

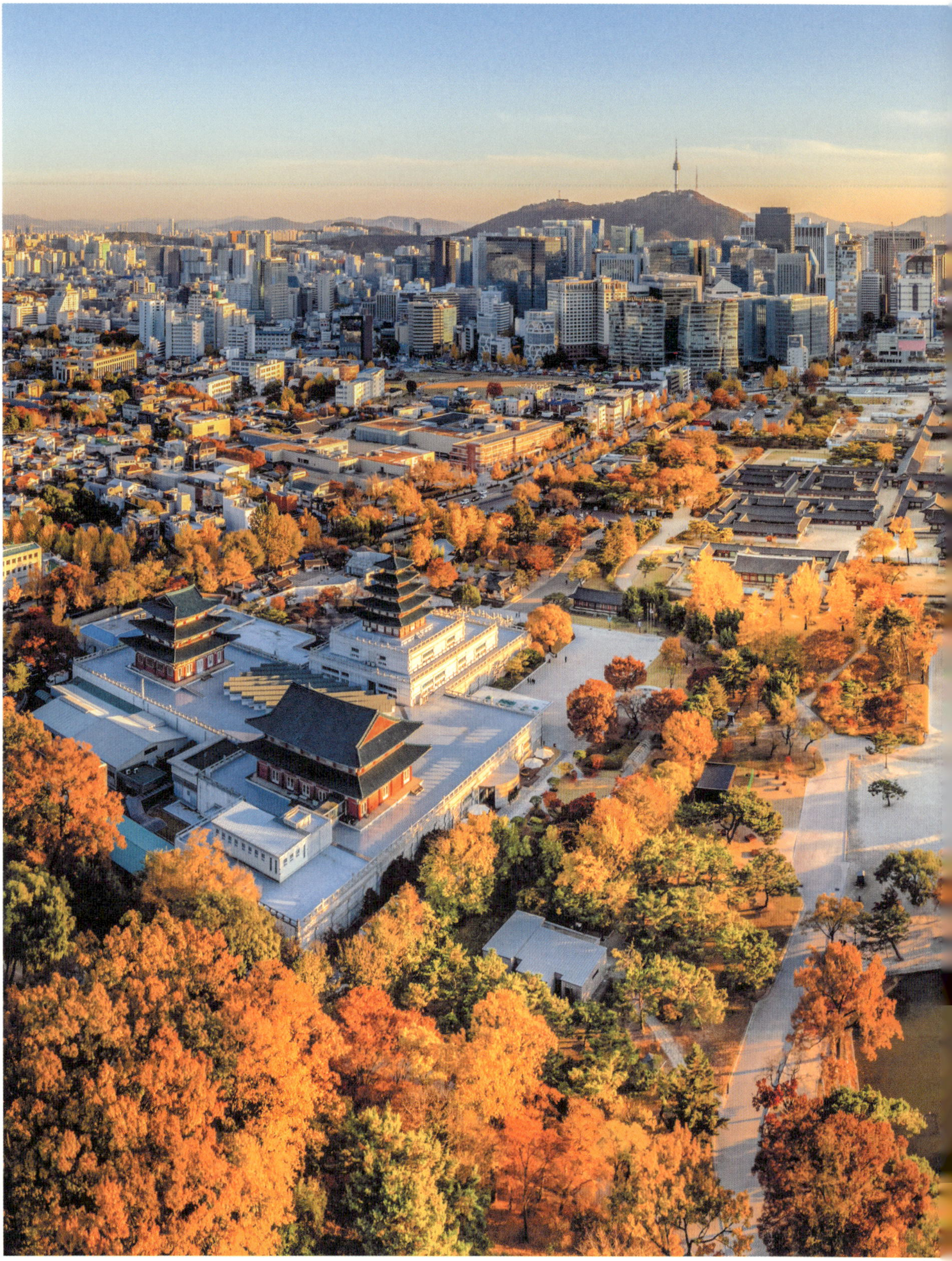

above: Gyeongbokgung Palace, Jongno District > The historic central palace of the Joseon Dynasty

previous spread: Changgyeongung Palace, Jongno District > Originally built by King Sejong for his retiring father, King Taejong

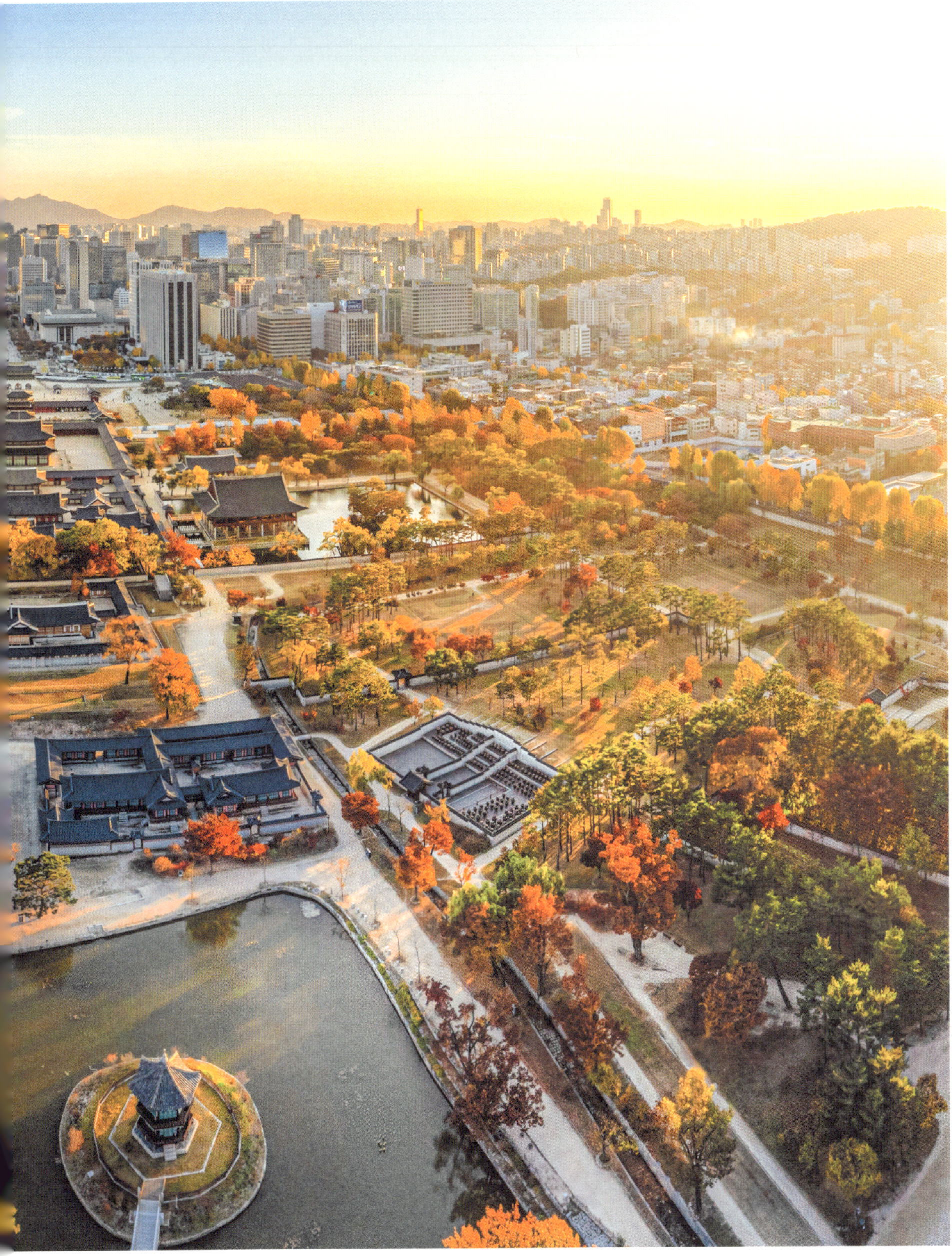

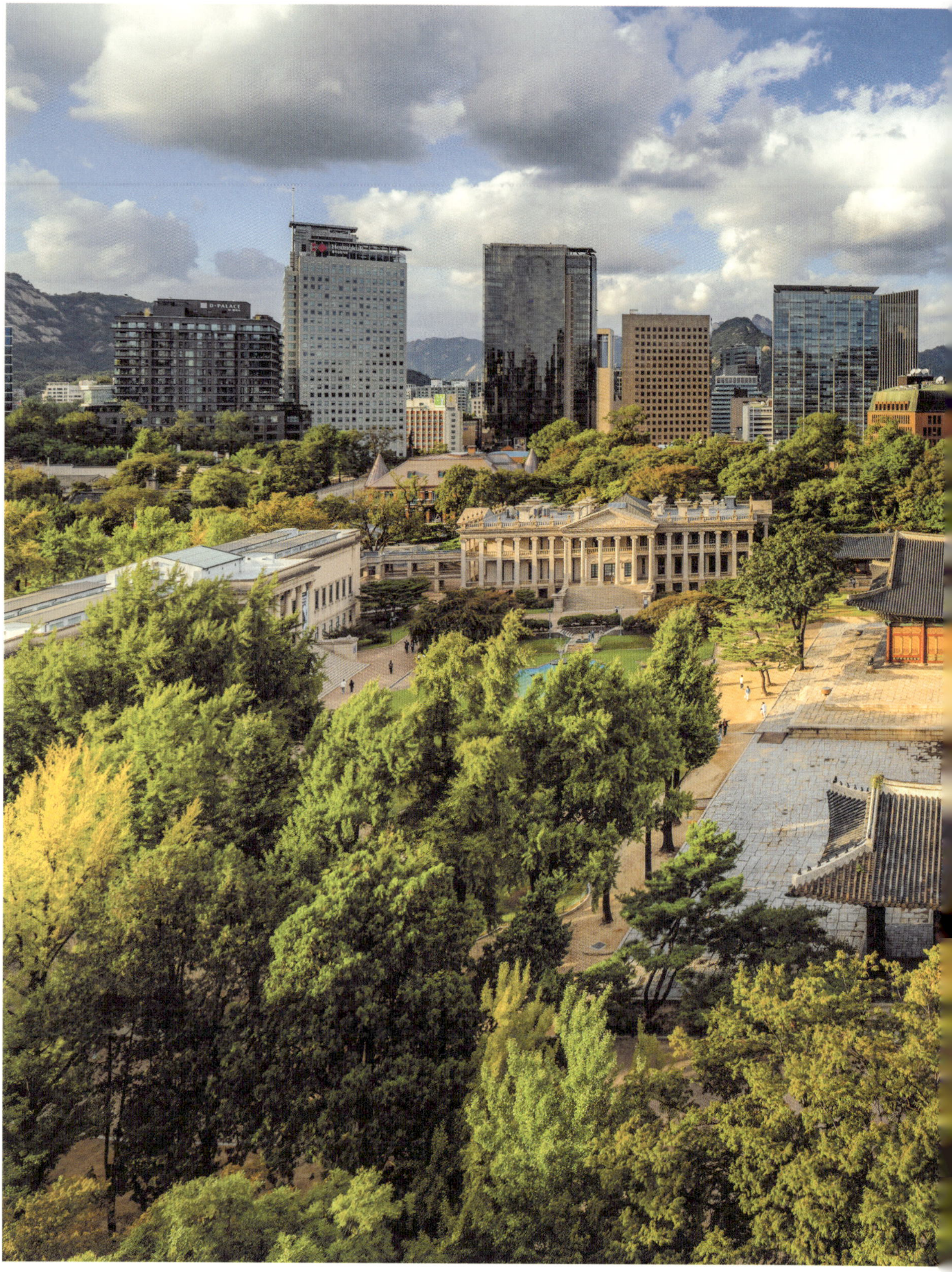


Deoksugung Palace, Jung District > One of five royal palaces that remains in Seoul

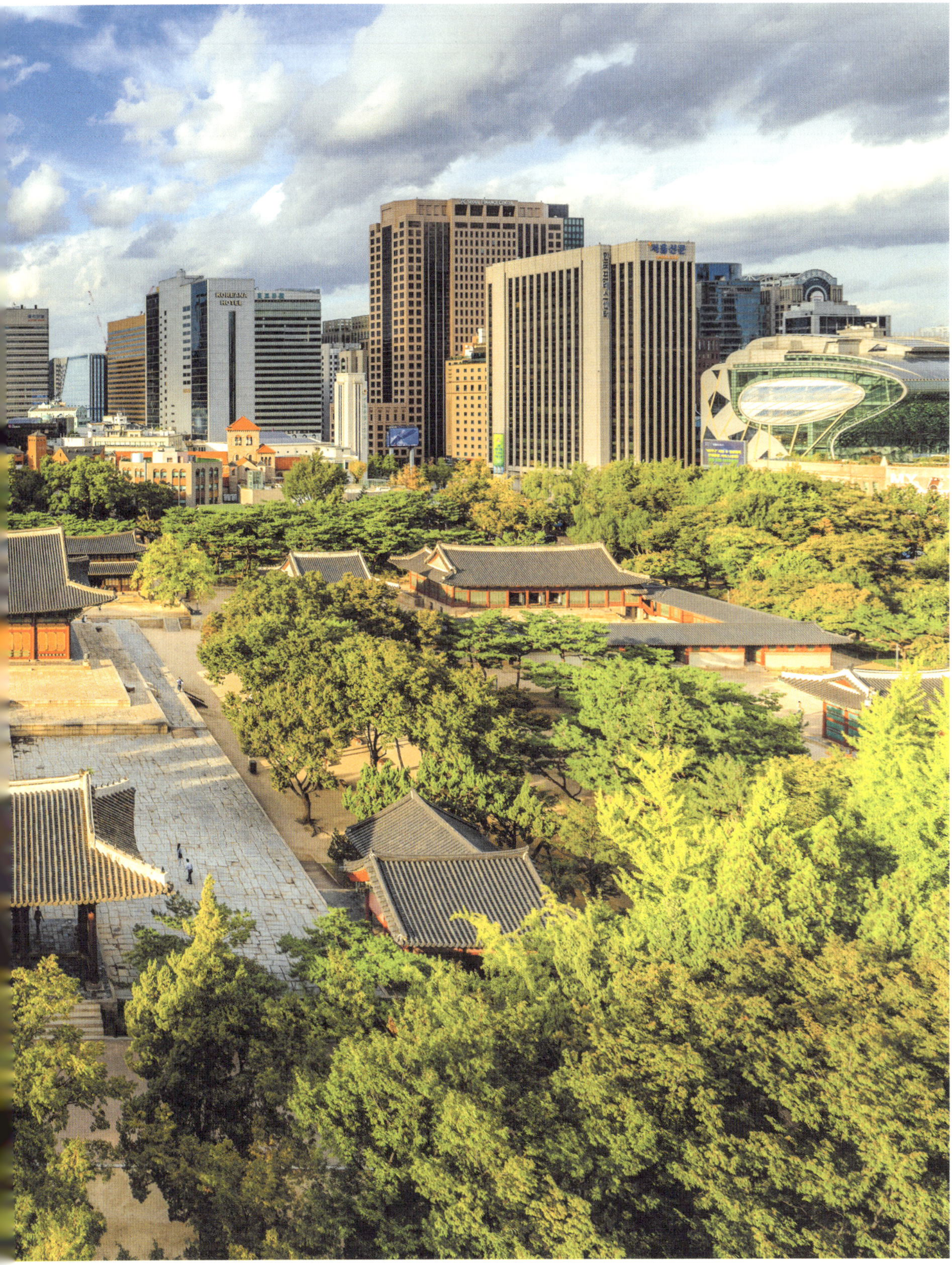
KOREANA HOTEL
서울신문

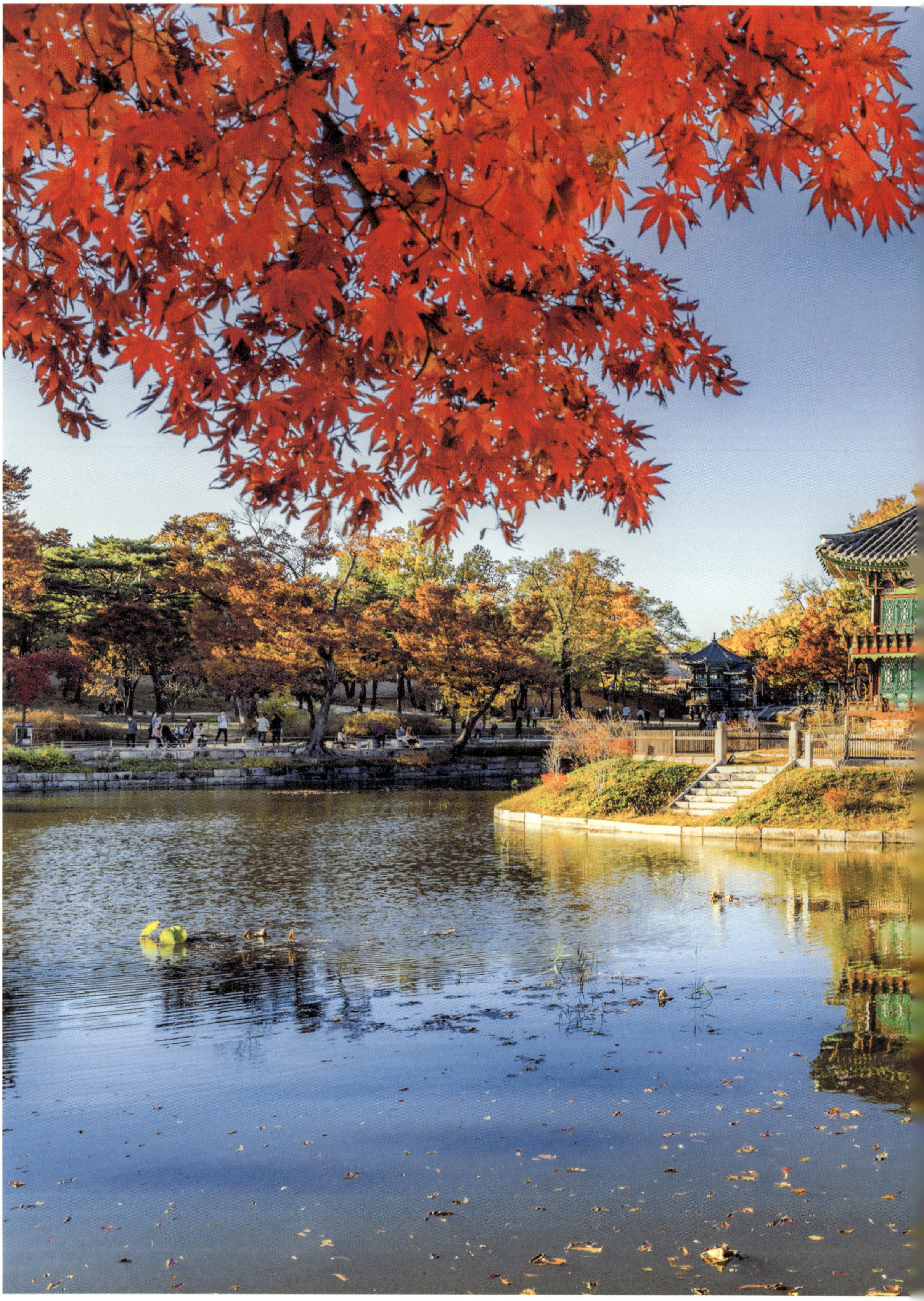

Hyangwonjeong Pavillion, Gyeongbokgung Palace, Jongno District

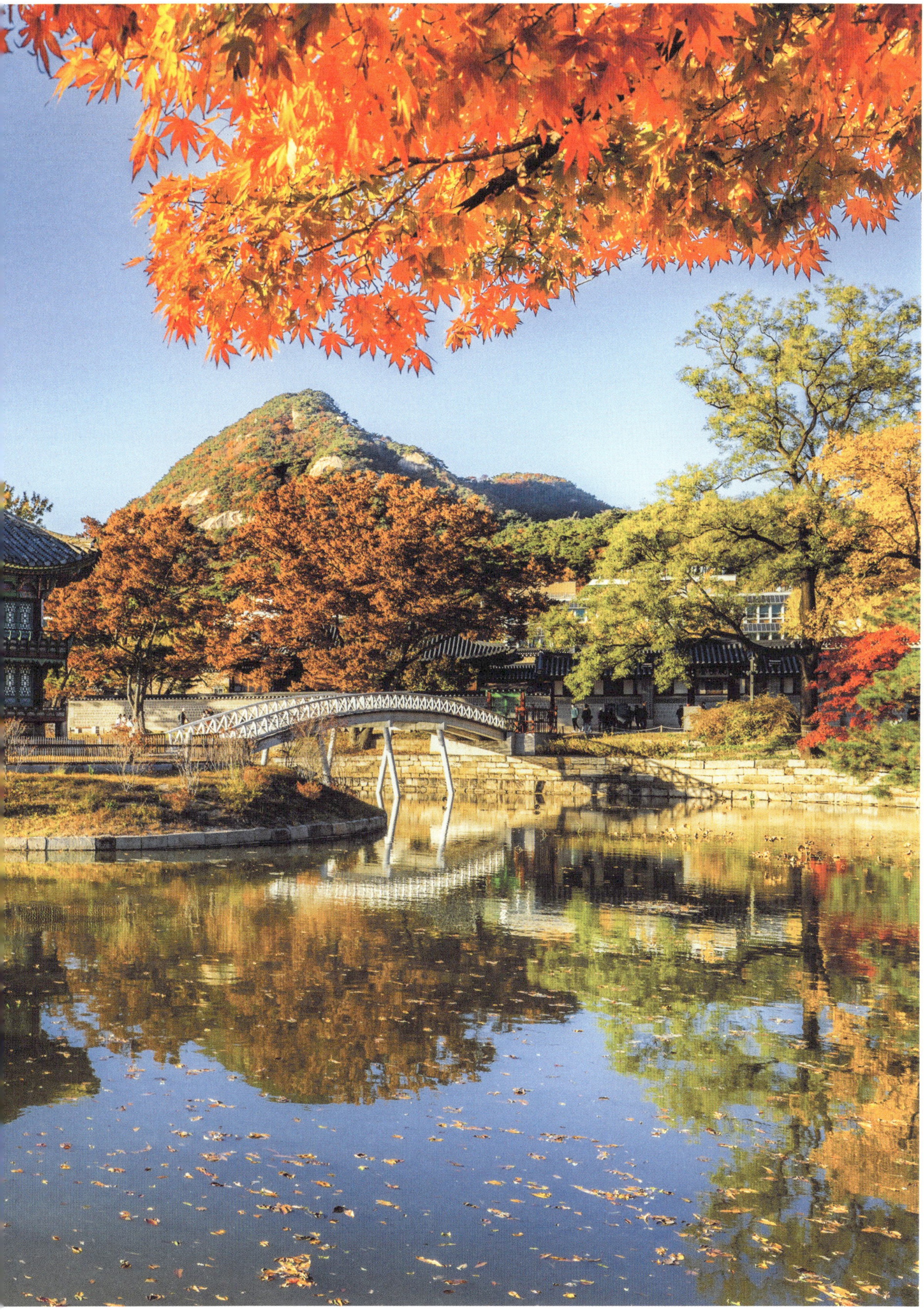

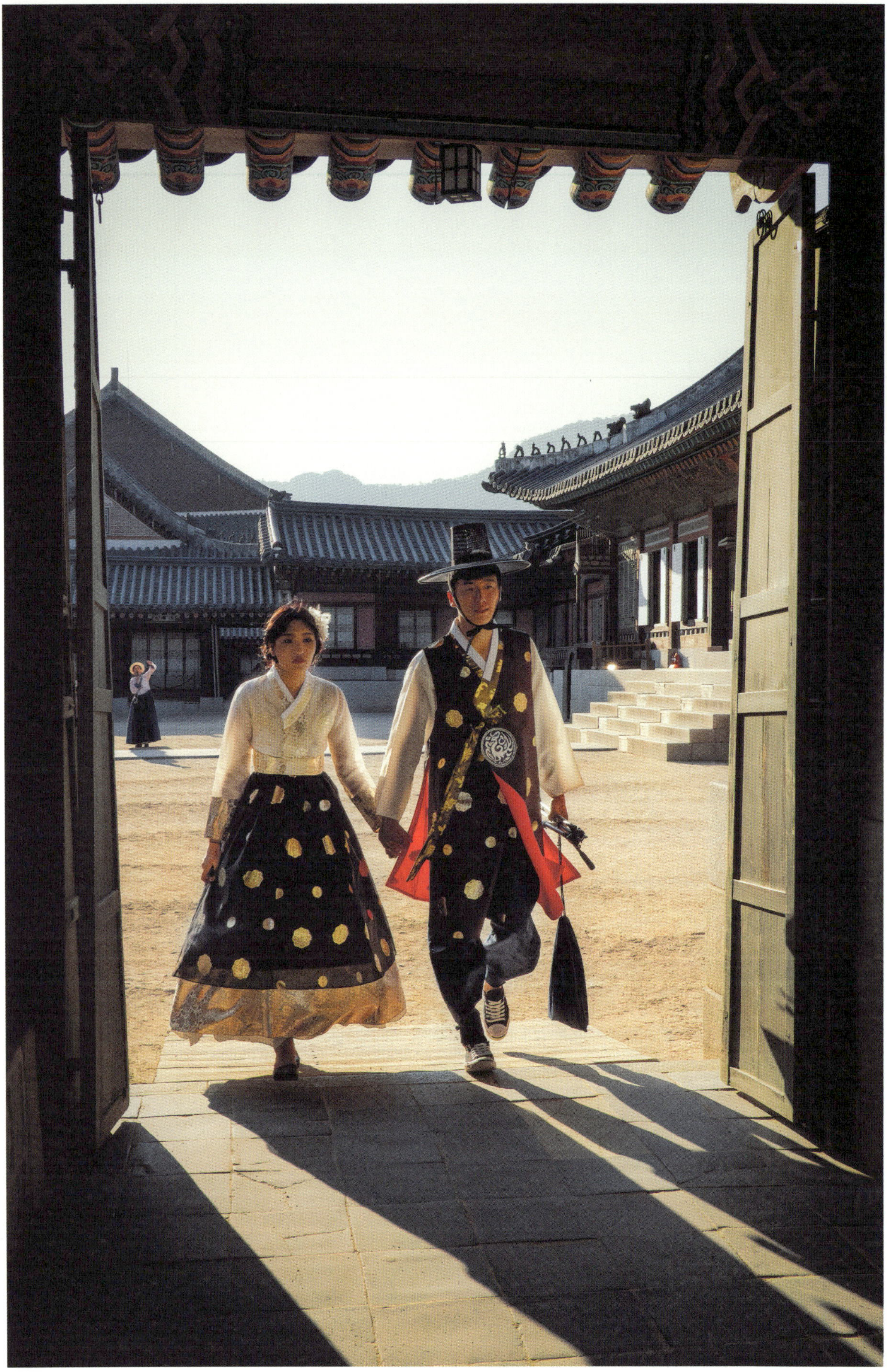

## JEONTONG

전통

(jen-tong) is the Korean word for "tradition." It represents the values, customs, and practices passed down through generations, from language, food, and clothing to art, architecture, and etiquette. But jeontong is more than preservation; it's about continuity—how the past lives within the present.

## HANBOK

한복

(hahn-bŏk) is traditional Korean clothing known for its vibrant colors, graceful lines, and elegant simplicity. Rooted in the Korean ideal of harmony with nature, it's often made from lightweight fabrics like silk or ramie. Hanboks are readily available for rentals and wearing one grants free visitor access to the palaces in Seoul.

Traditional values shape daily life in Seoul today. Respect for elders, bowing greetings, and celebrations of Chuseok—Korea's autumn harvest festival—and Seollal, the Lunar New Year, remain part of the city's cultural legacy. Across Seoul, traditional hanok homes constructed from wood and earth with distinctive tiled roofs stand beside glass towers. Hanbok is worn not only on holidays but also by locals and visitors walking through Bukchon or the palace grounds. Seeing people in hanbok in the middle of modern streets shows how traditional practices remain woven into everyday life in Seoul.

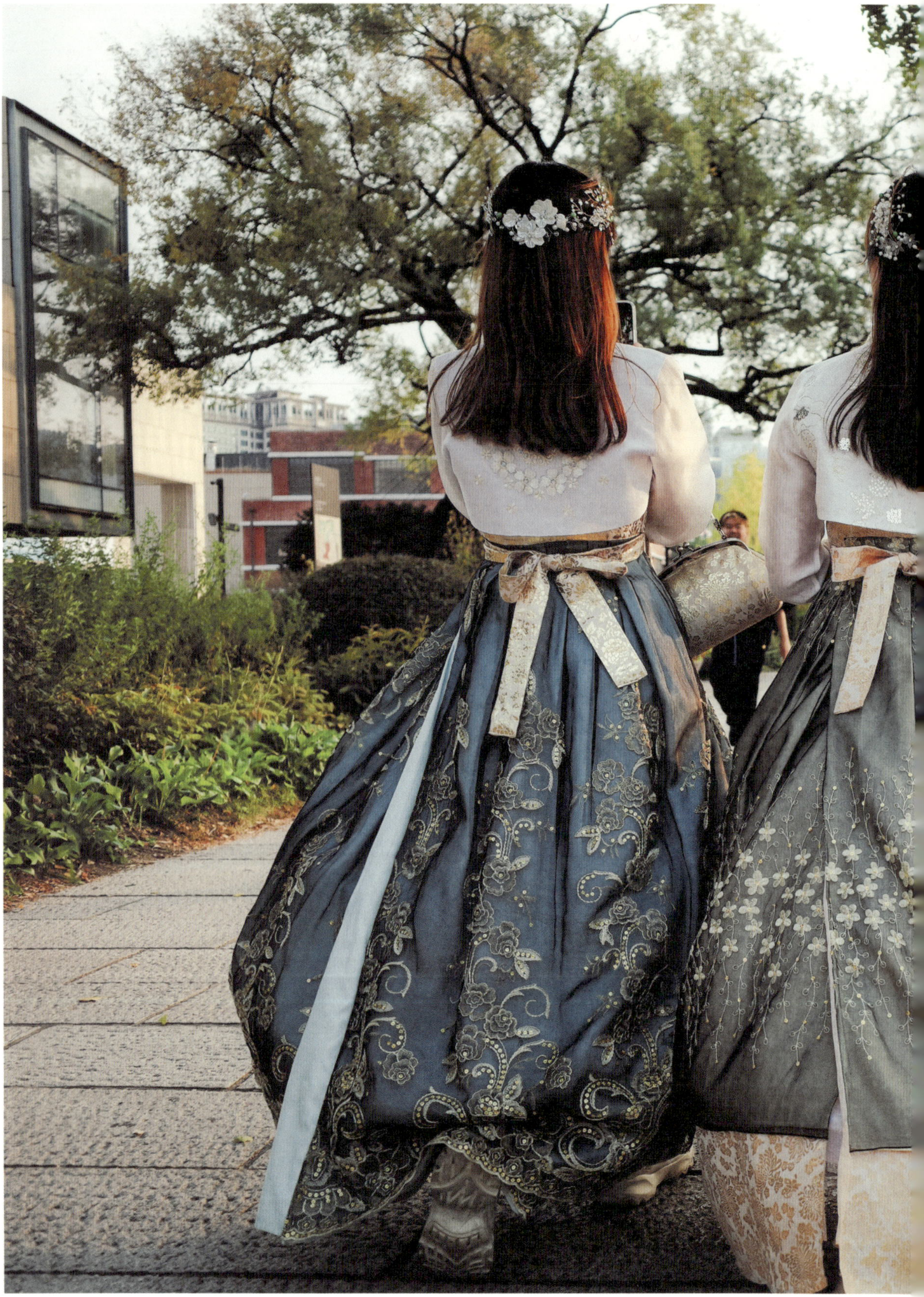

above: Samcheong-dong, Jongno District + previous spread: Gyeongbokgung Palace, Jongno District

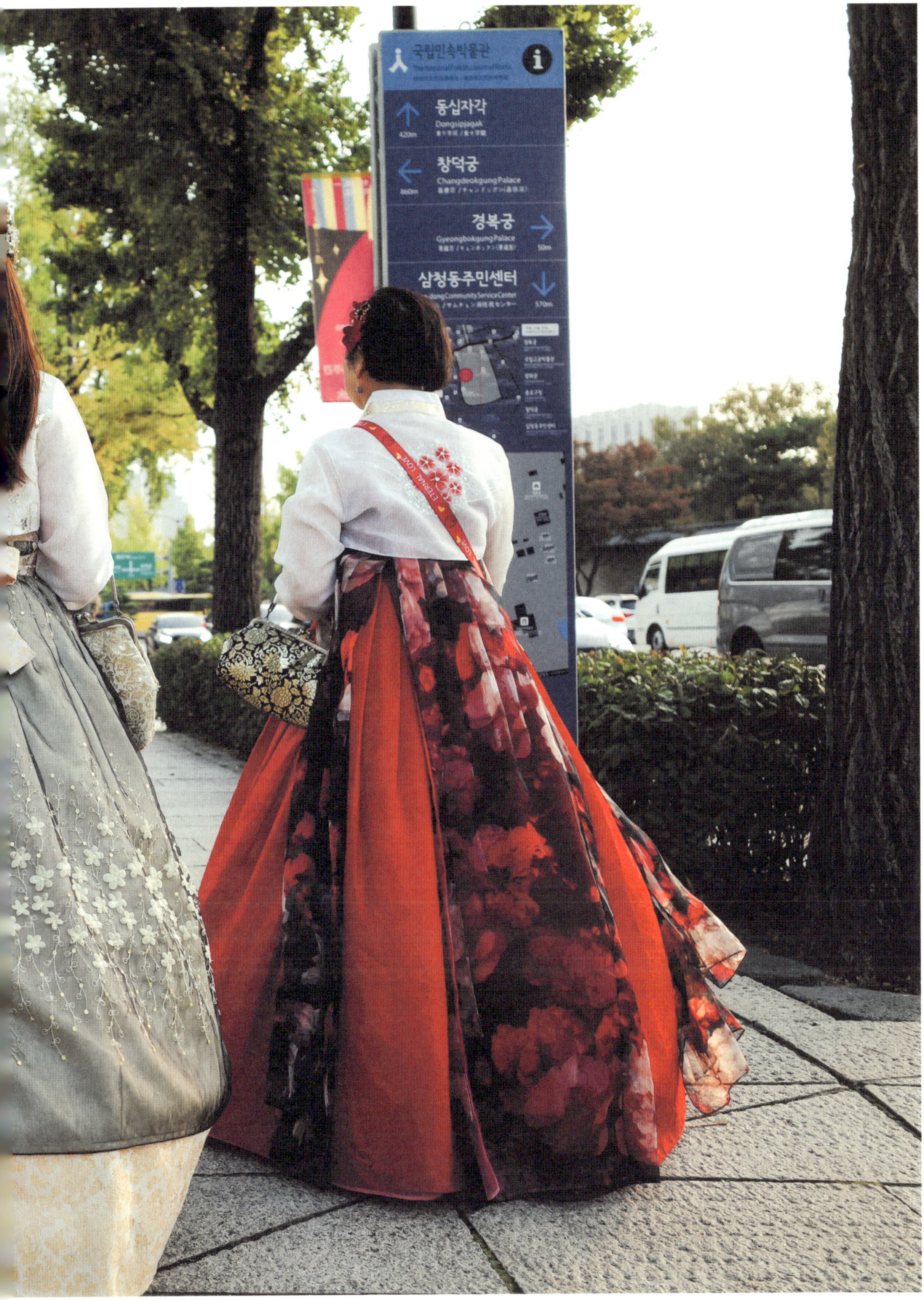
국립민속박물관
동십자각
Dongsipjagak
420m
창덕궁
Changdeokgung Palace
860m
경복궁
Gyeongbokgung Palace
50m
삼청동주민센터
570m
ETERNAL LOVE

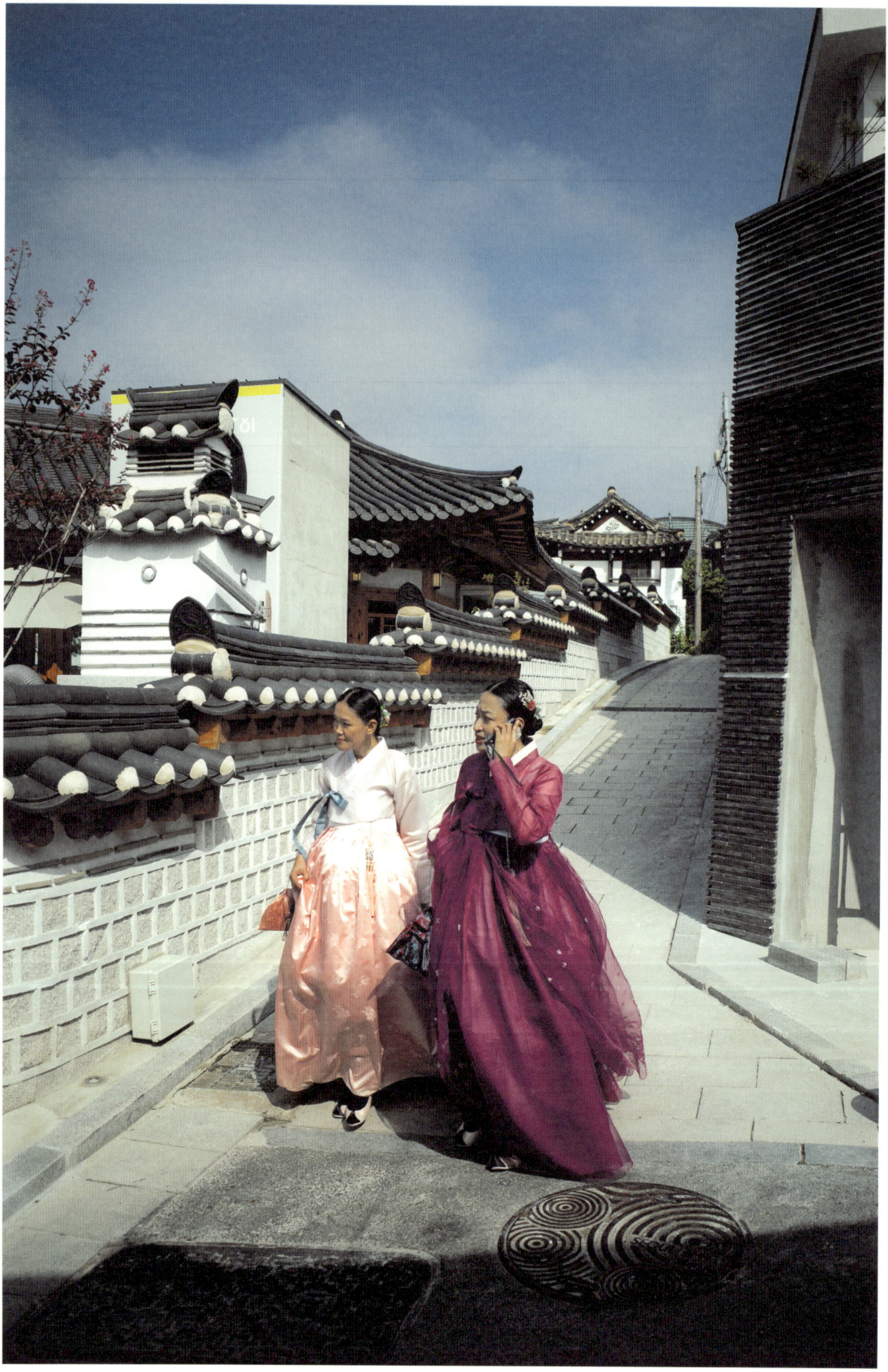

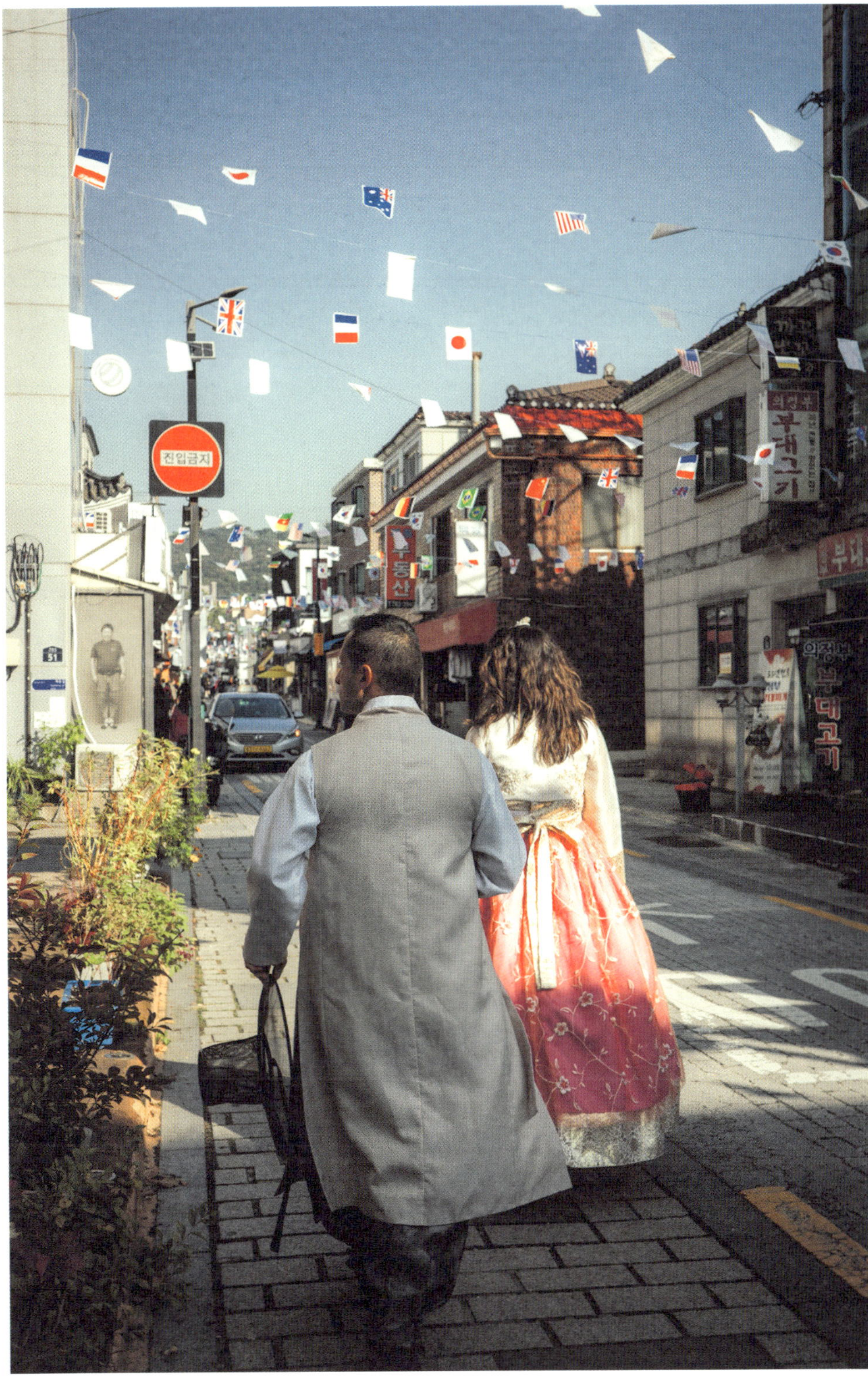


left + above: Samcheong-dong, Jongno District

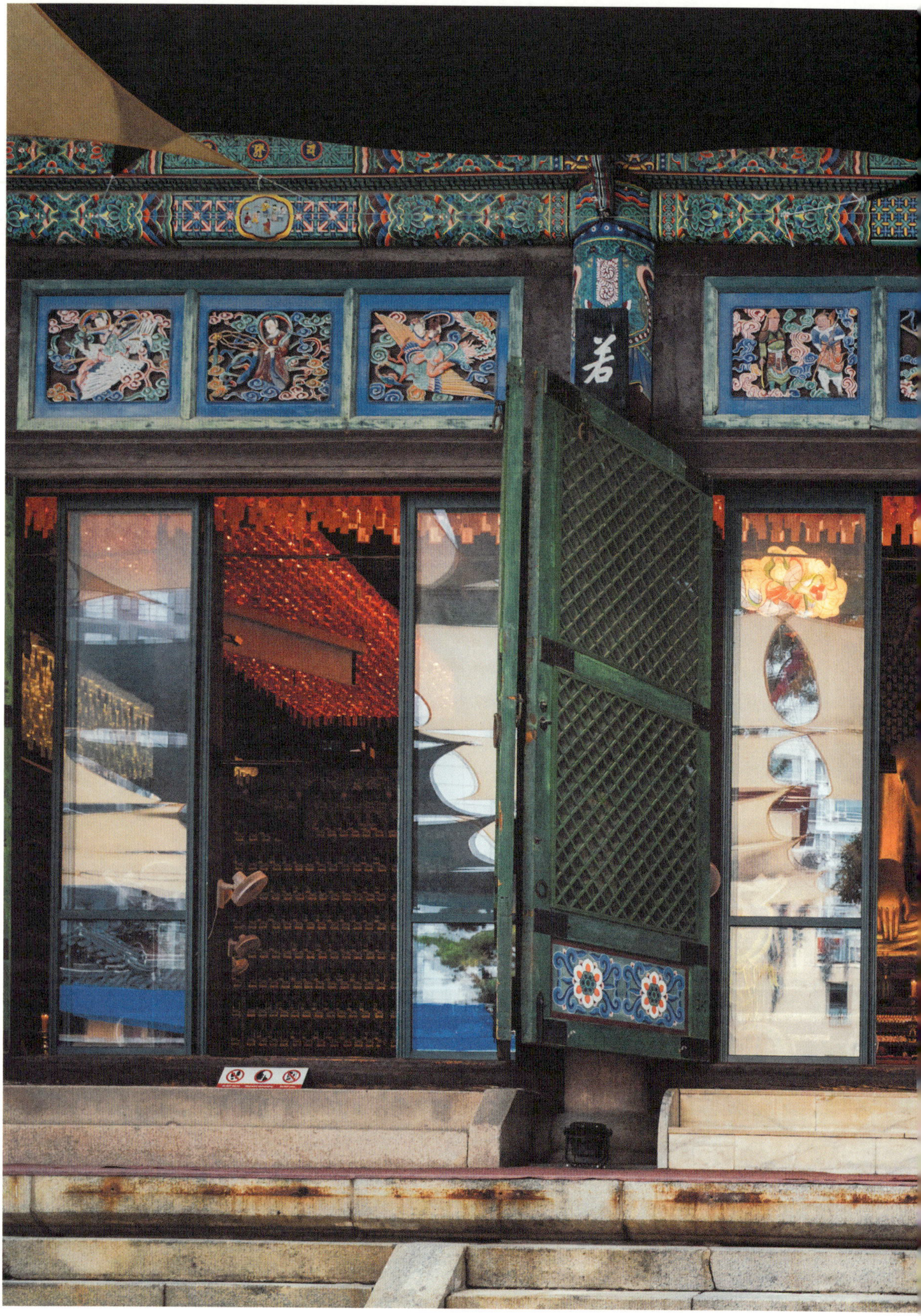


Jogyesa Temple, Daeungjeon, Jongno District > Chief temple of the Jogye Order of Korean Buddhism

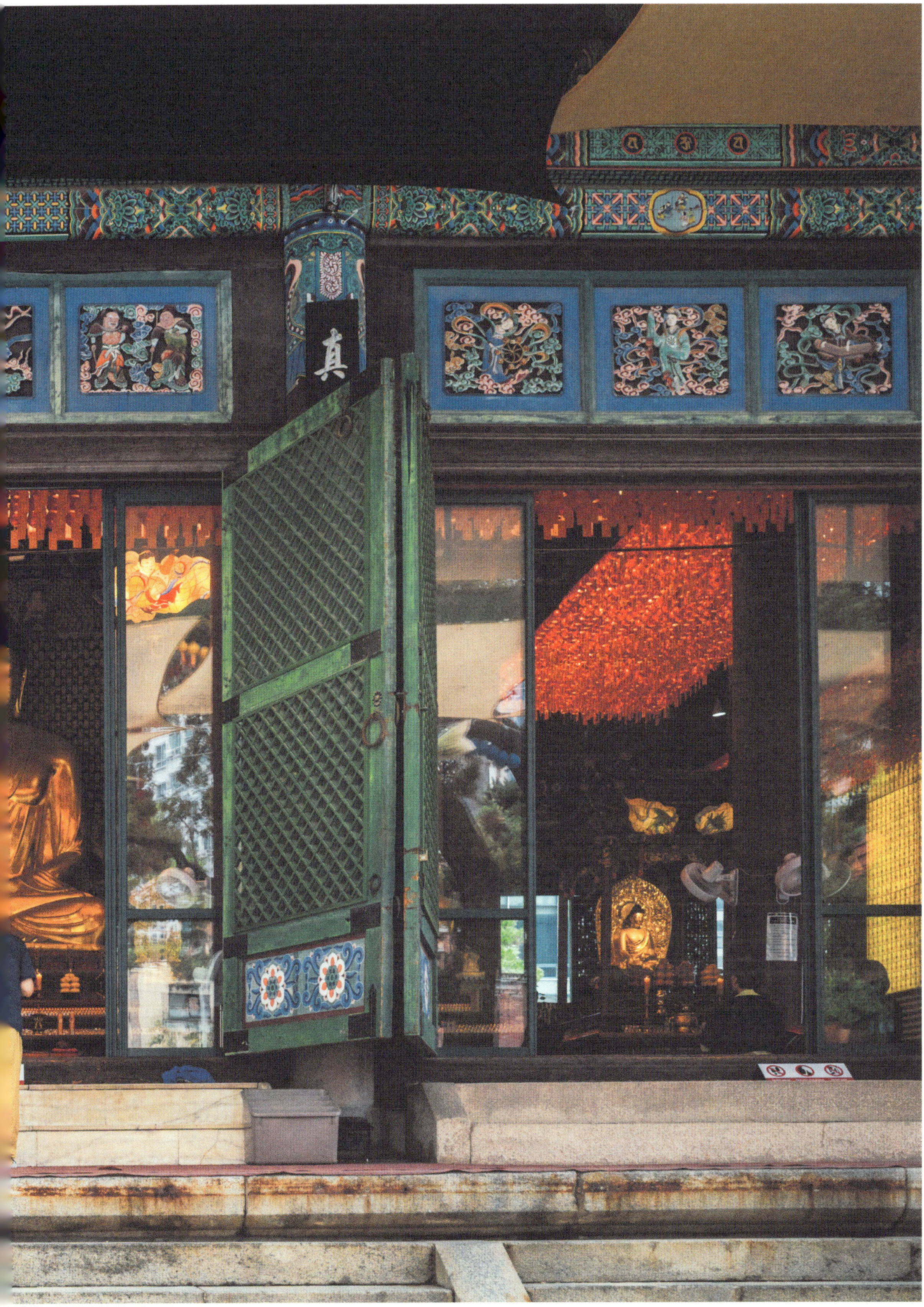
真

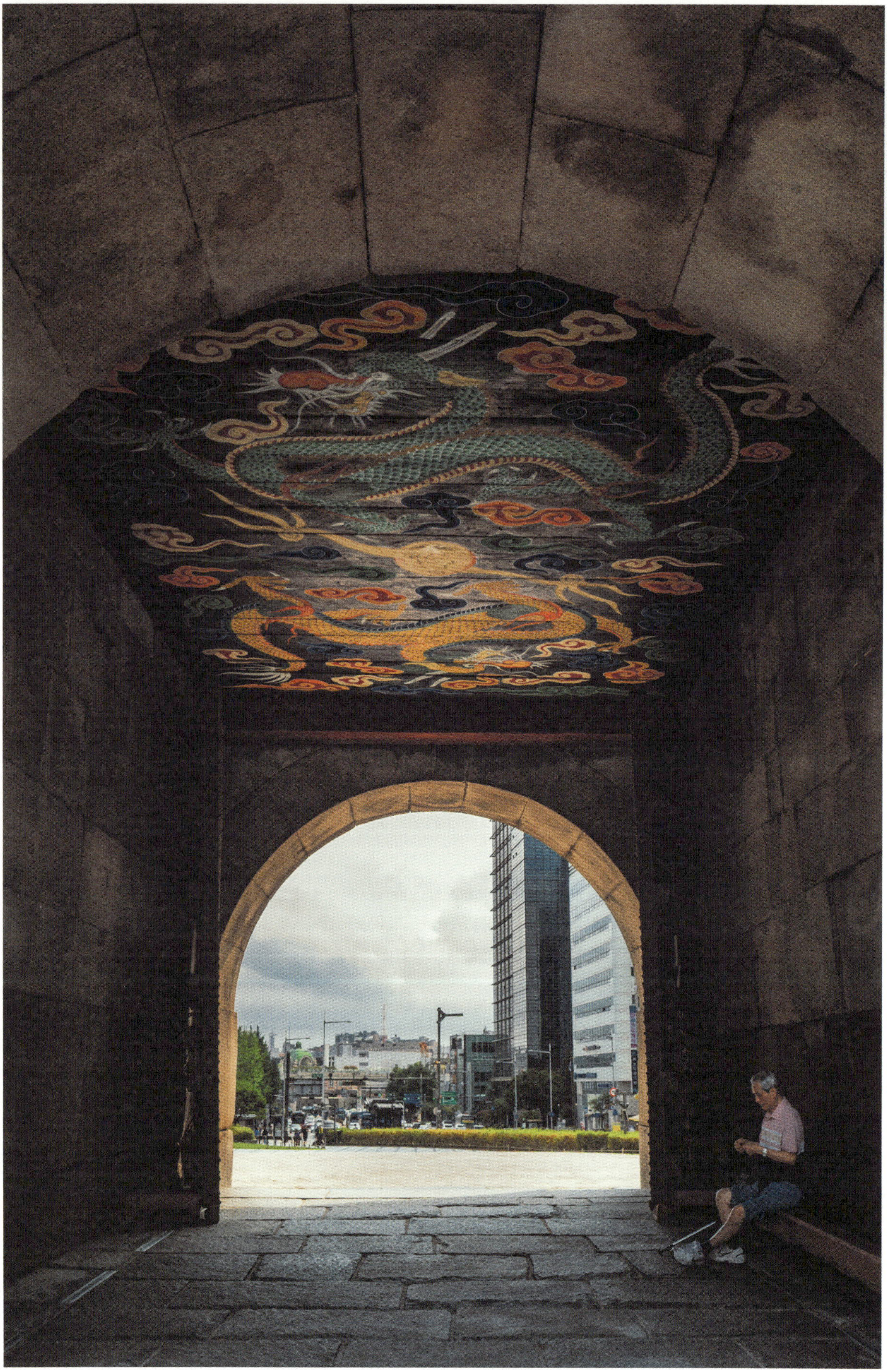

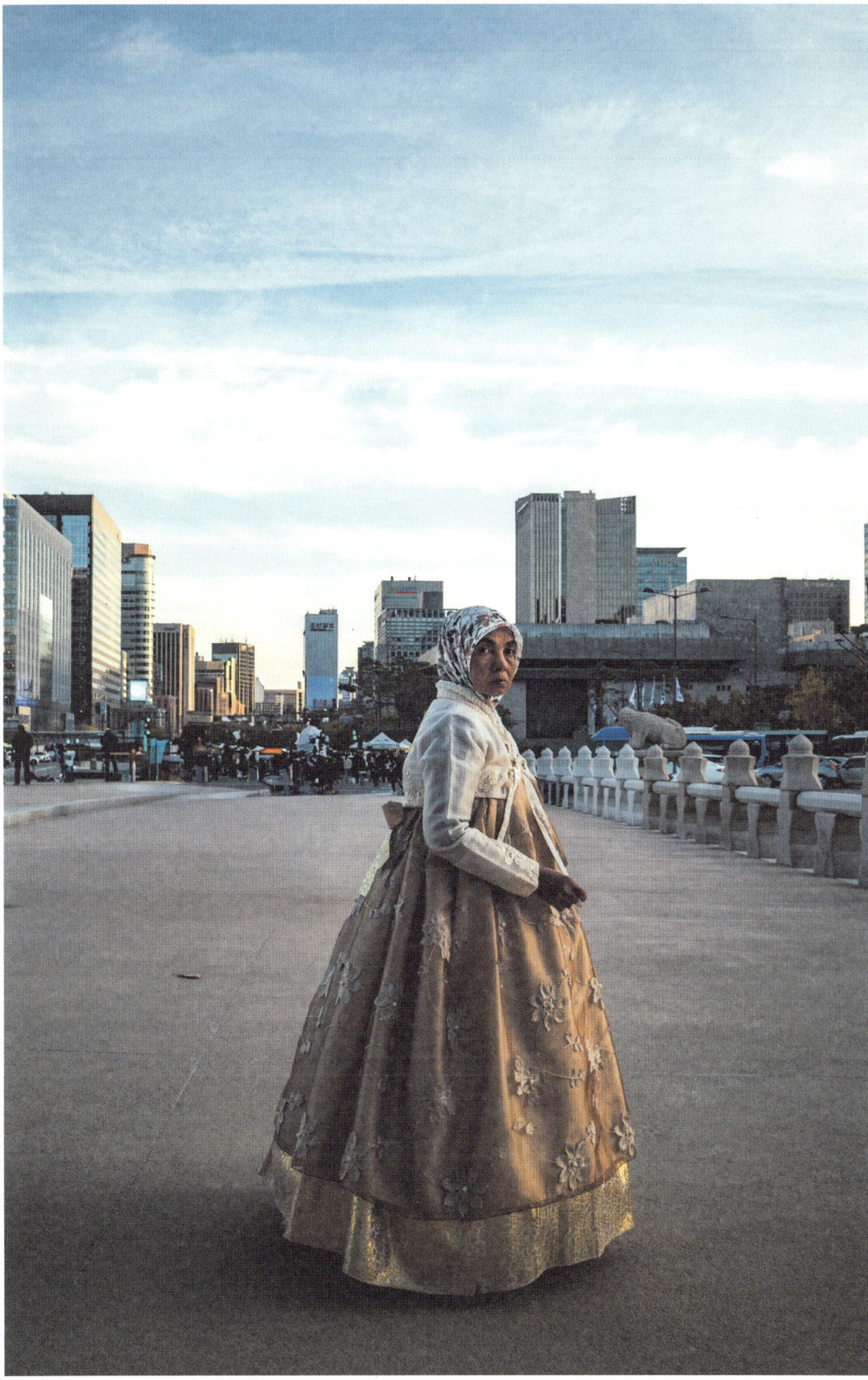

left + above: Gyeongbokgung Palace, Jongno District

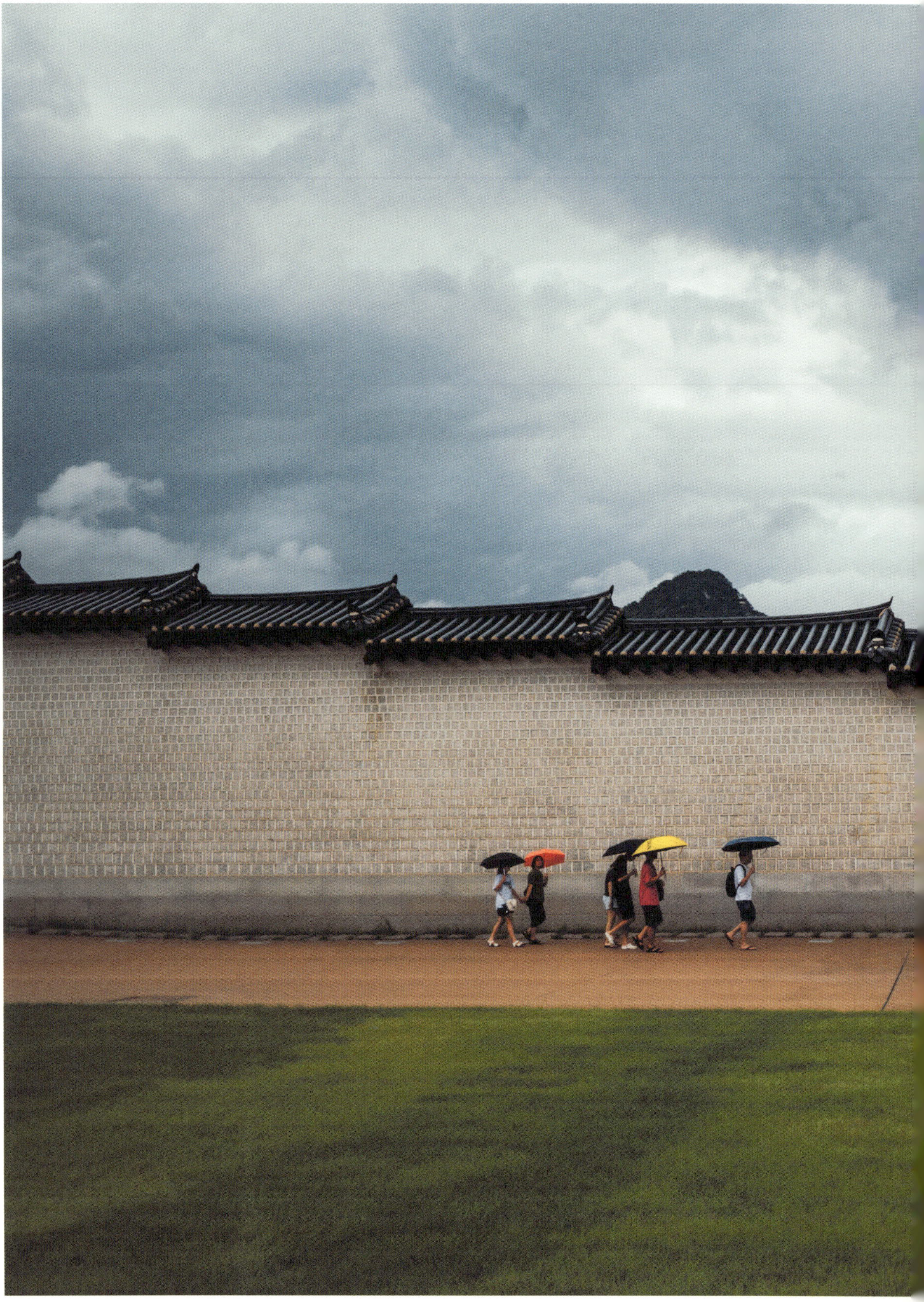

Gyeongbokgung Palace, Jongno District

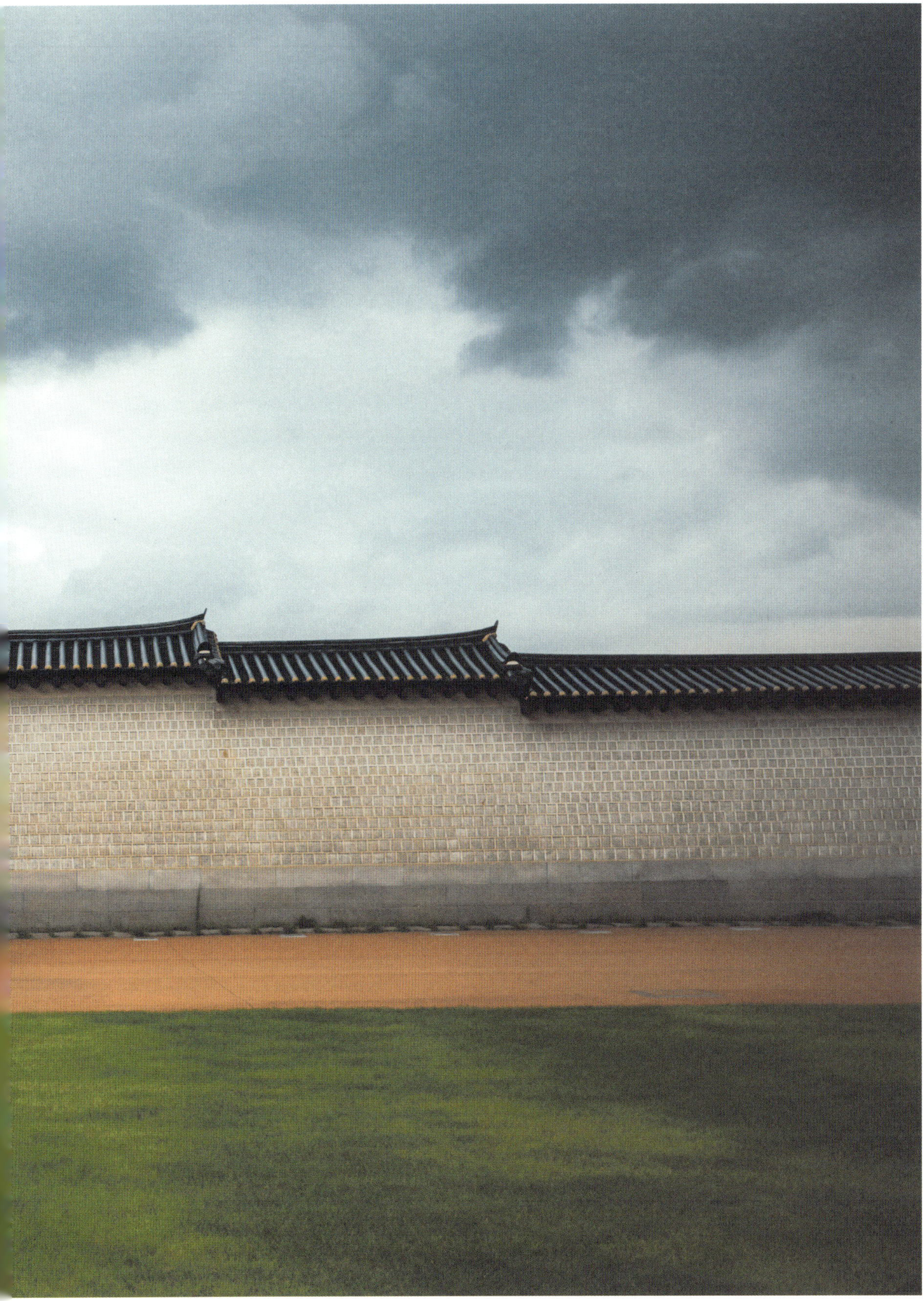

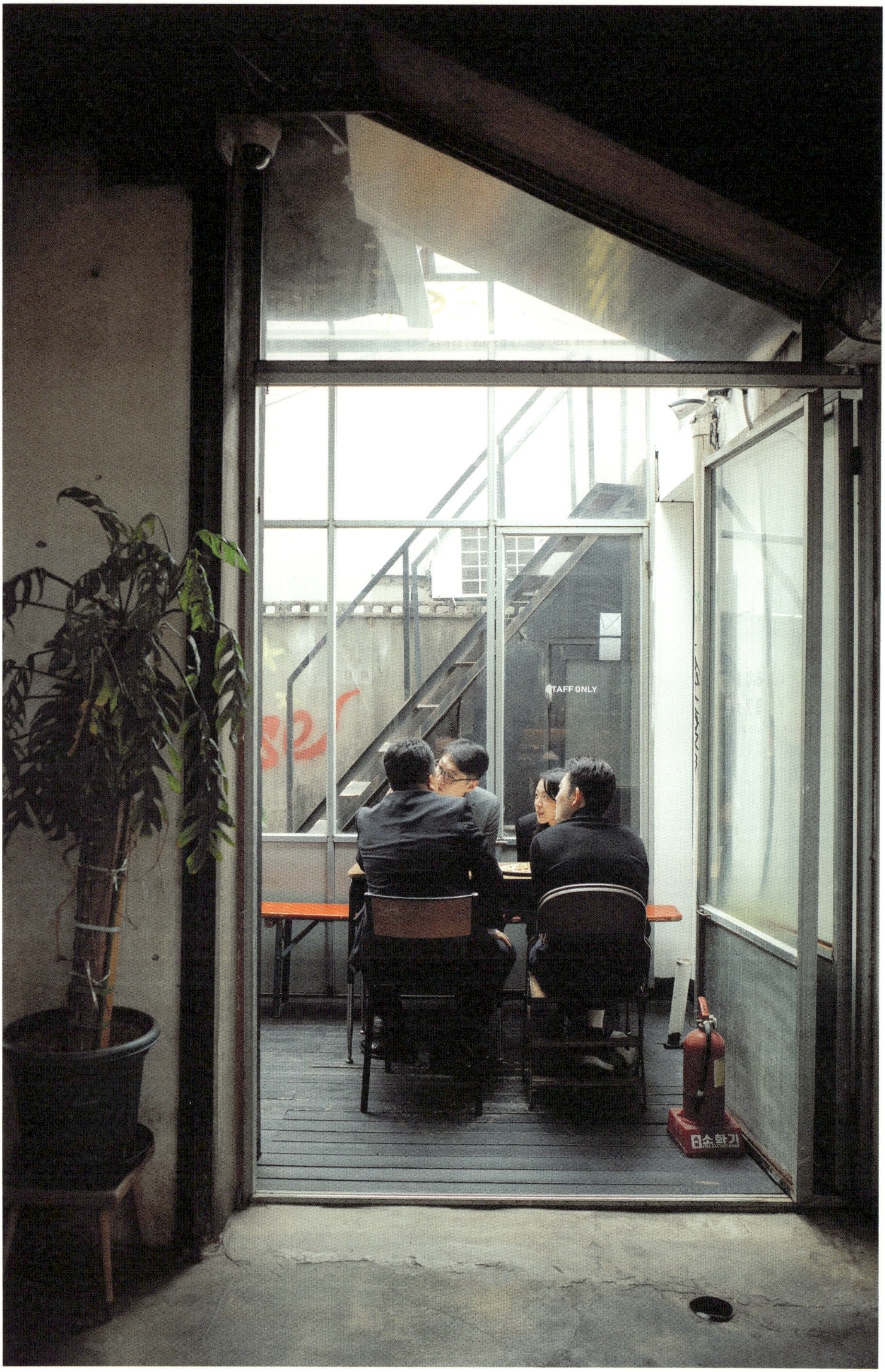
STAFF ONLY
소화기

# HWESIK

## 회식

(hway-shik) translates to "company dinner" or "staff dinner." It is a significant part of Korean work-place culture, traditionally involving after-work meals and multiple rounds of drinking with coworkers and superiors. The main purpose is to foster camaraderie, build a deeper sense of unity, and allow employees to bond with executives in a more relaxed, social setting outside of the formal office hierarchy.

Hwesik became deeply rooted in Korean work culture during the country's rapid industrialization, when long hours and tightly coordinated teams were viewed as essential to economic growth. Sharing food and drinks after work helped reinforce group cohesion, ease hierarchy, and create a sense of collective responsibility that carried back into the office. Over time, it became a near-standard expectation, treated as an extension of the workday and a way to maintain unity during periods of fast national and corporate change. Today, the tradition is still familiar, but its form is shifting; participation is becoming more optional, gatherings tend to be shorter, and many workplaces adjust the practice to reflect changing views on work–life balance. Even with these changes, hwesik continues to offer a space where colleagues can talk more openly and build connection outside the structure of the office.

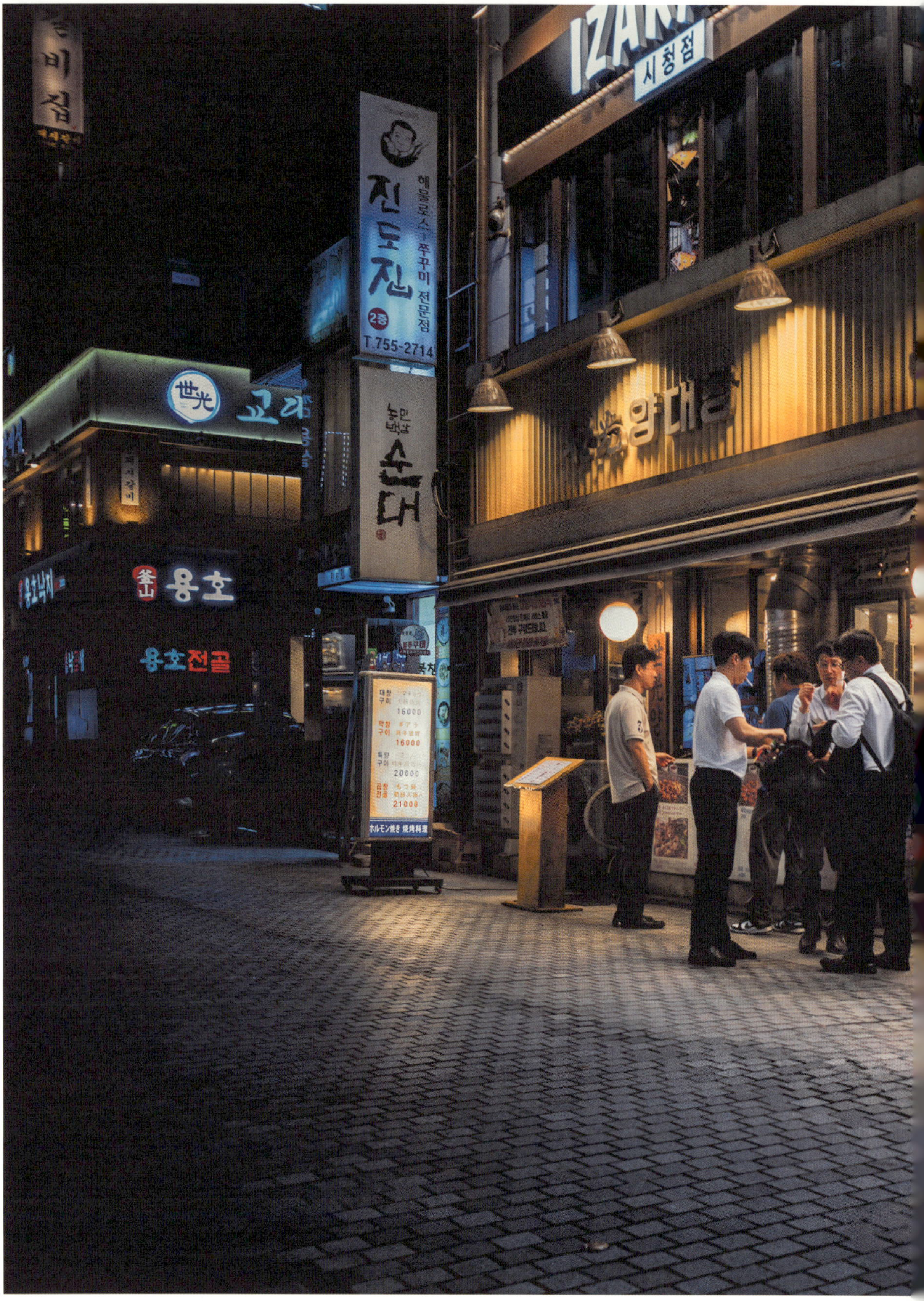


above: Bukchang-dong, Jung District + previous spread: Mullae-dong, Yeongdeungpo District

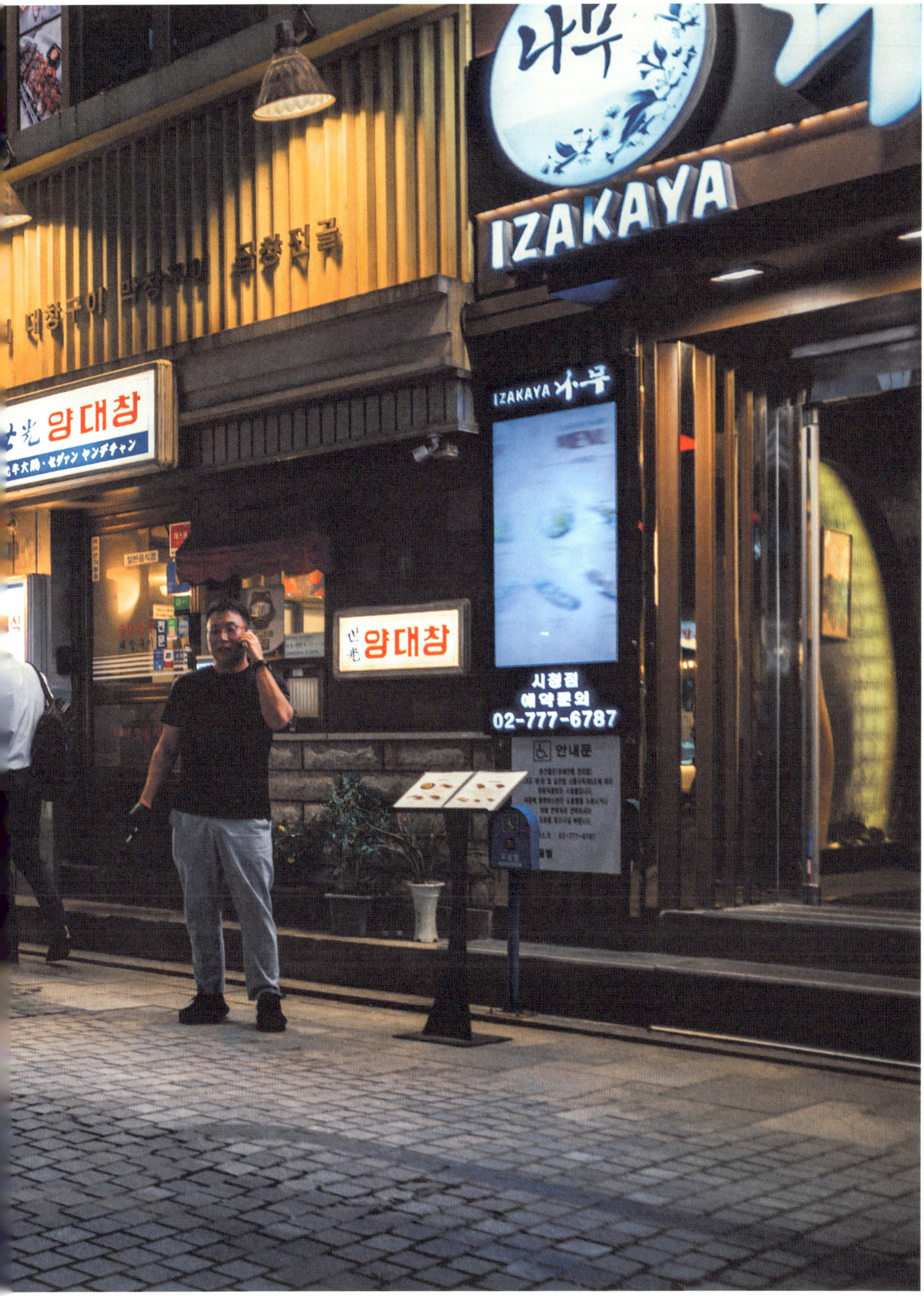
나무
IZAKAYA
양대창
IZAKAYA 나무
양대창
시청점
예약문의
02-777-6787
안내문

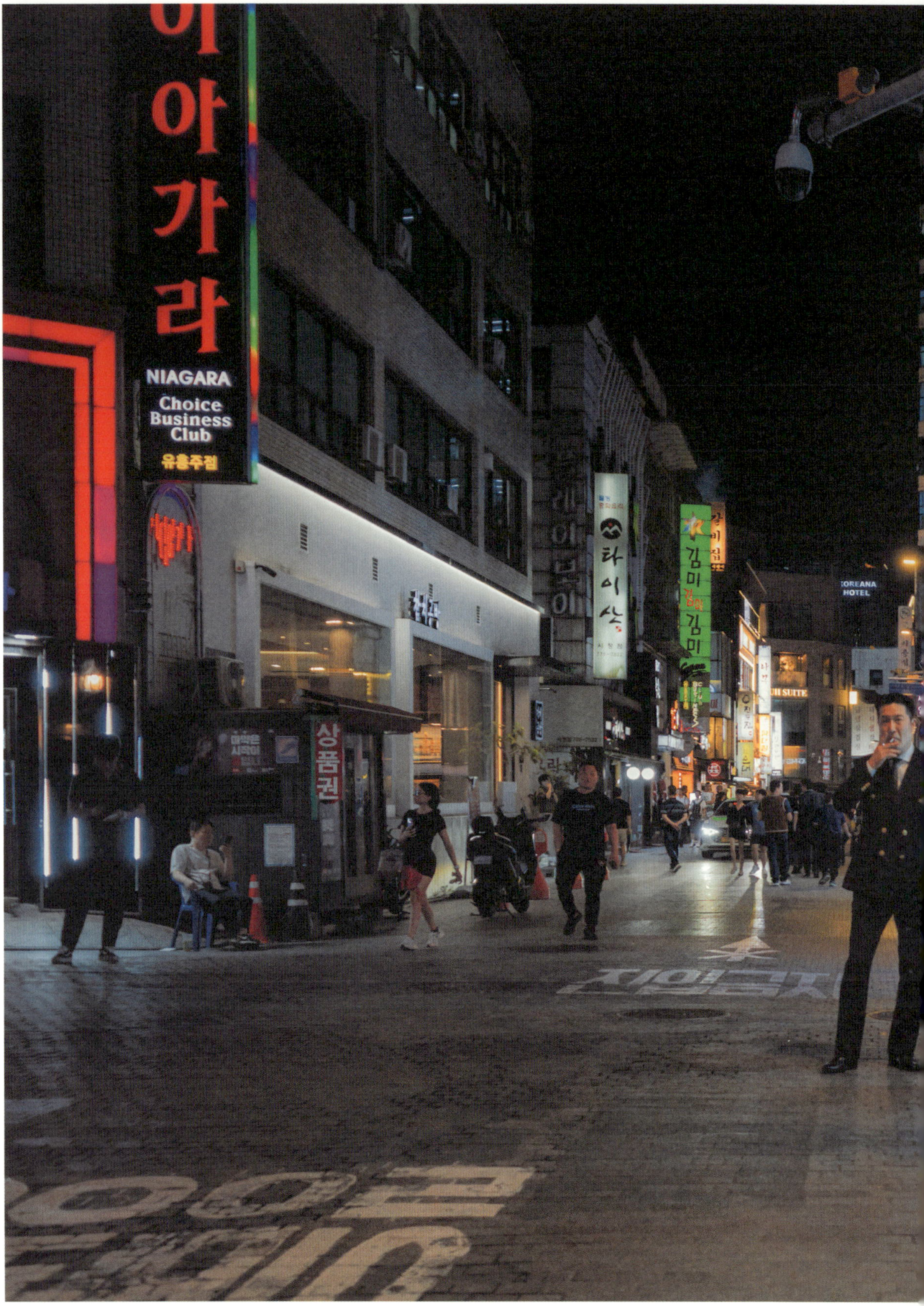


Bukchang-dong, Jung District

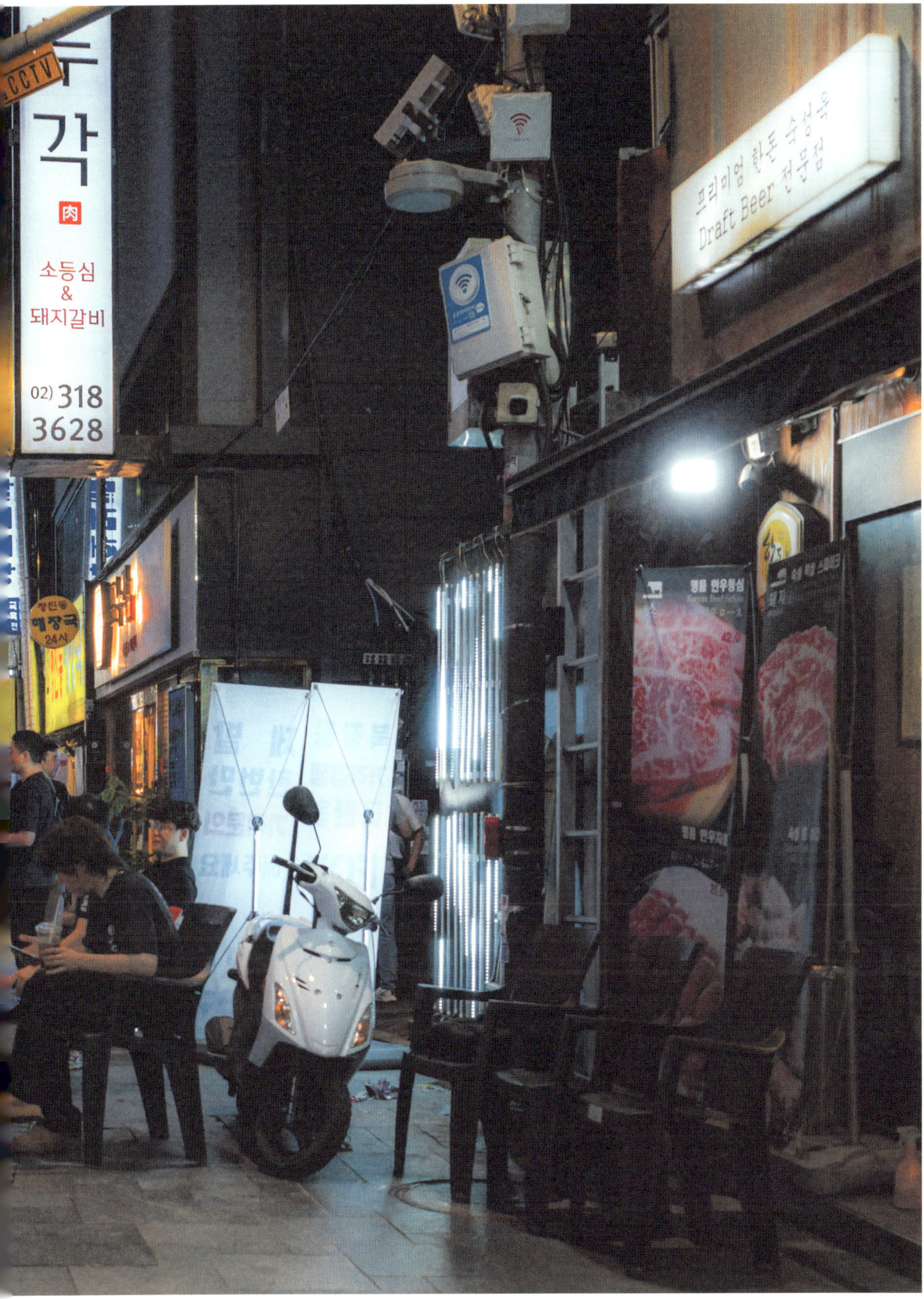
CCTV
각
肉
소등심
&
돼지갈비
02) 318
3628
프리미엄 한돈 숙성육
Draft Beer 전문점
해장국
24시

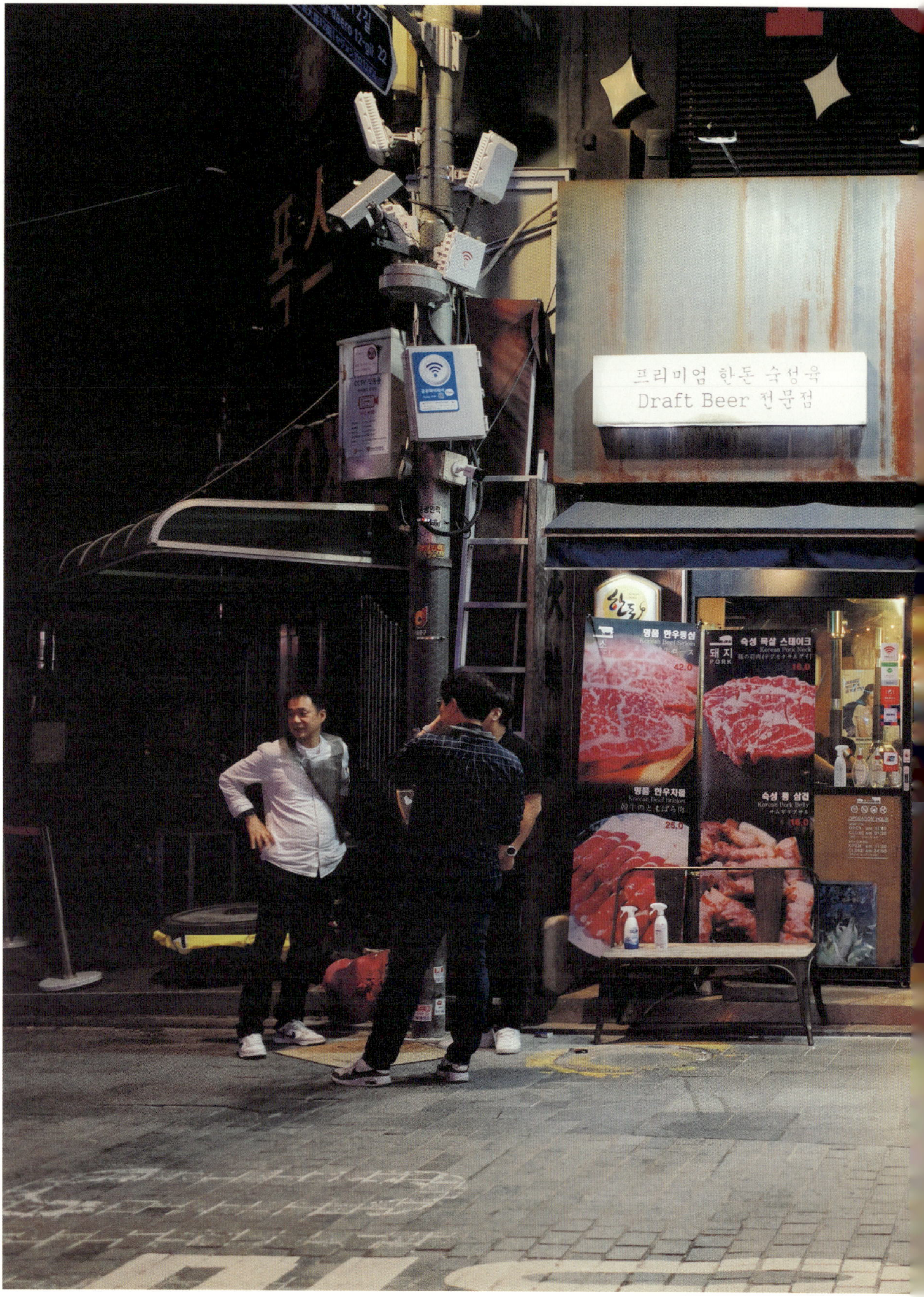


Bukchang-dong, Jung District

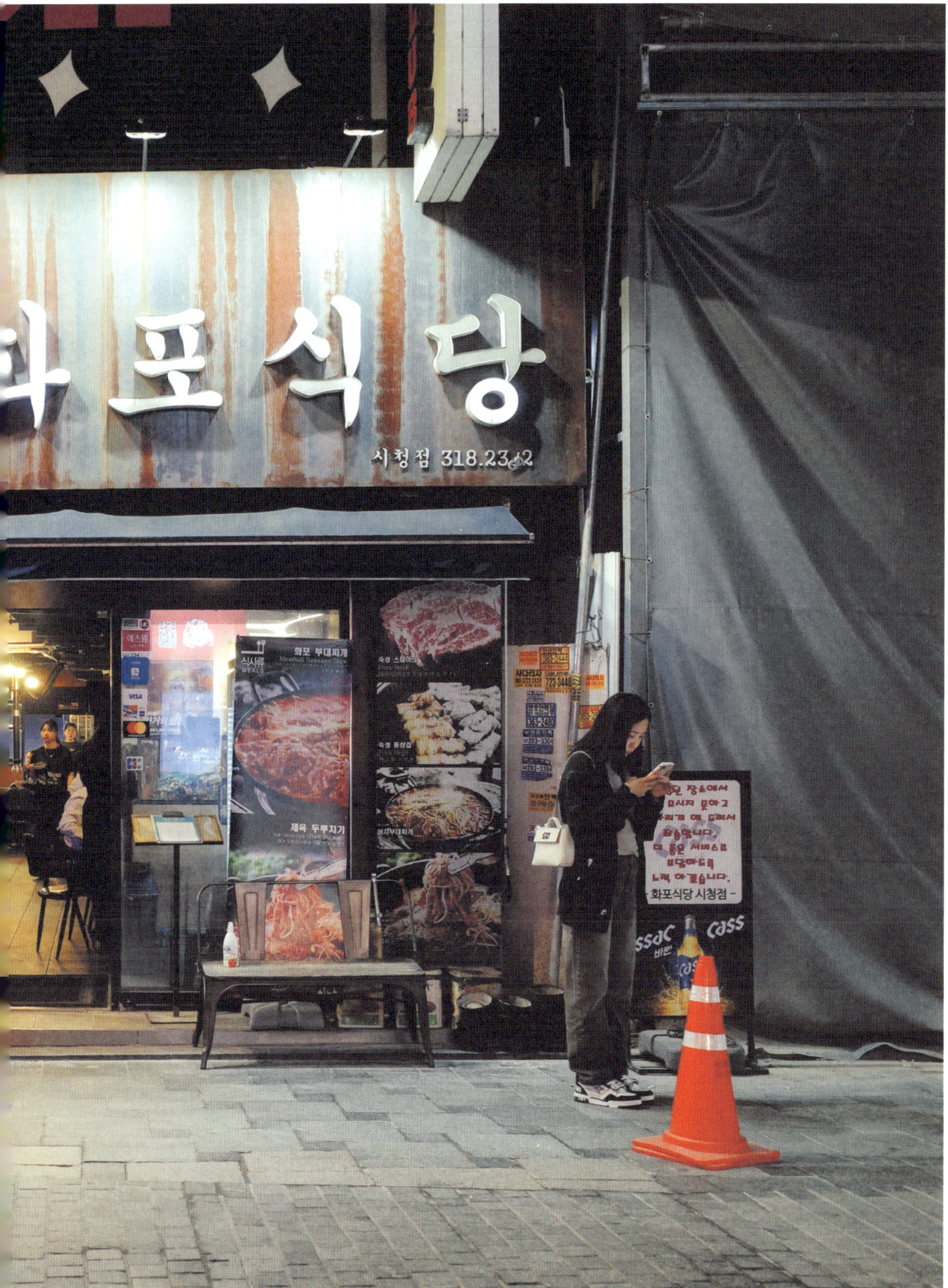
포식당
화포식당 시청점 -
cass

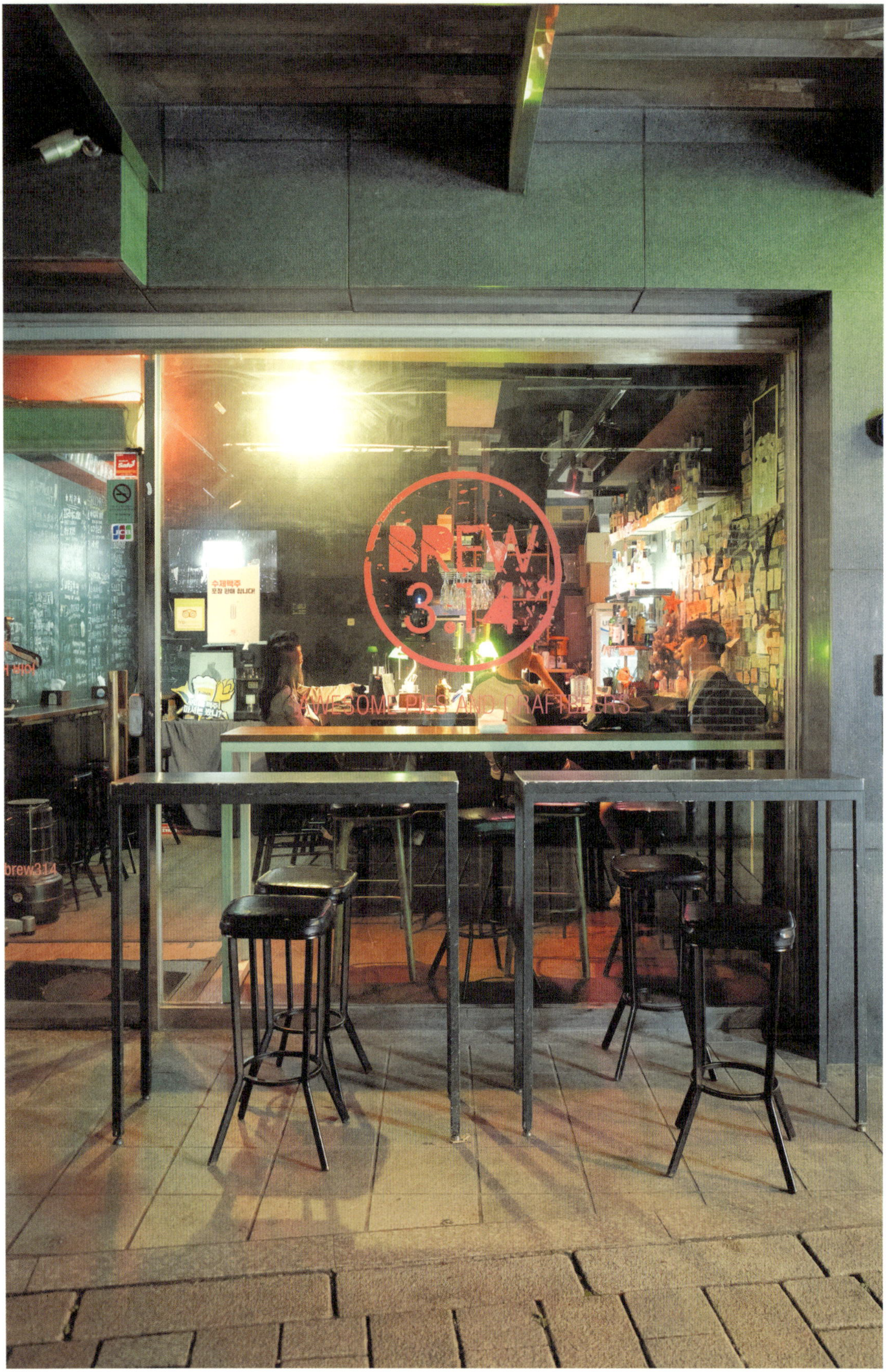
BREW
3.14
AWESOME PIES AND CRAFTBEERS
수제맥주
포장 판매 합니다!
brew314

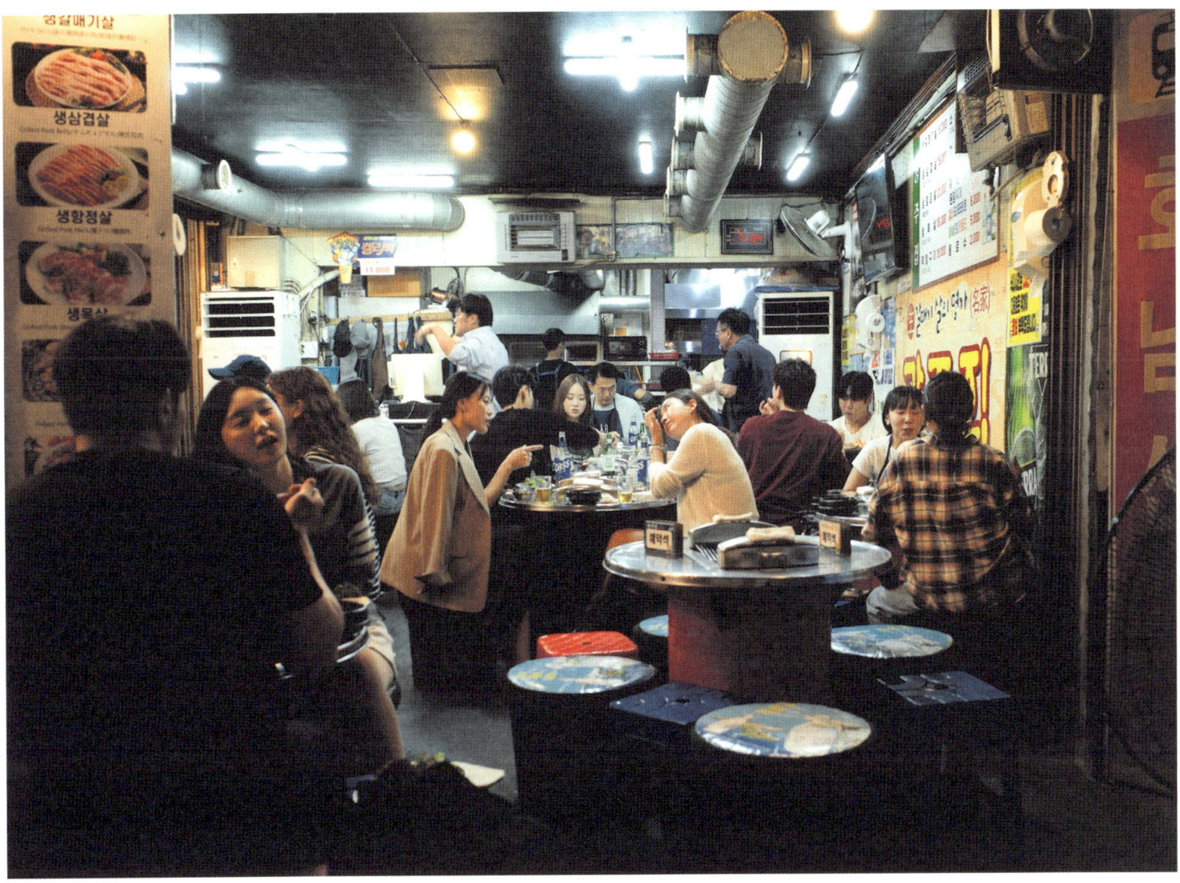


left + above: Ikseon-dong, Jongno District

# SIJANG

## 시장

(see-jang) is a term used broadly to encompass all kinds of markets—from open-air traditional markets to large, covered food markets. In modern Seoul, sijang carries more than a literal meaning; it evokes warmth, familiarity, and a sense of local identity. Many Koreans associate their neighborhood sijang with childhood memories, the smell of street food, and local community.

Markets in Seoul are vibrant reflections of the city's history, places where commerce, community, and culture have intertwined for centuries. Rooted in the trading hubs of the Joseon dynasty, these markets once supplied the royal court and citizens alike, growing alongside Seoul itself. Gwangjang Market, established in 1905, became one of Korea's first permanent marketplaces and still thrives with vendors selling bindaetteok and mayak gimbap. Namdaemun Market, dating to the 15th century, remains a maze of seafood, ginseng, and fabrics, open nearly all hours. Near Gyeongbokgung Palace, Tongin Market preserves older customs with its brass coin lunchboxes, while Mangwon and Majang Markets show how tradition evolves, blending heritage foods with modern cafés and design.

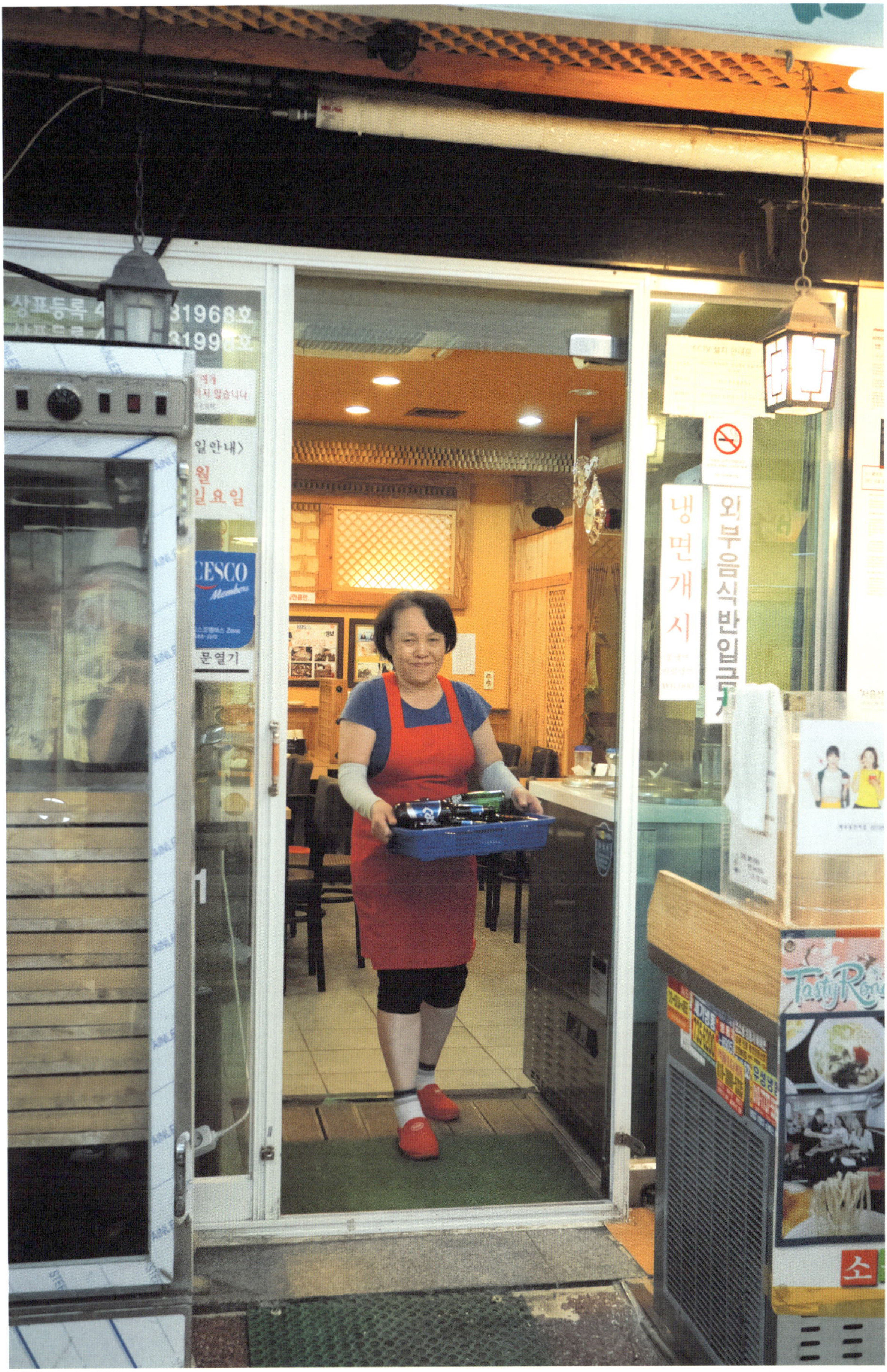
냉면개시
CESCO
Members
문열기
Tasty Road

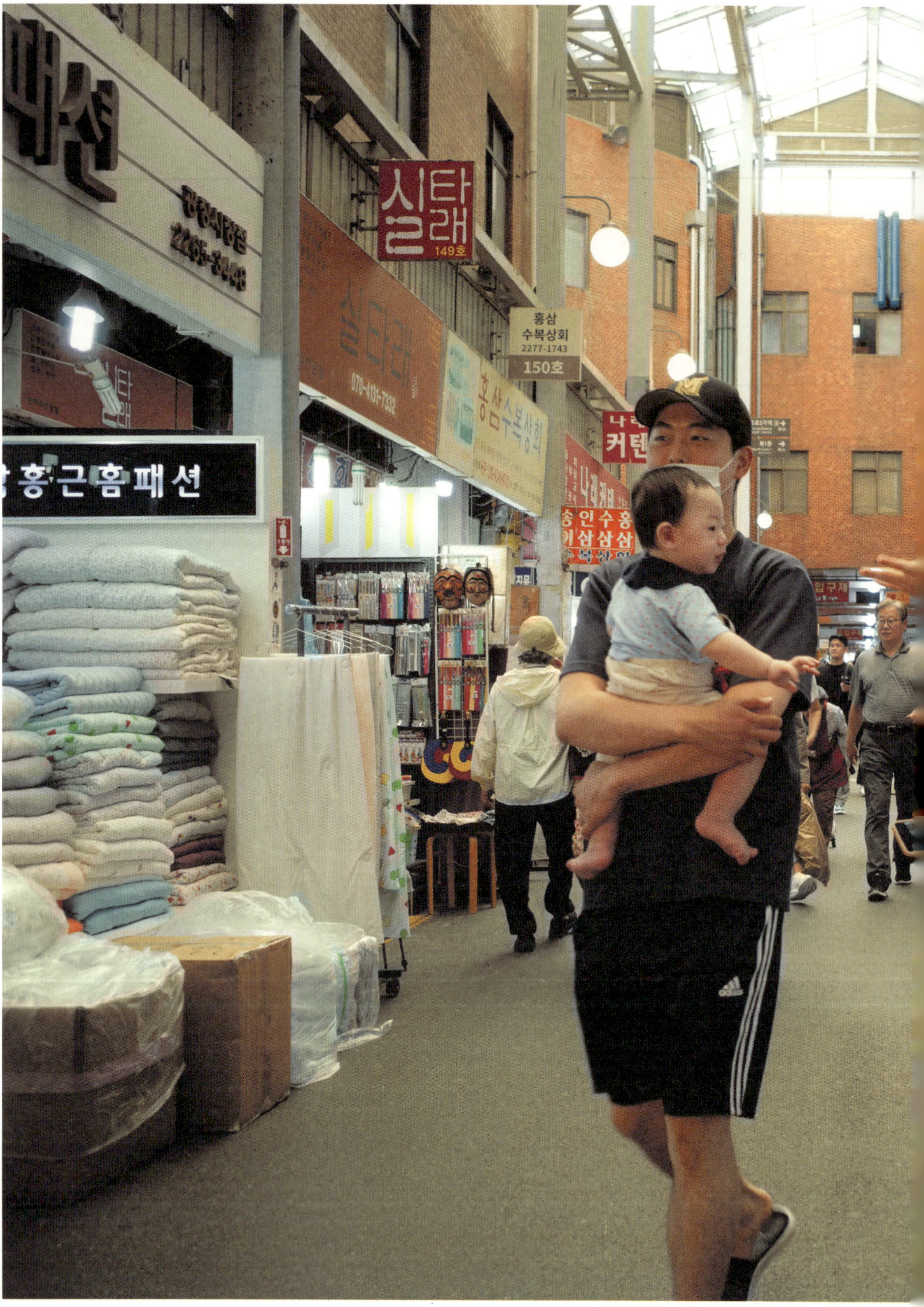


above: Gwangjang Market, Jongno District + previous page: Tongin Market, Tongin-dong, Jongno District

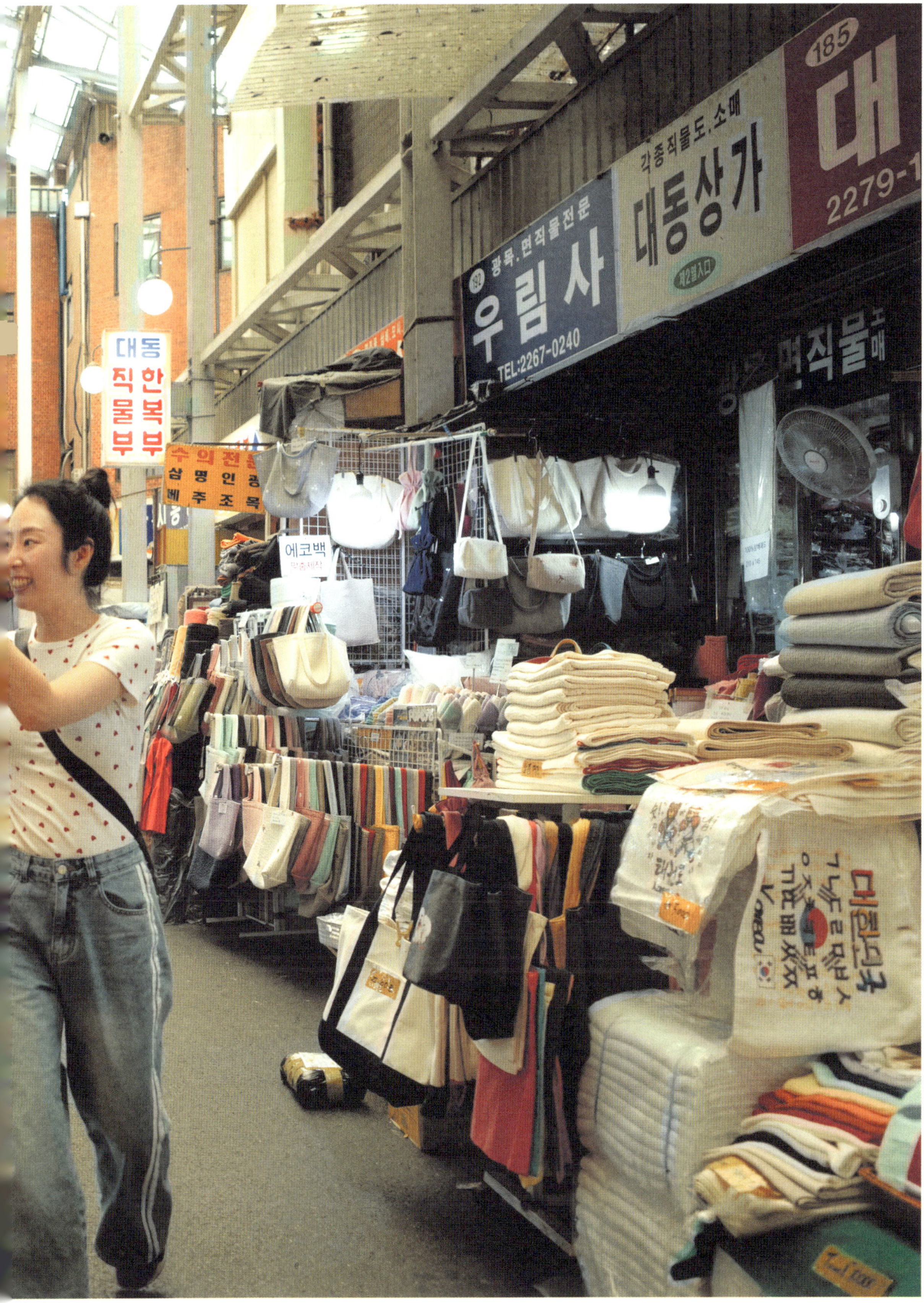
185
대
각종직물도.소매
대동상가
광목.면직물전문
우림사
TEL:2267-0240
대동
직물부
한복부
에코백

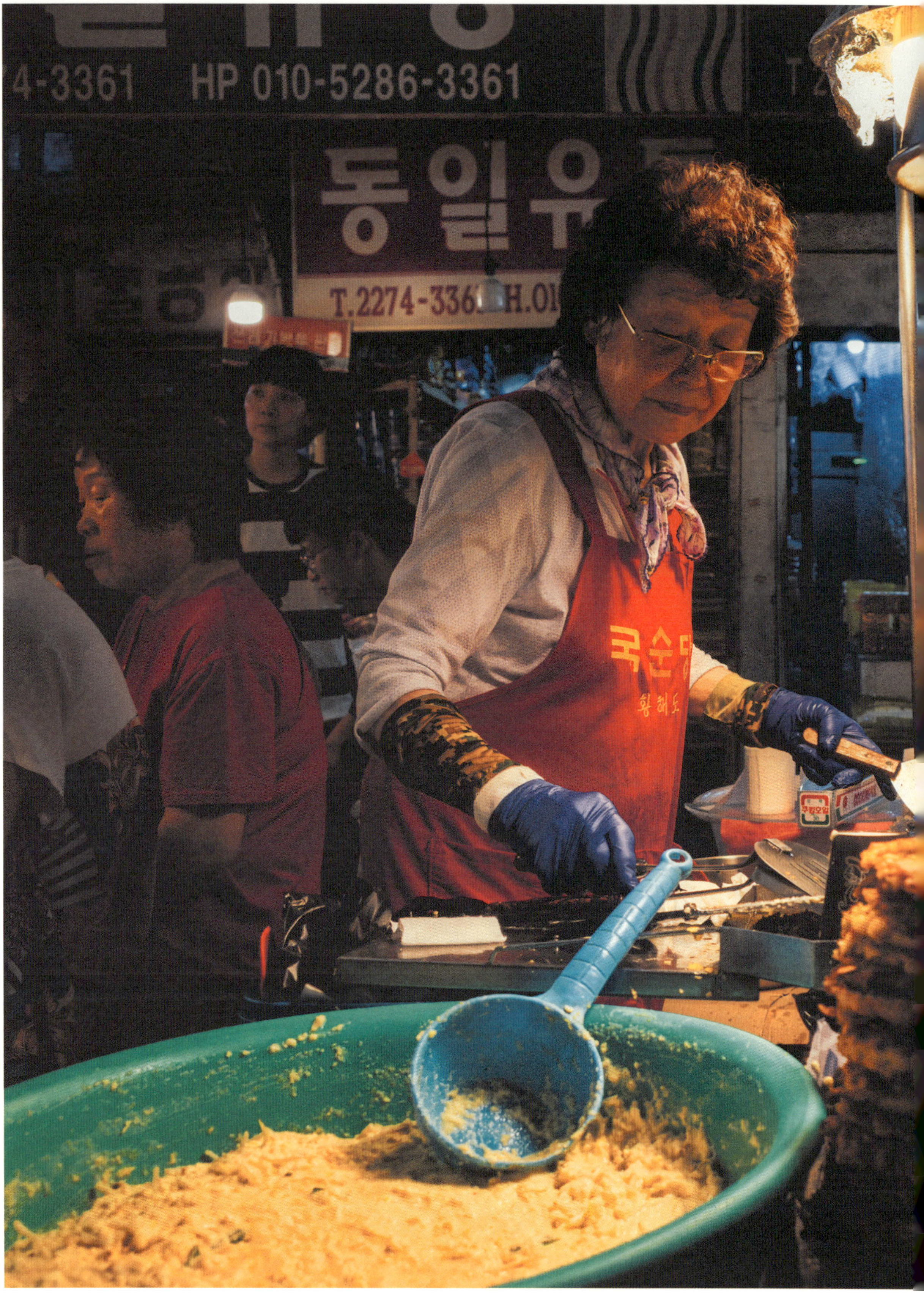


Gwangjang Market, Jongno District

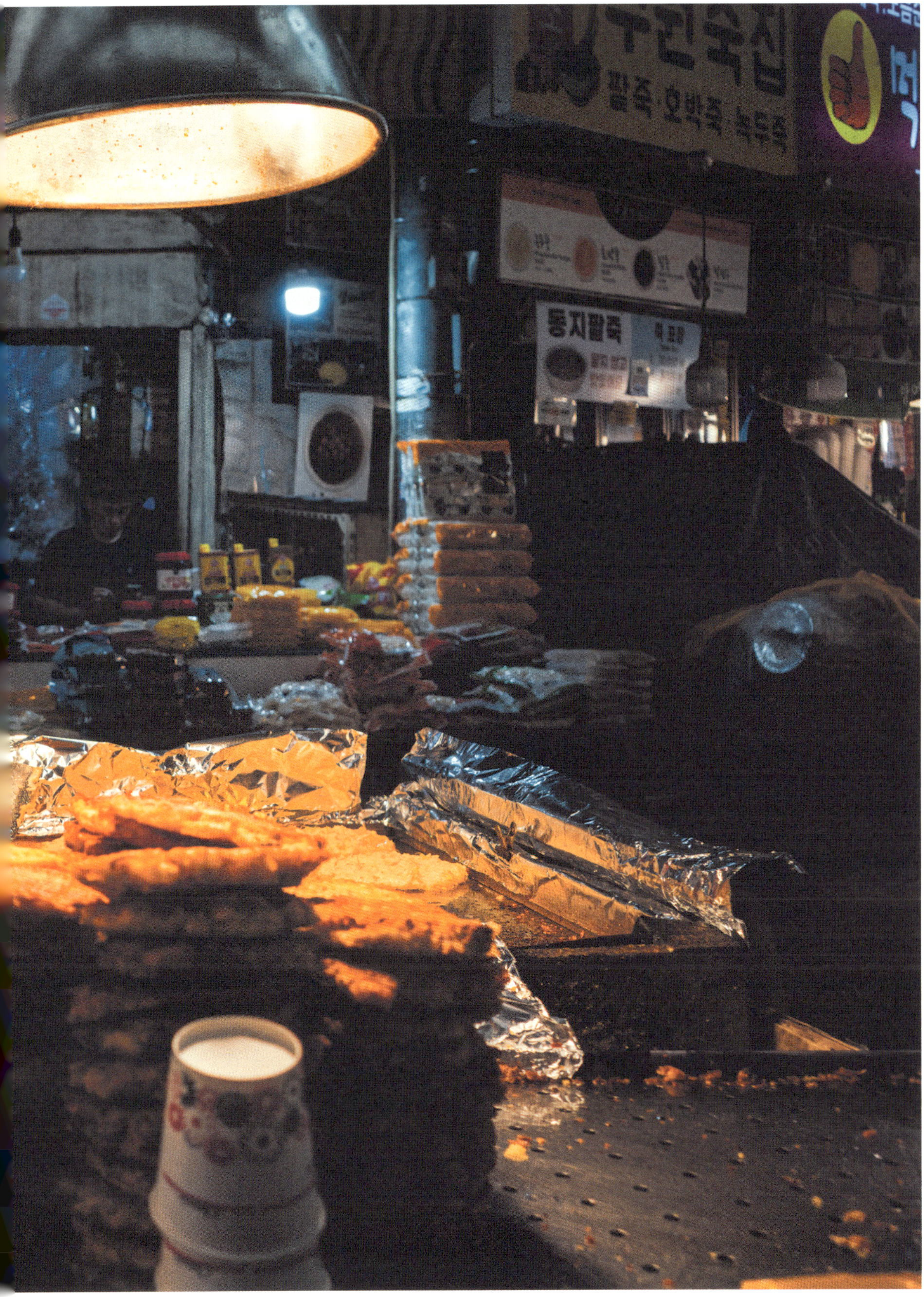
팥죽·호박죽·녹두죽
동지팥죽

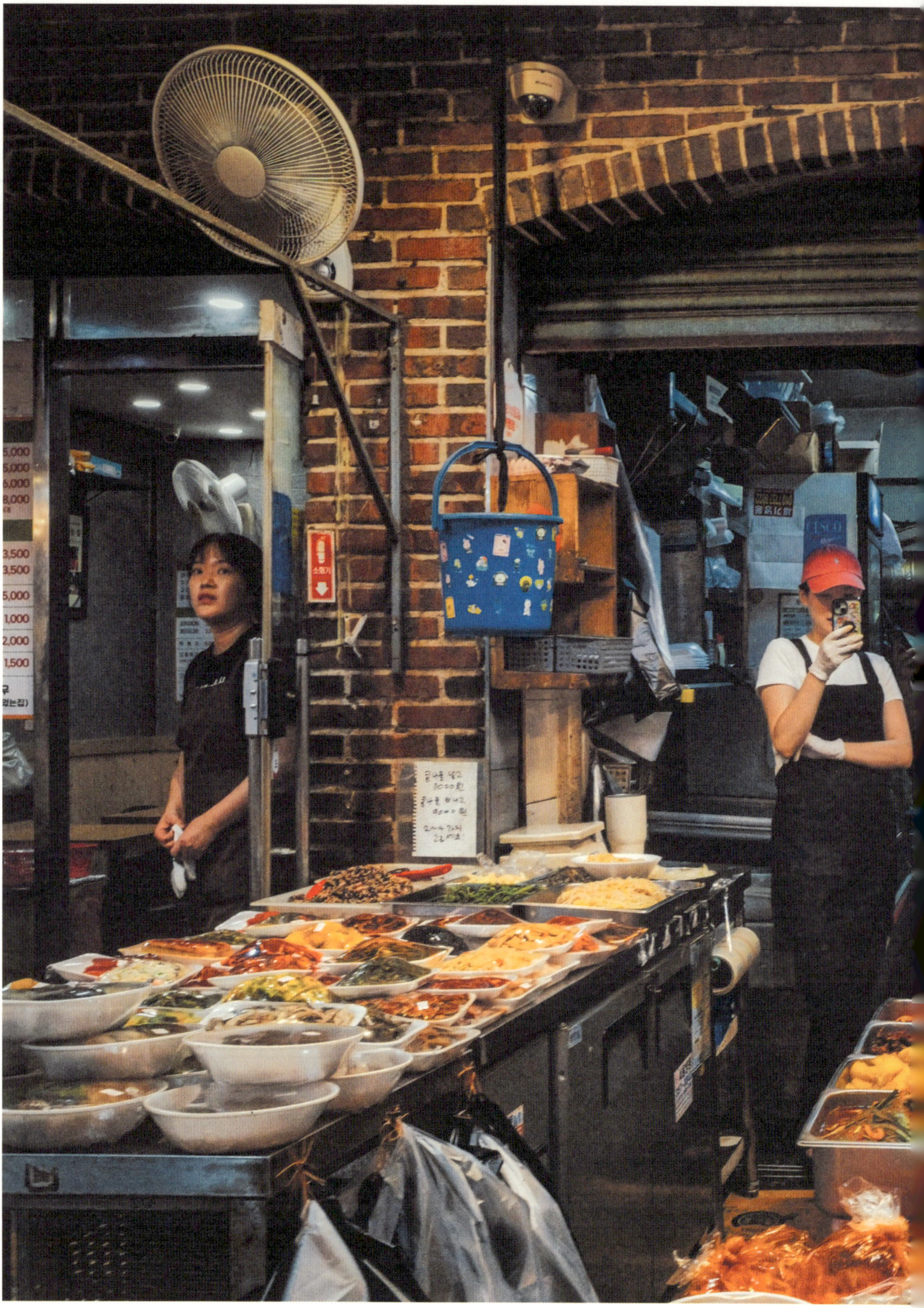

Mangwon Market, Mapo District

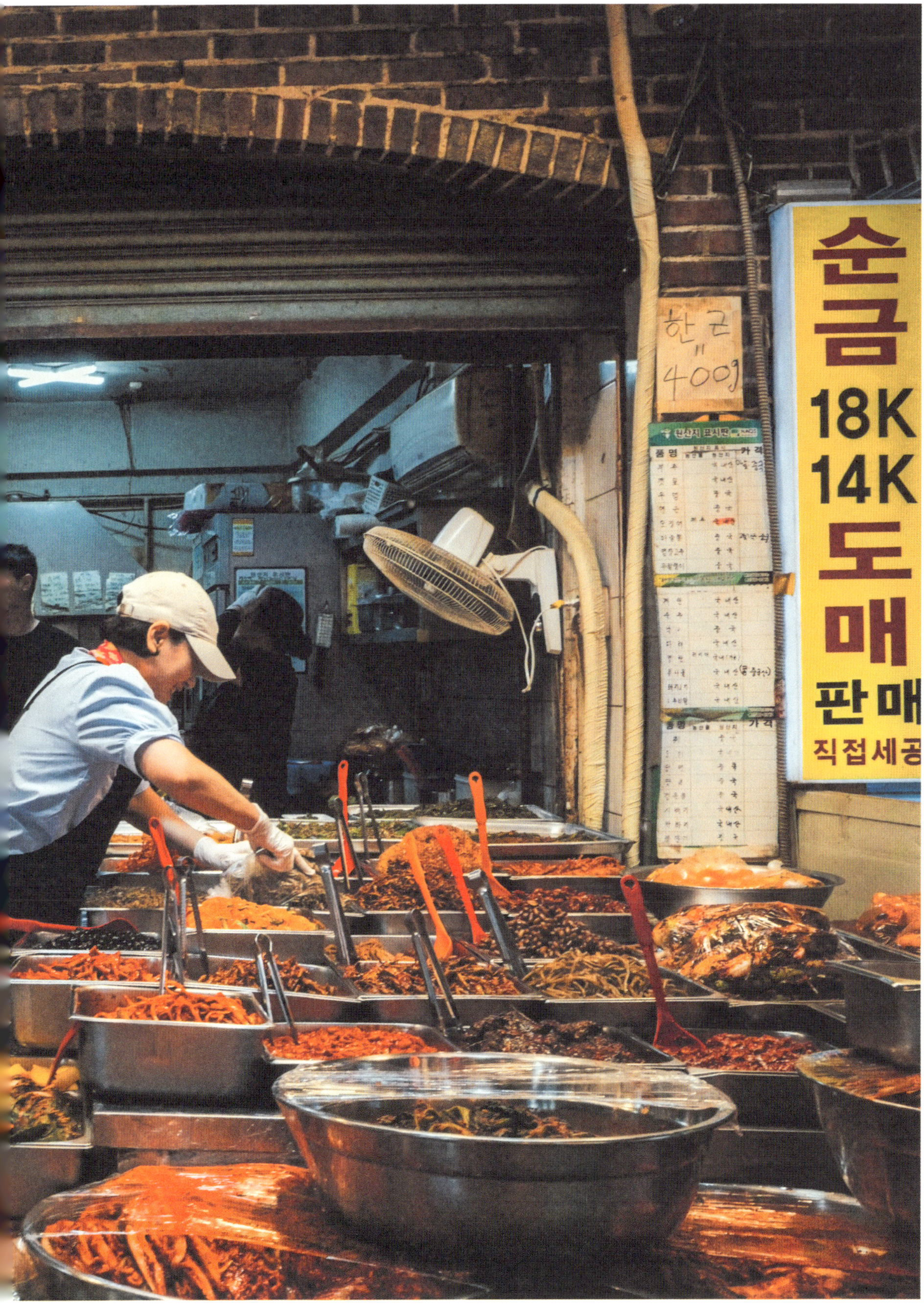
순금
18K
14K
도매
판매
직접세공
한근
400g

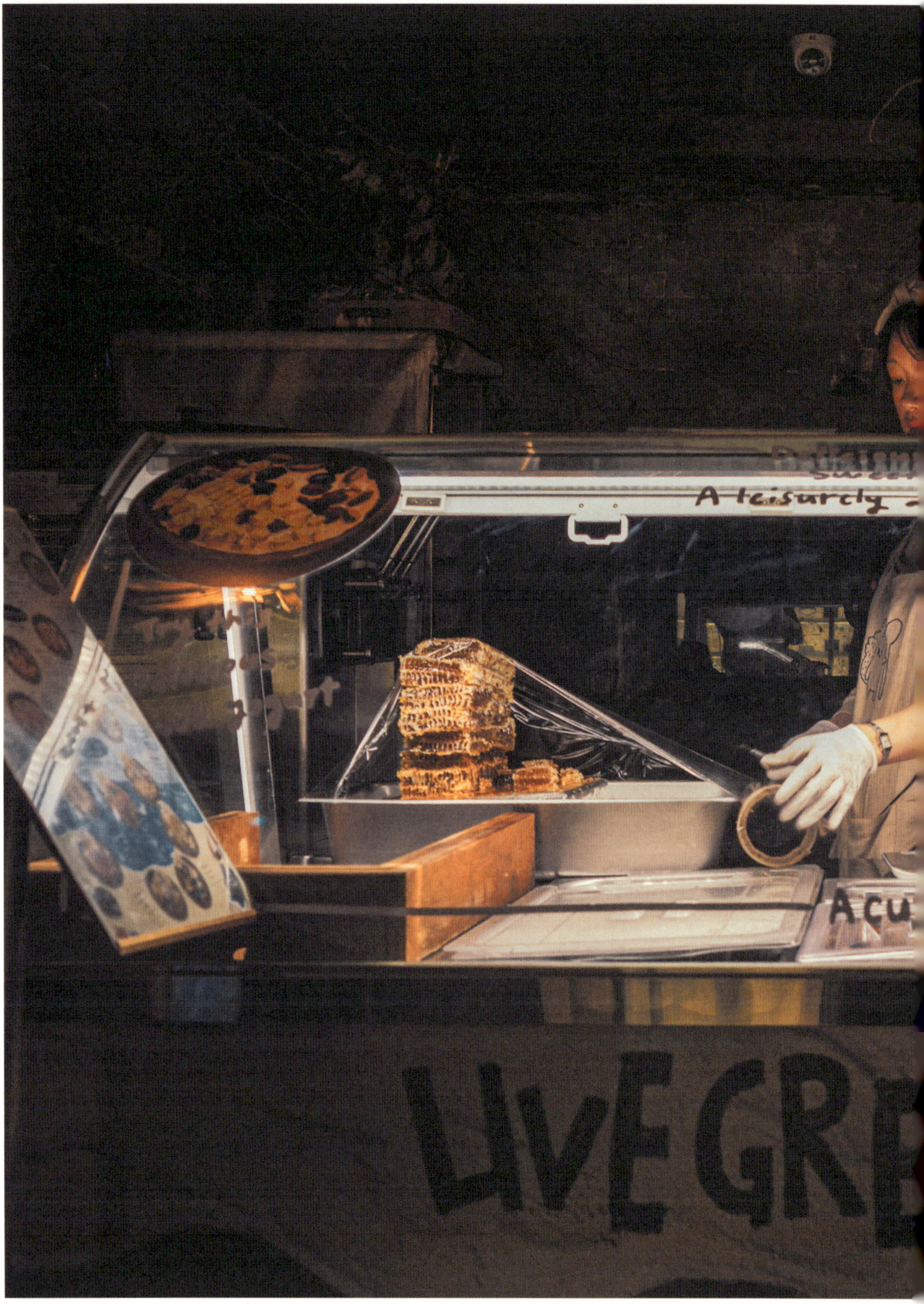


Samgagji, Yongsan District

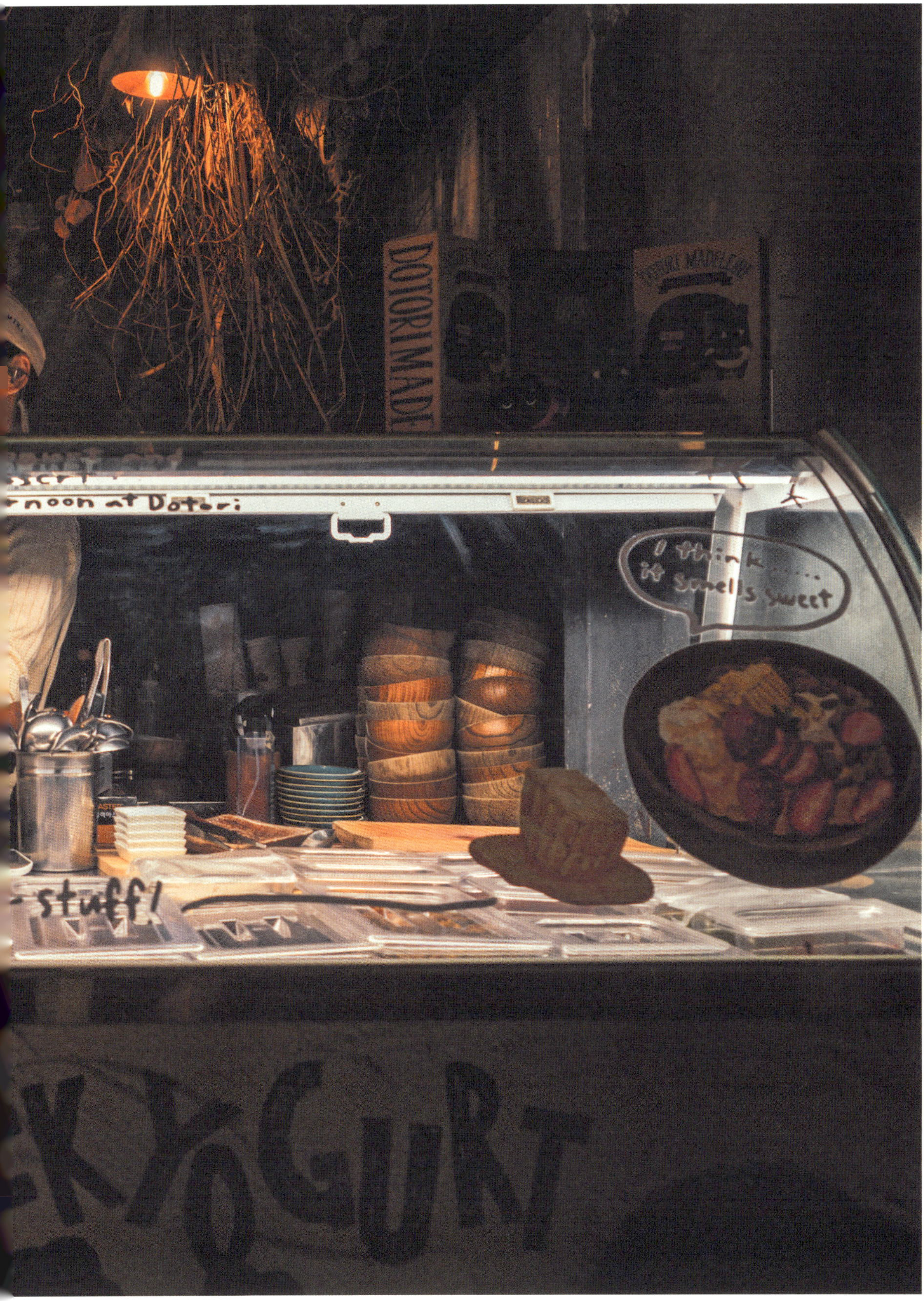
DOTORIMADE
noon at Dotori
I think ......
it smells sweet
stuff!
YOGURT

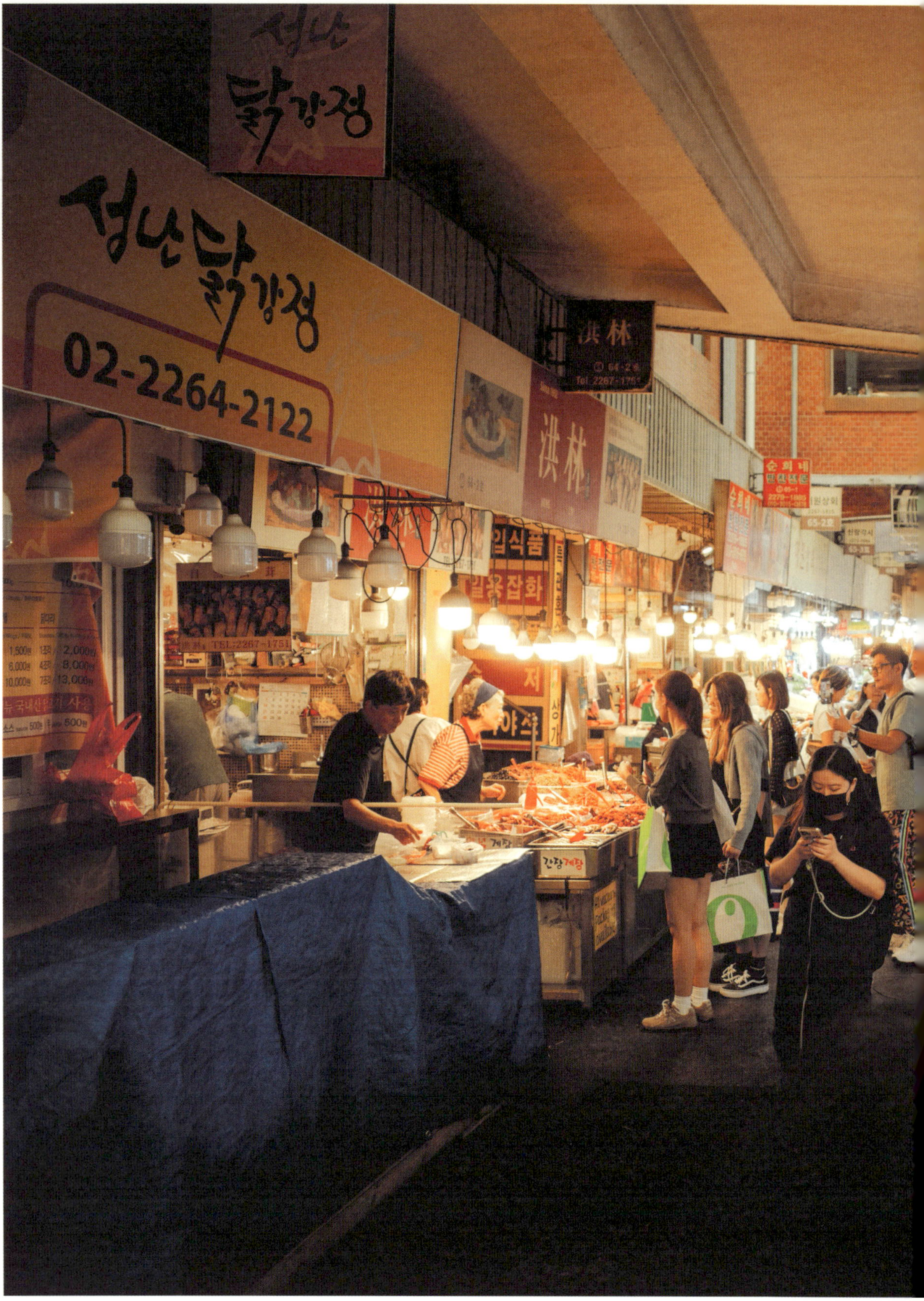


Gwangjang Market, Jongno District

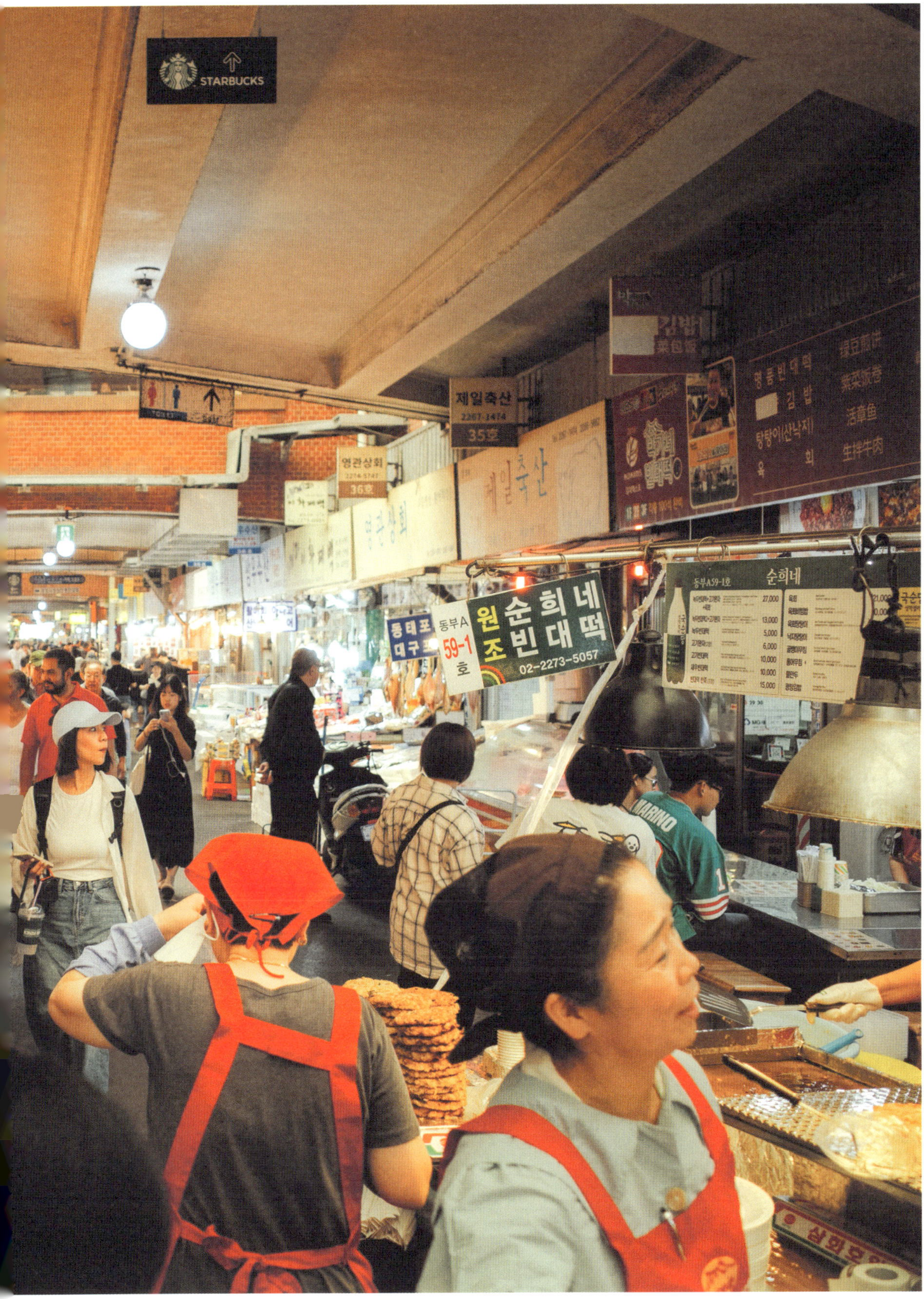
STARBUCKS
제일축산
35호
영관상회
36호
동부A
59-1
호
원조
순희네
빈대떡
02-2273-5057
동부A59-1호
순희네
김밥
탕탕이(산낙지)
육회
MARINO

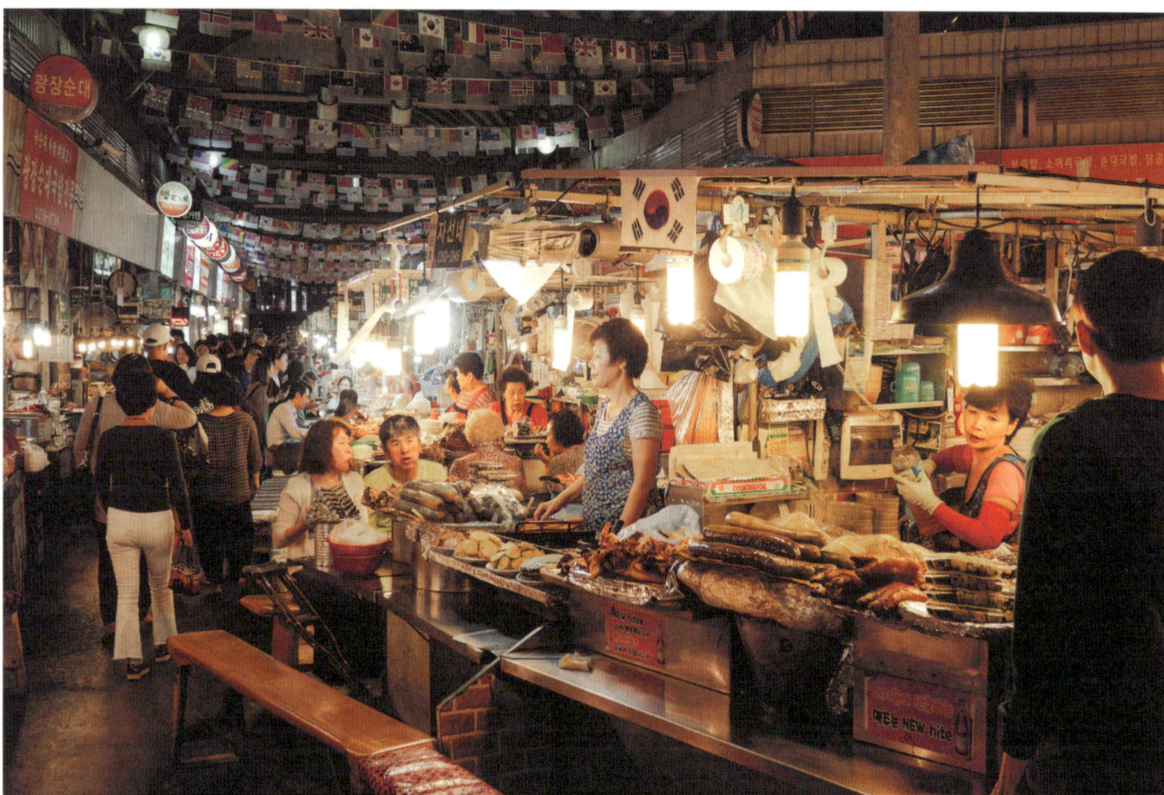


Gwangjang Market, Jongno District

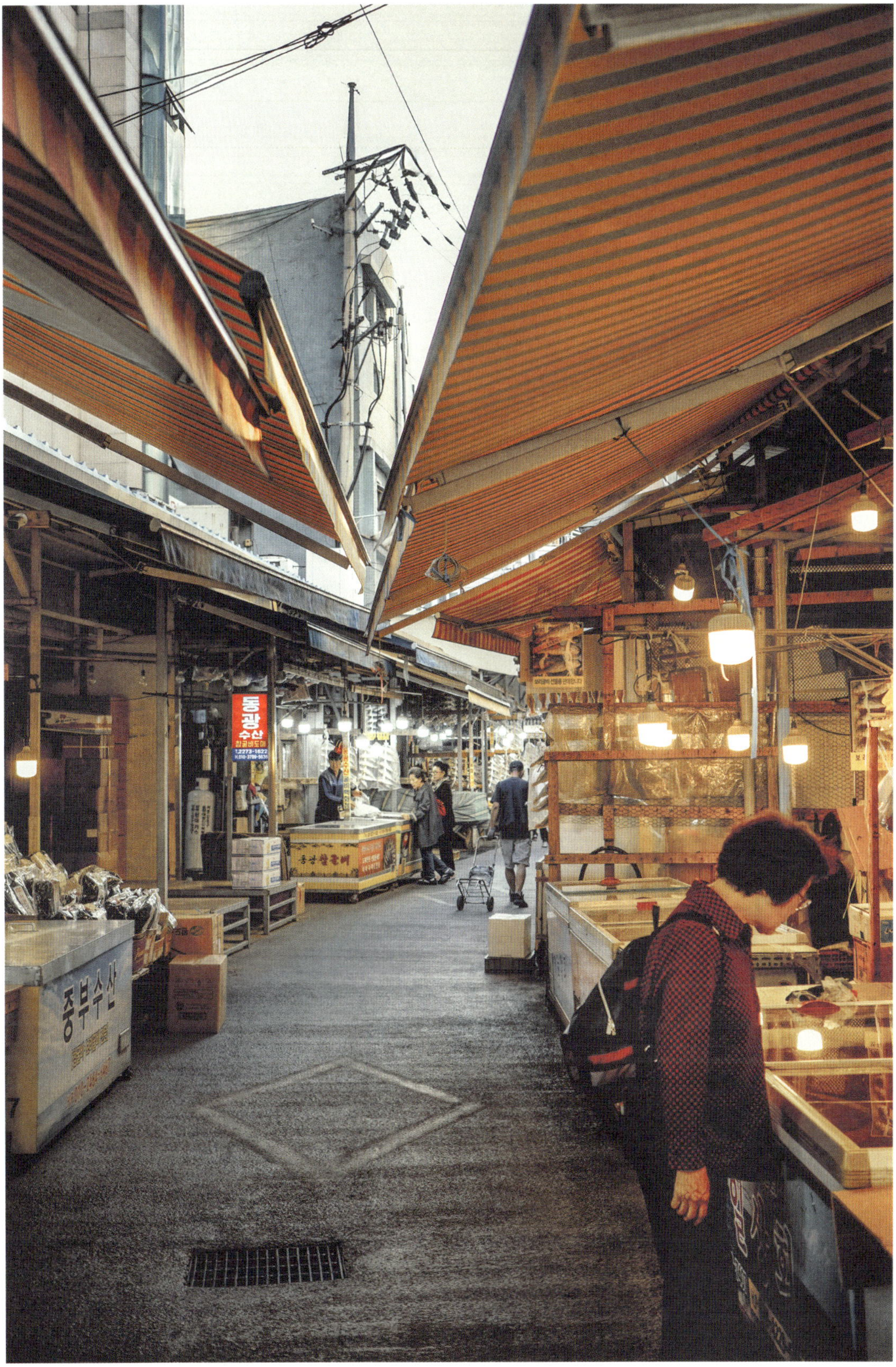


Euljiro Jungbu Market, Euljiro 5-ga, Jung District

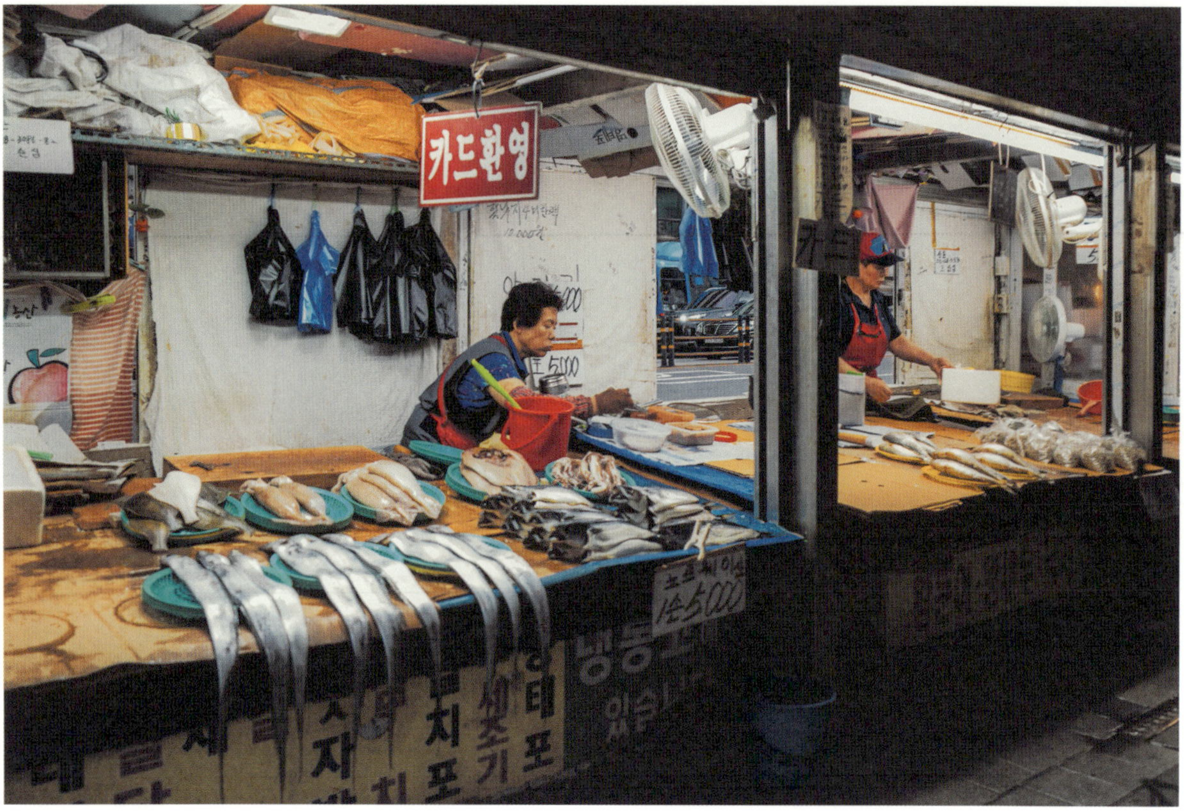


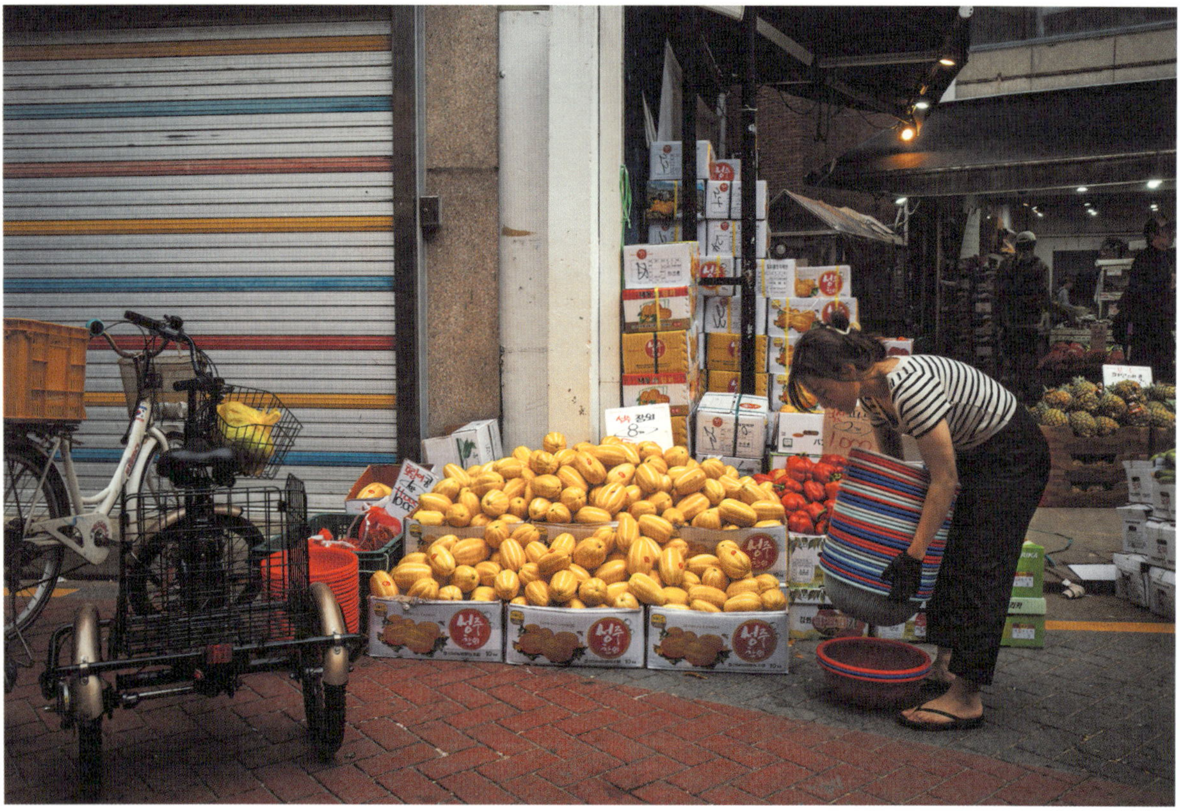


above: Dongdaemun Market, Jung District + below: Mangwon Market, Mapo District

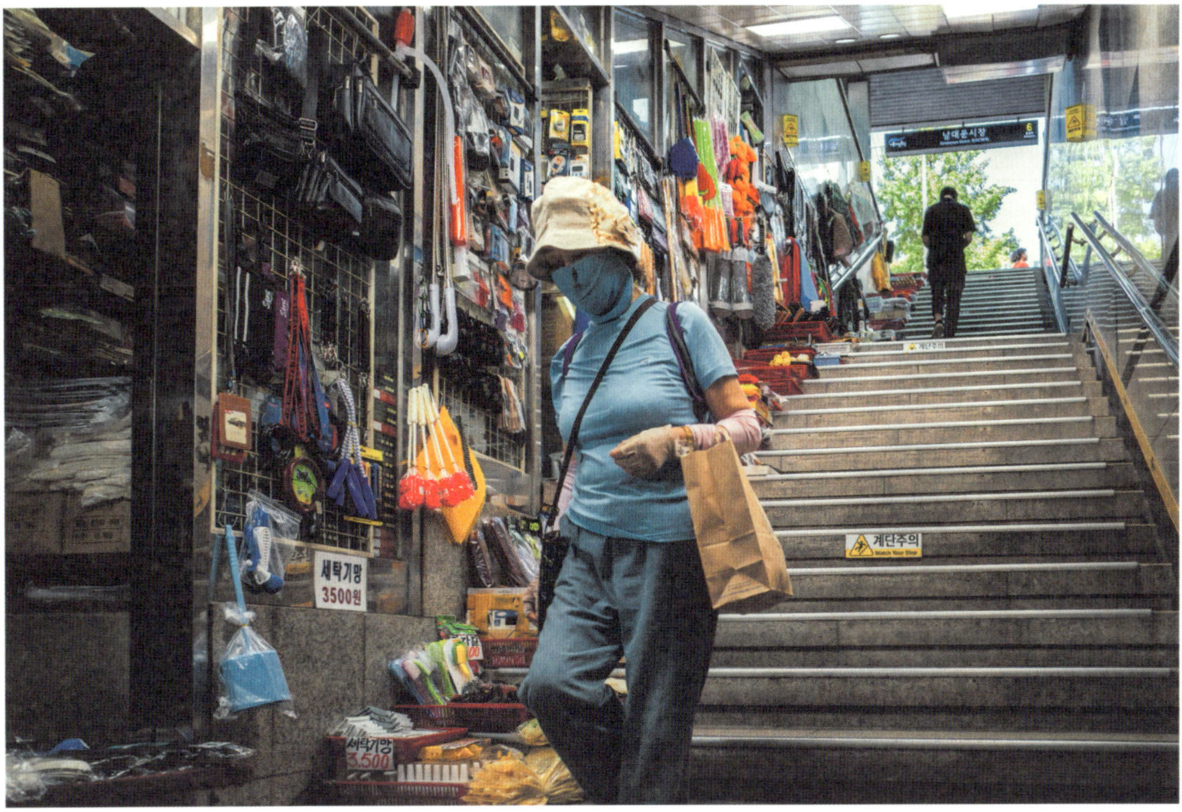


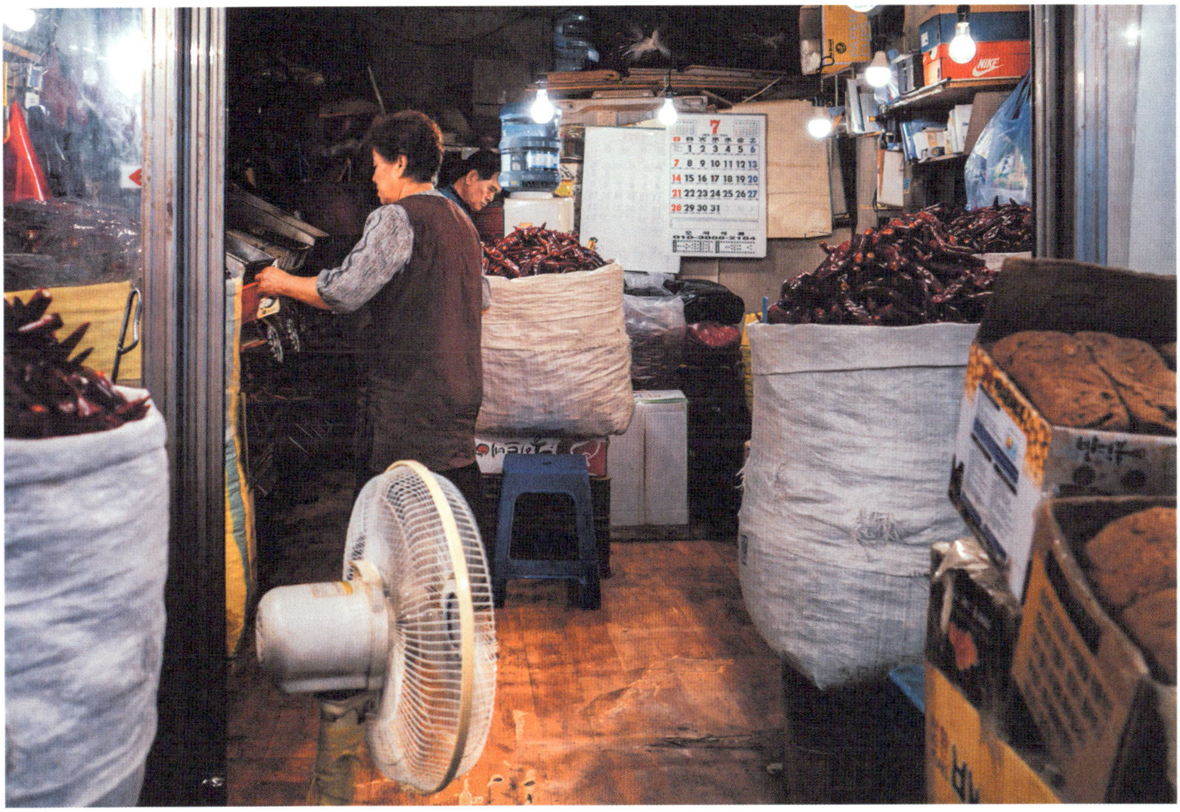


above: Namdaemun Market, Jung District + below: Dongdaemun Market, Jung District

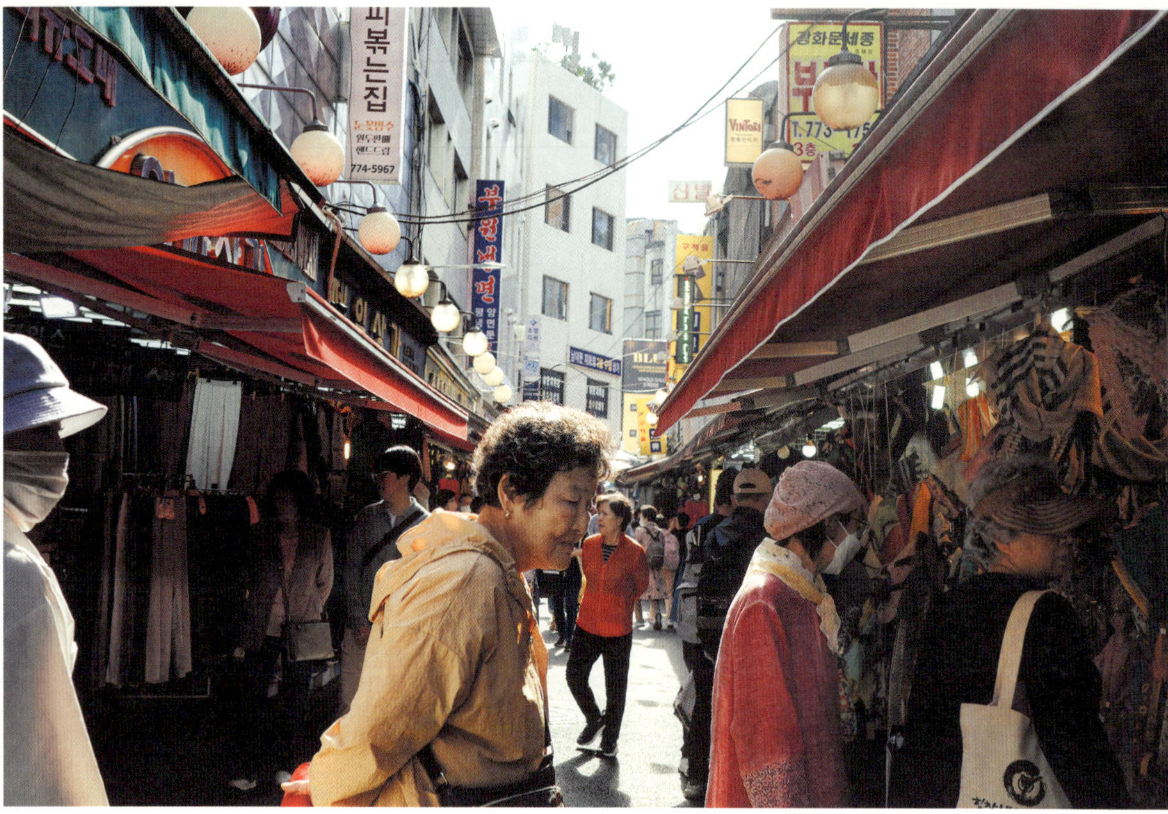


above + right: Namdaemun Market, Jung District

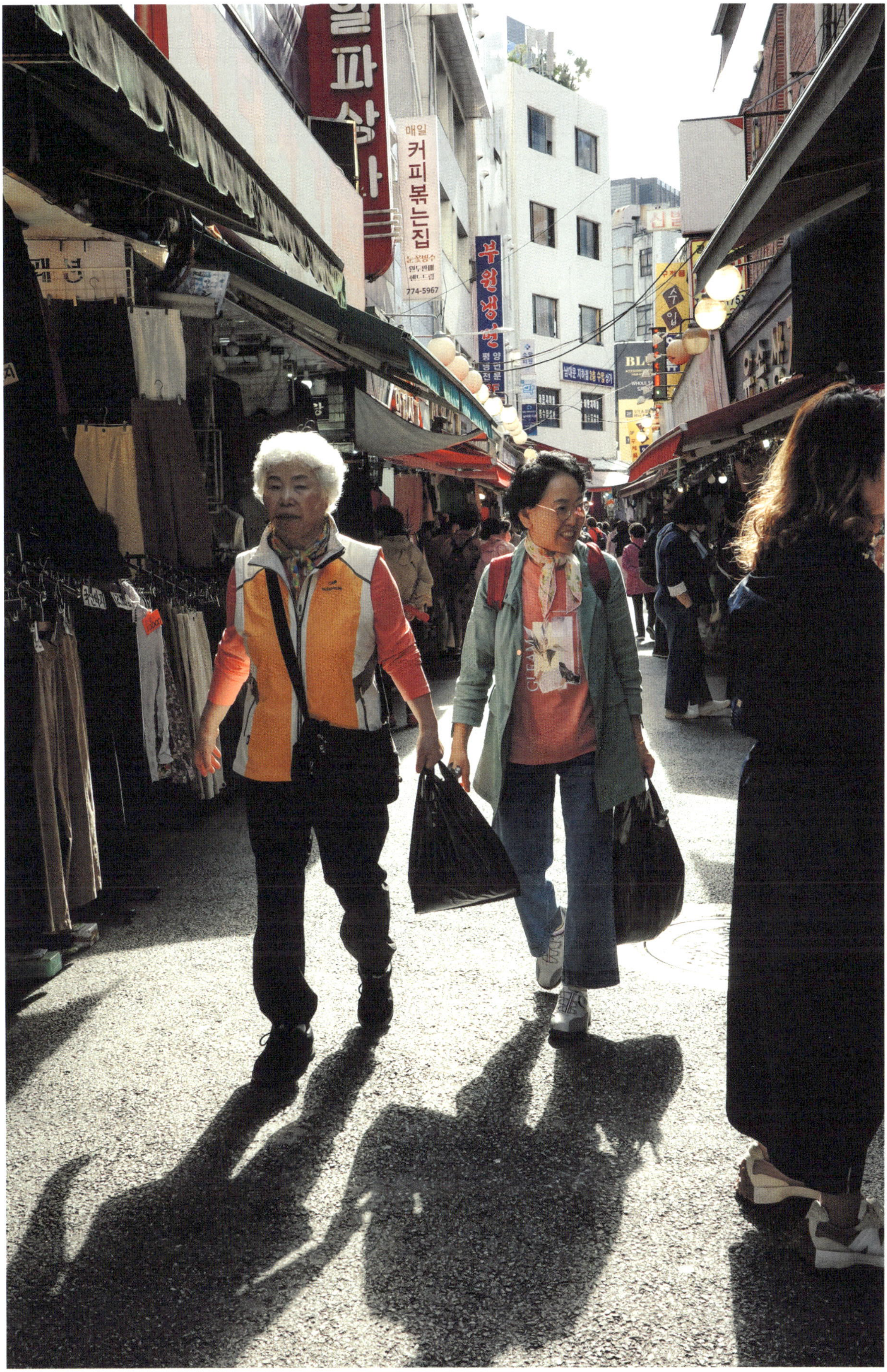
매일
커피볶는집
774-5967
부원냉면

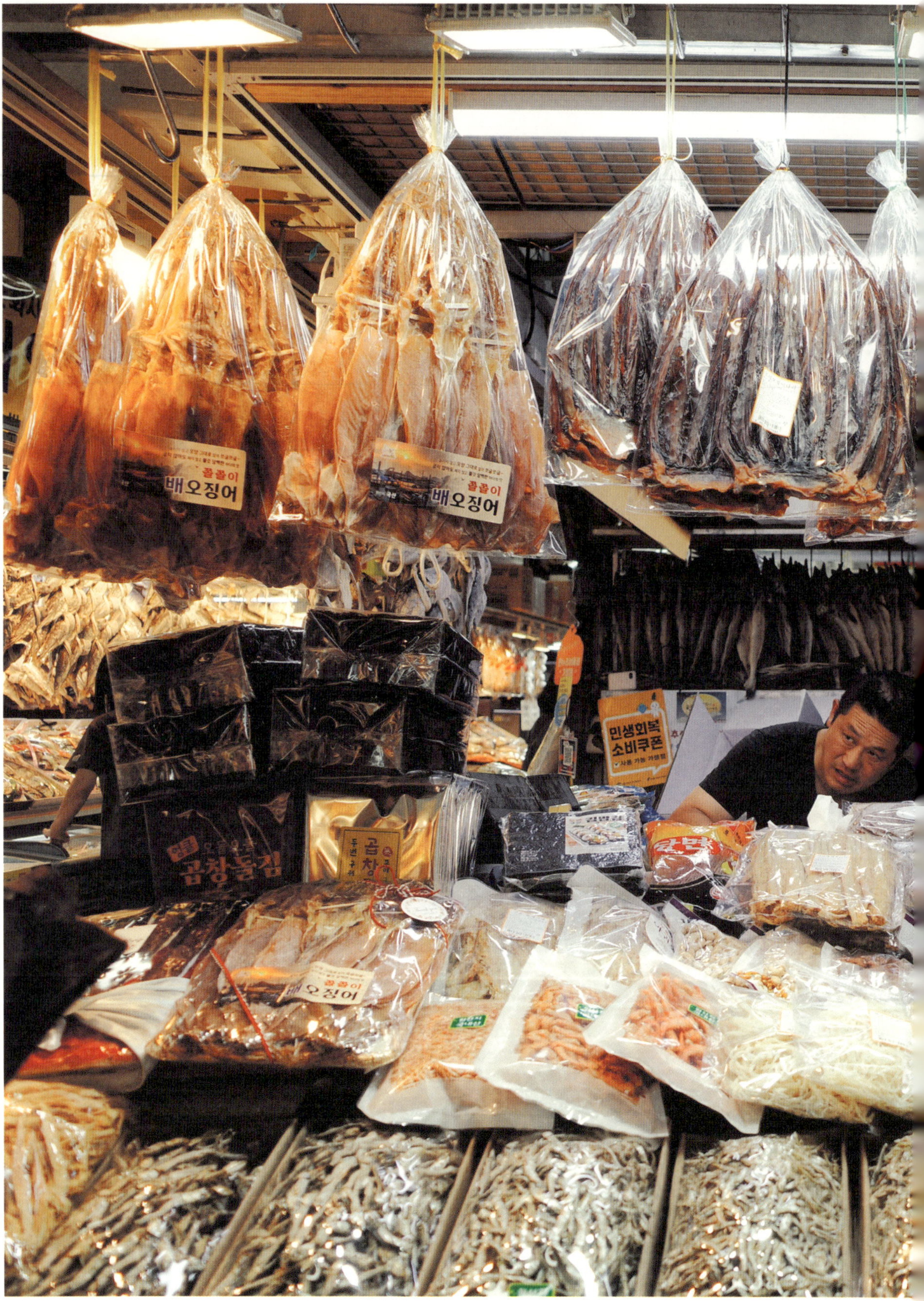


Garak Market, Garak-dong, Songpa District

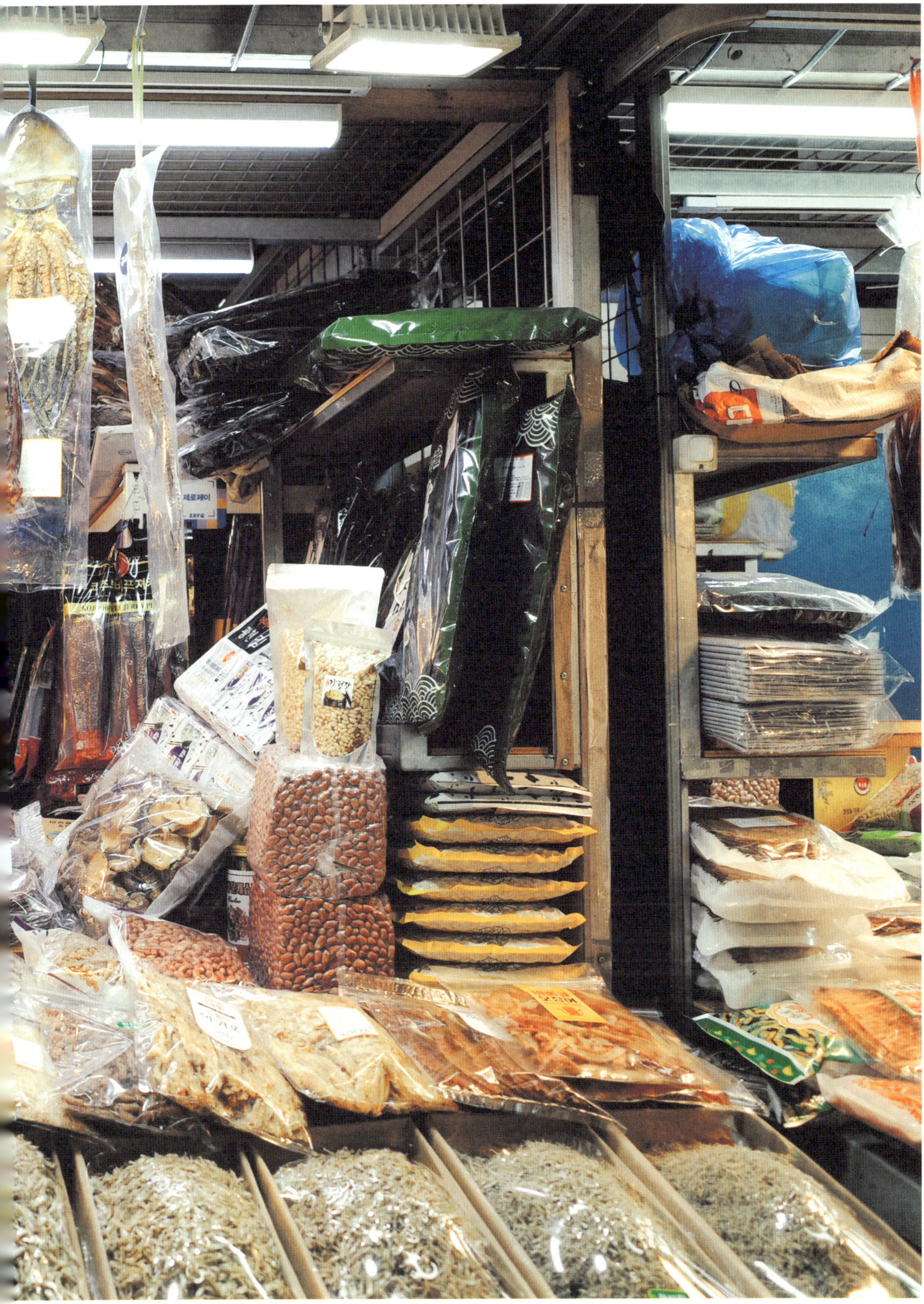

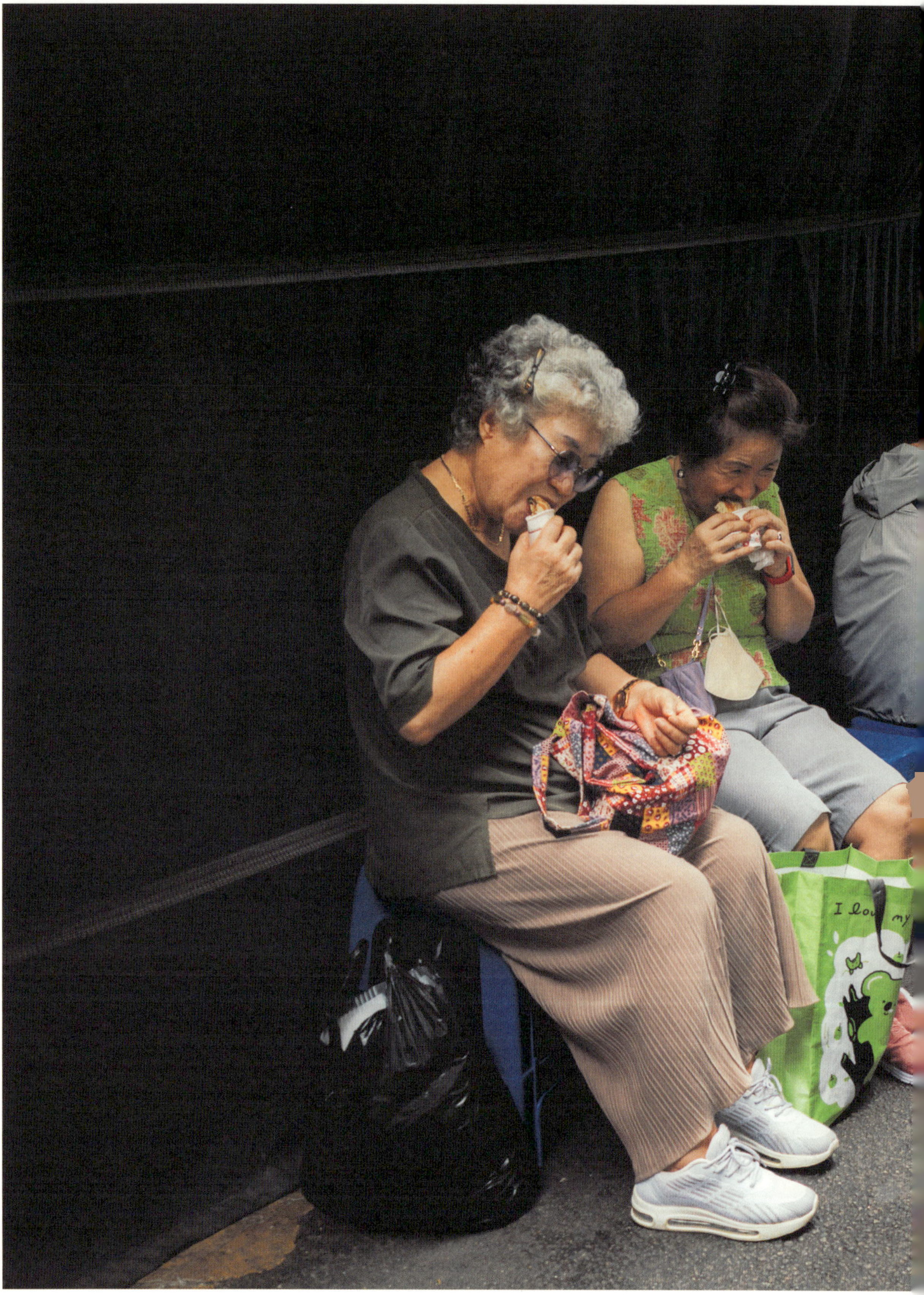


Namdaemun Market, Jung District

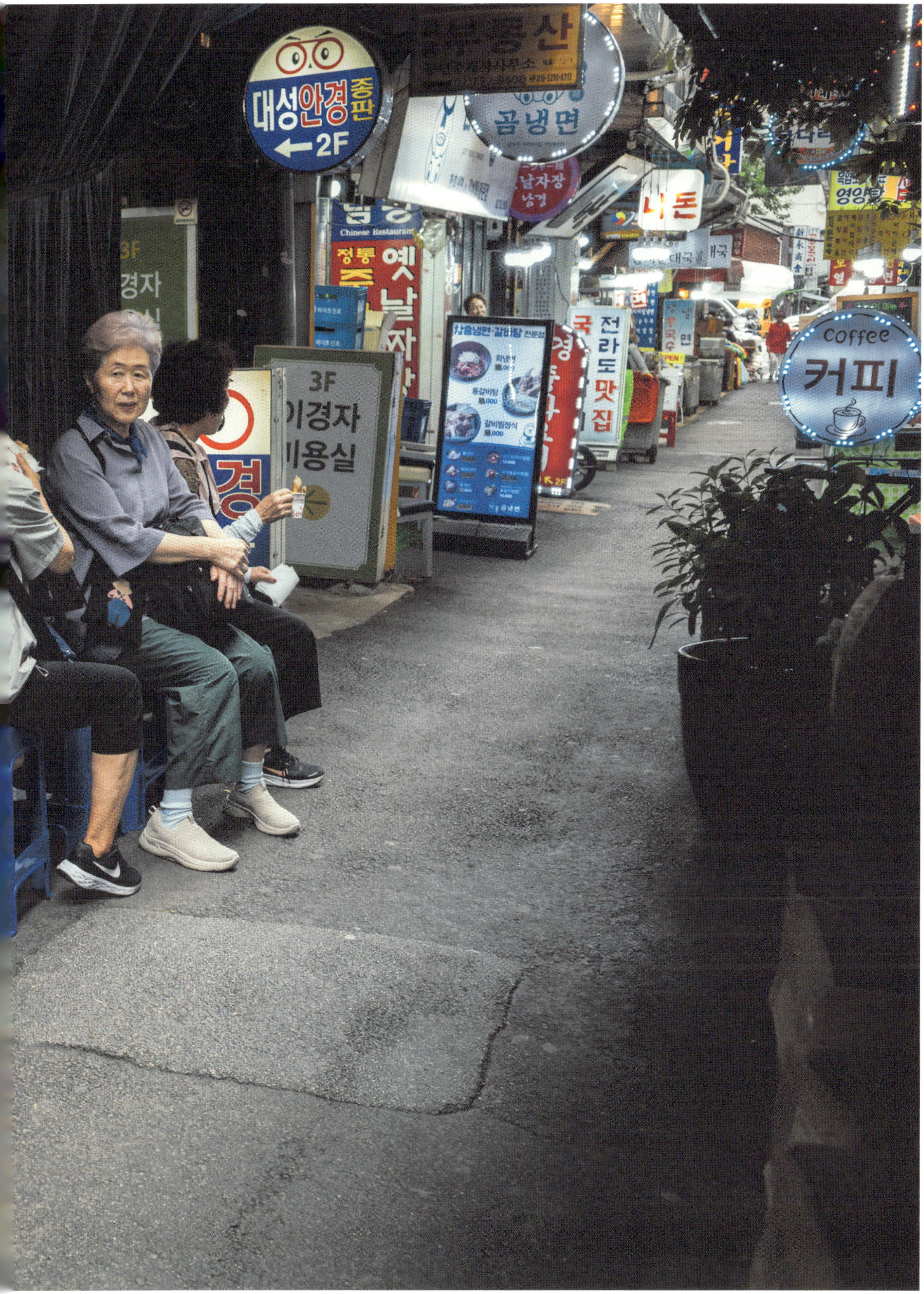
대성안경
2F
곰냉면
Chinese Restaurant
3F
이경자
전라도
맛집
Coffee
커피

# INYEON

## 인연

(in-ye-on) is a Korean concept that refers to fate, destiny, or a predestined connection between people, often with the implication of karmic ties formed over many lifetimes. Inyeon is understood as the accumulated connections that cause two people to meet and influence each other. A common proverb, "even if you just brush sleeves with someone, it is inyeon," illustrates how even fleeting encounters are seen as a product of fate.

In contemporary Seoul, inyeon remains a familiar way of understanding how relationships take shape, even if people reference it more casually than in the past. The idea often comes up when explaining unexpected reunions, long-lasting friendships, or the sense that certain connections carry more weight than simple coincidence. In a dense city where millions cross paths each day, inyeon provides a framework for seeing meaning in encounters that might otherwise feel accidental. While modern life is faster and more fluid, the concept continues to underscore how relationships, brief or enduring, are part of a larger thread. In this way, inyeon offers a quiet counterbalance to the pace of Seoul, reminding people that connection is as much about circumstance and timing as it is about intention.

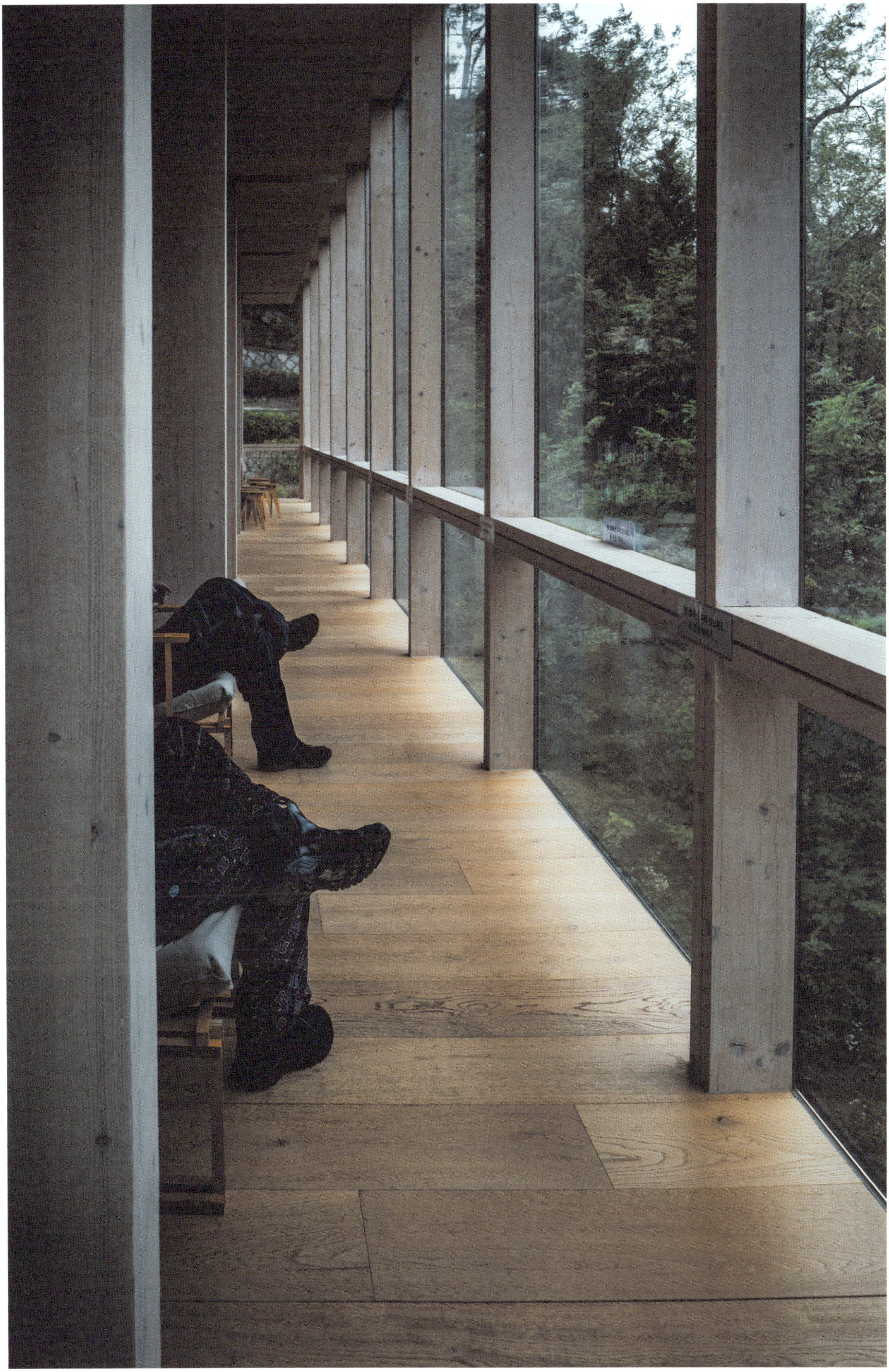

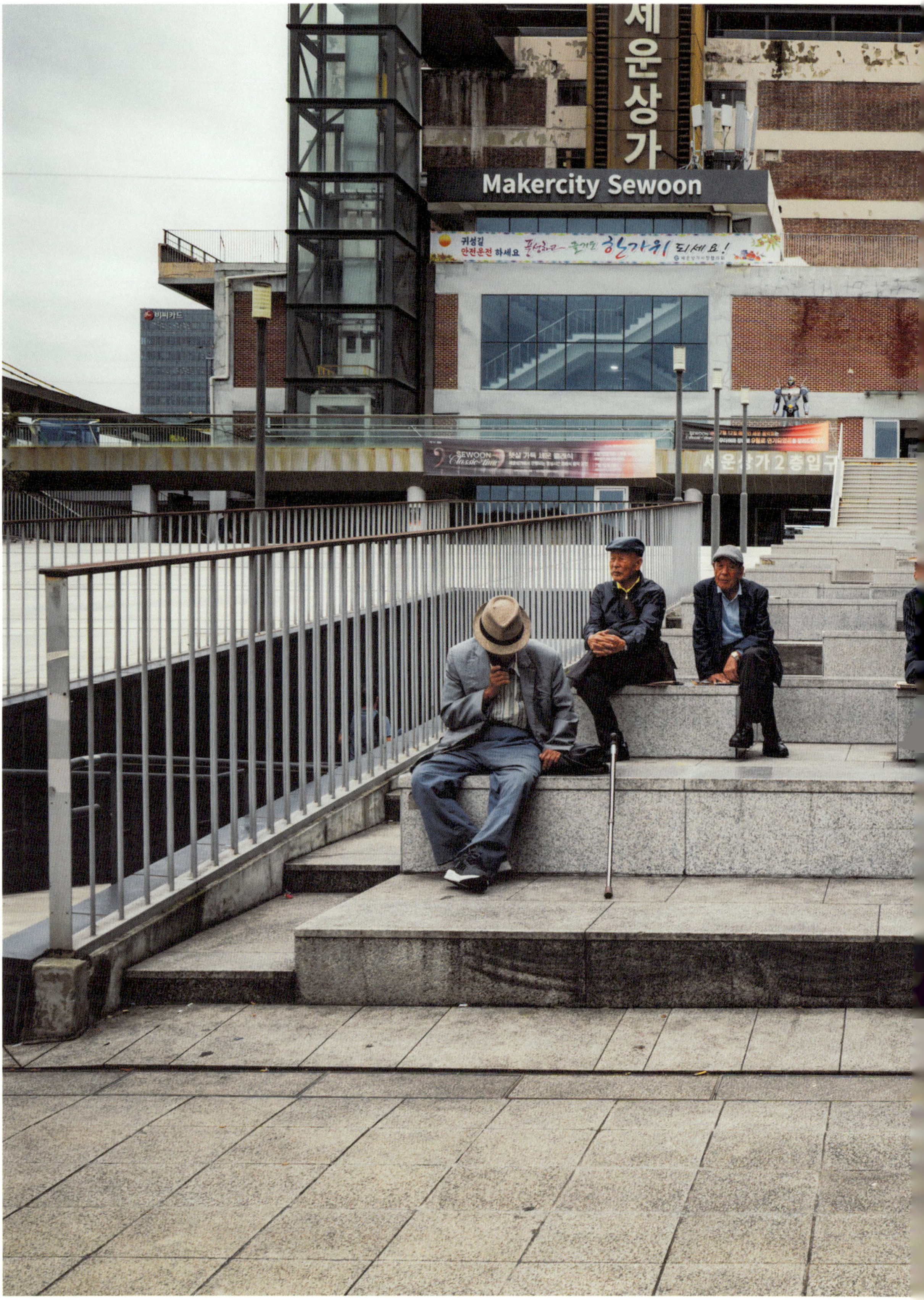


above: Jongno 3-ga, Jongno District + previous page: Inwangsan Mountain, Jongno District

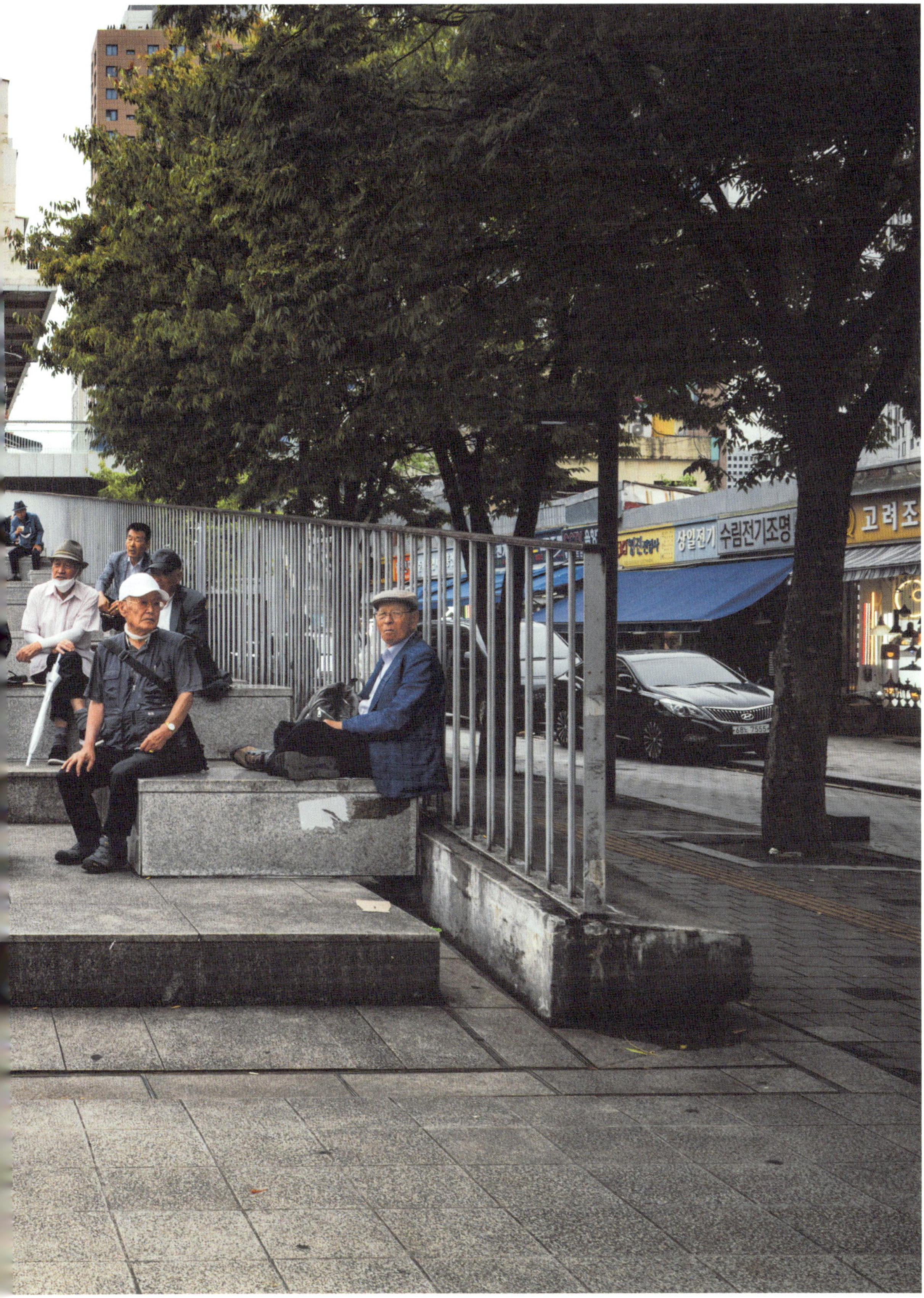

상일전기
수림전기조명
고려조

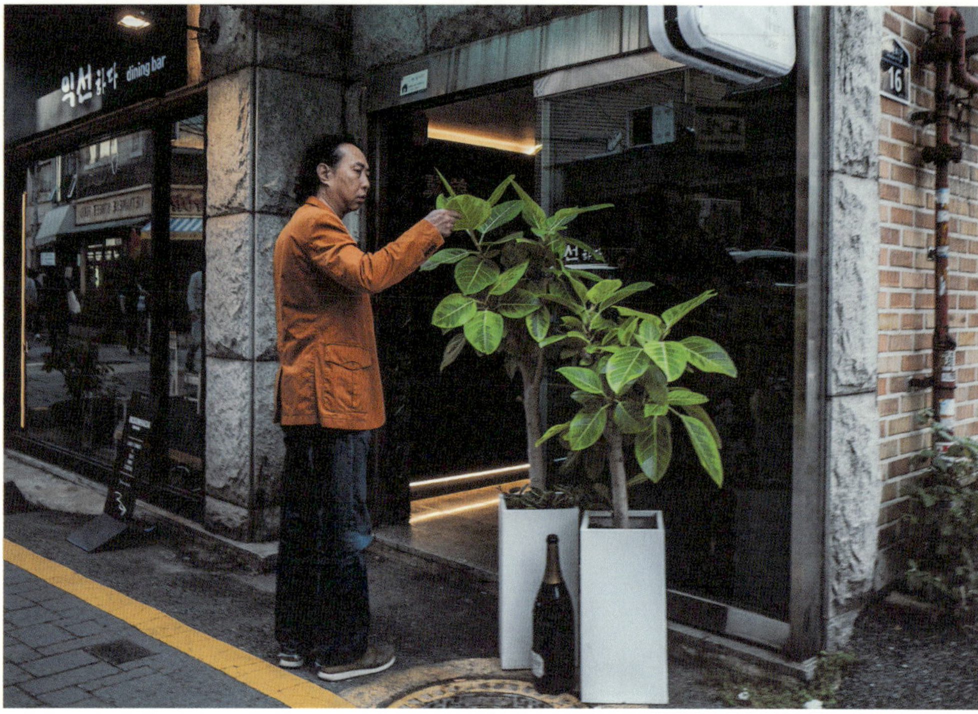


above + right: Seochon, Jongno District

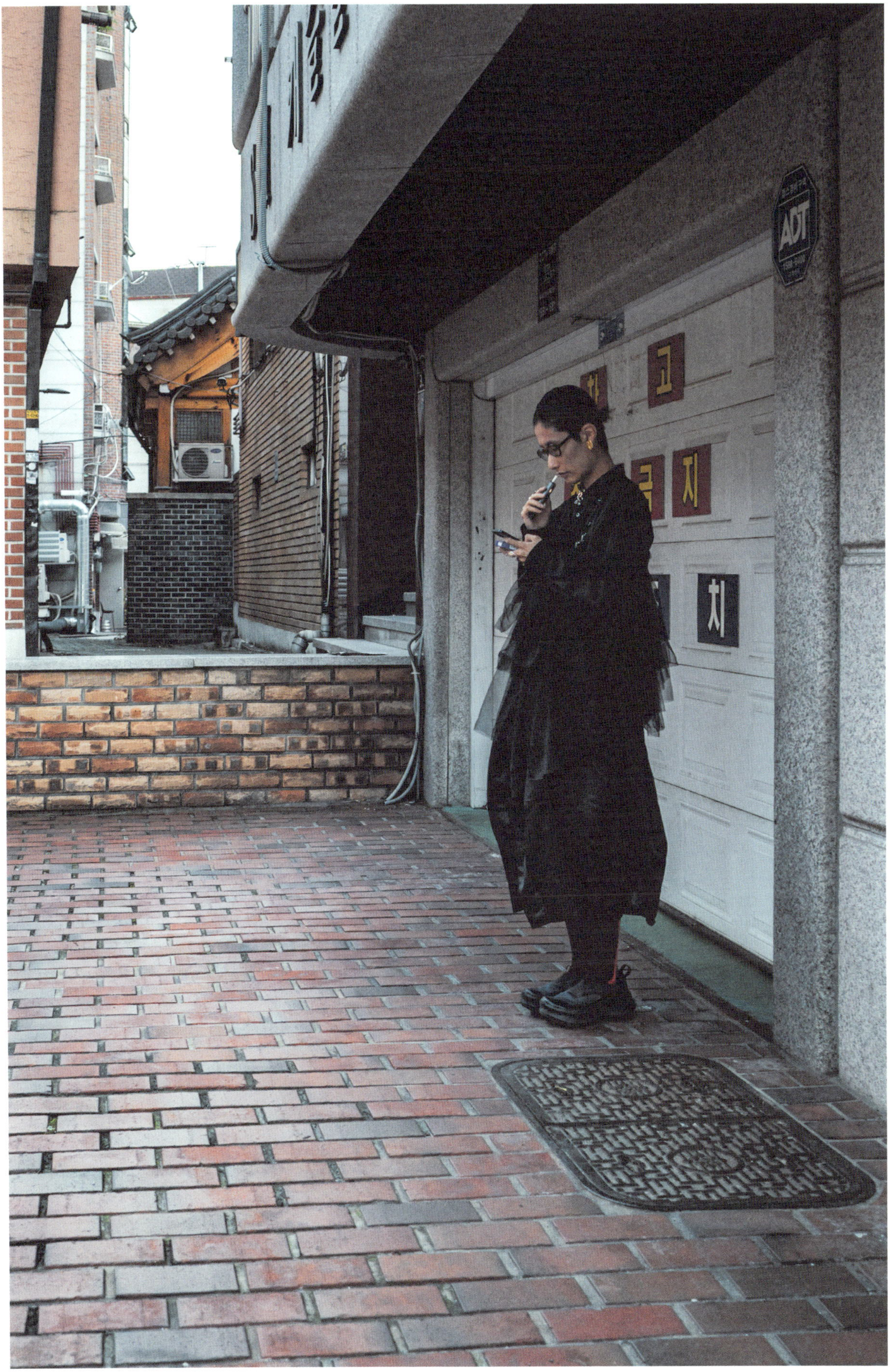
ADT

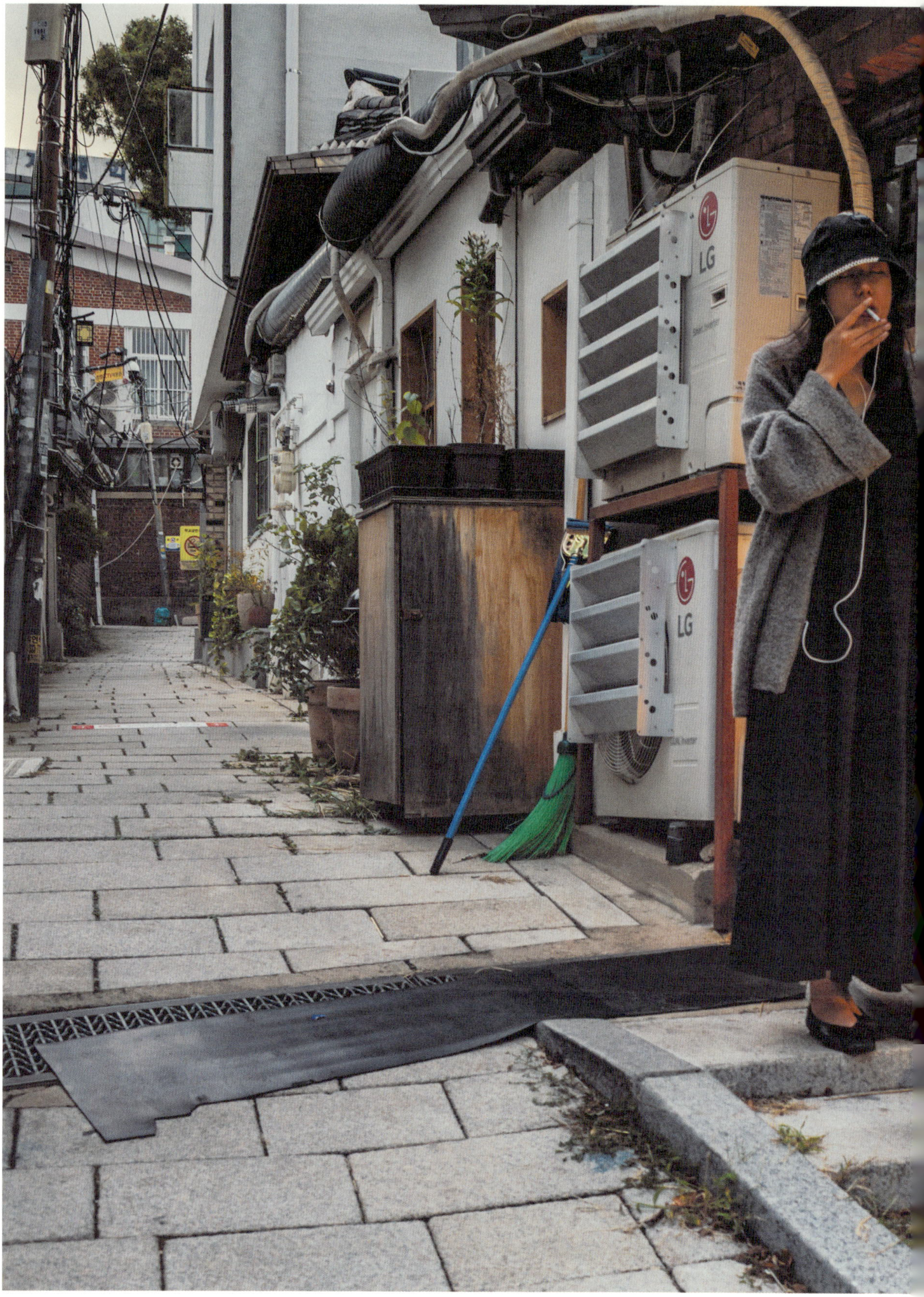


Seochon, Jongno District

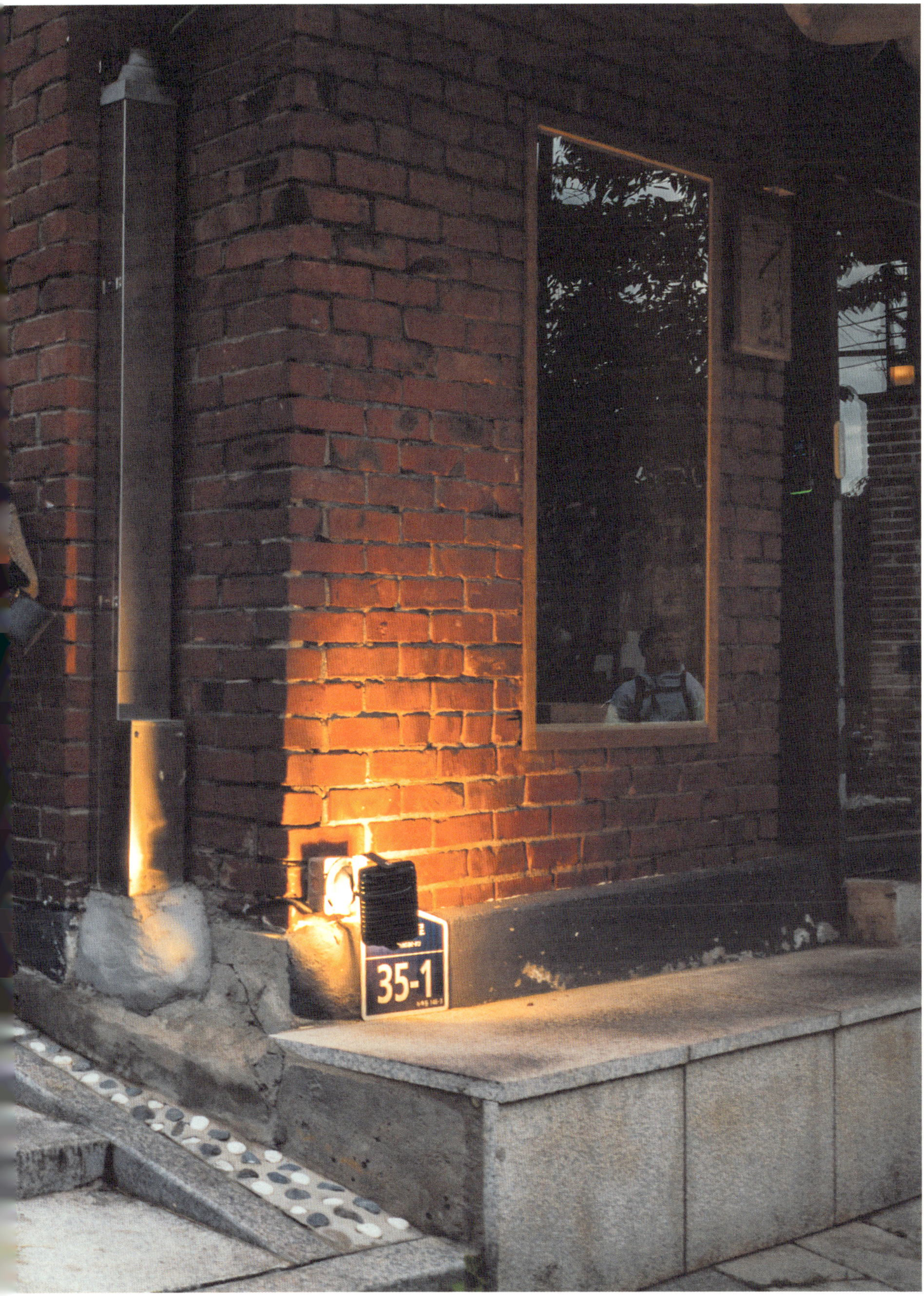
35-1

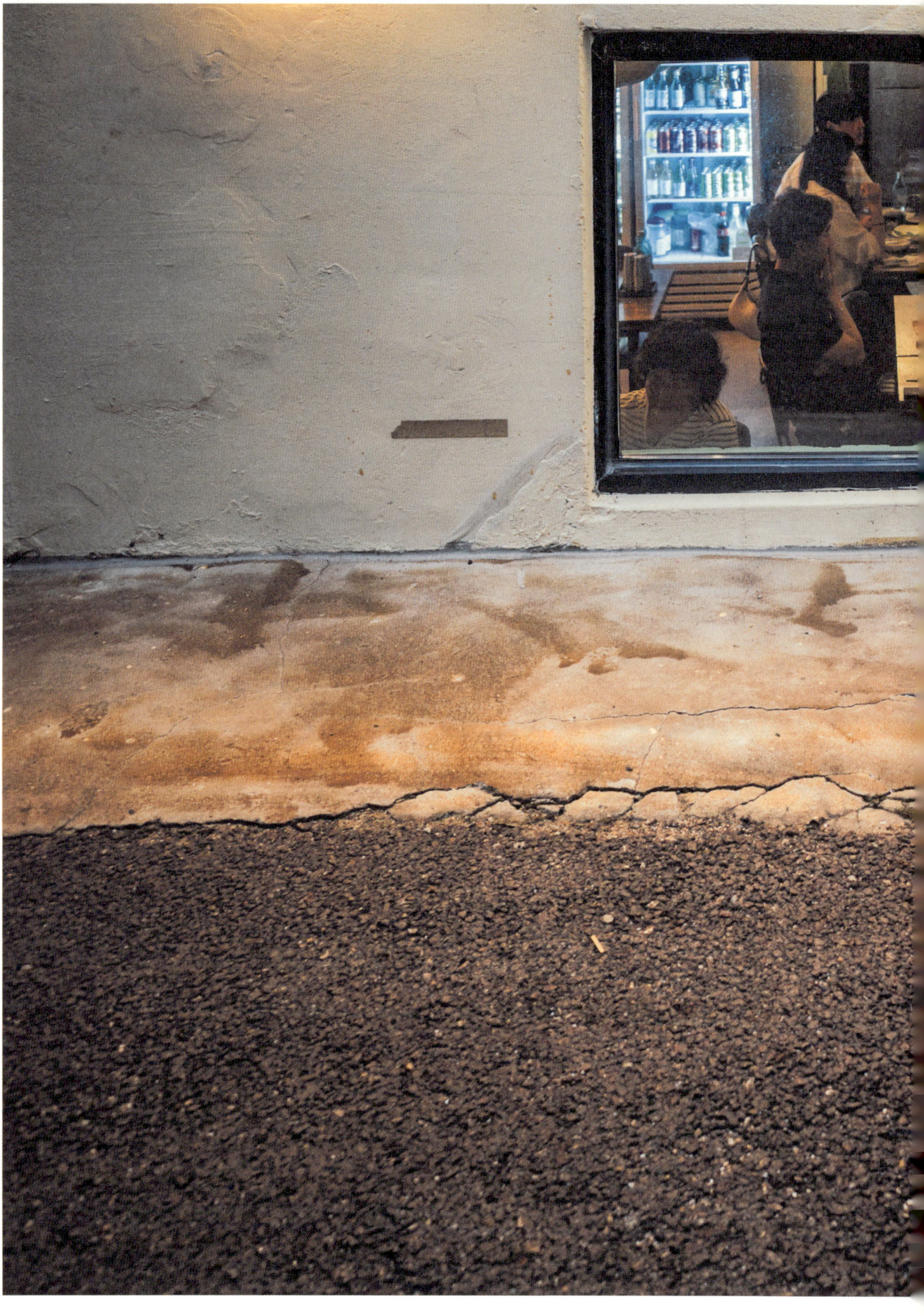

Seochon, Jongno District

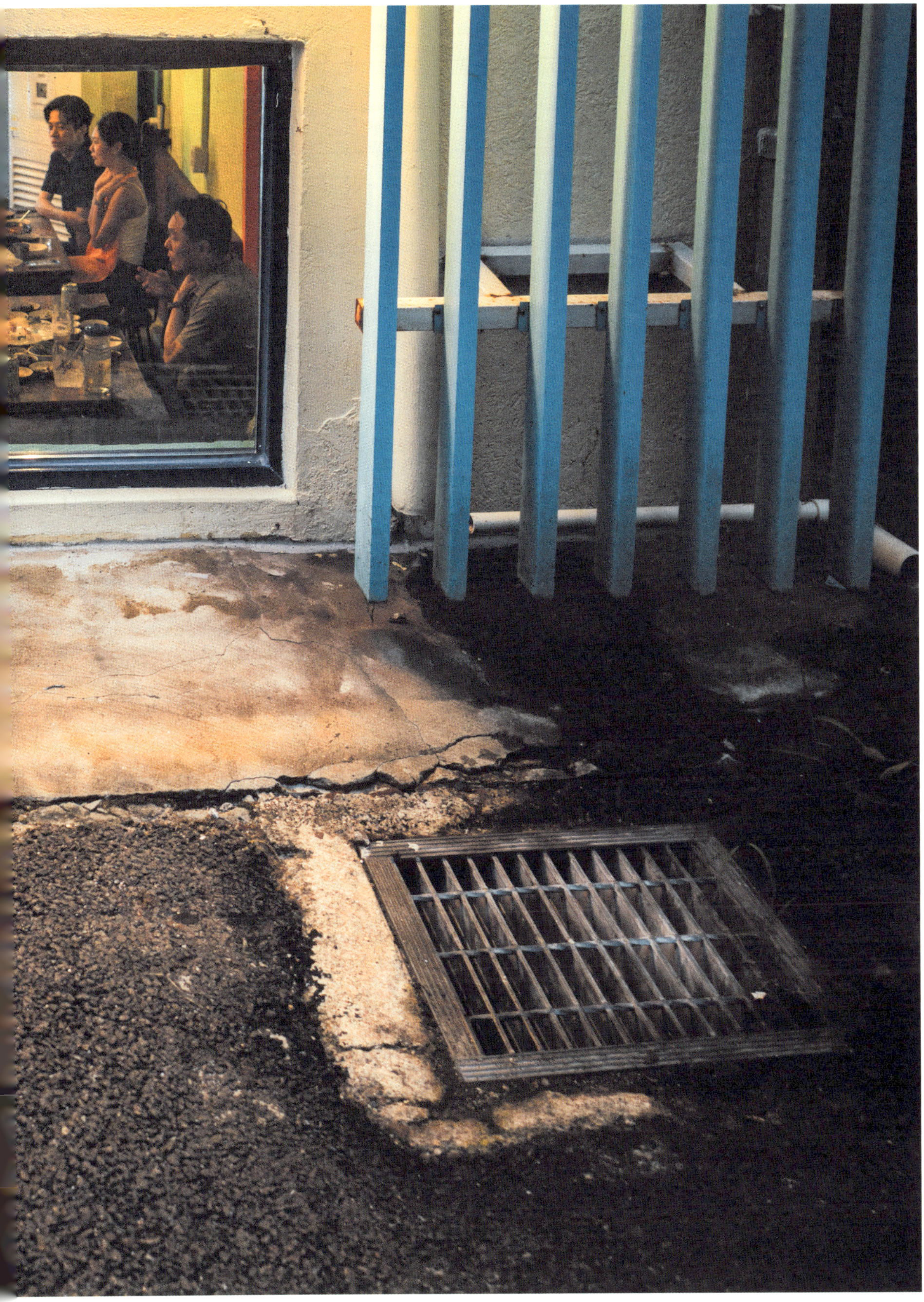

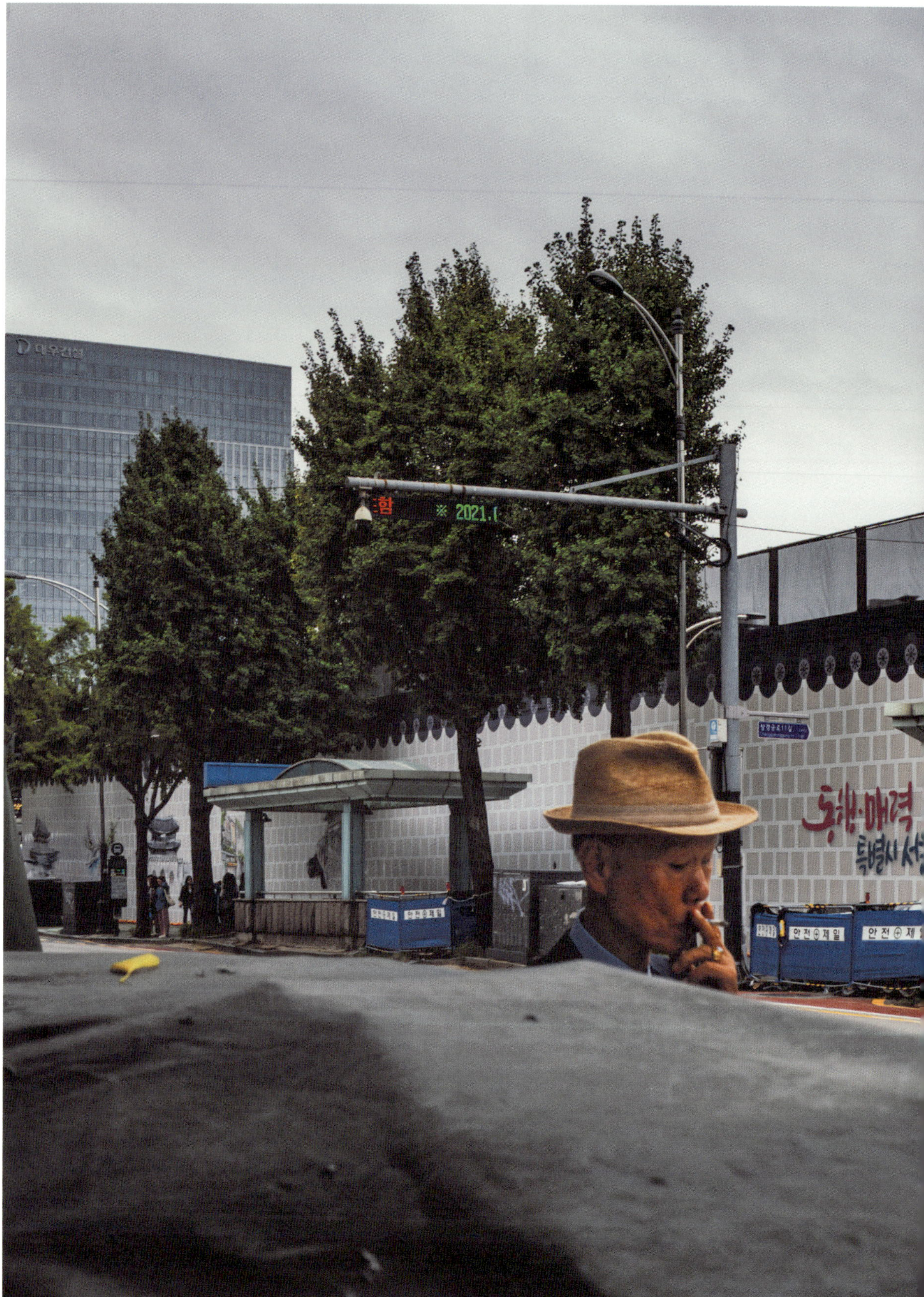


Jongno 4-ga, Jongno District

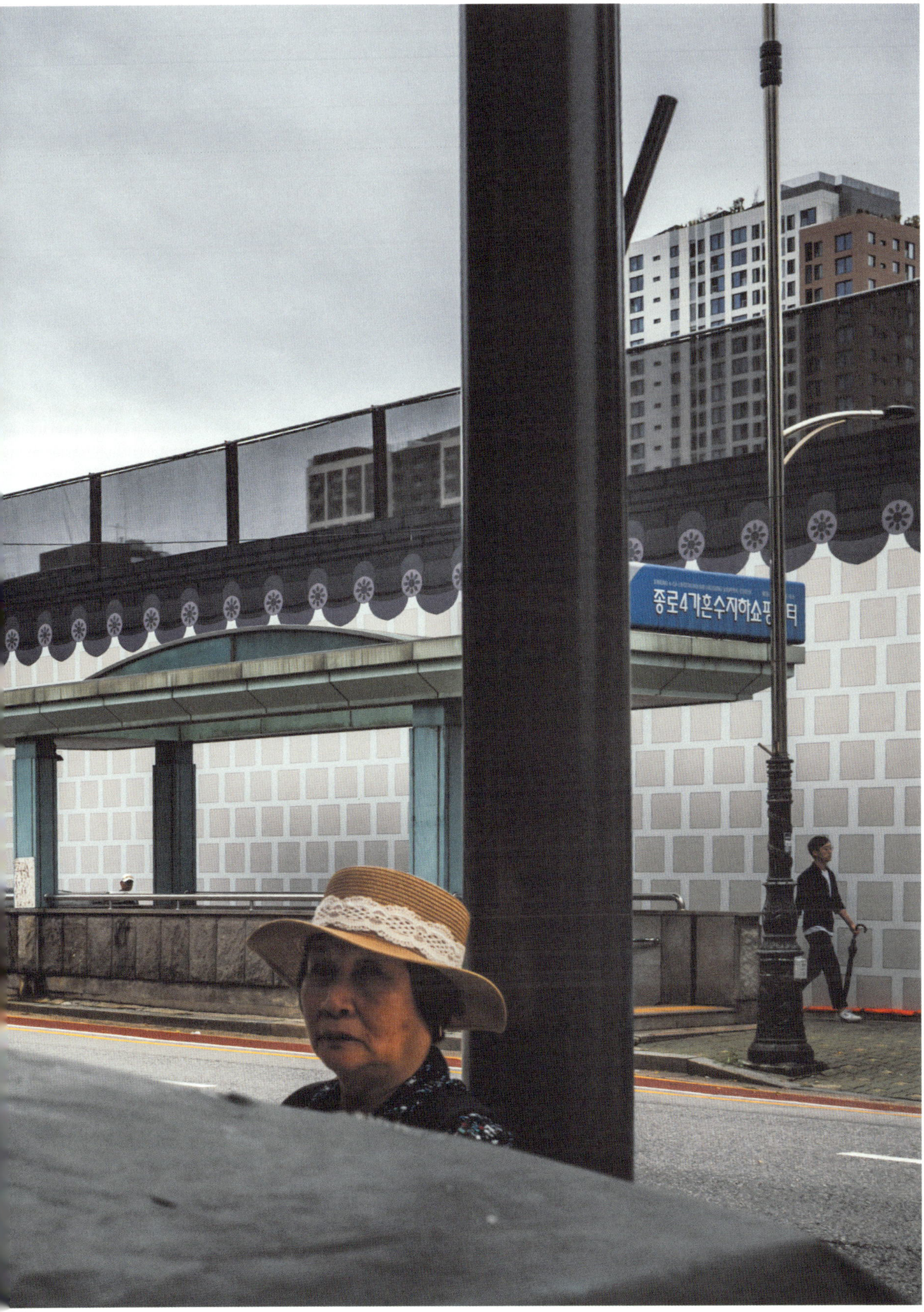
종로4가혼수지하쇼핑
터

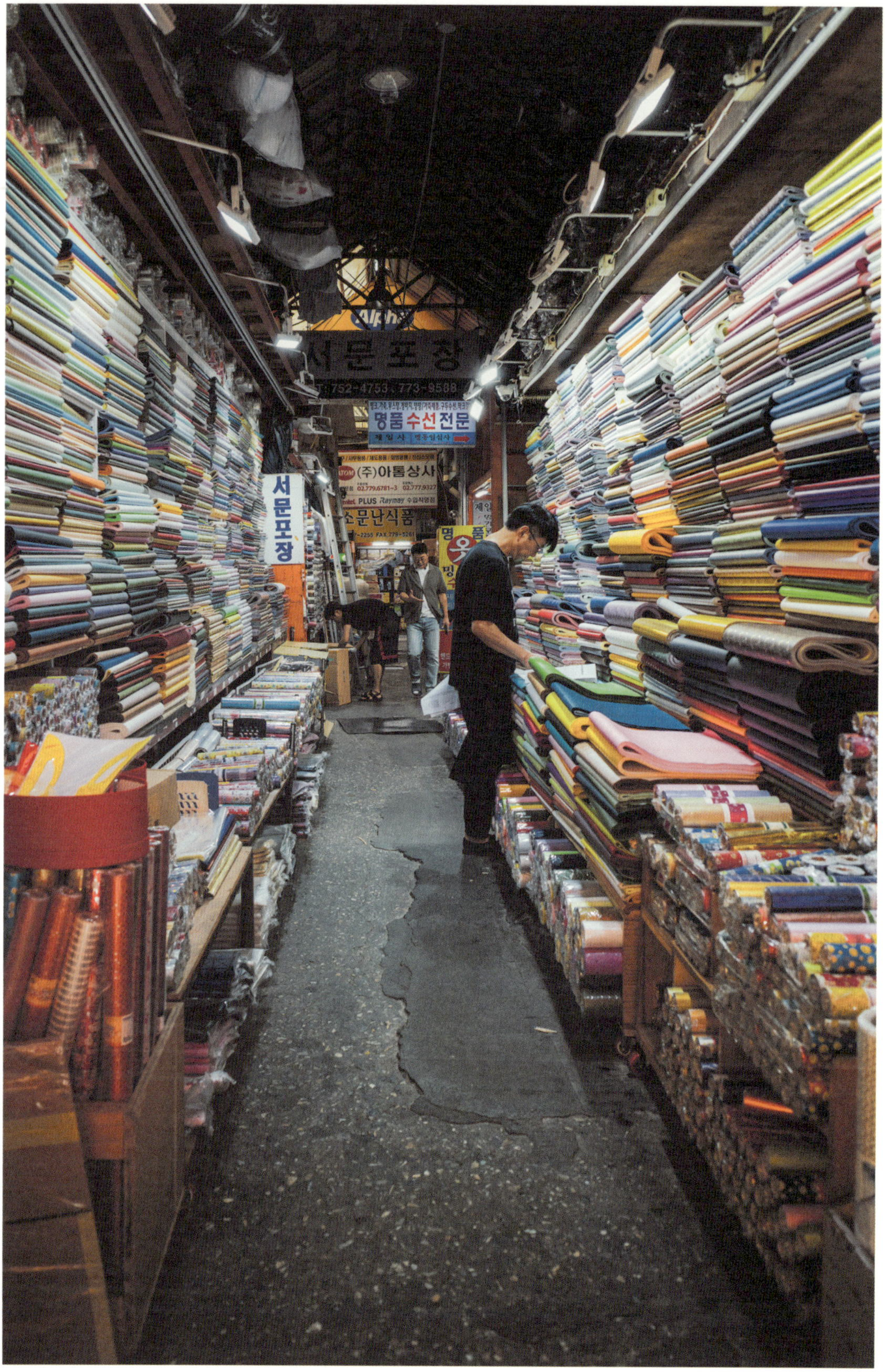


Hoehyeon-dong, Jung District

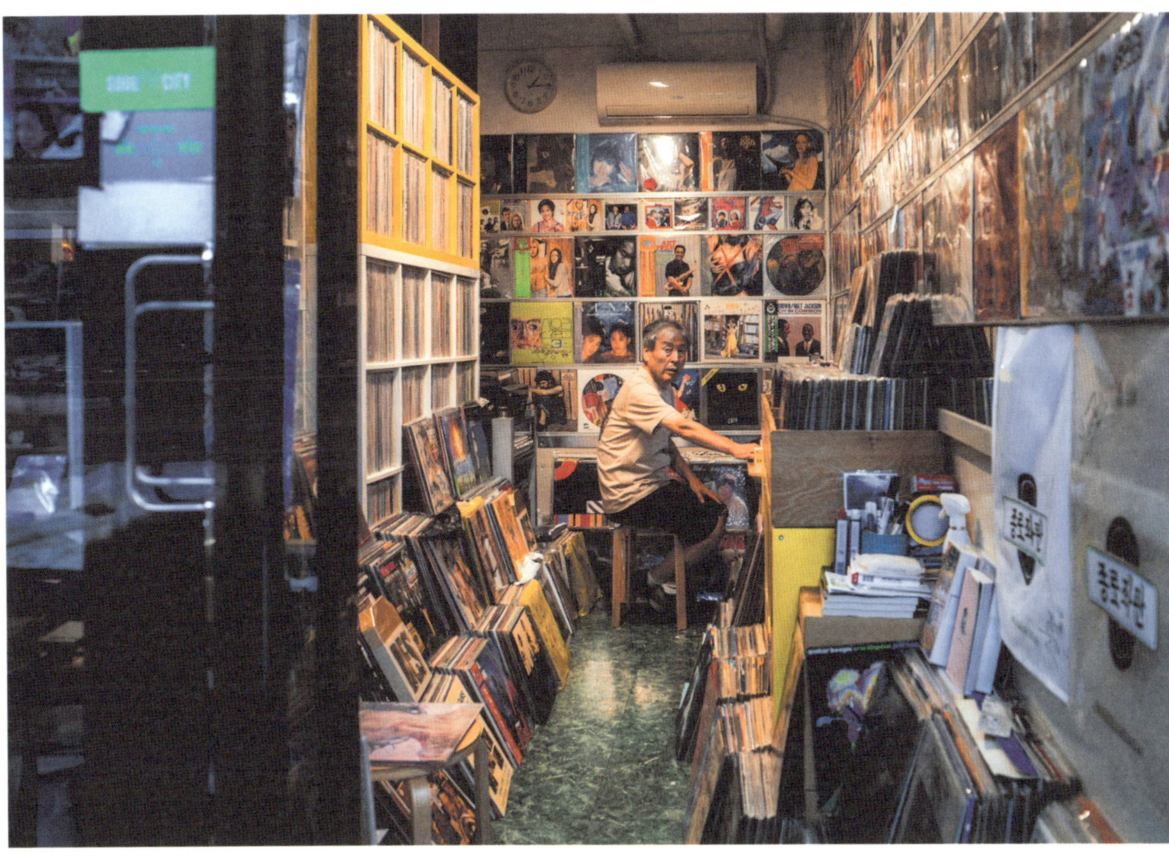

Sewoon Plaza, Jongno 3-ga, Jongno District

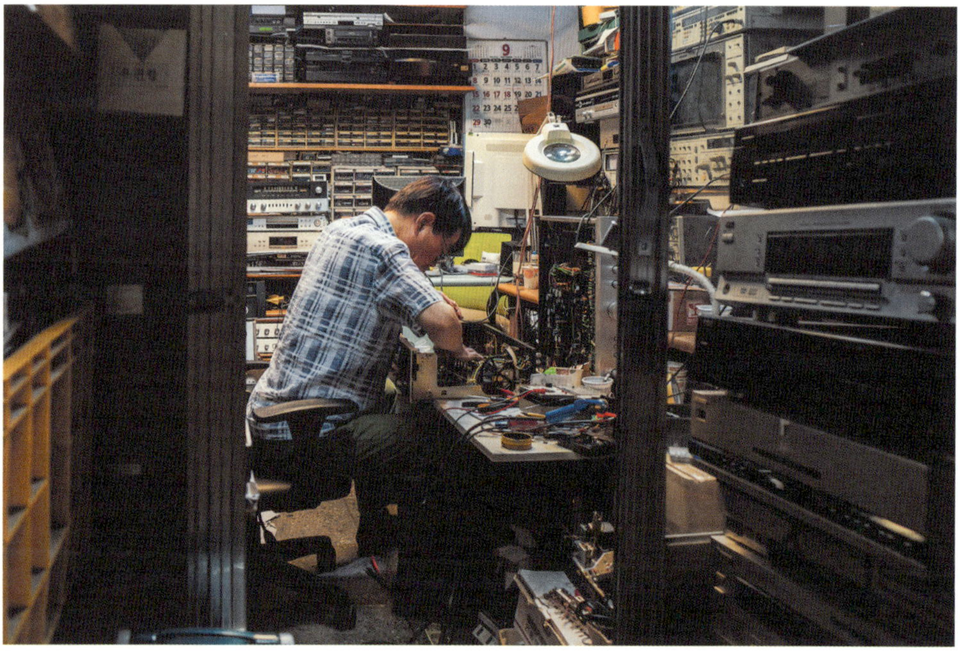

above + right: Sewoon Plaza, Jongno 3-ga, Jongno District

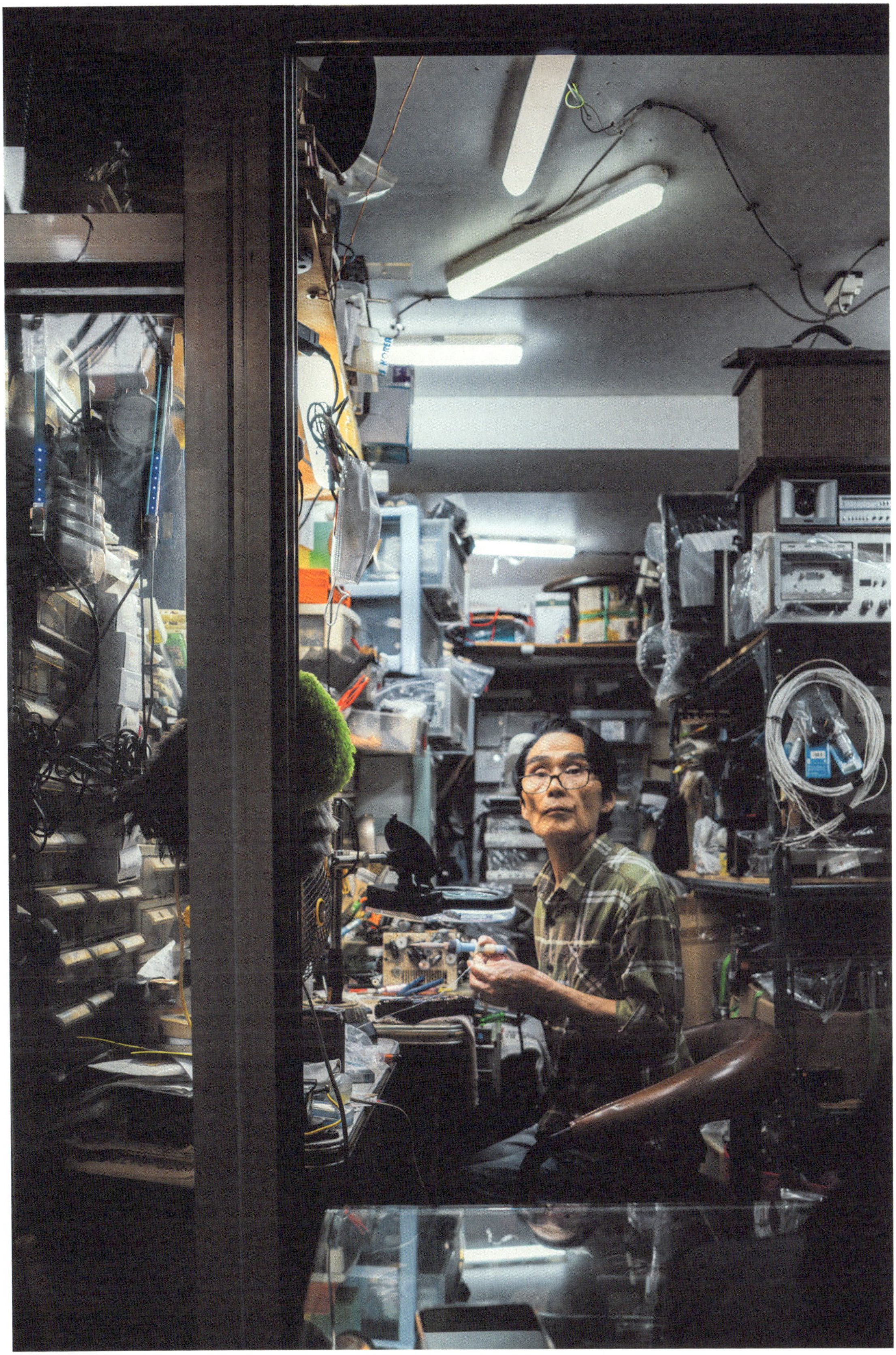

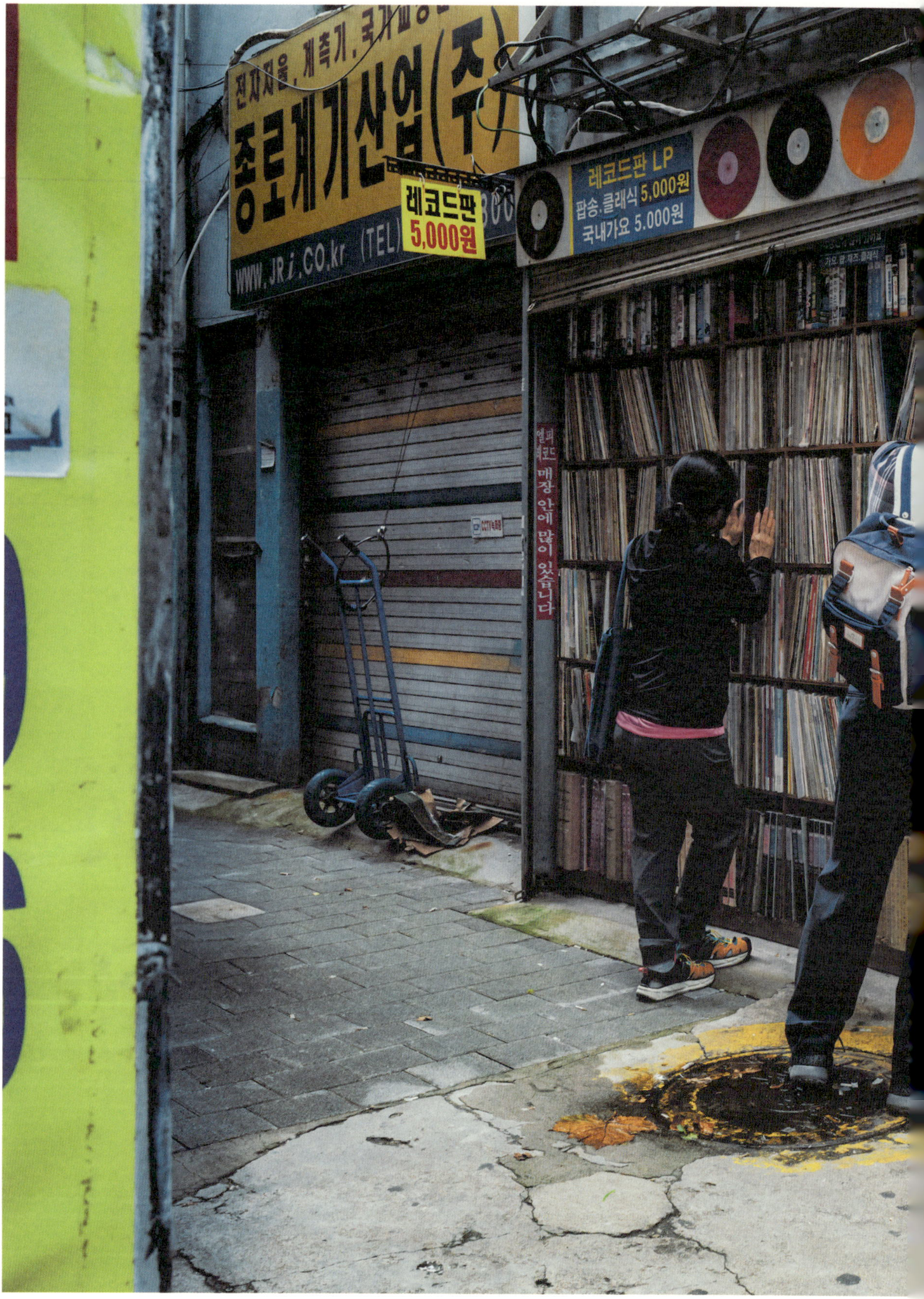


Jongno 1-ga, Jongno District

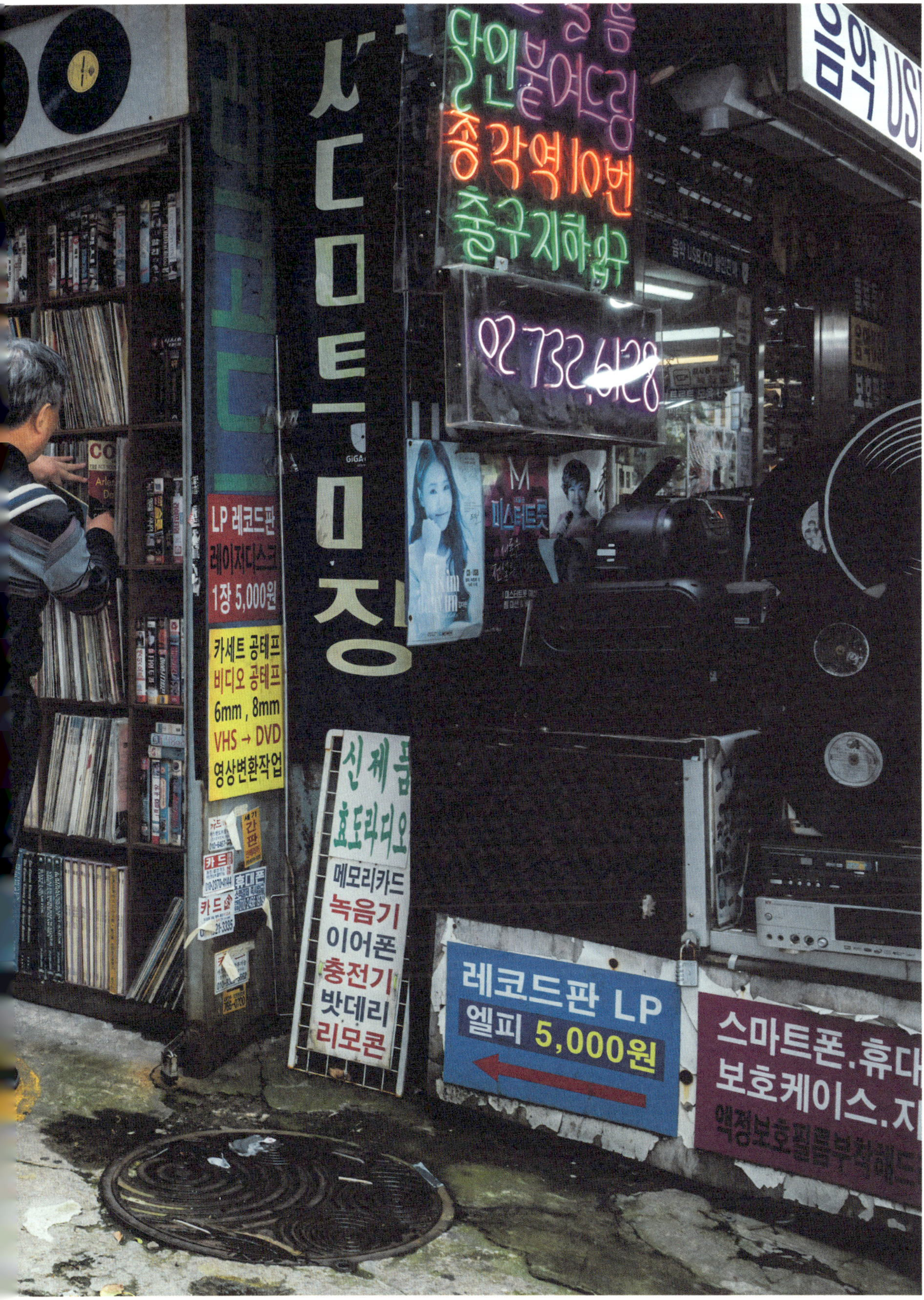
종각역10번
02 732 6128
LP 레코드판
레이저디스크
1장 5,000원
카세트 공테프
비디오 공테프
6mm, 8mm
VHS → DVD
영상변환작업
신제품
효도라디오
메모리카드
녹음기
이어폰
충전기
밧데리
리모콘
레코드판 LP
엘피 5,000원

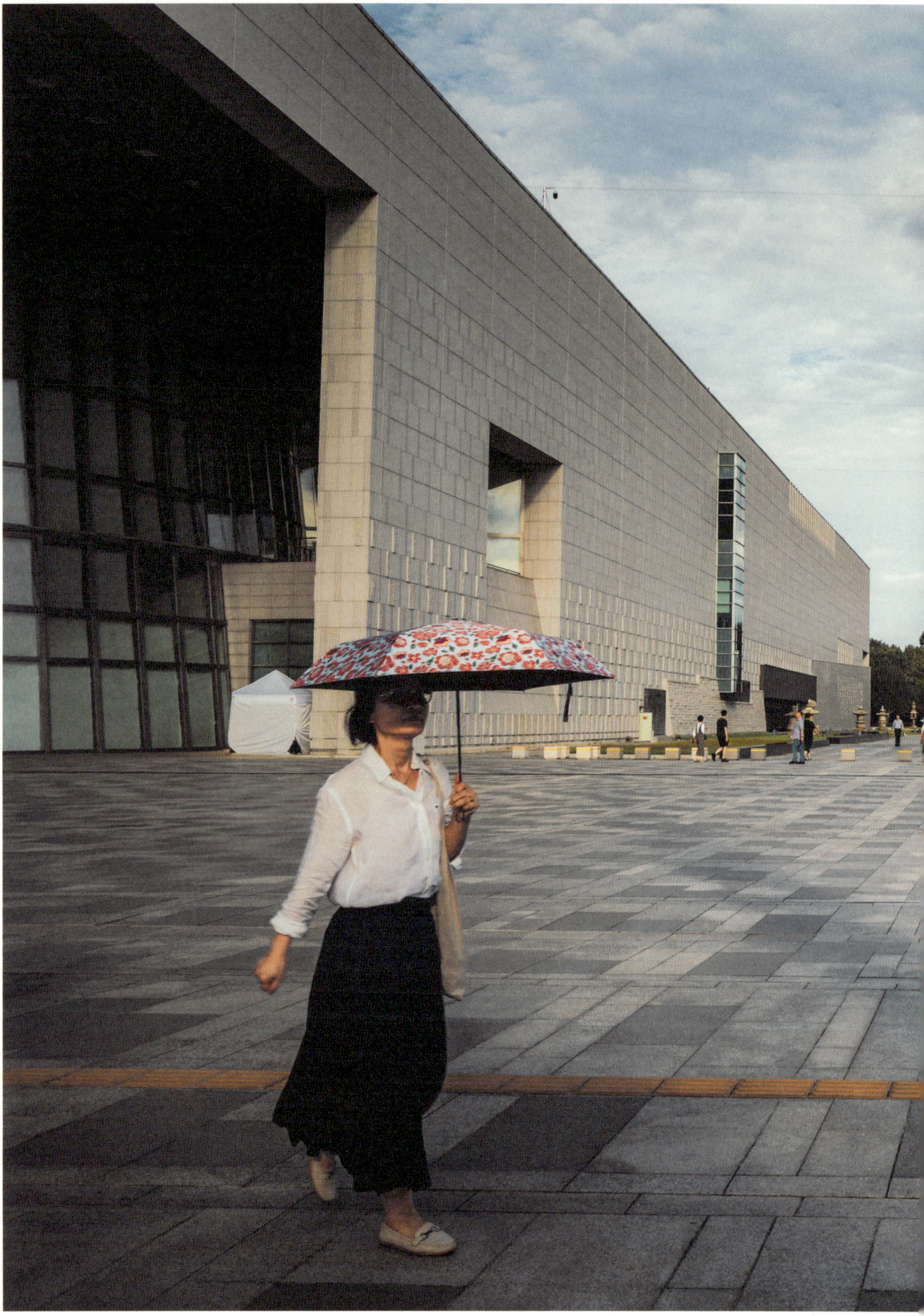

National Museum of Korea, Seobinggo-dong, Yongsan District

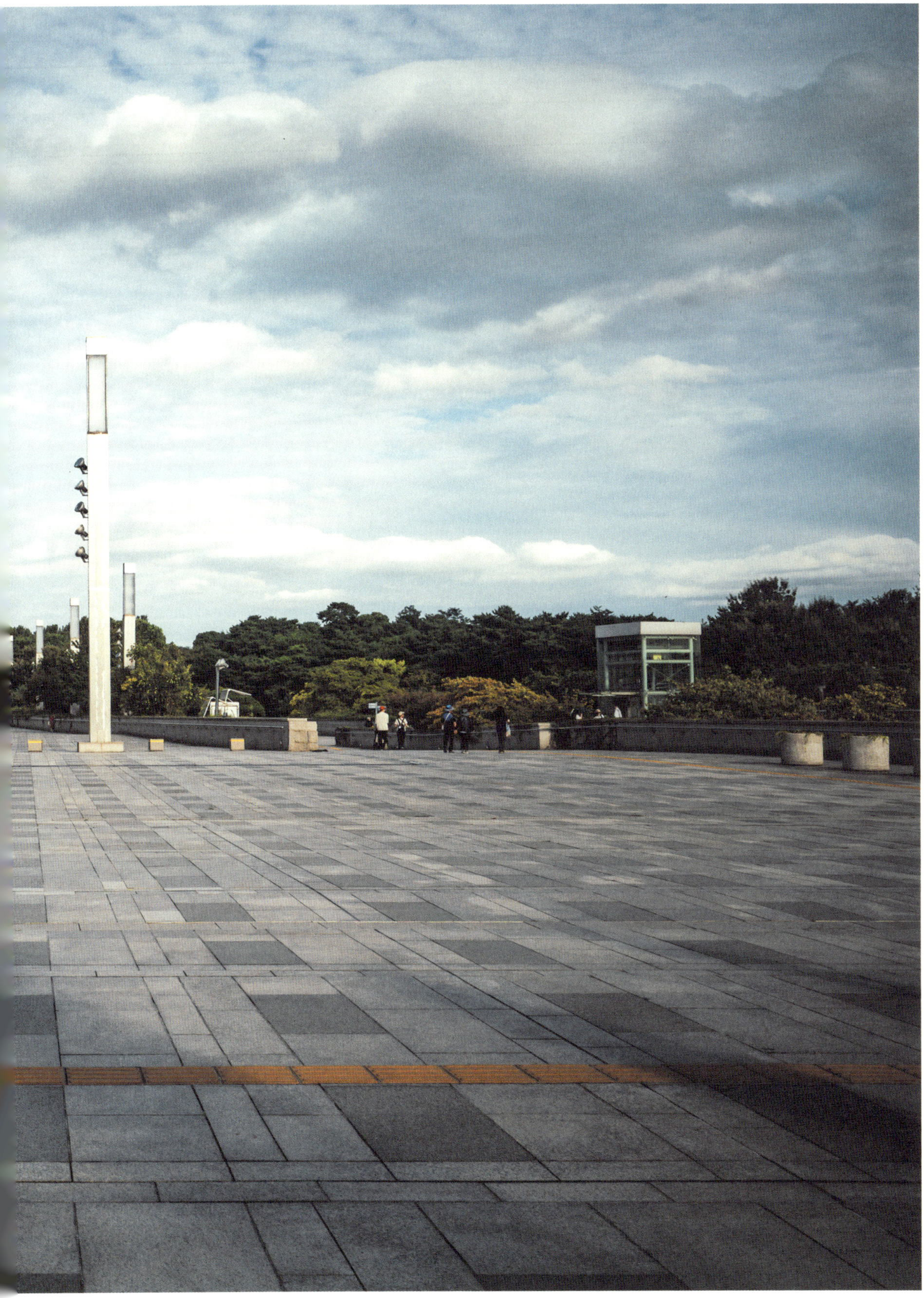

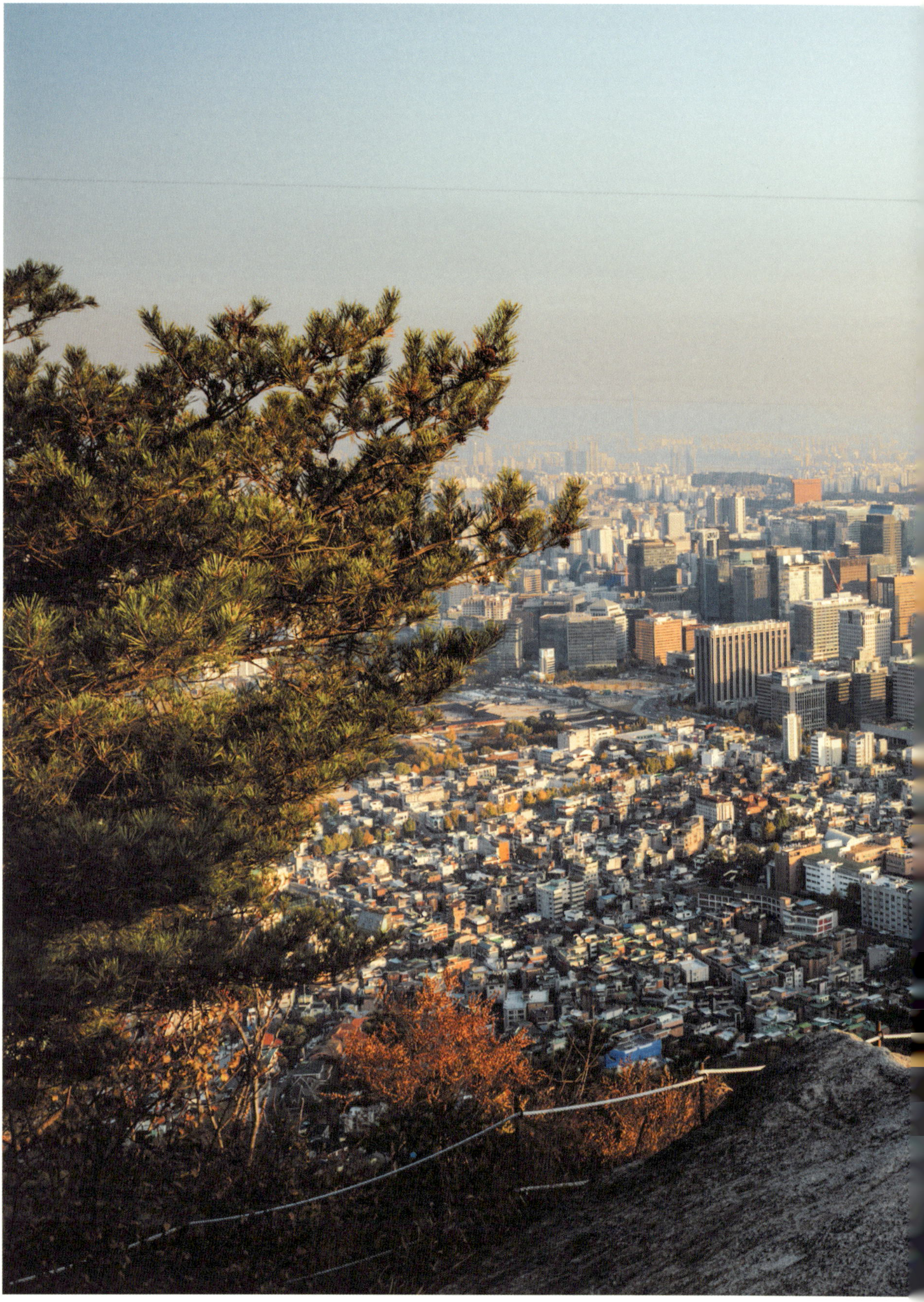

Inwangsan Mountain, Jongno District

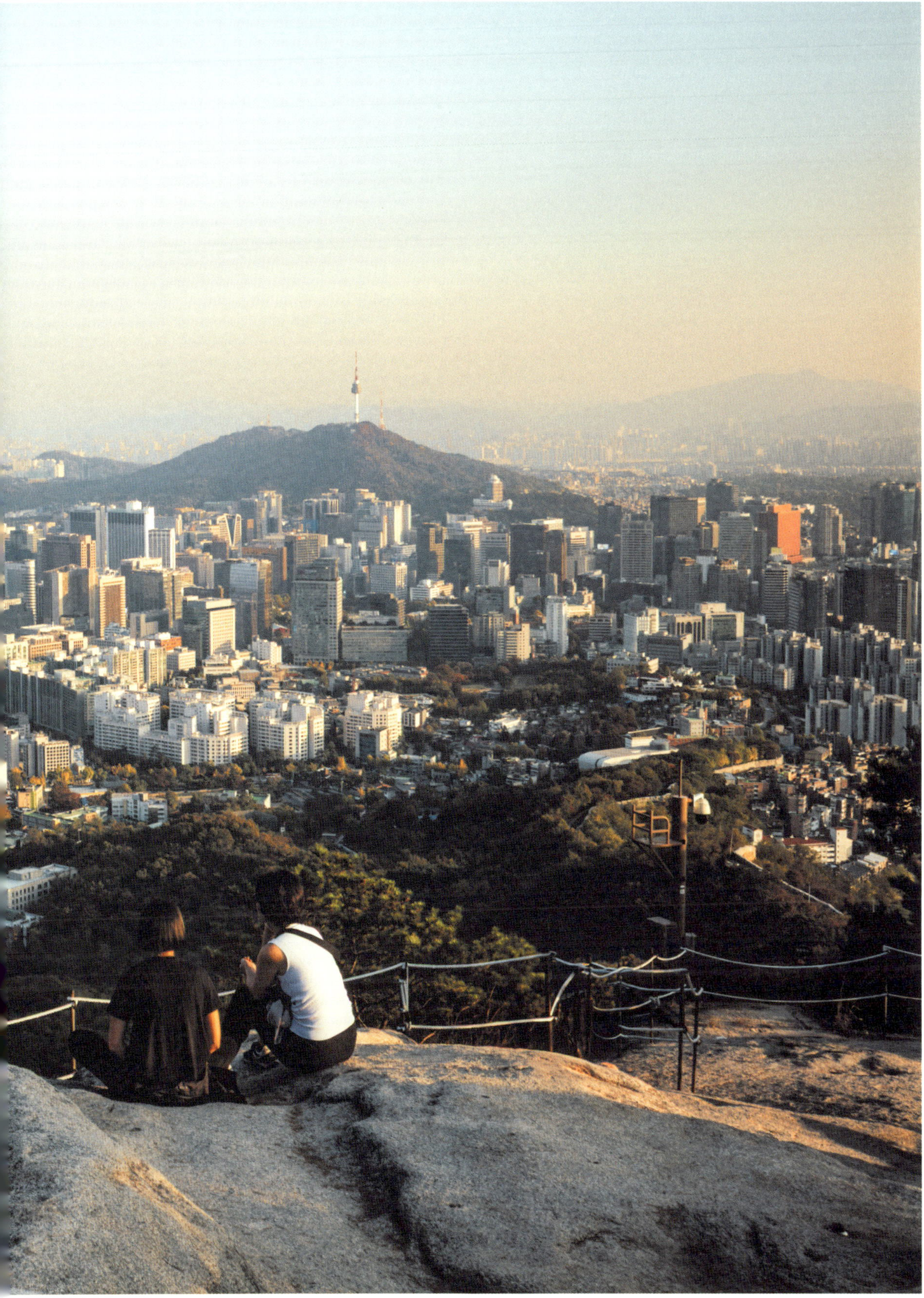

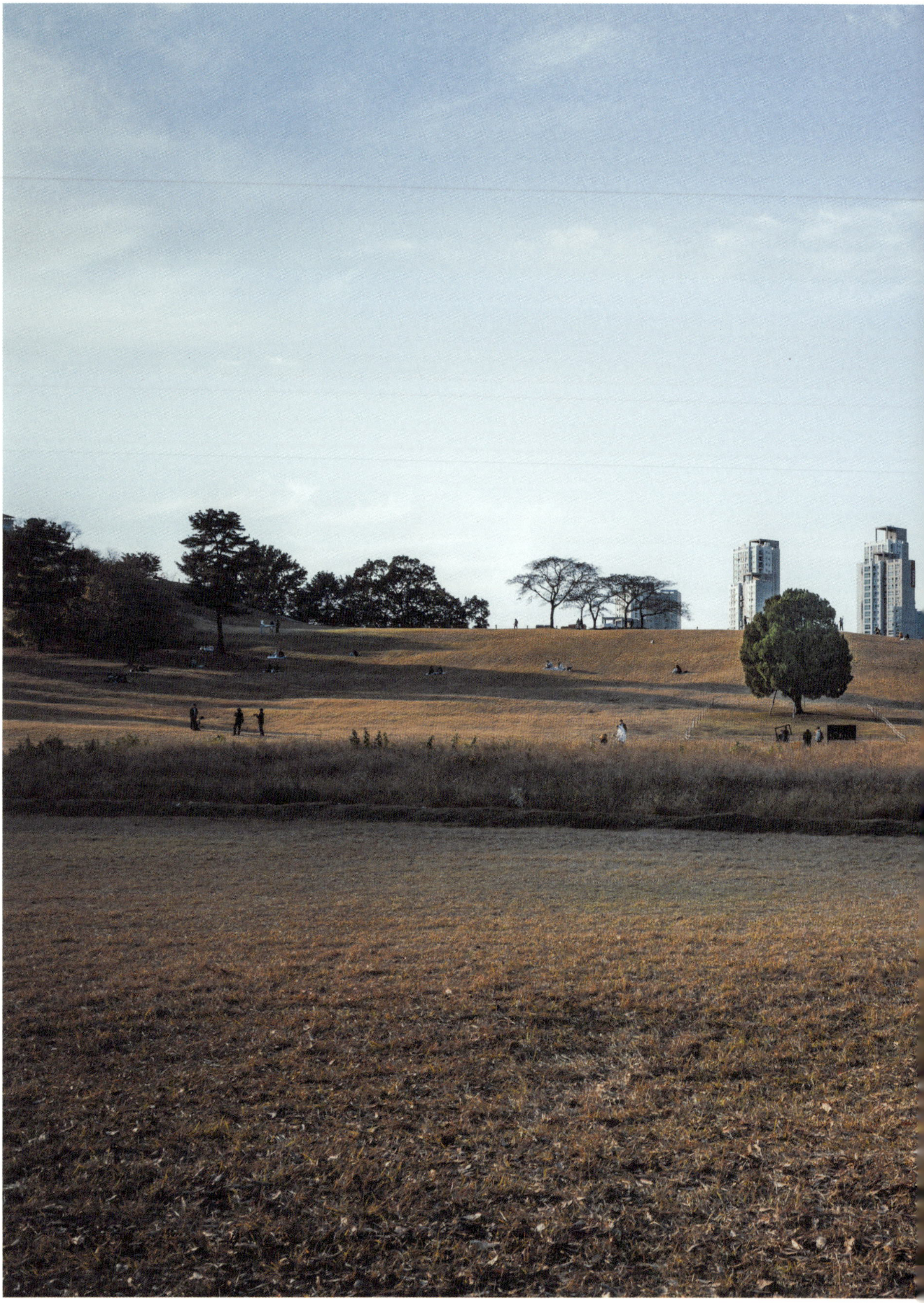

Olympic Park, Bangi-dong, Songpa District > Legacy Park developed for the 1988 Seoul Olympics

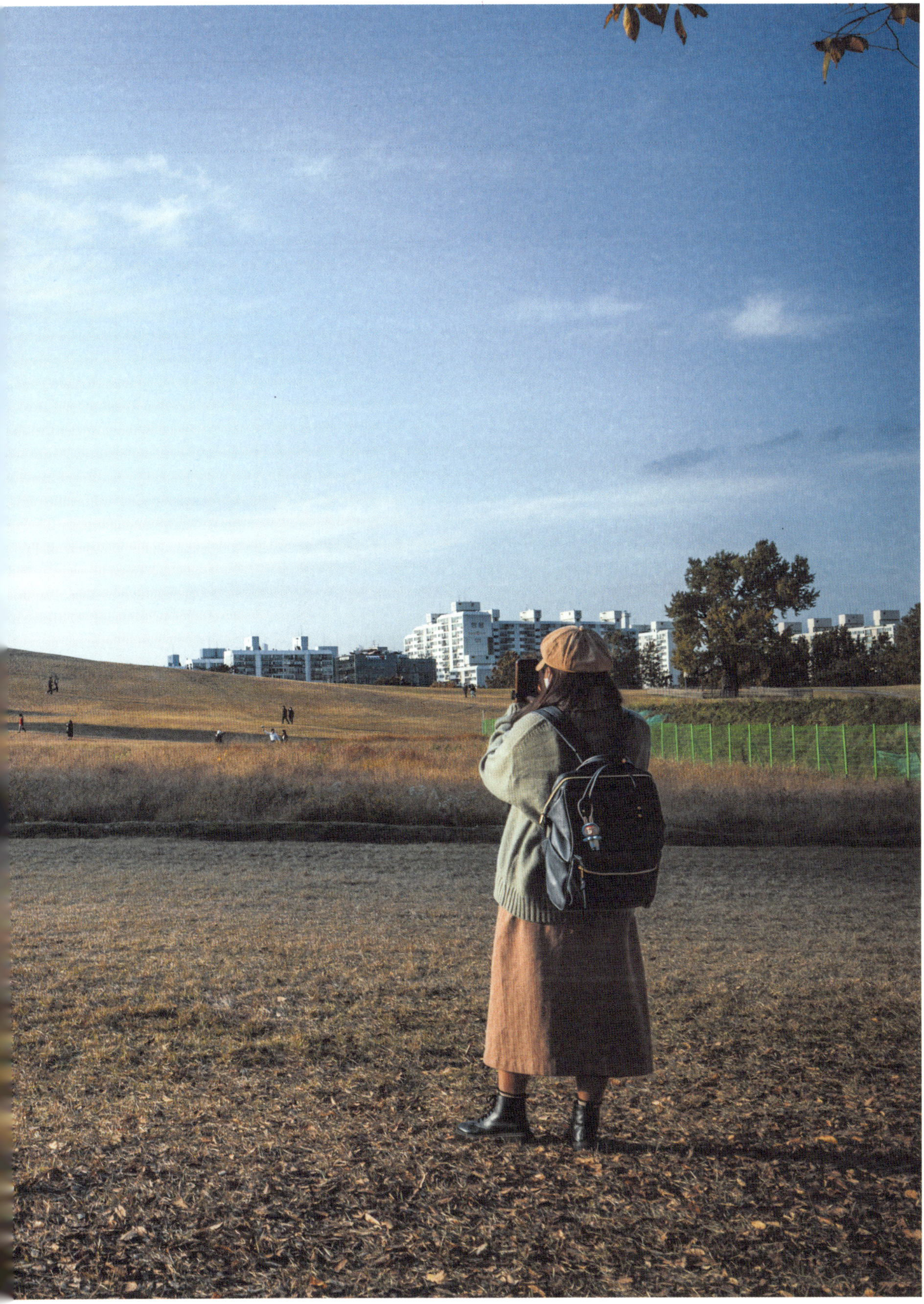

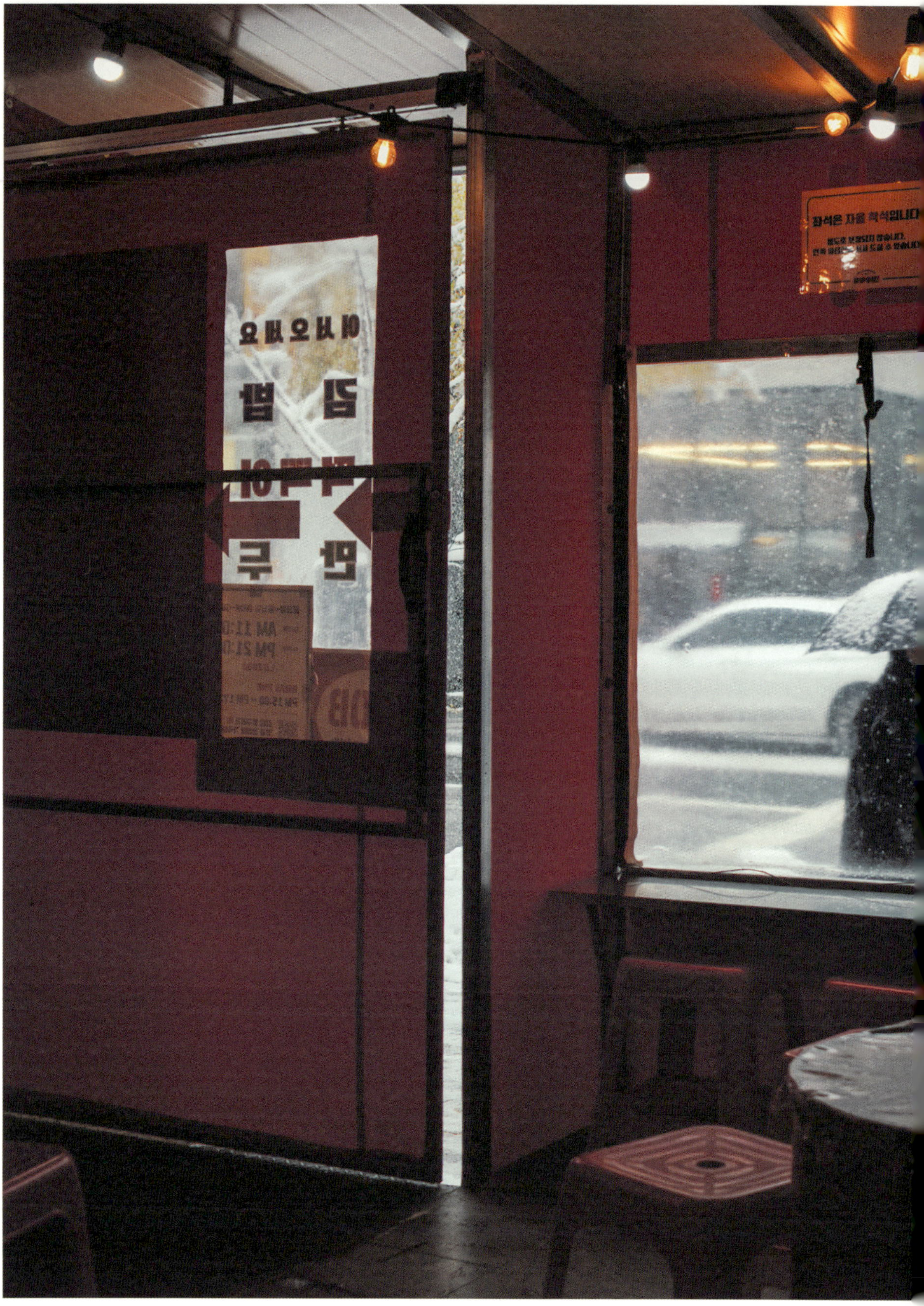

Itaewon, Yongsan District

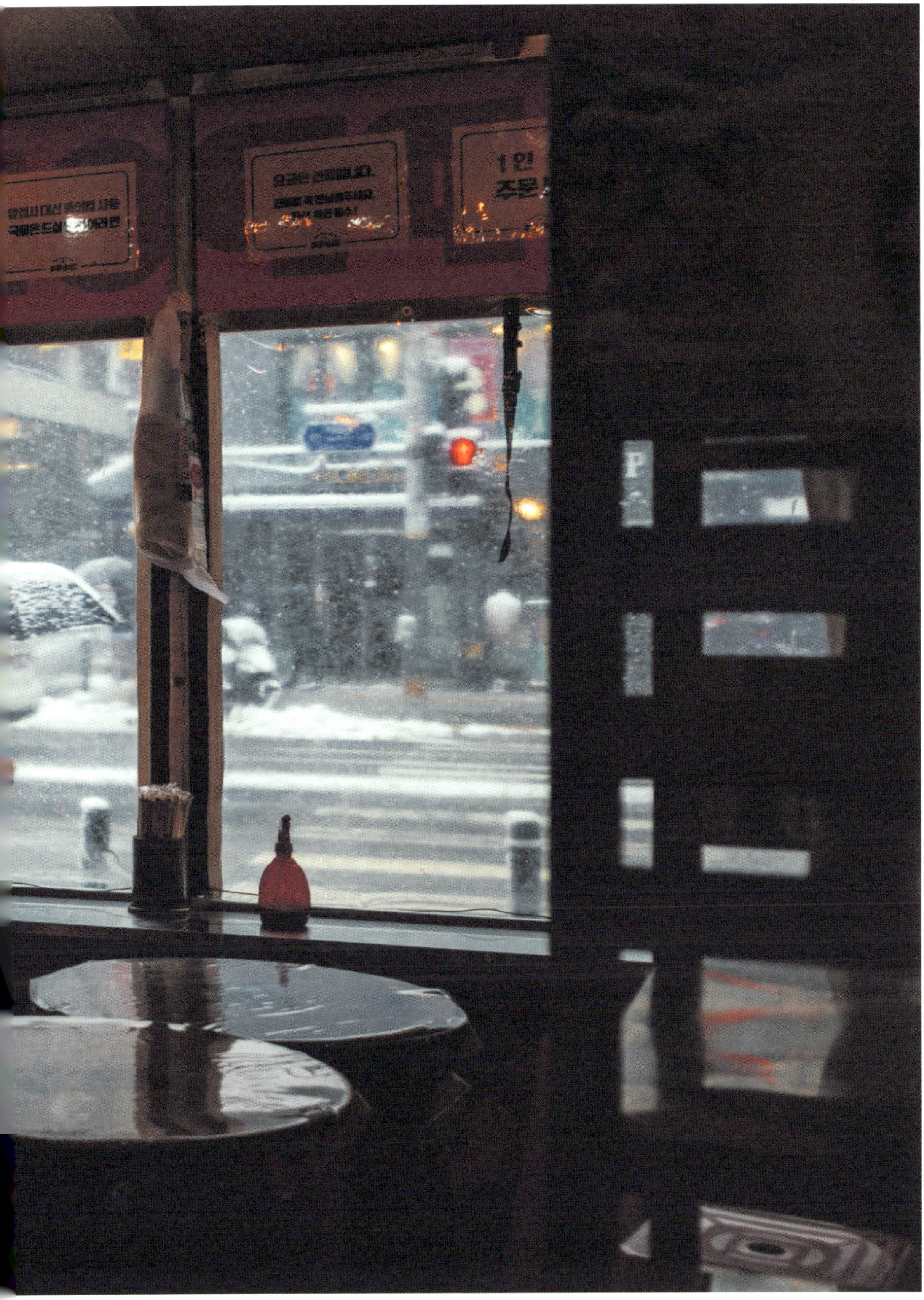
1인
주문

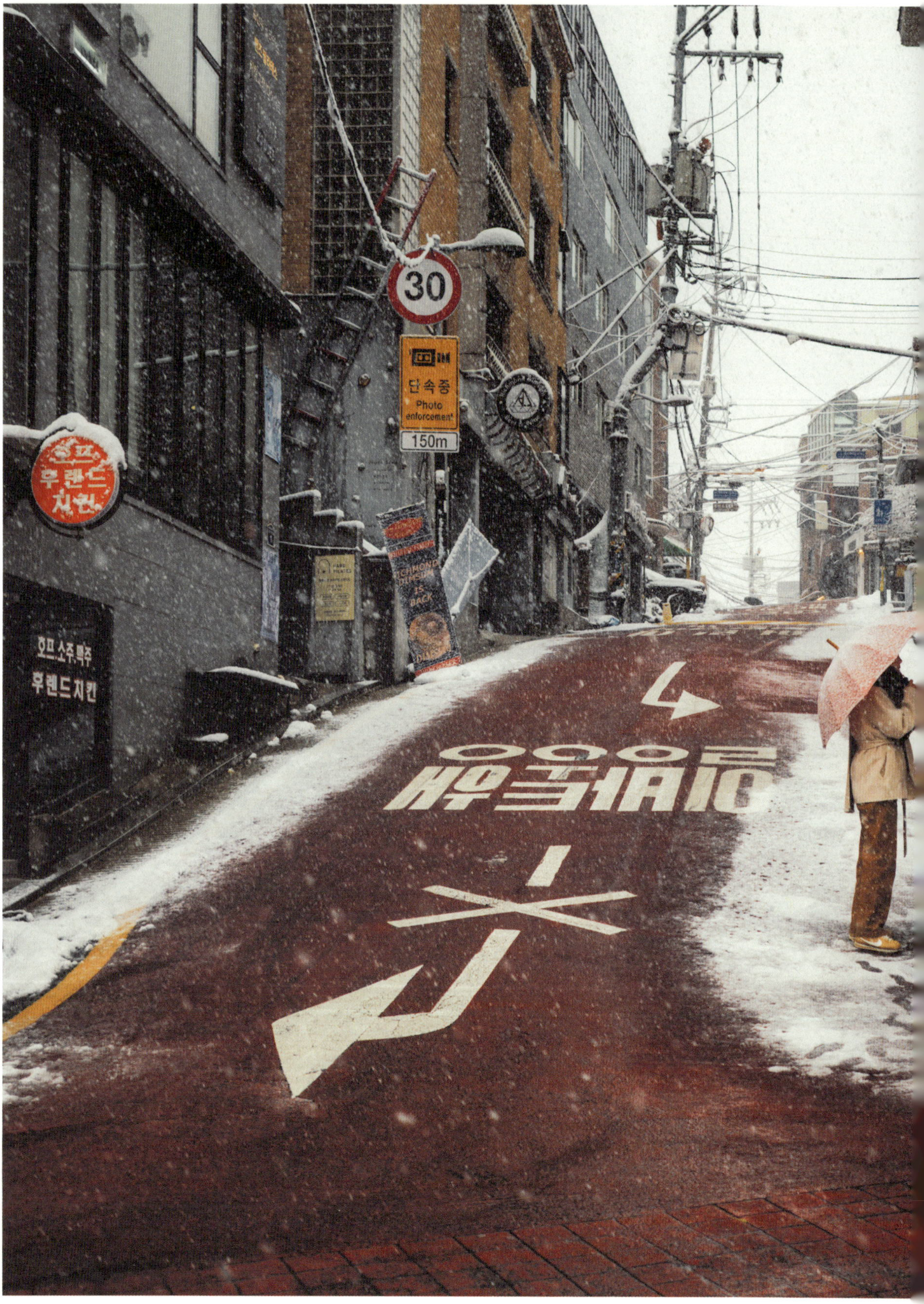


Itaewon, Yongsan District

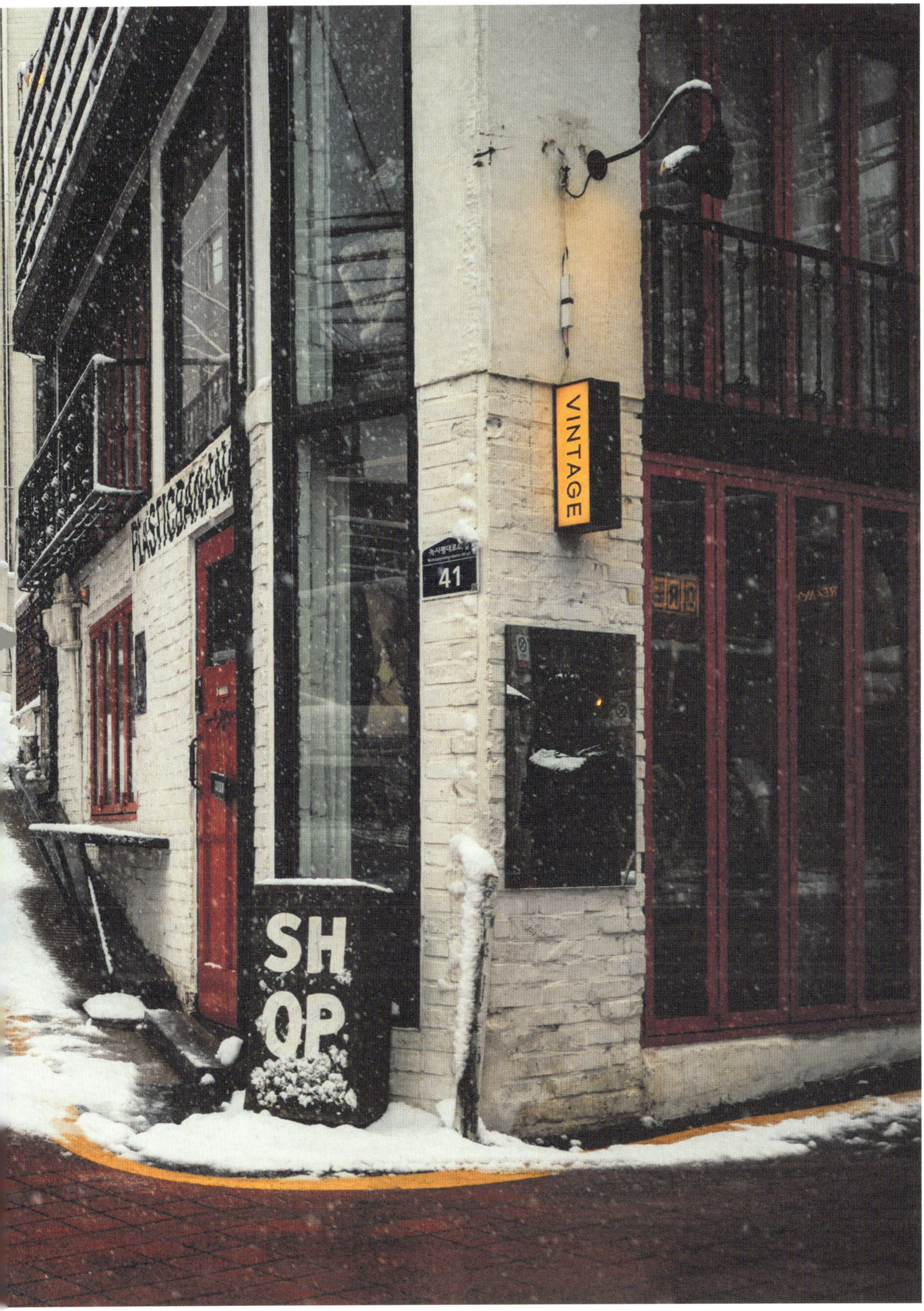
VINTAGE
41
SH
OP

# BEONGAE

## 번개

(beon-gae) by definition, literally means "lightning" and is a slang term for an impromptu or spur-of-the-moment social gathering with friends or close acquaintances, often arranged quickly via text or a group chat.

Seoul changes character after dark. The formality of the day, the suits and measured greetings, softens as people spill from offices into the streets. Restaurants fill with coworkers sharing soju and grilled meat in the ritual of hwesik, where hierarchy fades and laughter replaces titles. Seoulites move on to izakaya style bars, fried chicken restaurants, and late cafés that stay lively past midnight. An ease settles over the city as couples walk the Hangang River, friends gather at convenience store patios, and music drifts from upstairs bars. The Seoul that moved in focused precision by day transforms into something more human at night: open, unguarded, and alive with conversation.

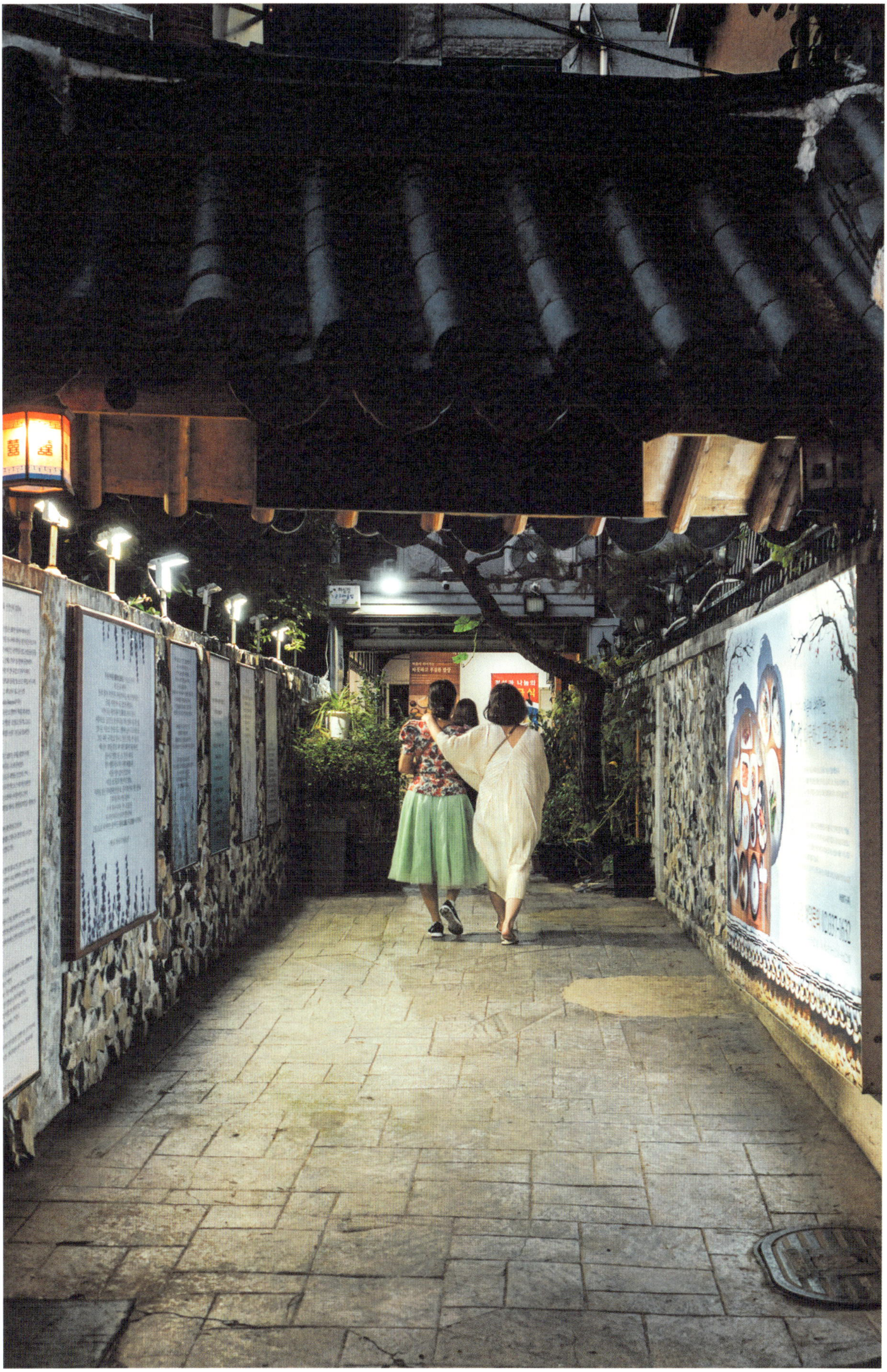

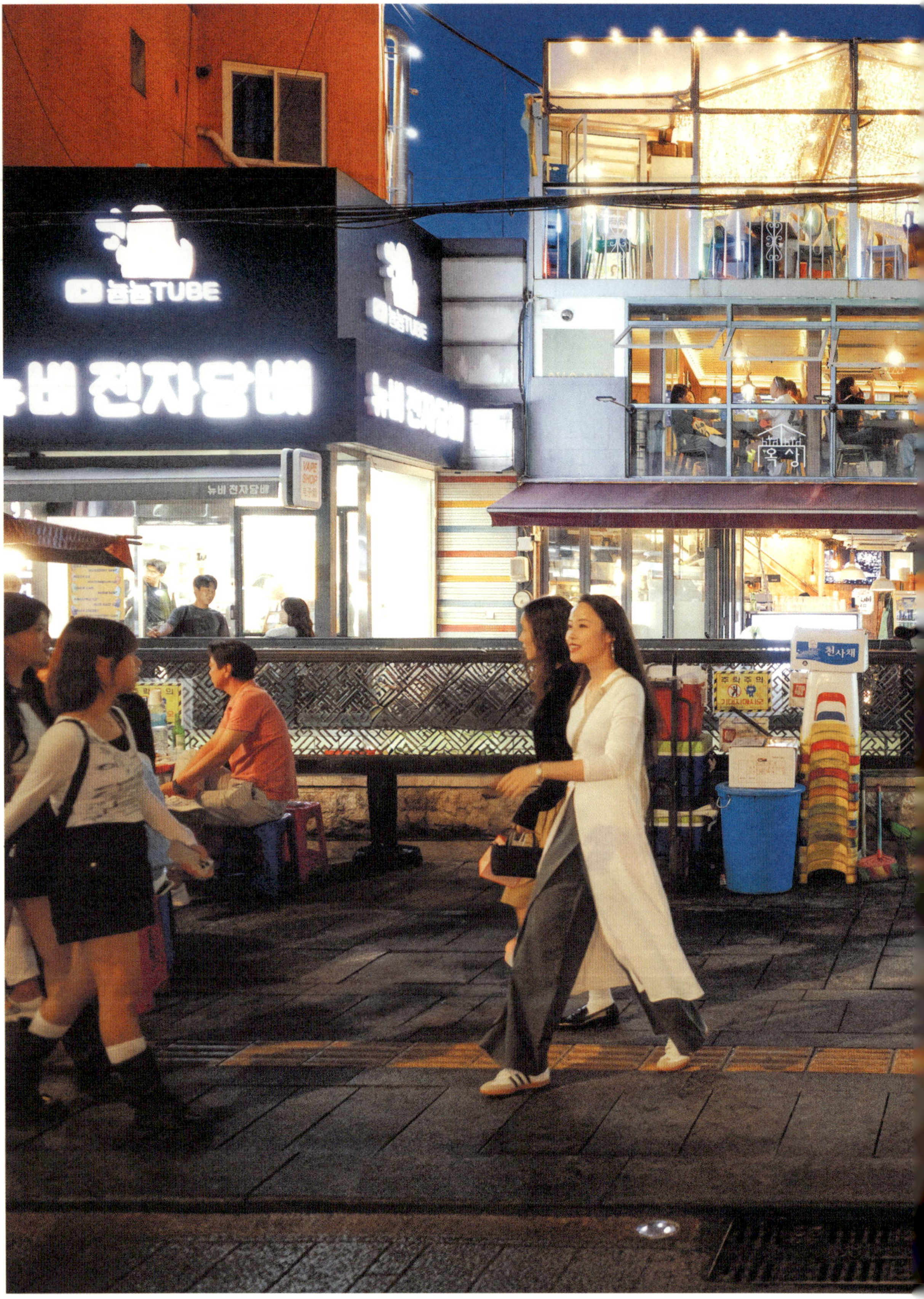


above: Ikseon-dong, Jongno District + previous page: Mangwon-dong, Mapo District

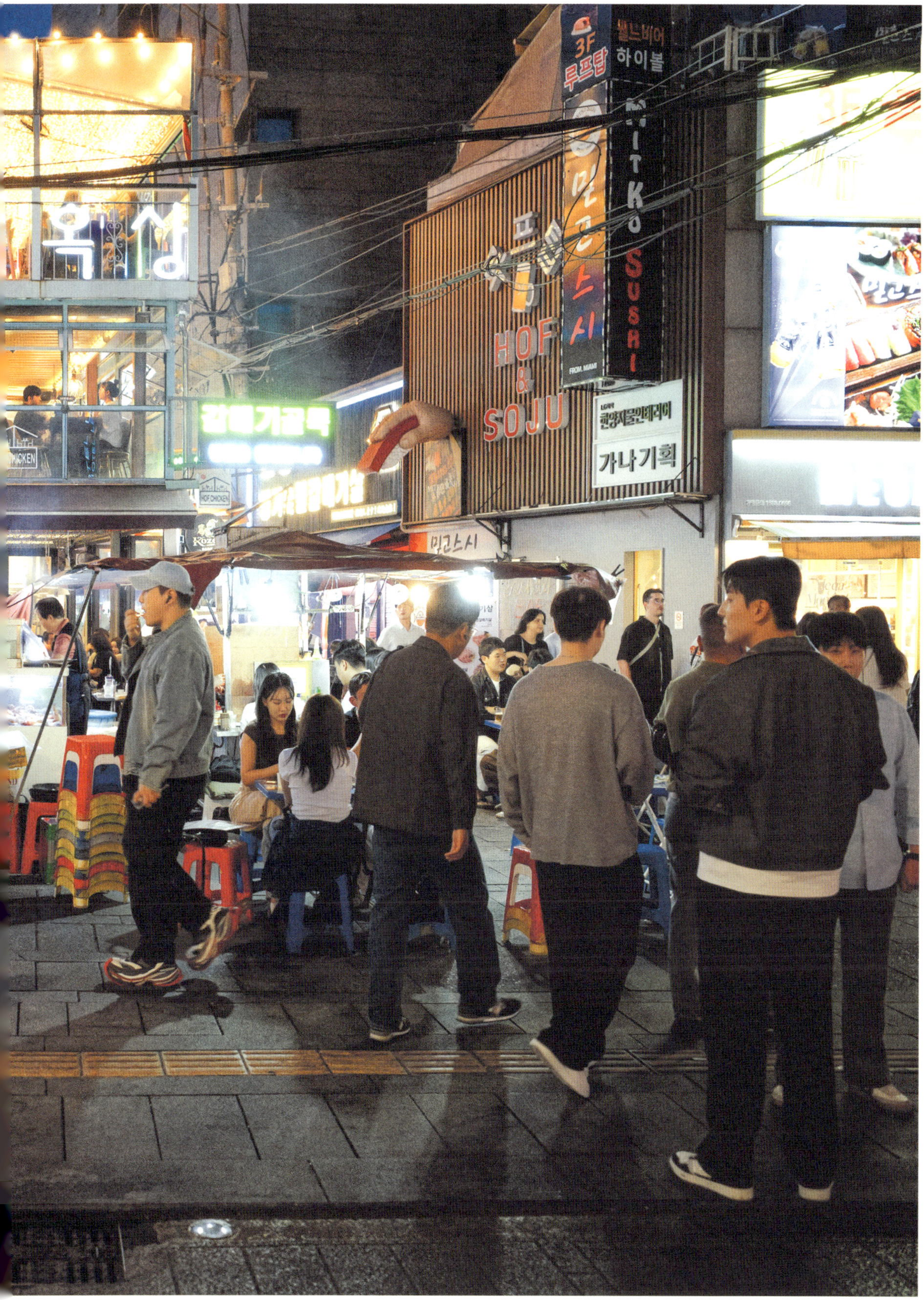
3F
루프탑
하이볼
HOF & SOJU
가나기획

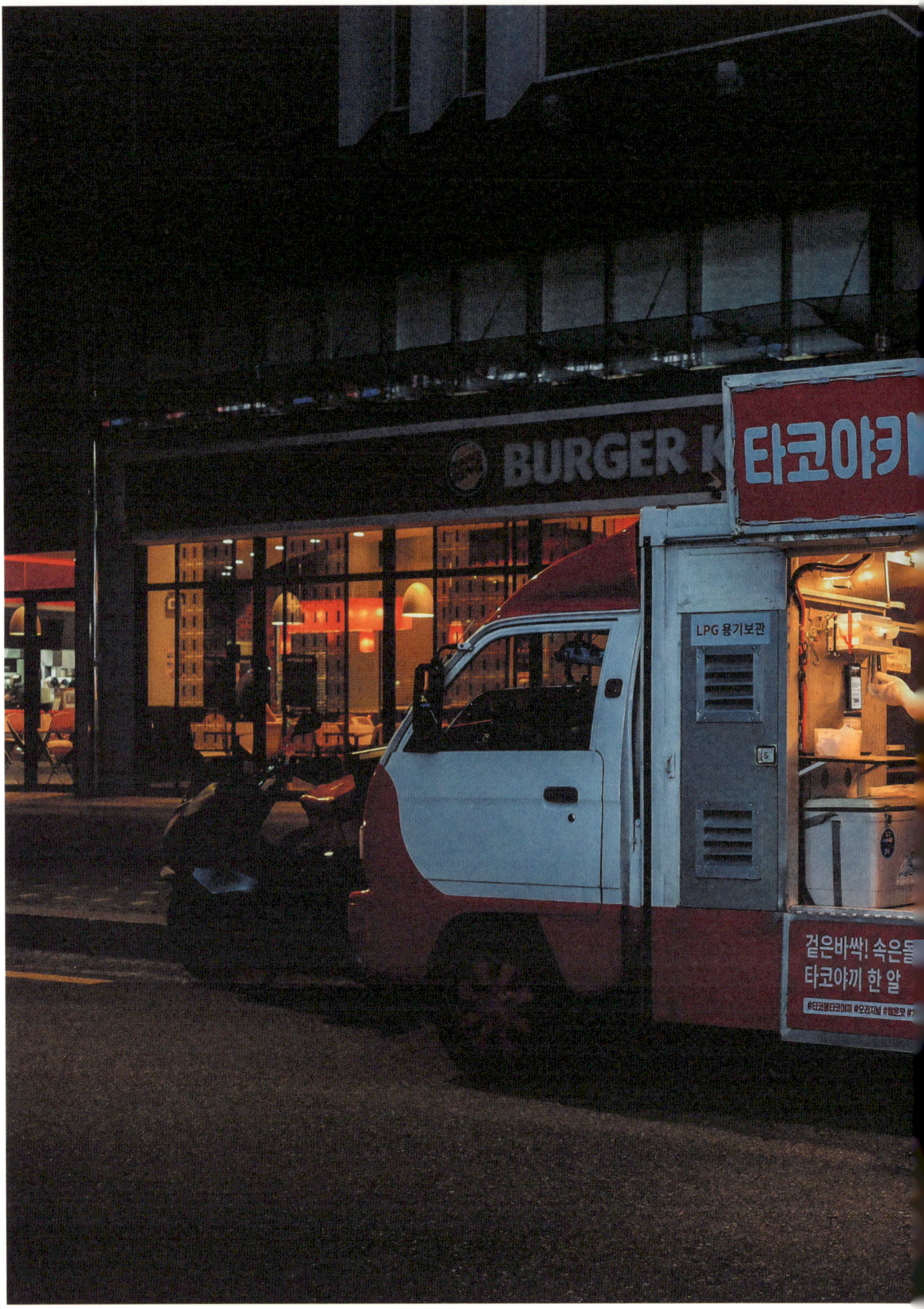


Dangsan-dong, Yeongdeungpo District

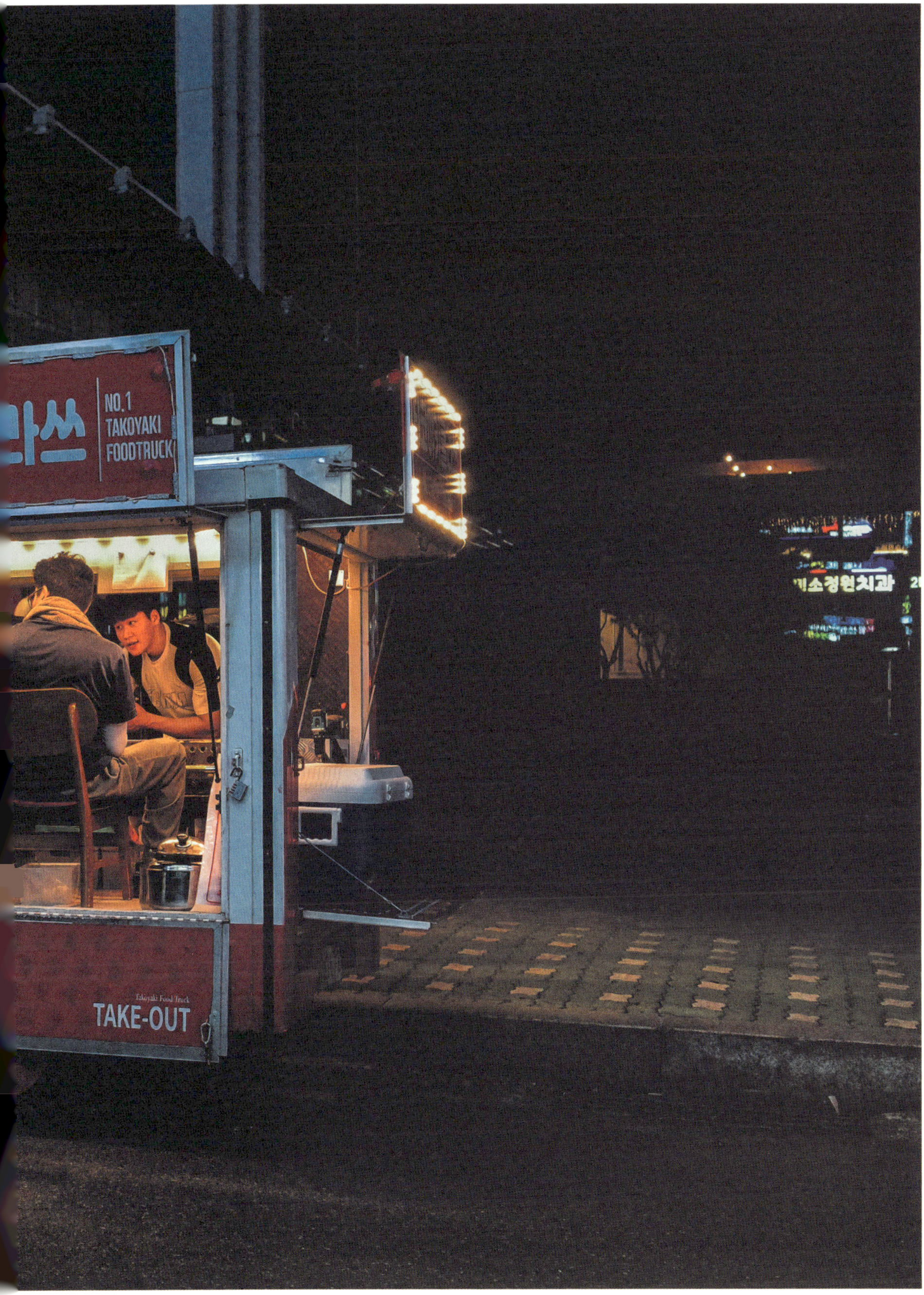
타쓰
NO.1
TAKOYAKI
FOODTRUCK
Takoyaki Food Truck
TAKE-OUT

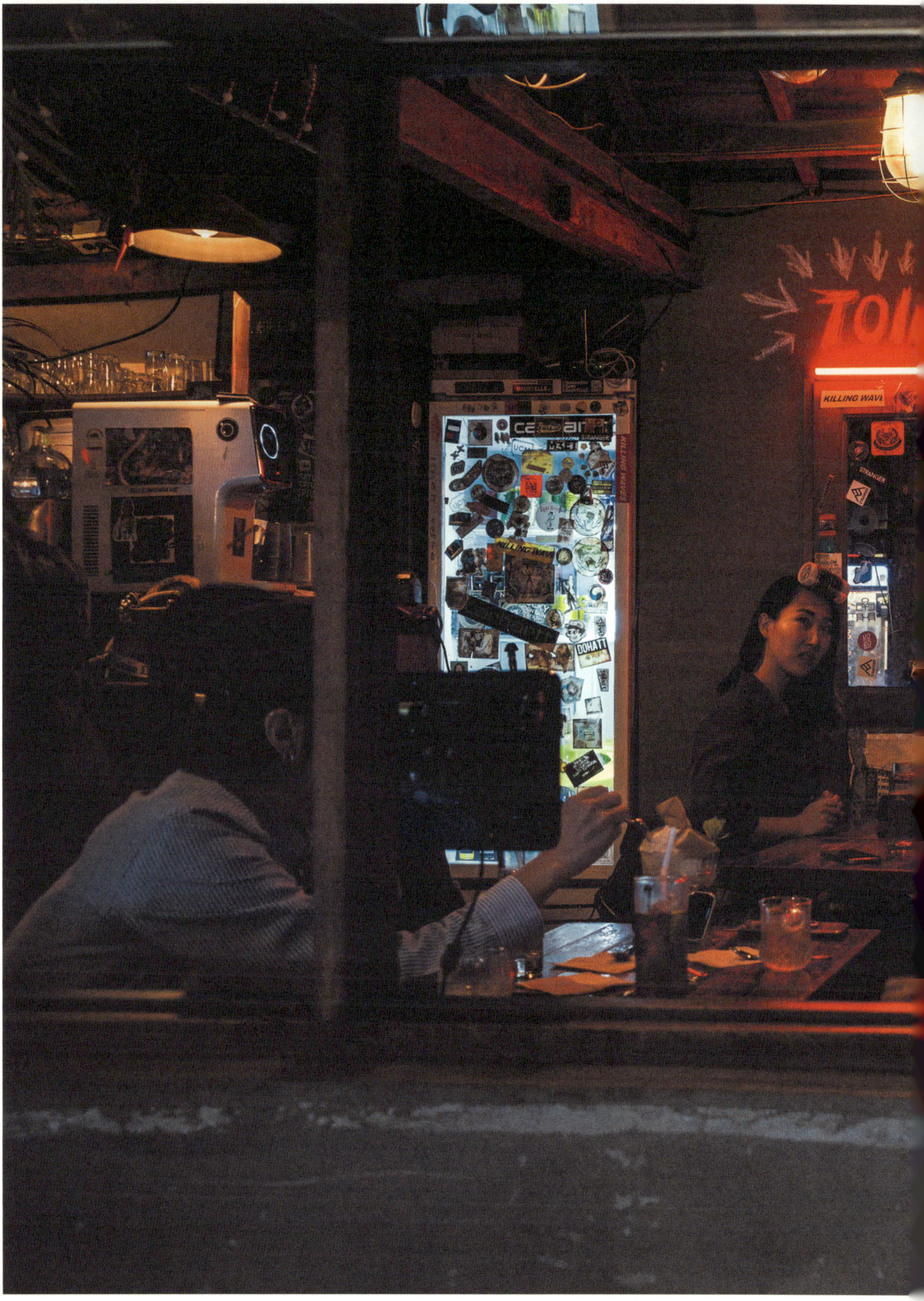


Seochon, Jongno District

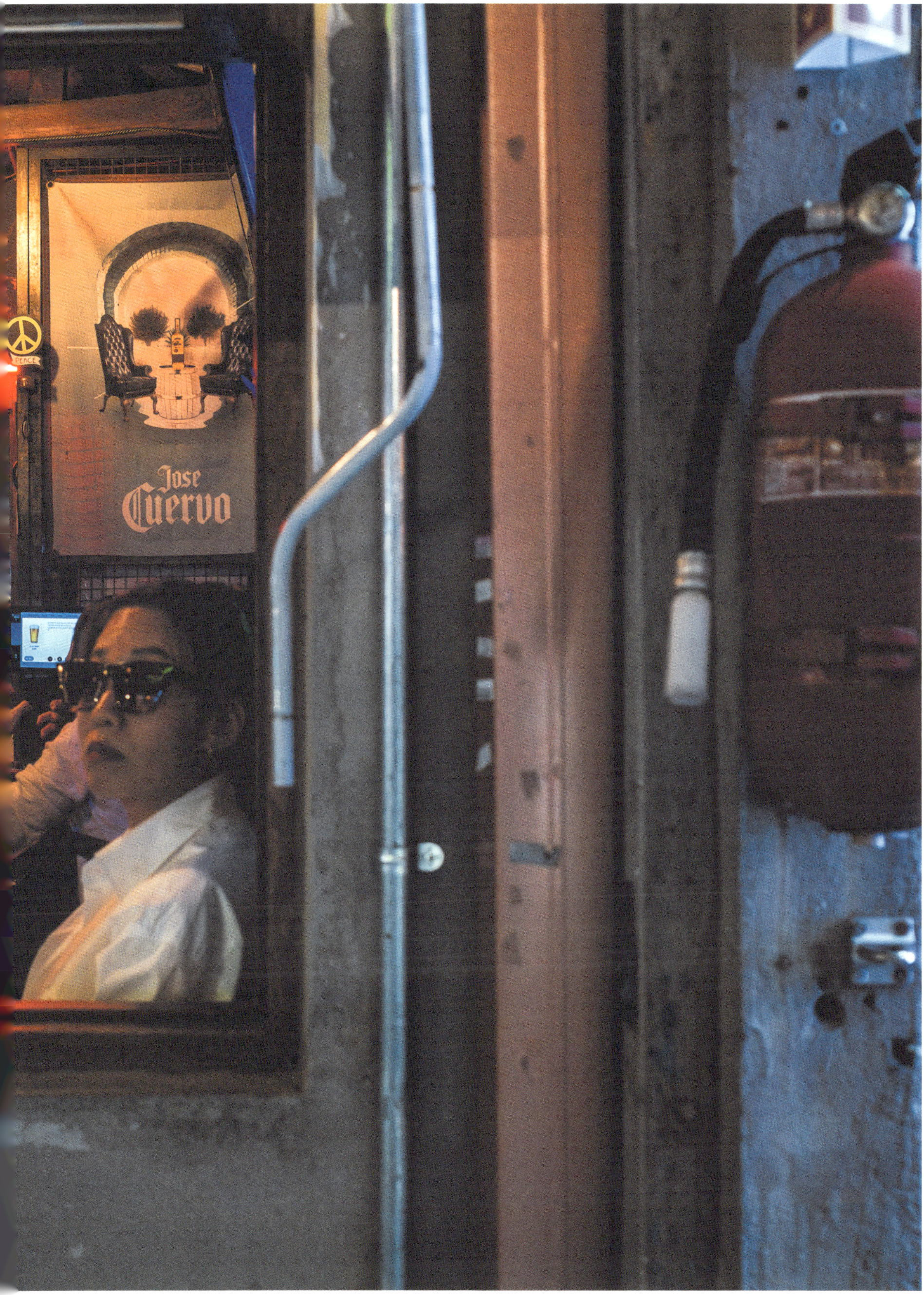
Jose
Cuervo

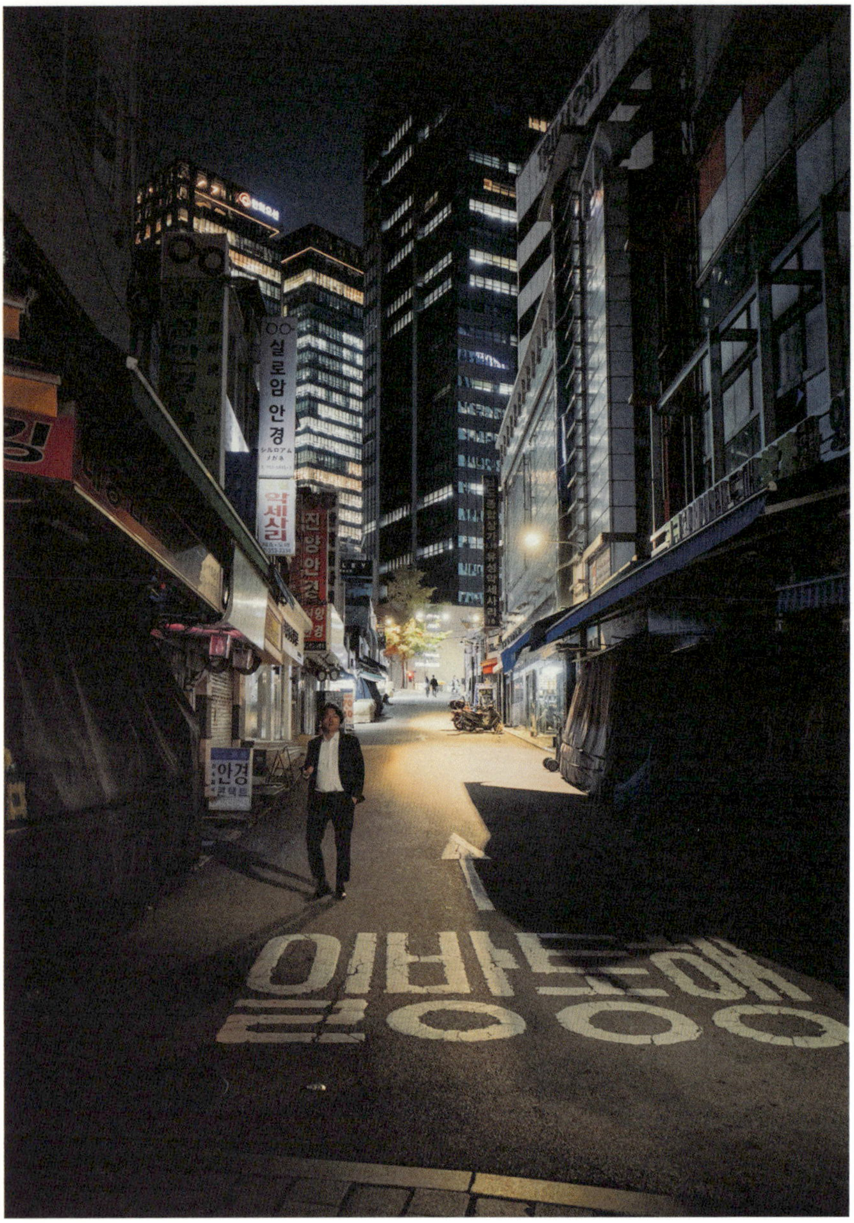


left: Bukchang-dong, Jung District

right: Itaewon, Yongsan District

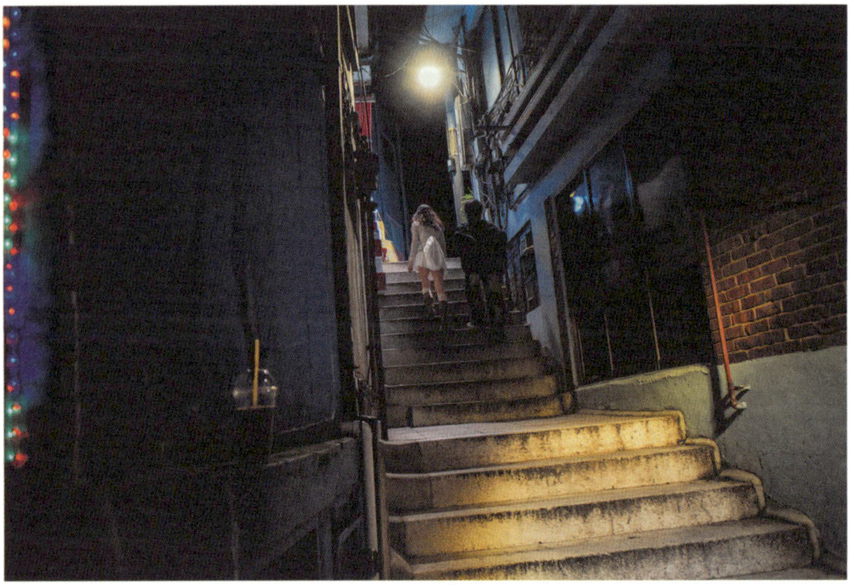

left: Haebangchon, Yongsan Distric

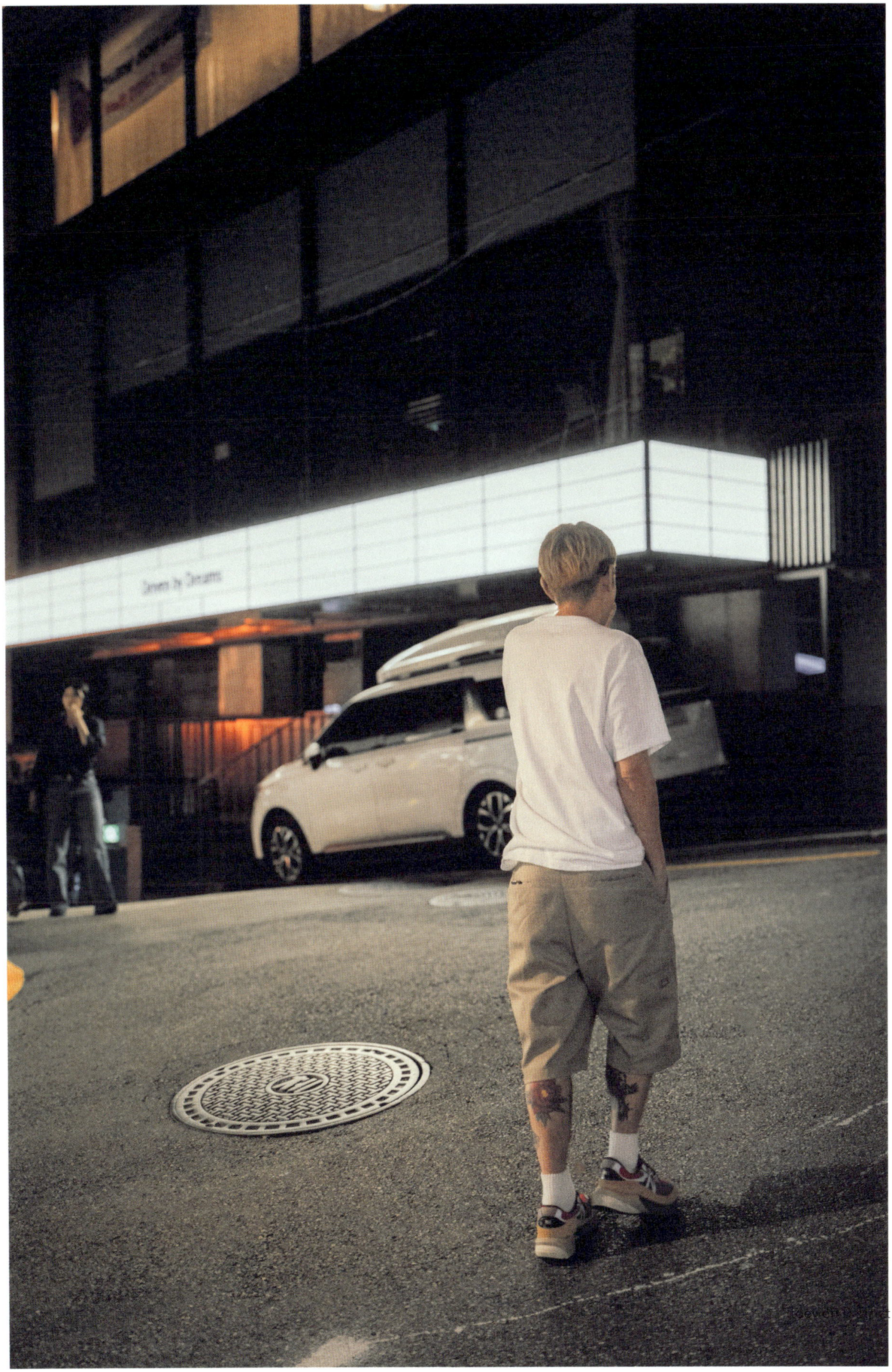

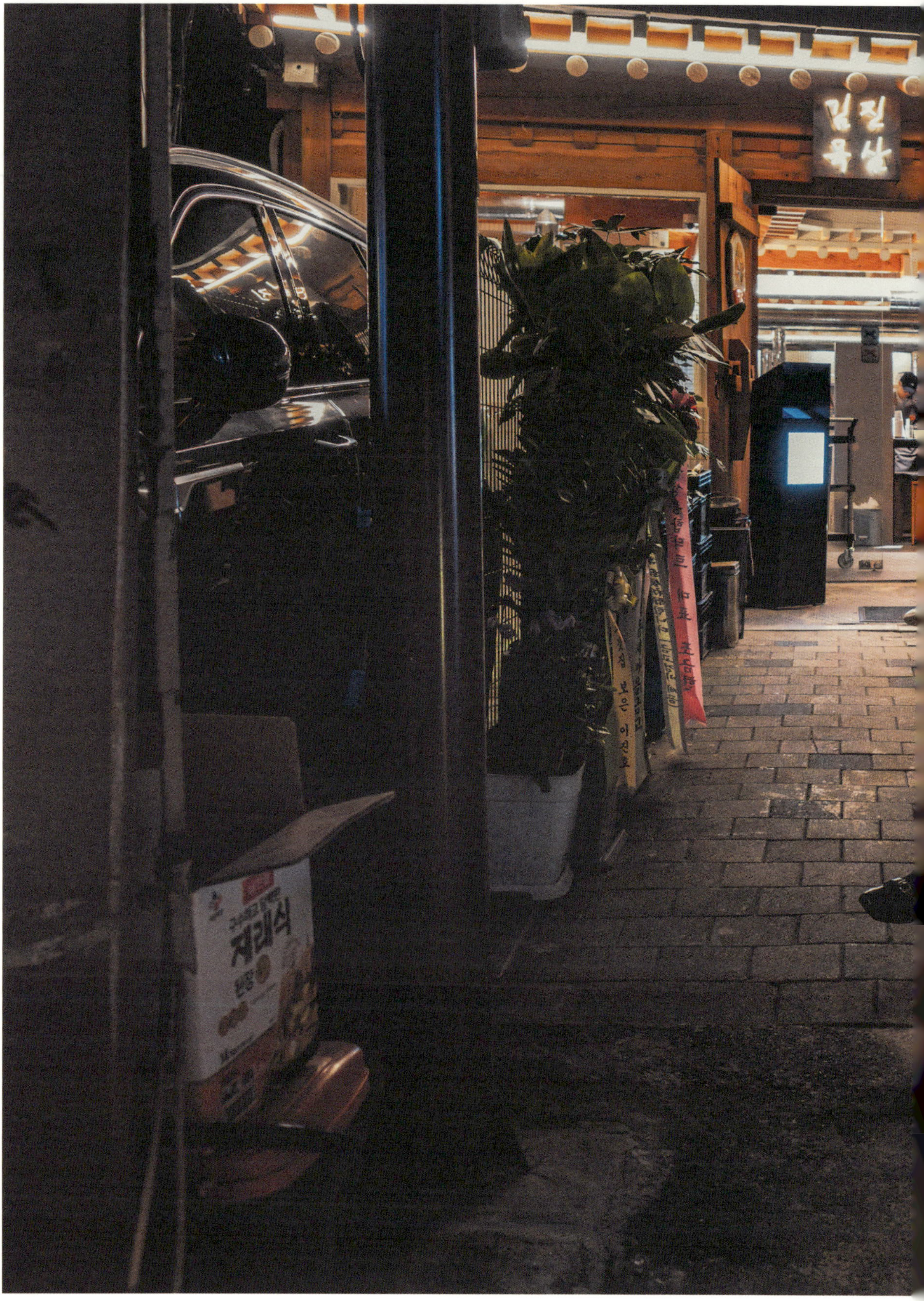

Seochon, Jongno District

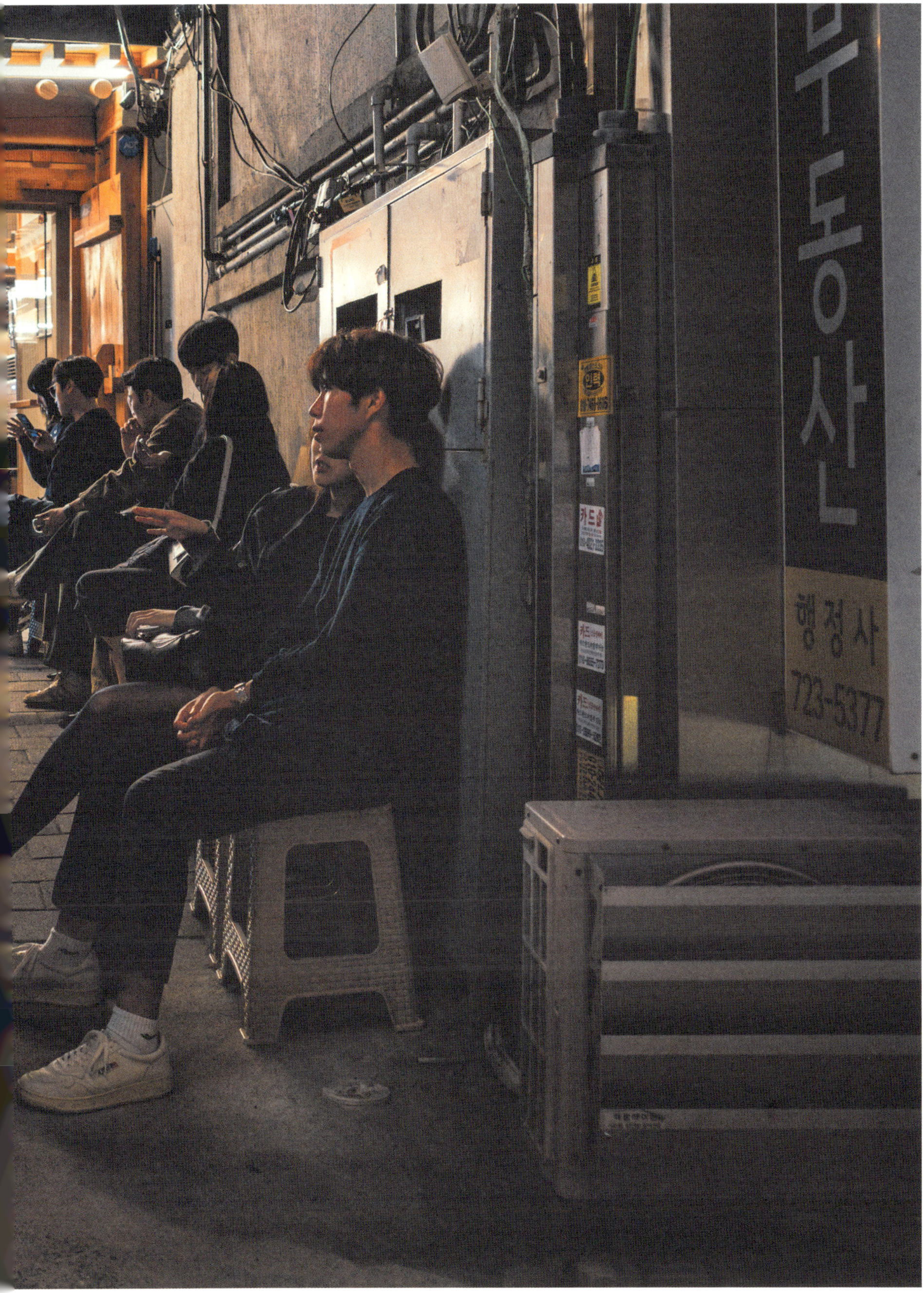
행정사
723-5377

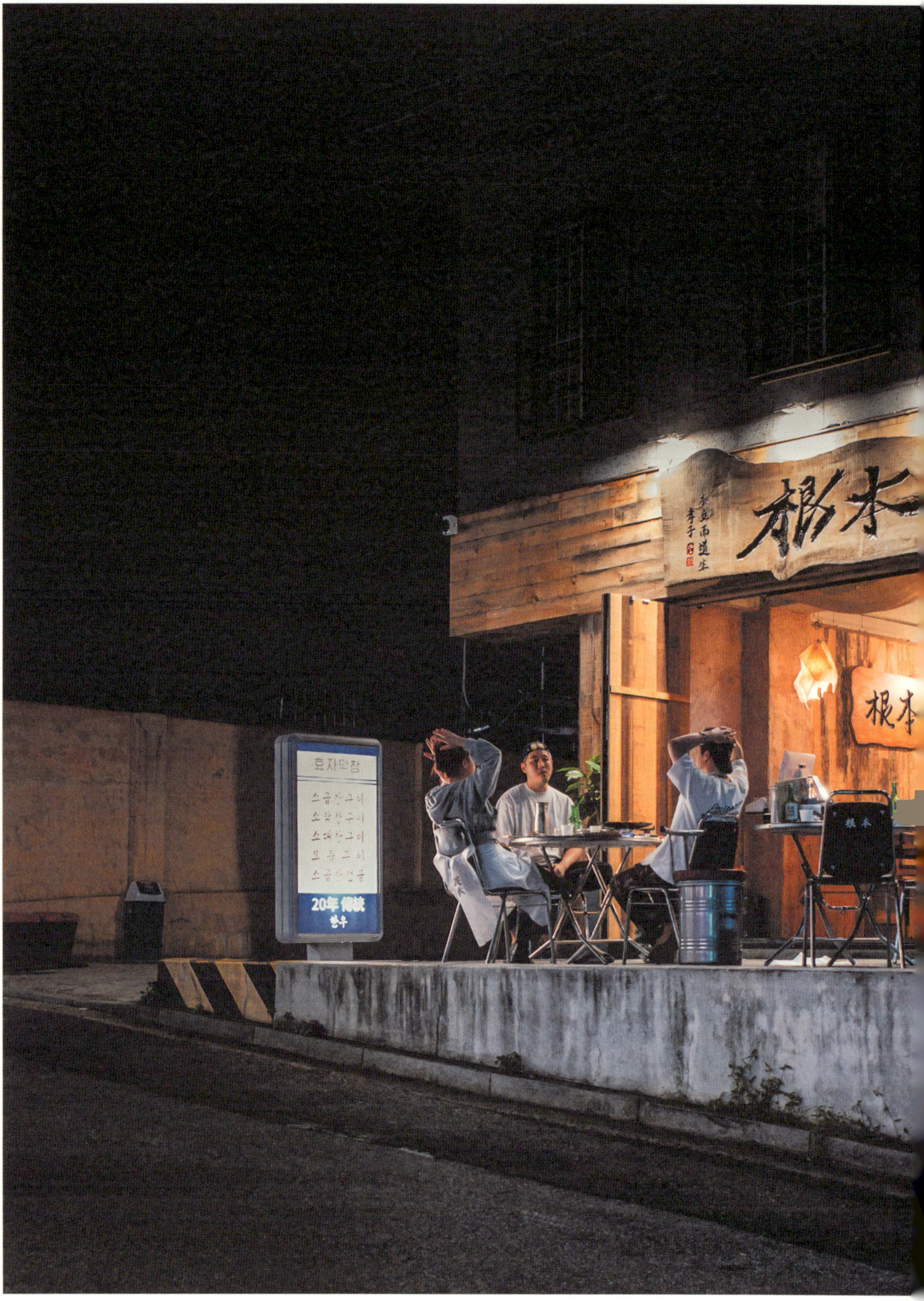


Mangwon-dong, Mapo District

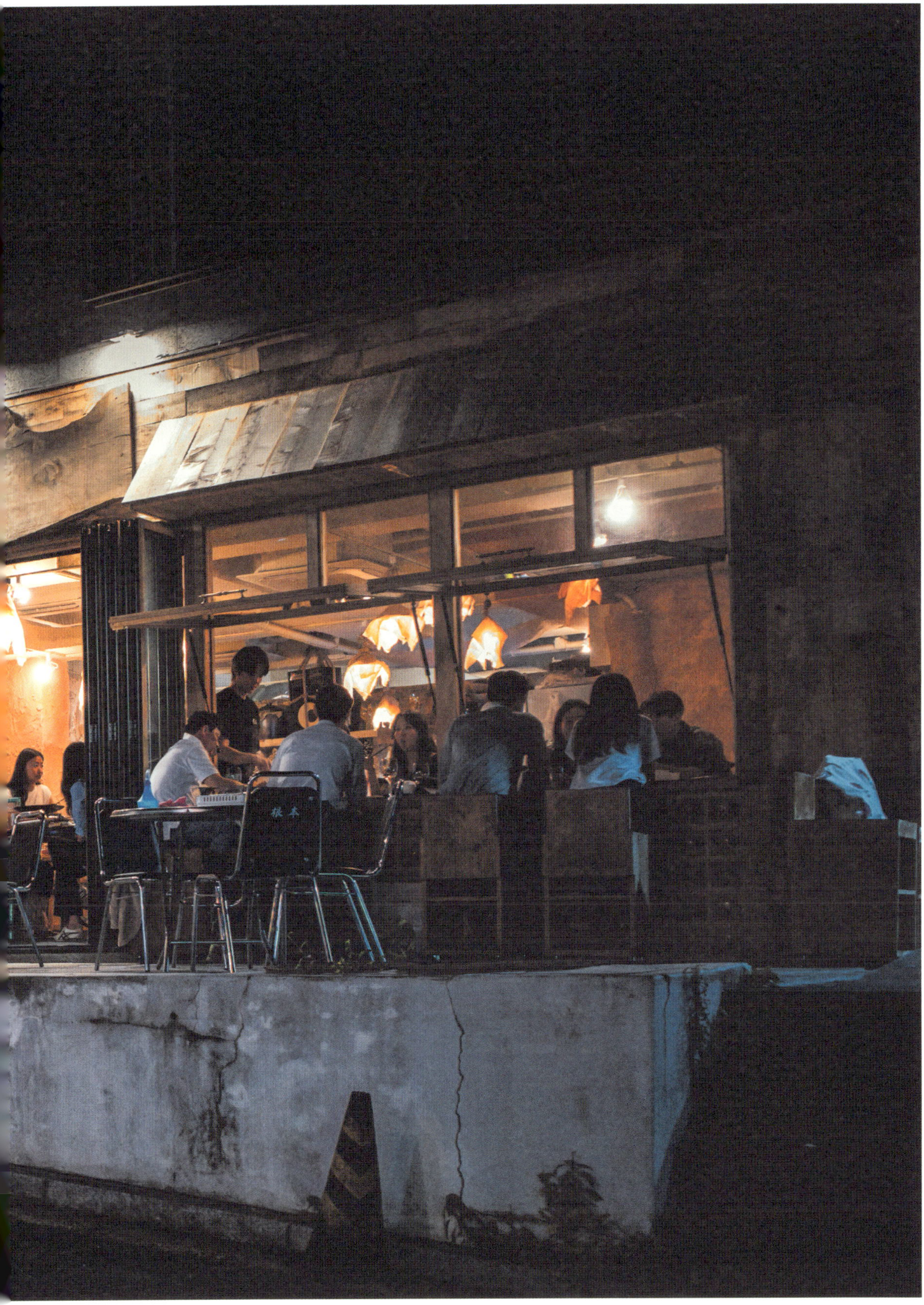

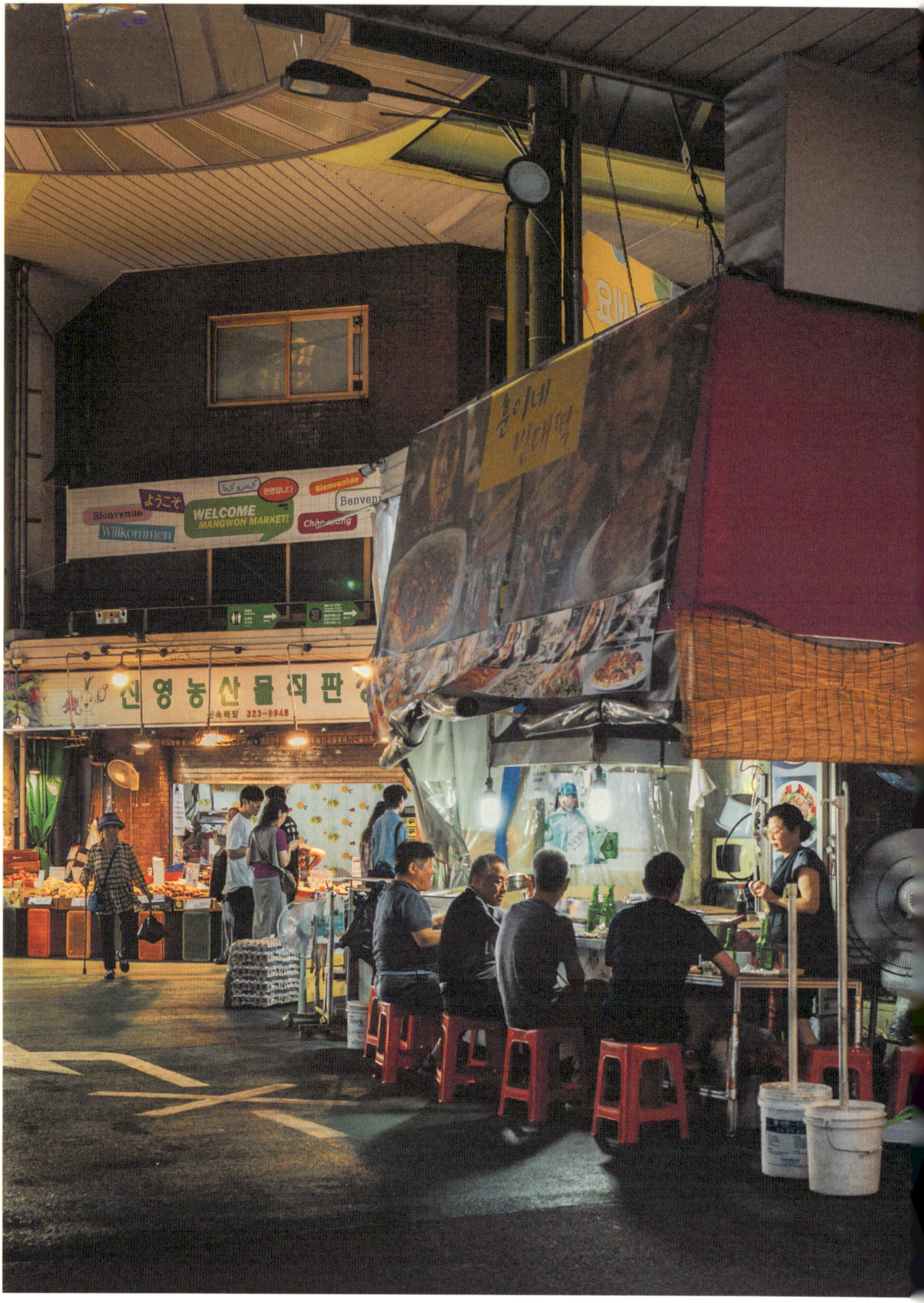


Mangwon Market, Mangwon-dong, Mapo District

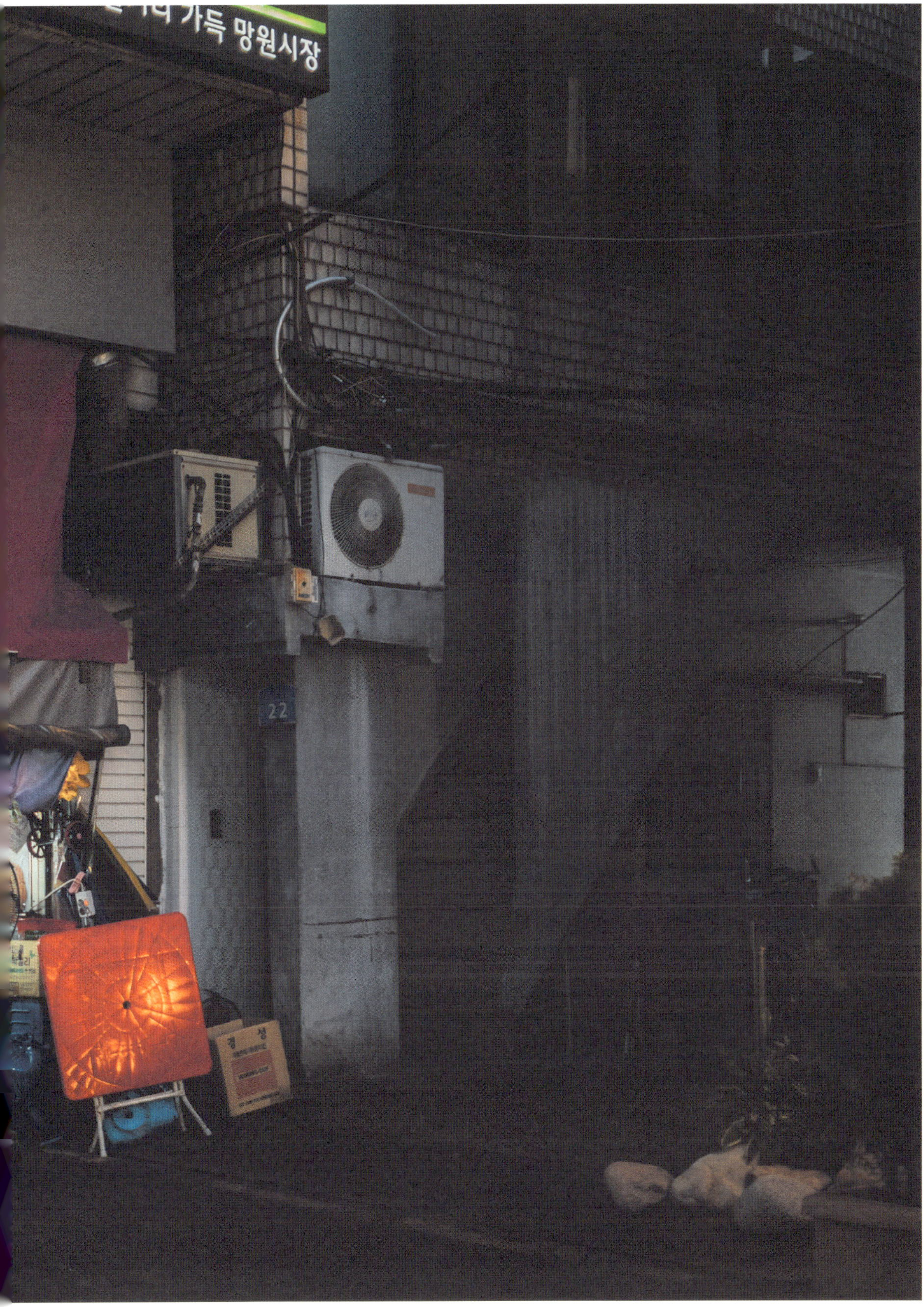
가득 망원시장
22

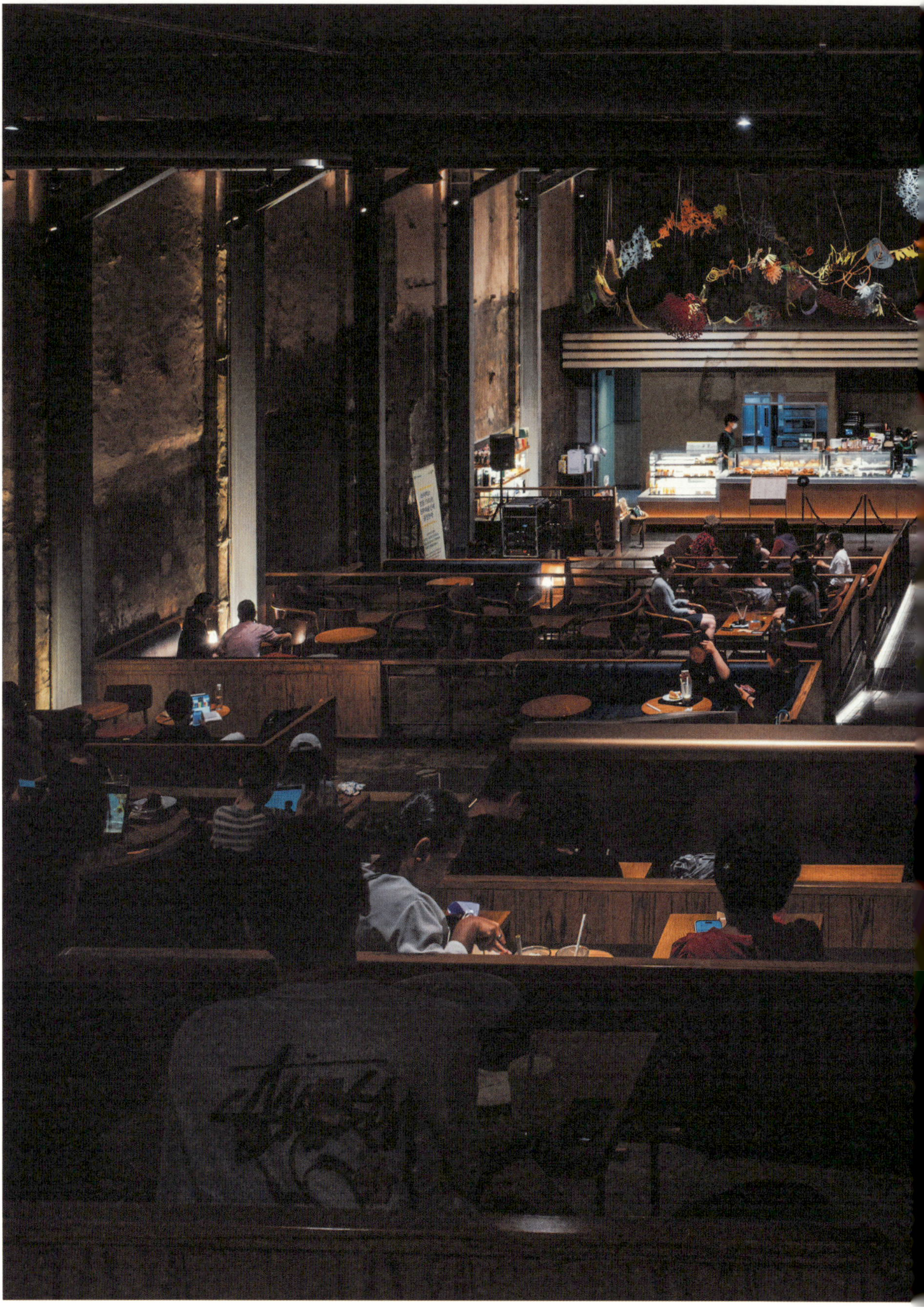

Gyeongdong Market, Jegi-dong, Dongdaemun District

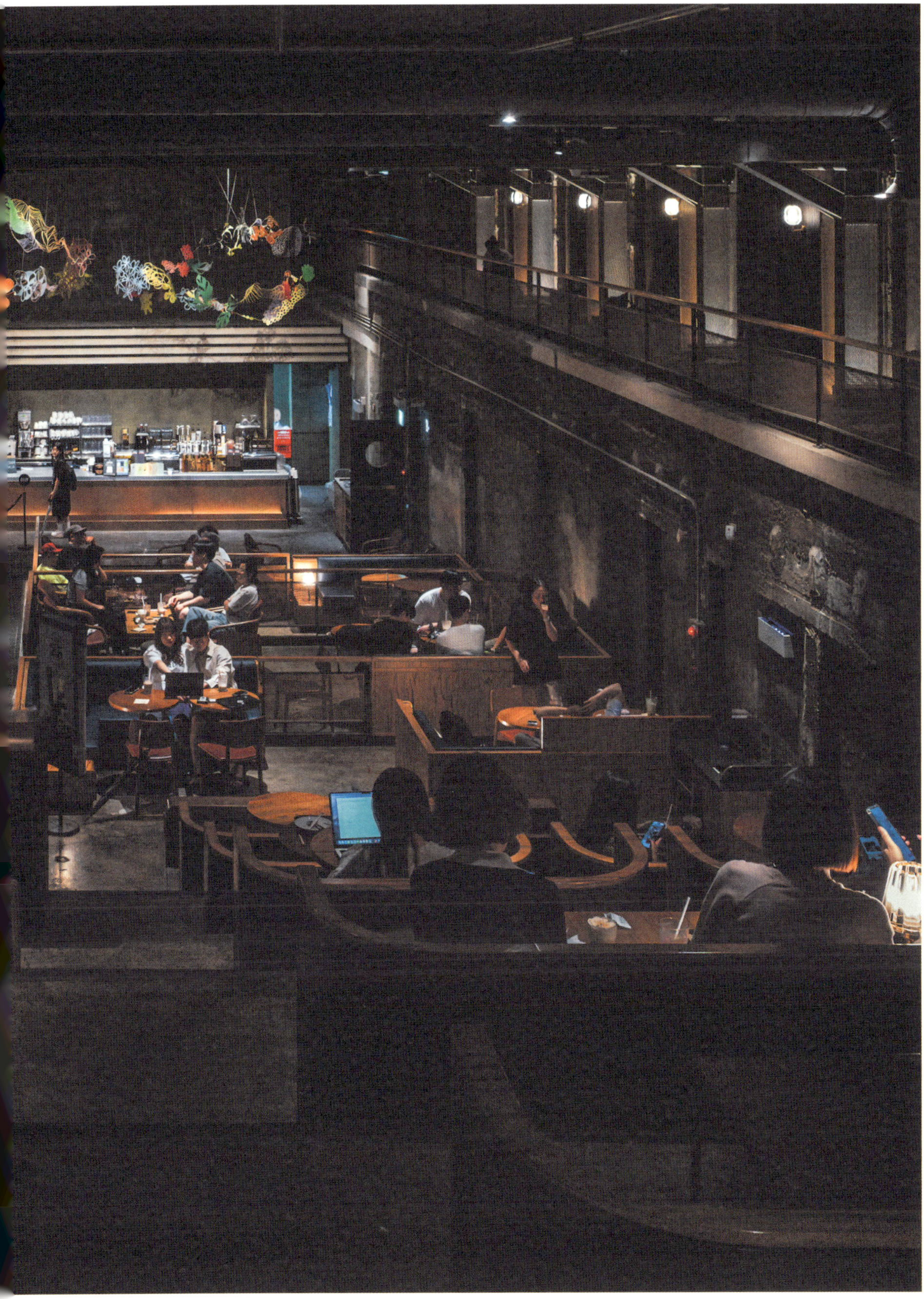

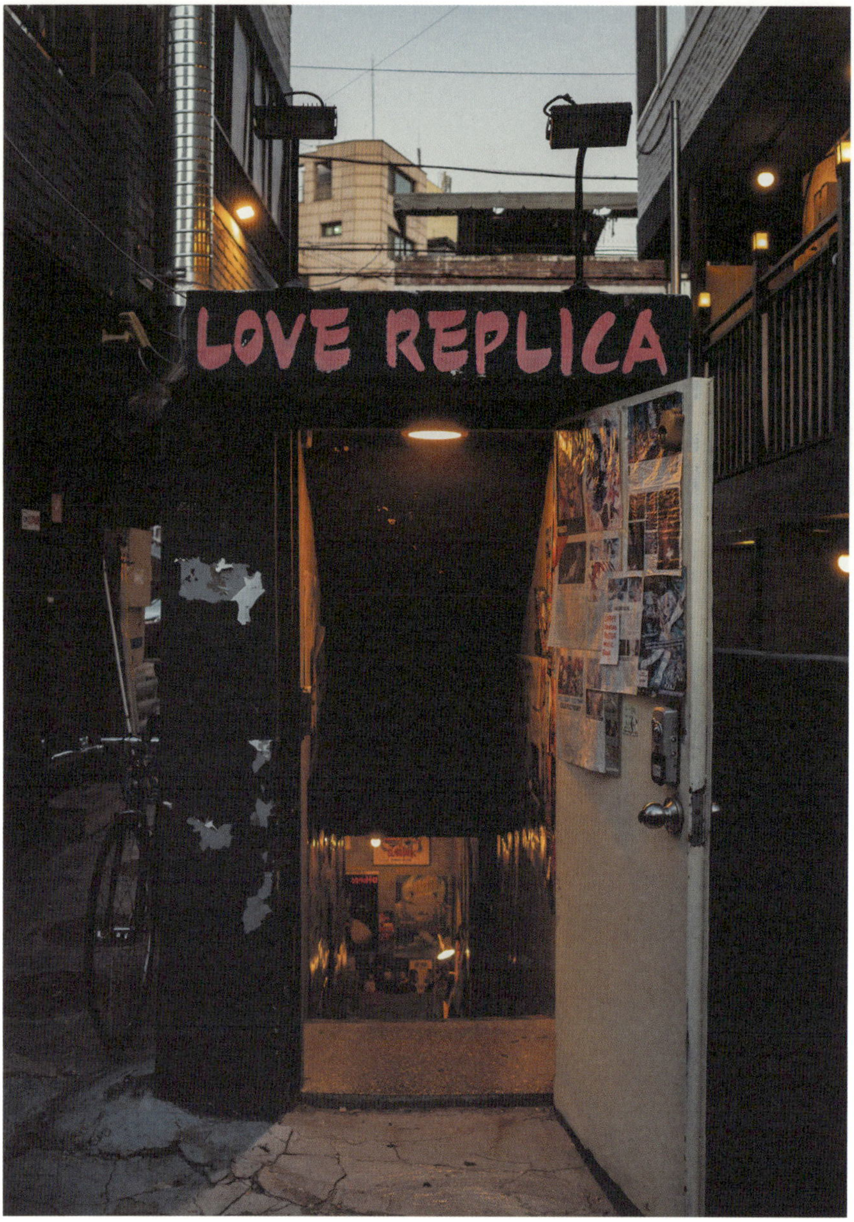


left: Mangwon-dong, Mapo District

right: Itaewon, Yongsan District

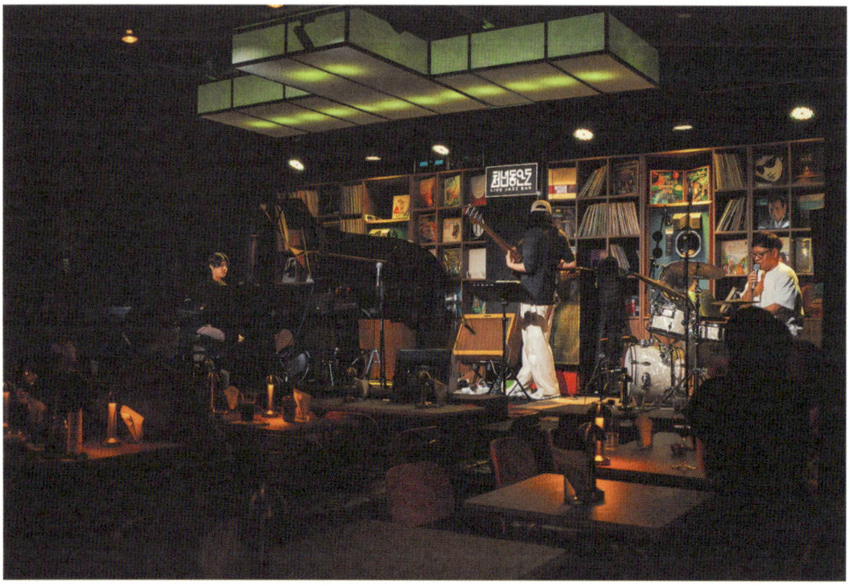

left: Itaewon, Yongsan District

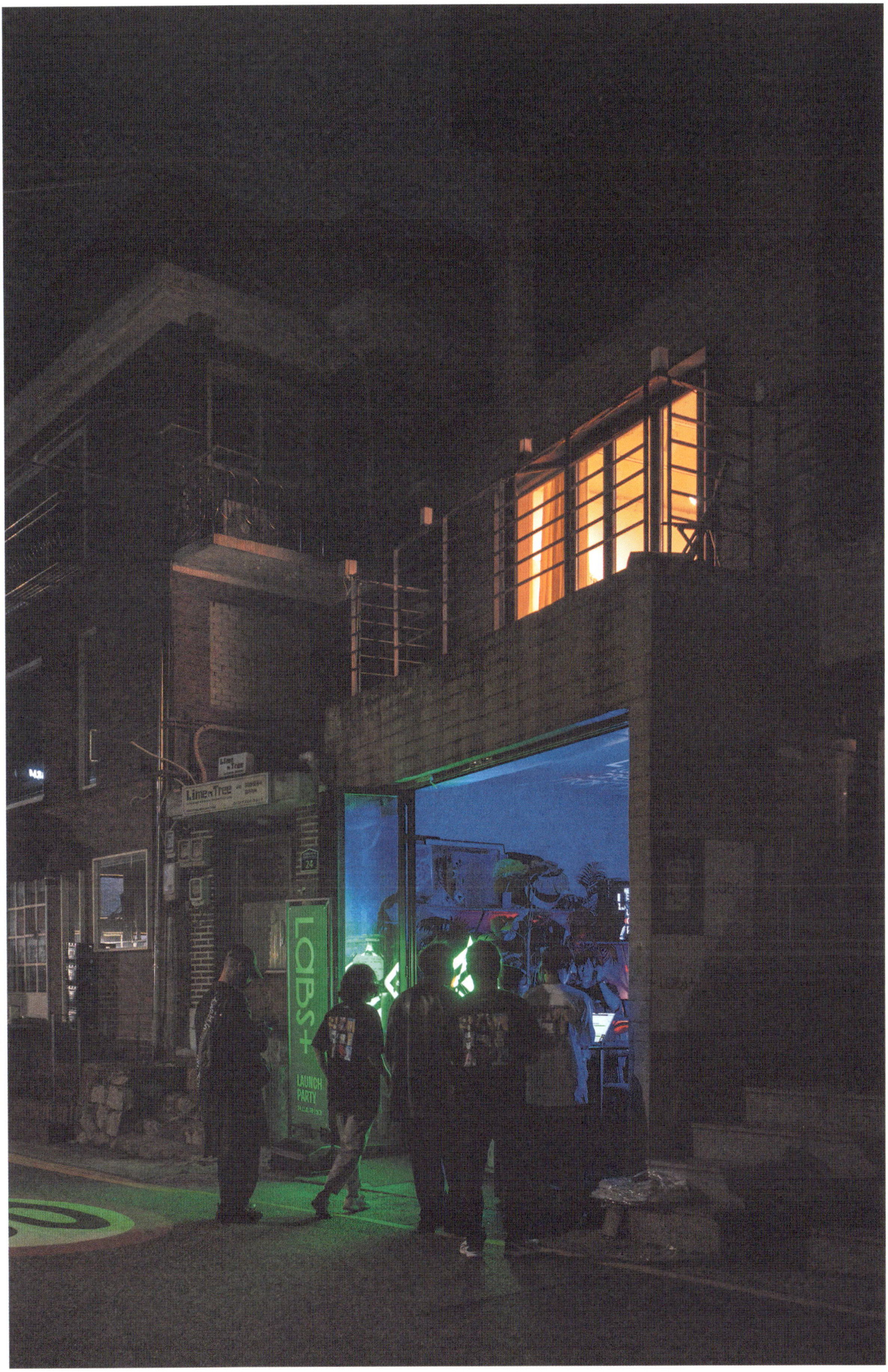
Lime Tree
24
LABS+
LAUNCH
PARTY

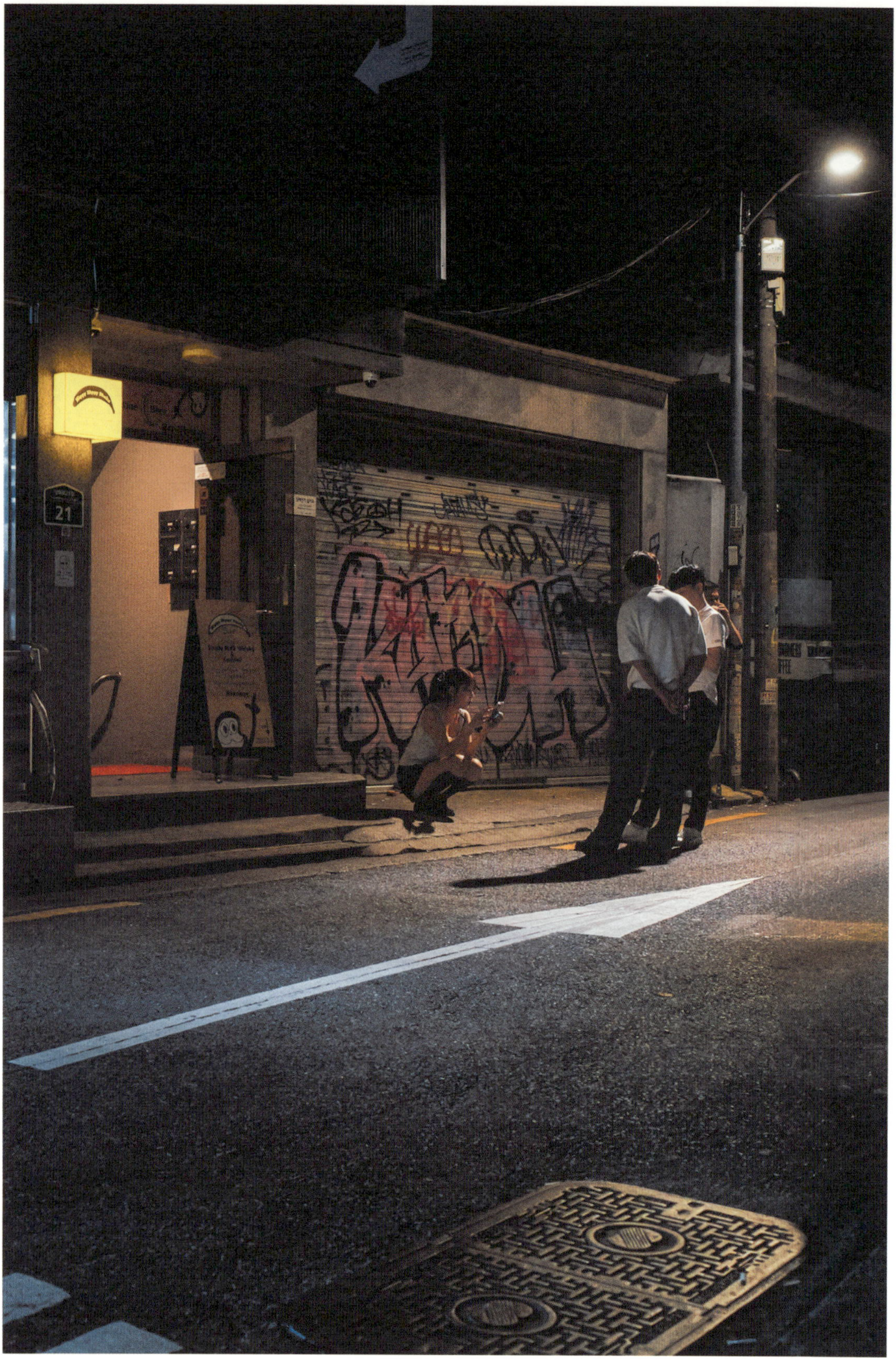

Hongdae, Mapo District

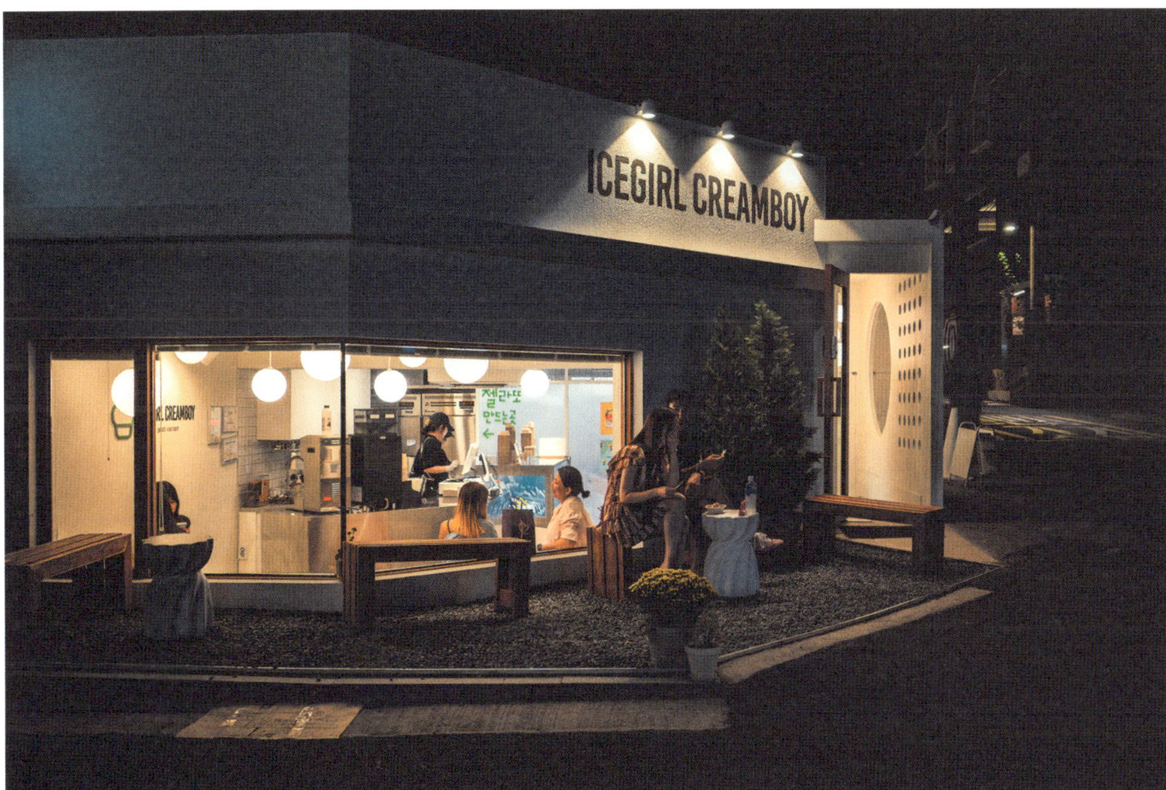


Yongnidan-gil, Yongsan District

# ABOVE SEOUL

하늘

From above, Seoul reveals its structure and scale, a city built within a ring of mountains and bisected by the Hangang River. Seoul is one of the world's most densely populated capitals, where modern towers rise beside compact neighborhoods that trace centuries of growth. At its center, Lotte World Tower reaches 555 meters, the tallest building in Korea and the sixth tallest in the world. It is a symbol of Seoul's ambition and ascent on the global stage. Nearby, Namsan Tower offers a view from Bukhansan in the north to Gwanaksan in the south, revealing how the city fits into its terrain. The mountains that surround Seoul create a natural boundary, giving the city its shape and influencing how it has developed over time.

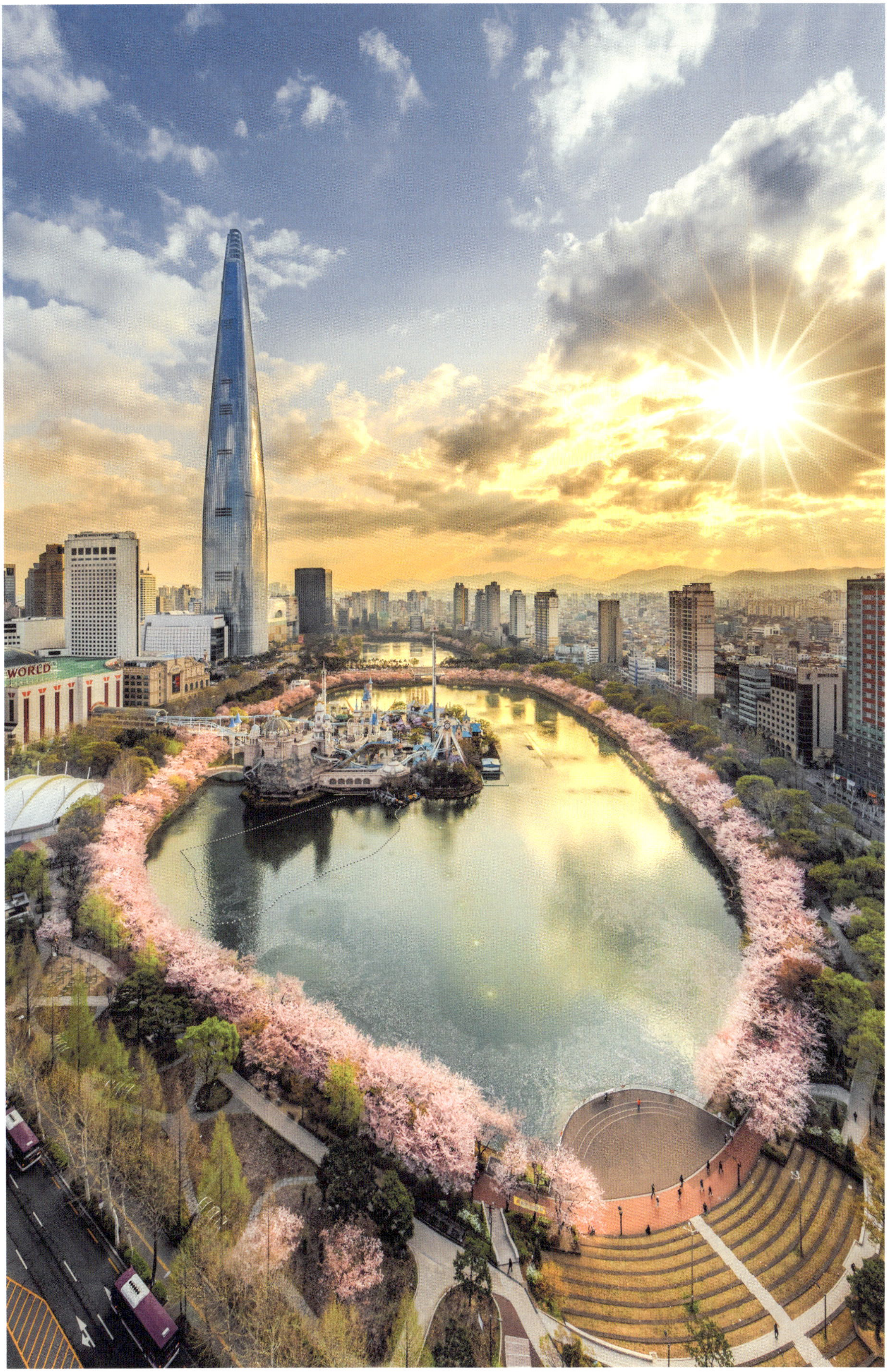
WORLD

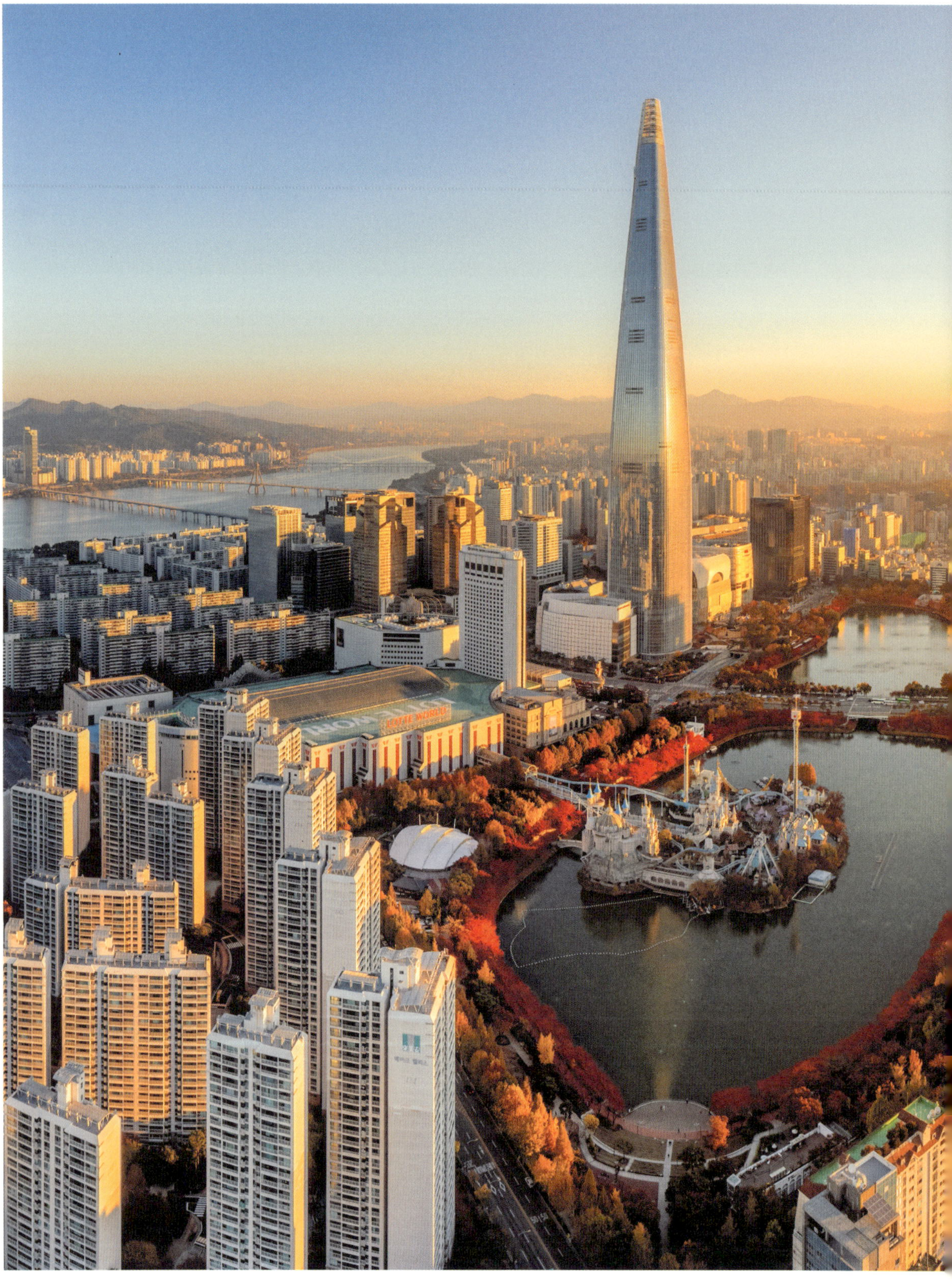

above + previous page: Lotte World Tower, Jamsil-dong, Songpa District

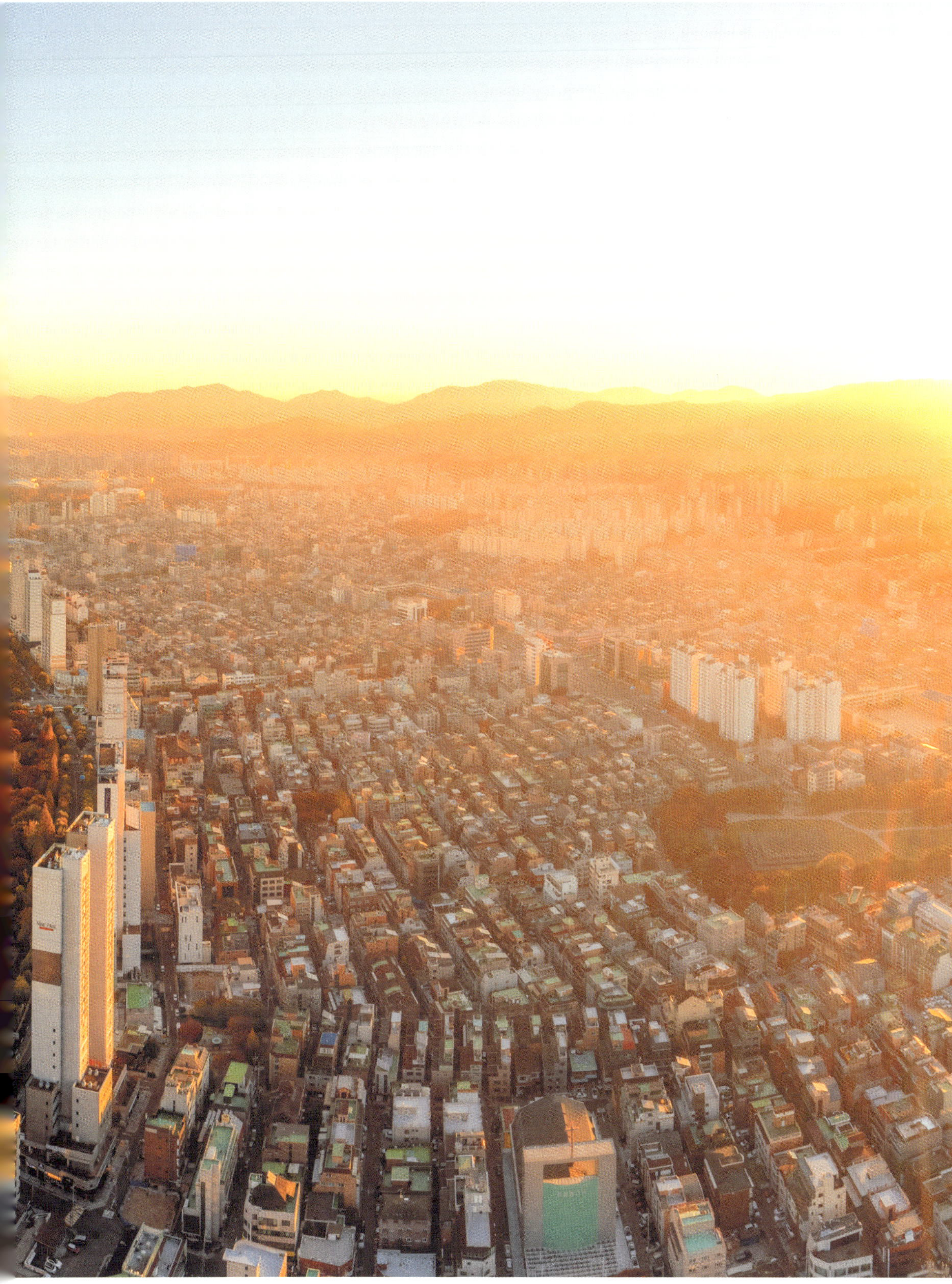

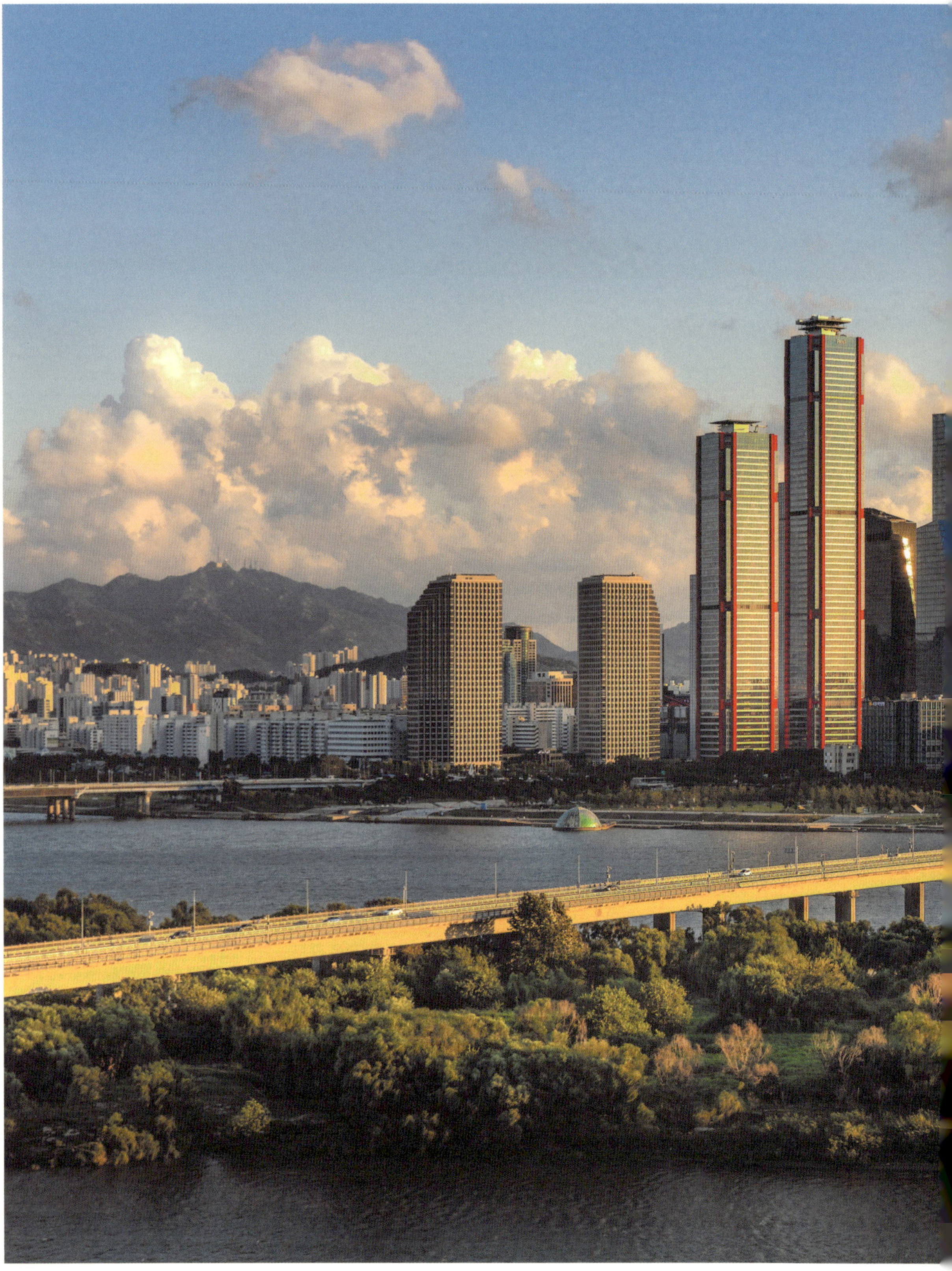

Seogang Bridge, Yeouido, Yeongdeungpo District

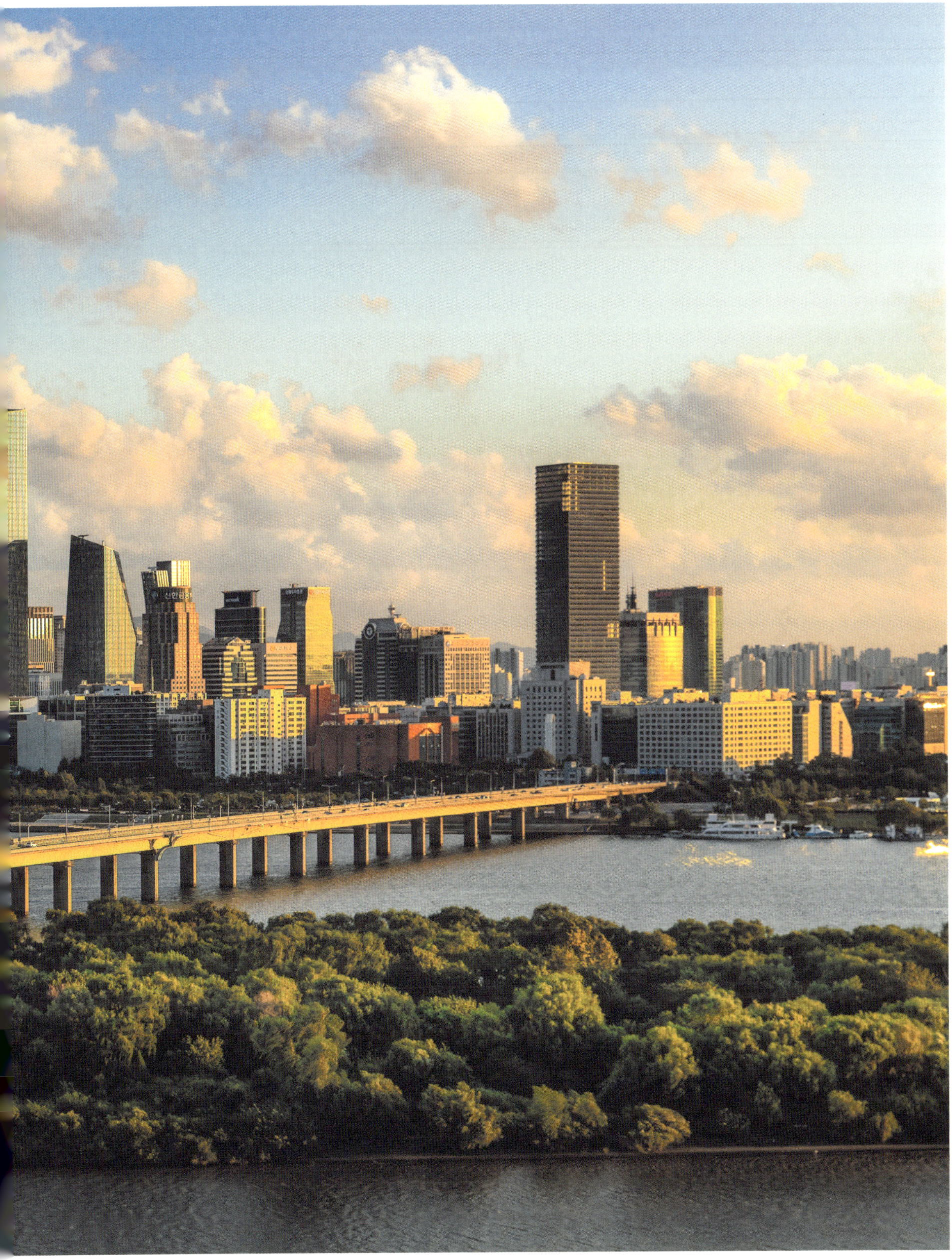

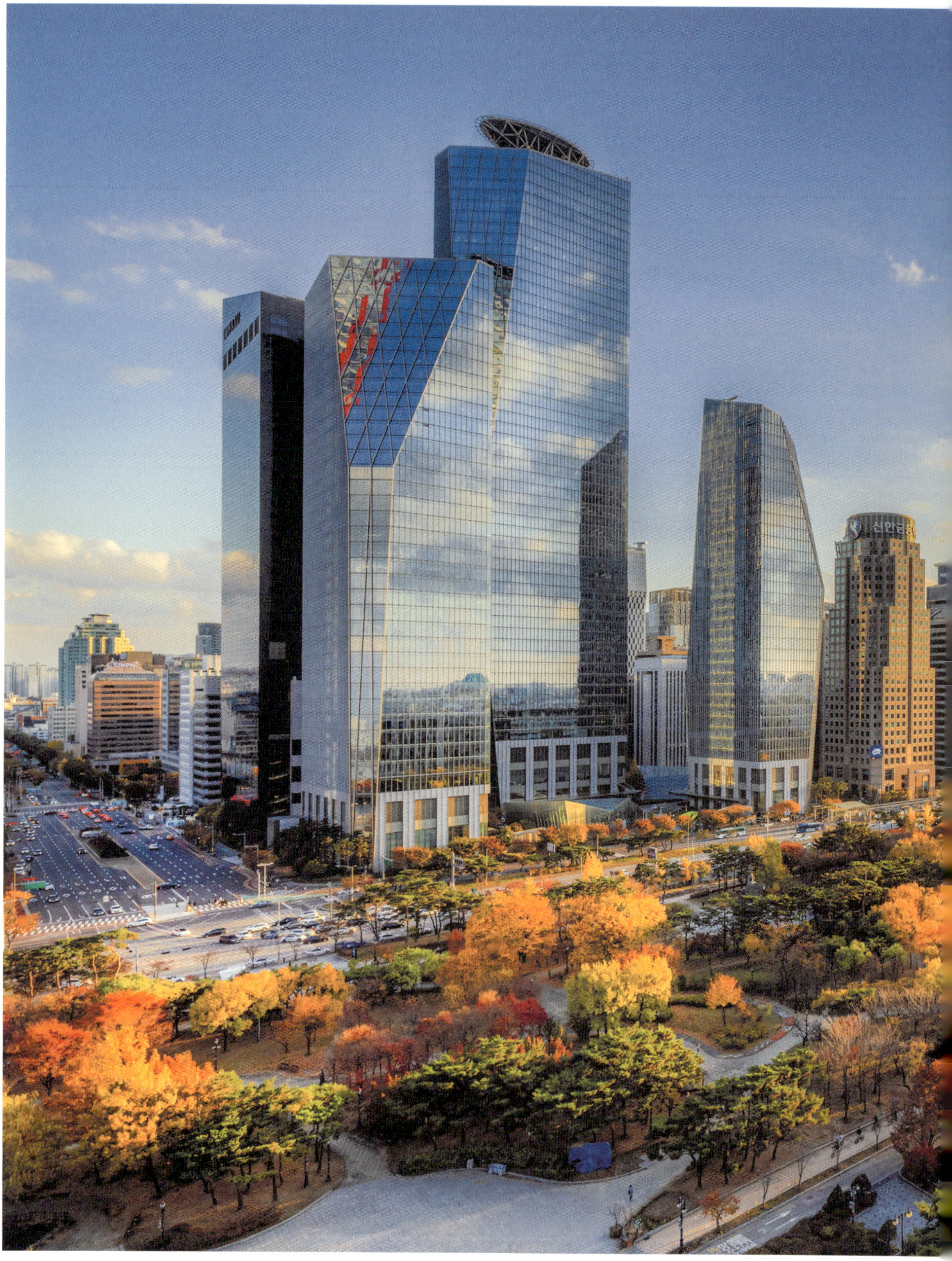


Yeouido Park, Yeouido, Yeongdeungpo District

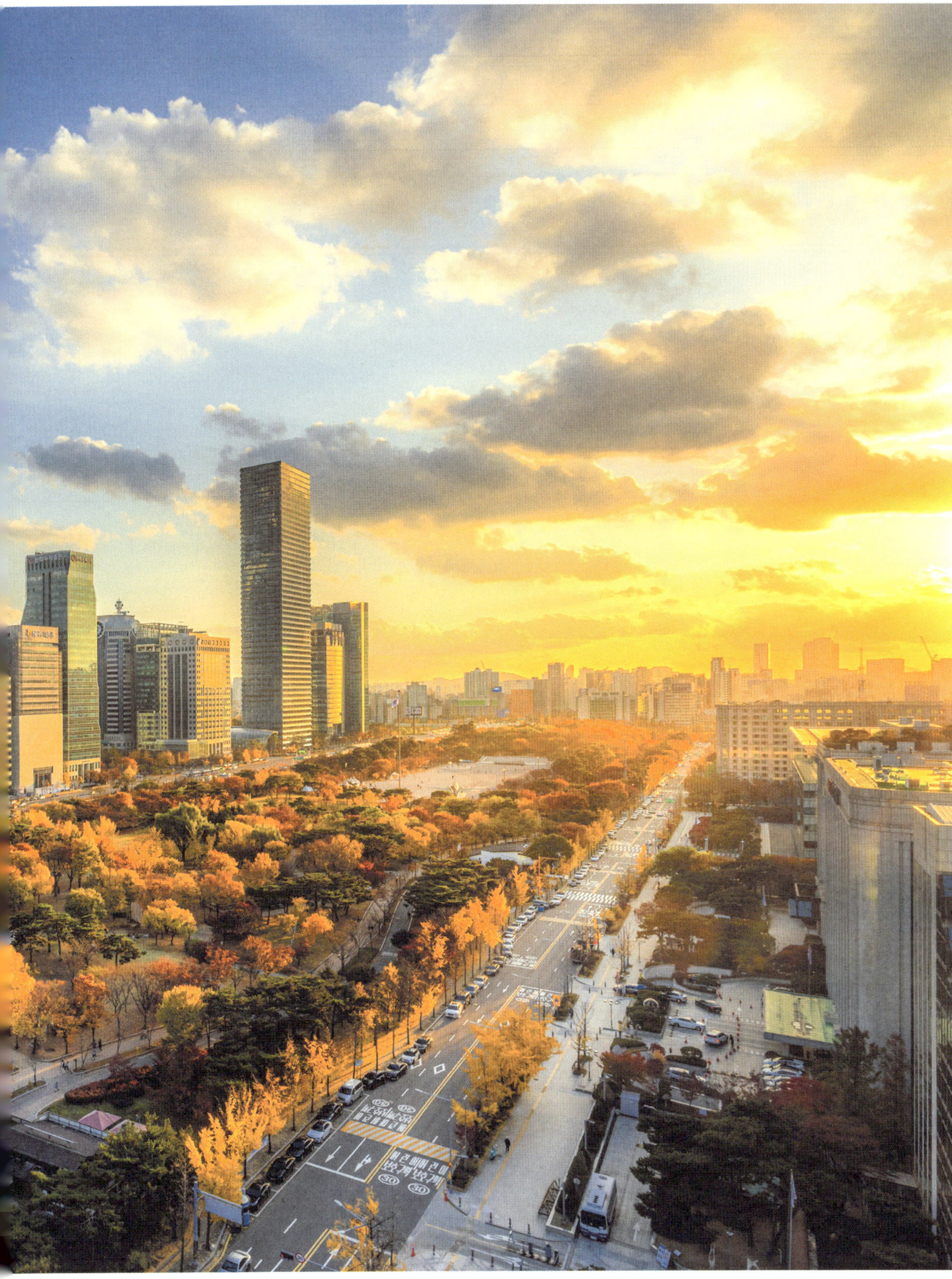

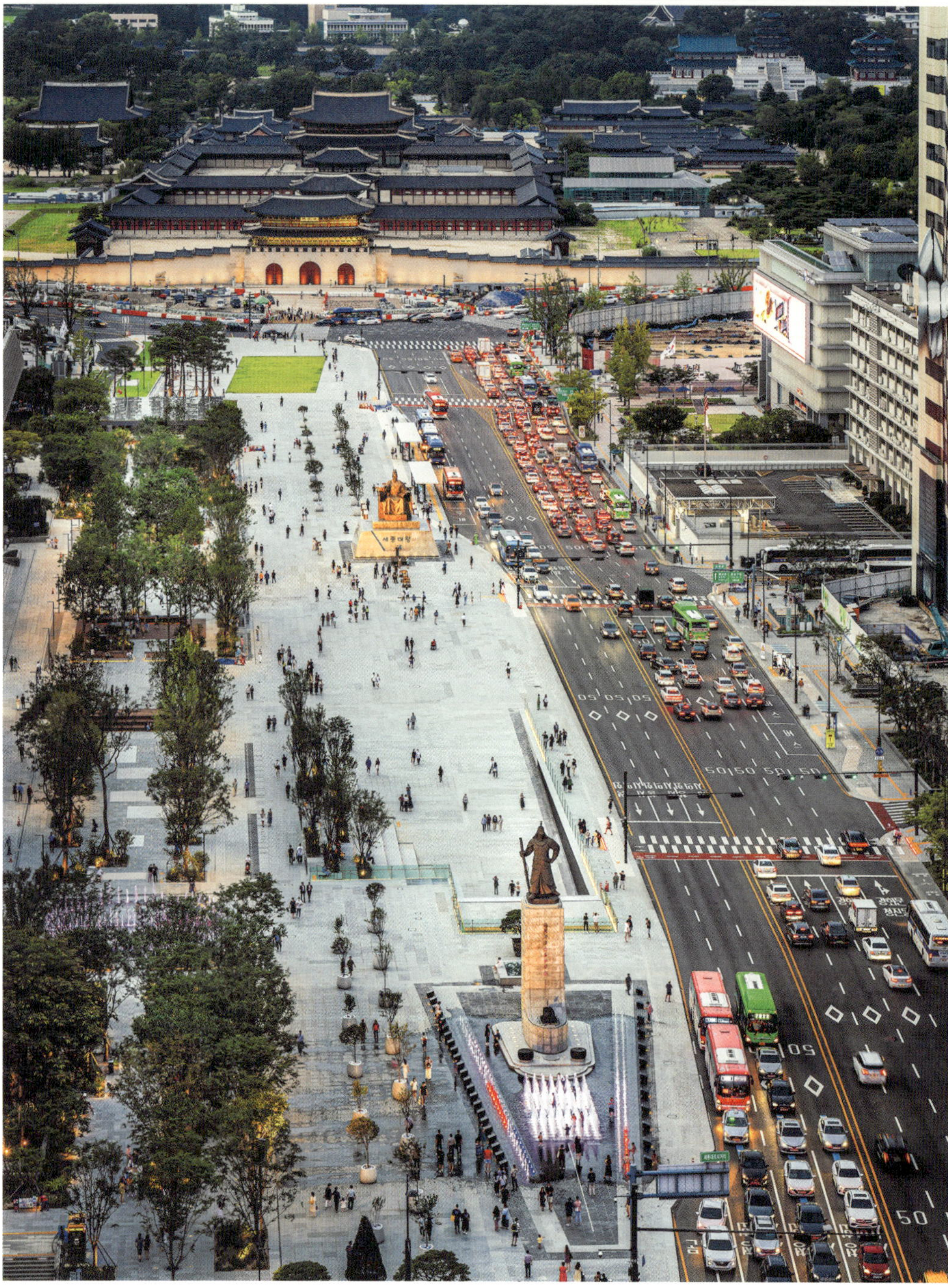

Gwanghwamun Square, Jongno District

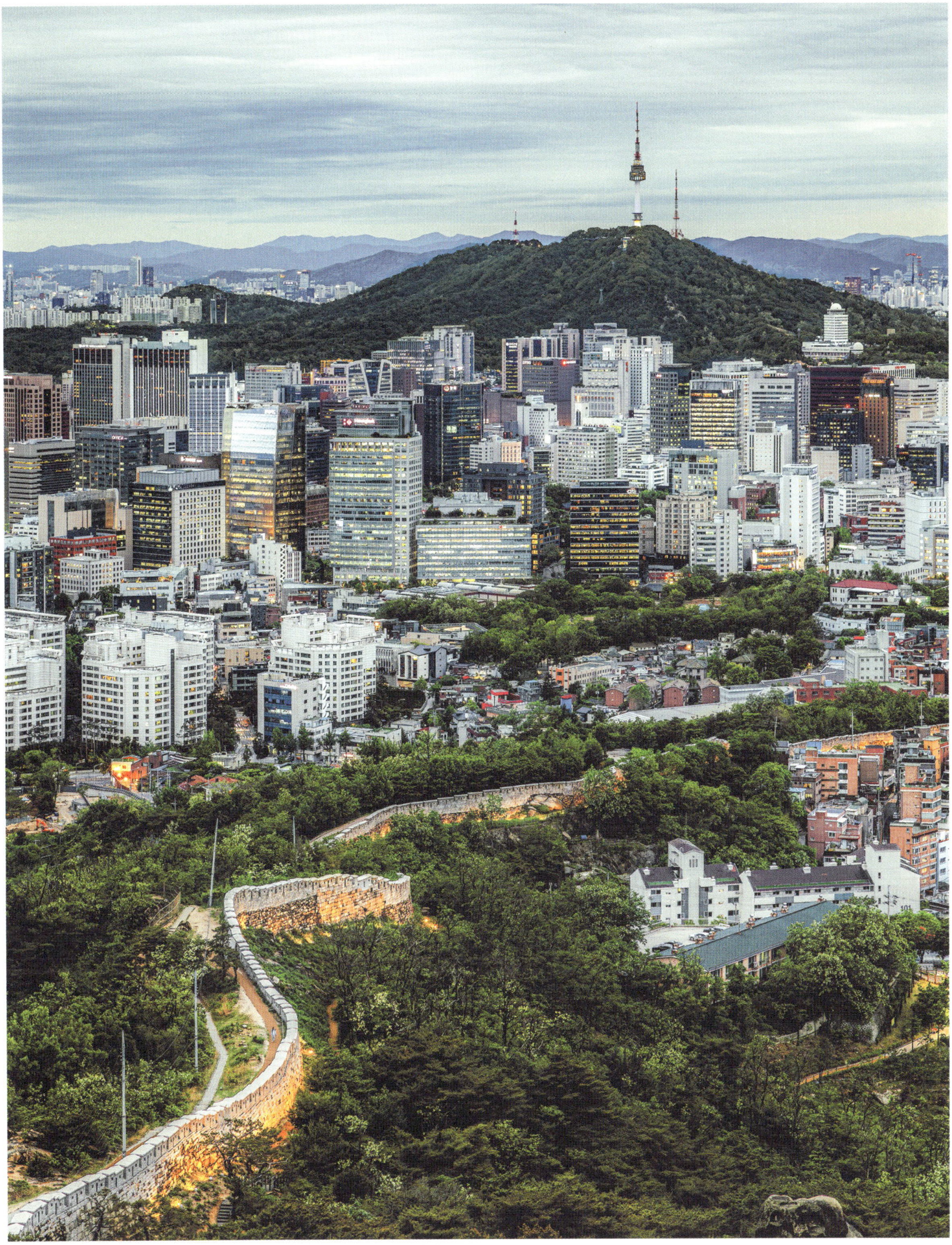

Seoul City Wall, Myeong-dong, Jung District

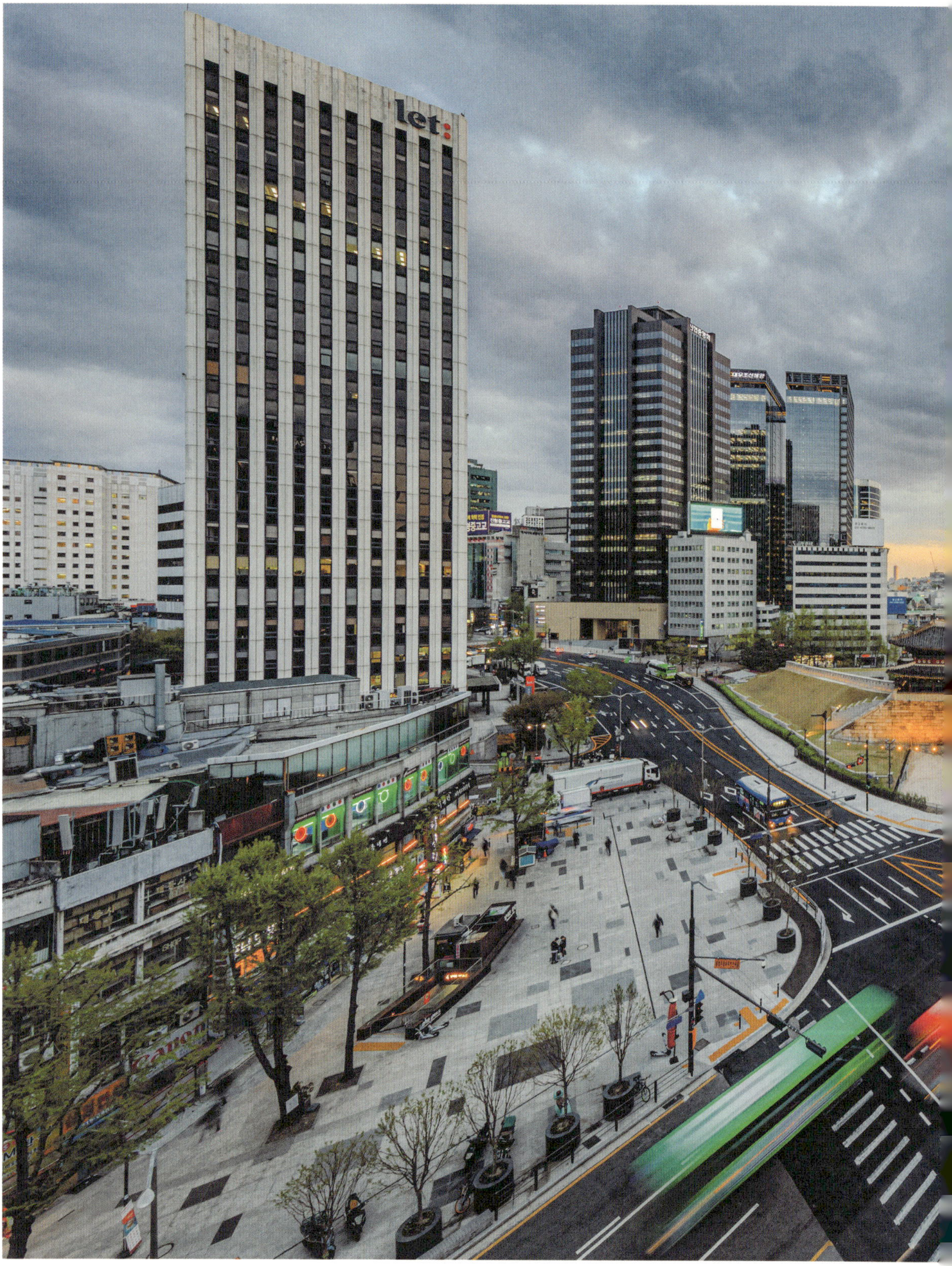


Namdaemun South Great Gate, Jung District > One of the eight gates of the old fortress wall of Seoul, built in the Joseon Dynast

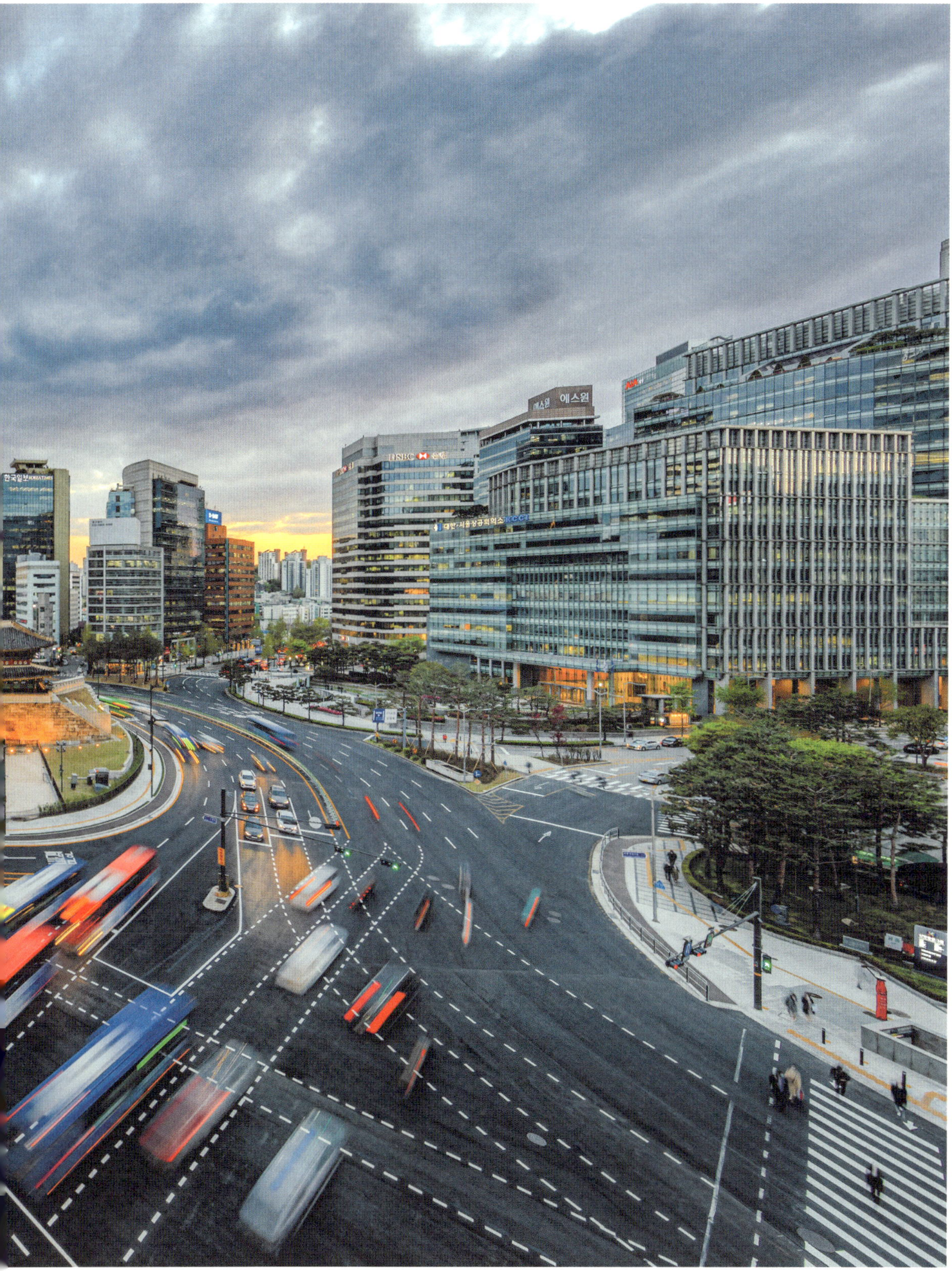
에스원

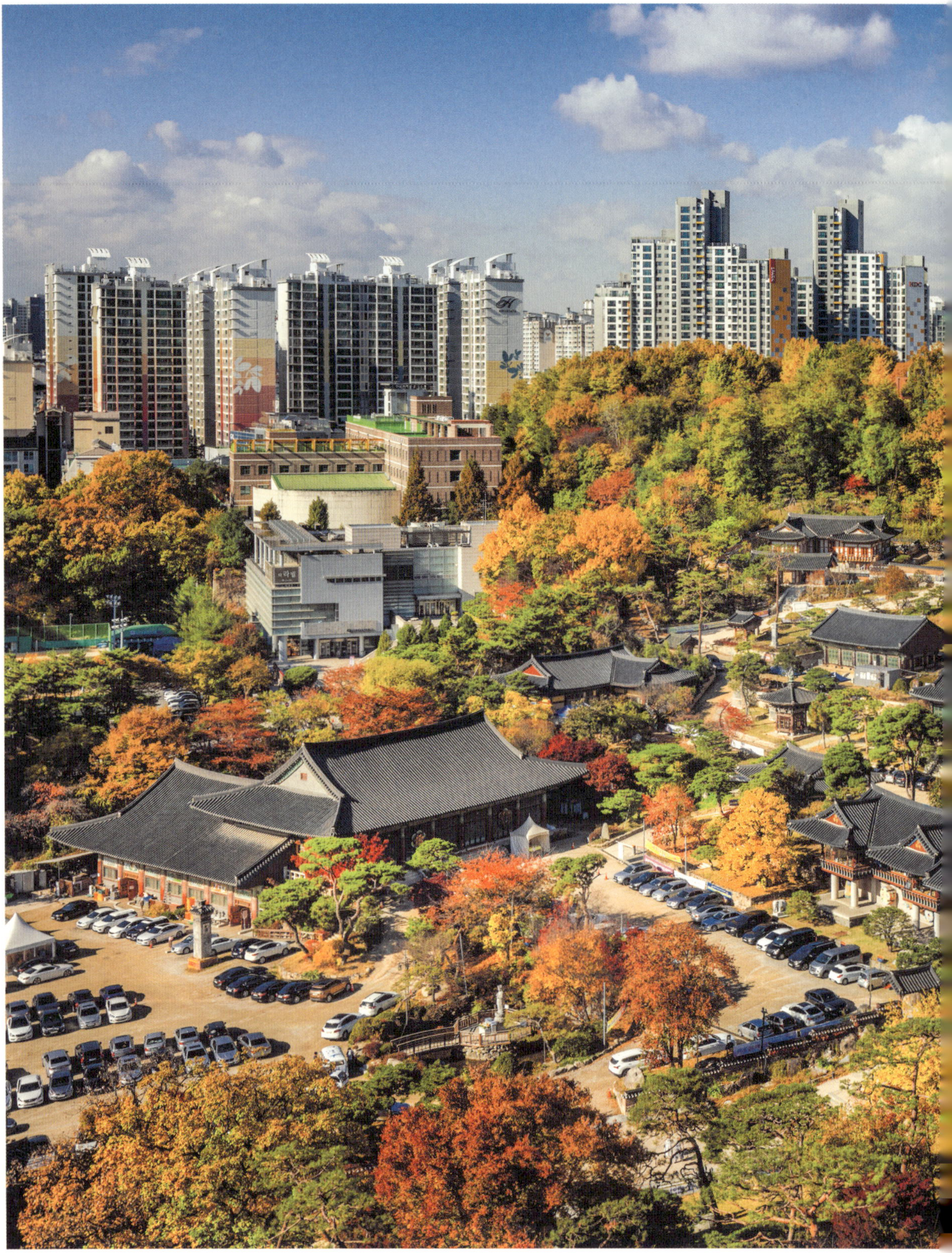

Bongeunsa Temple, Samseong-dong, Gangnam District > Historic Buddhist temple built in the year 794

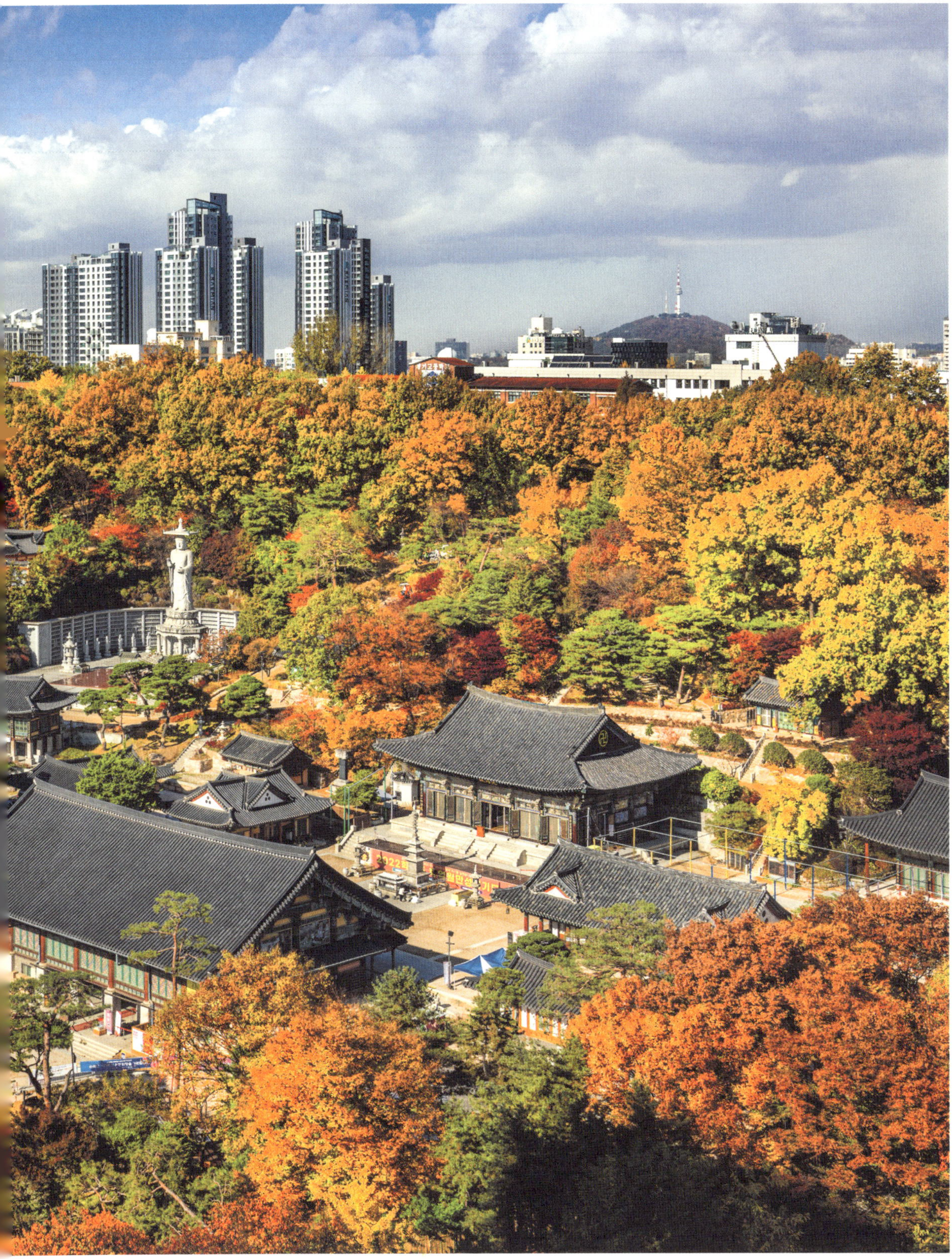

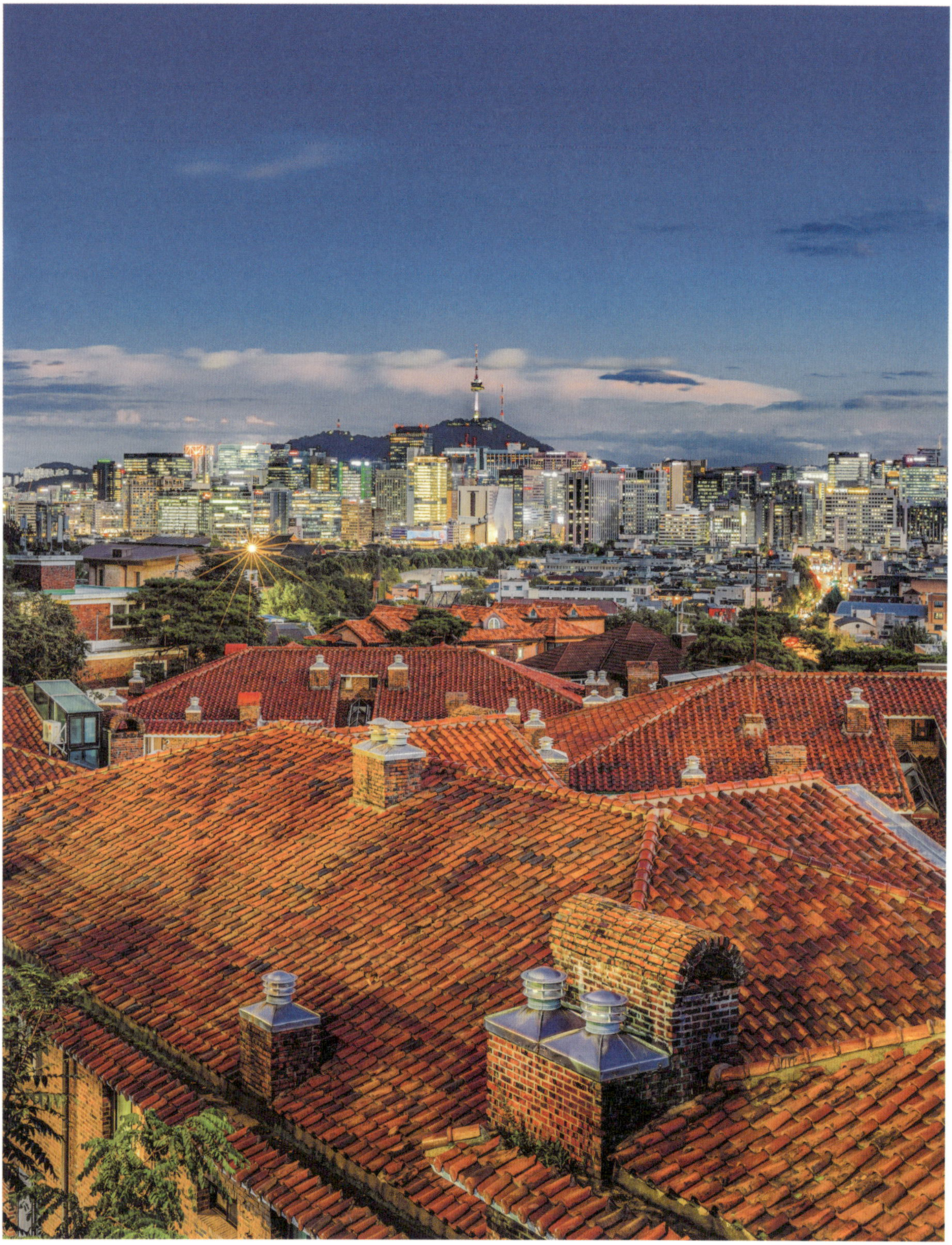

Seochon, Jongno District

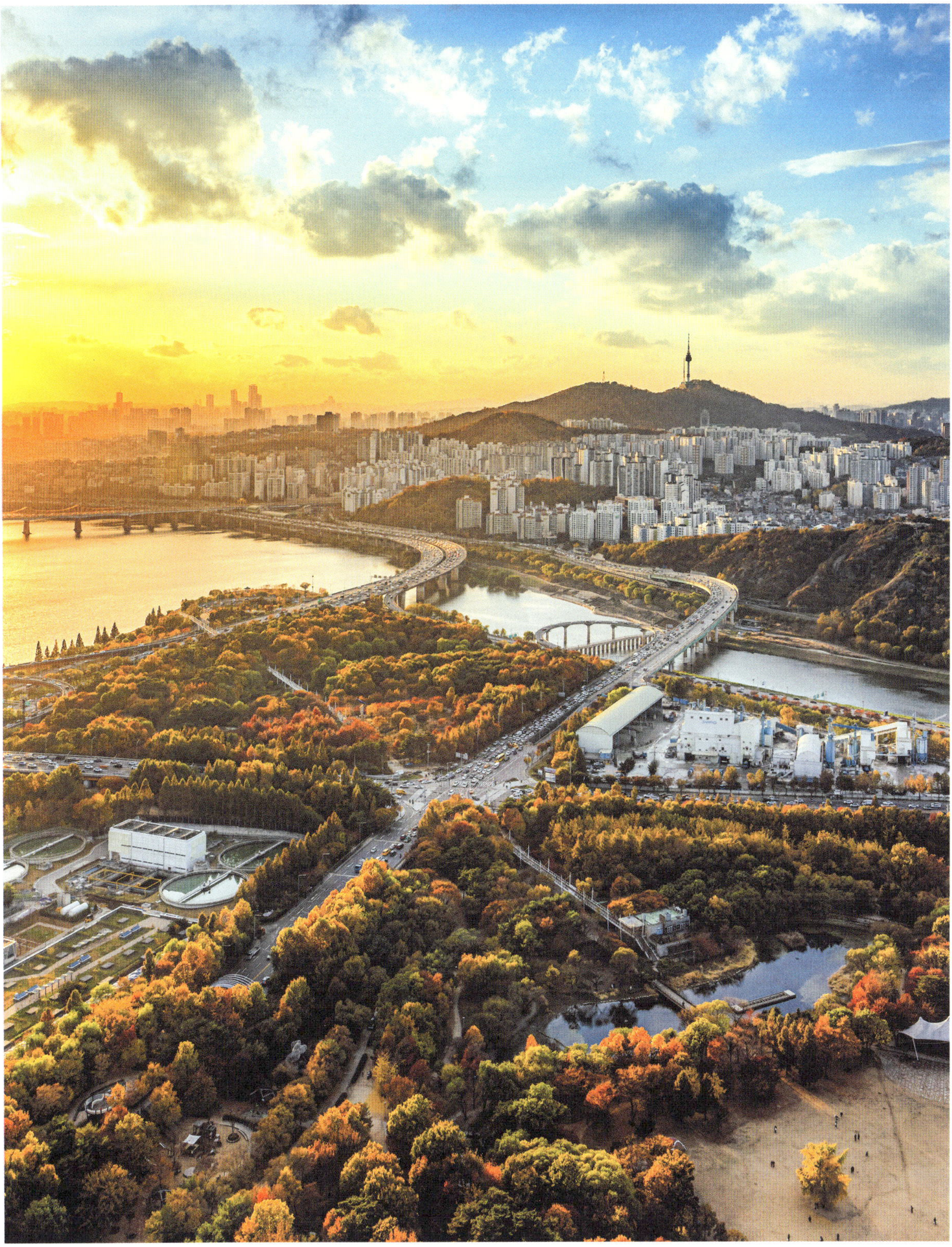

Seoul Forest Park, Seongsu-dong, Seongdong District

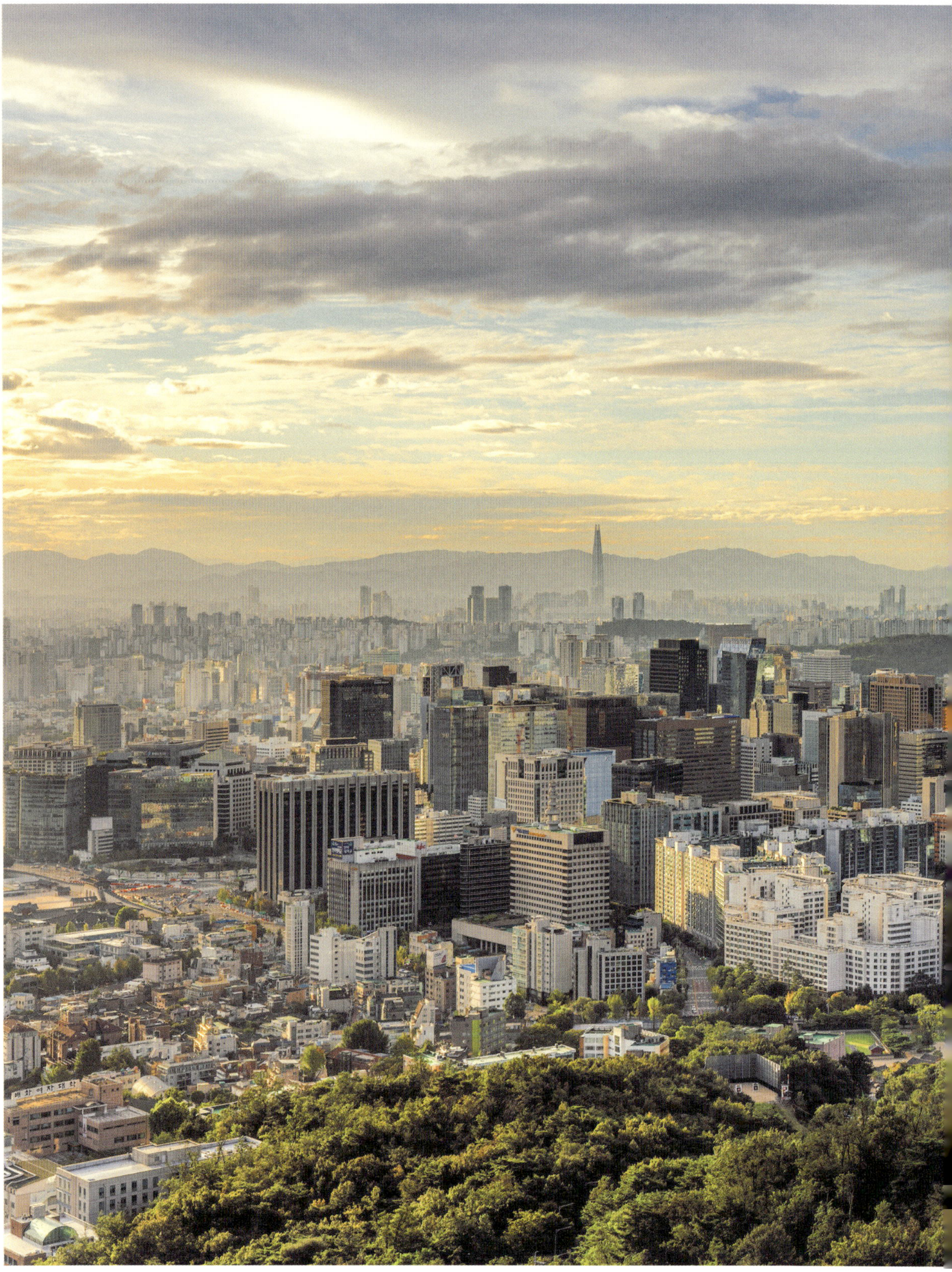

Jongno District > Seoul City Wall: Significant sections of the fortress wall built during the Joseon Dynasty still remain in Seoul

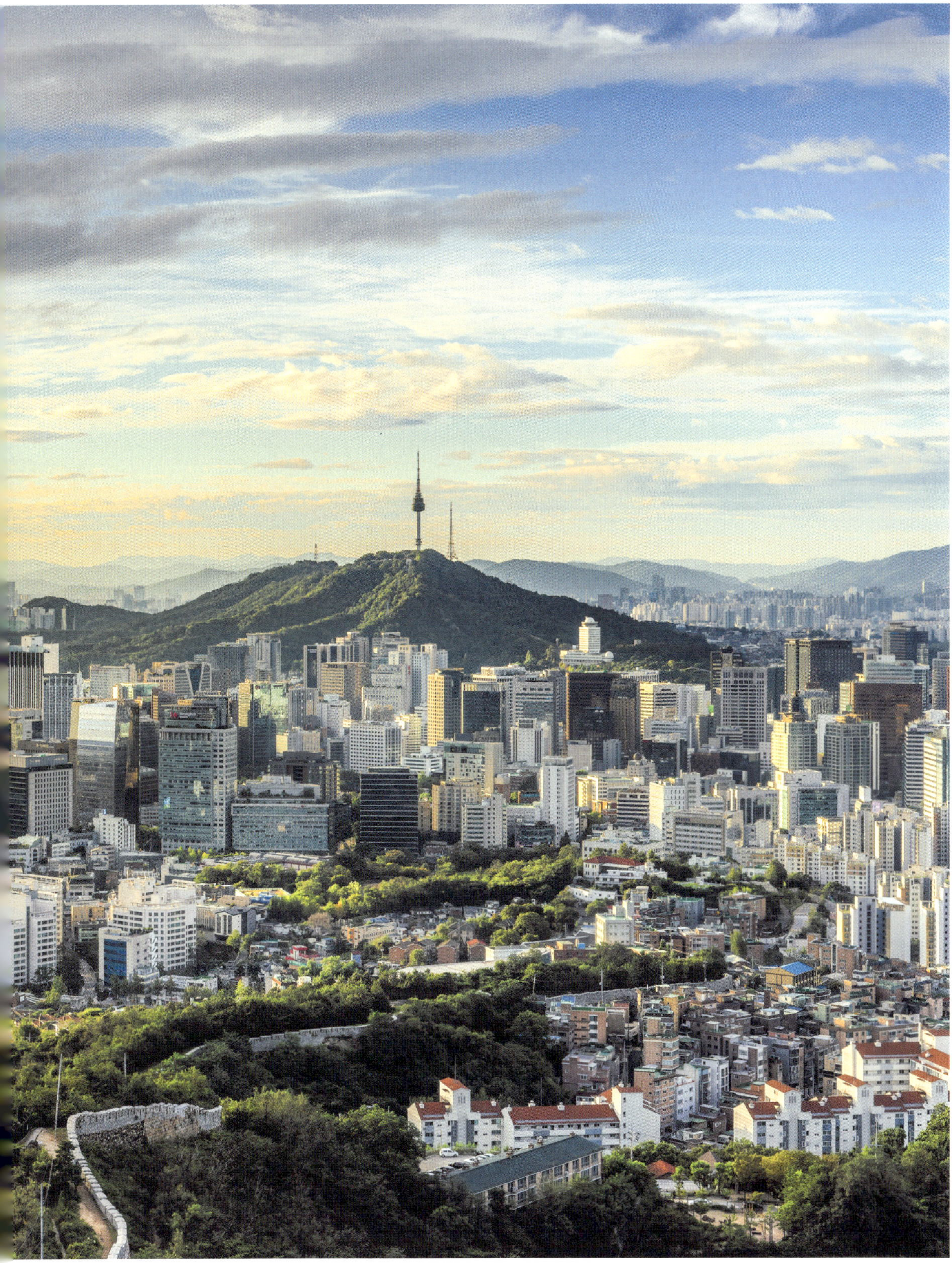

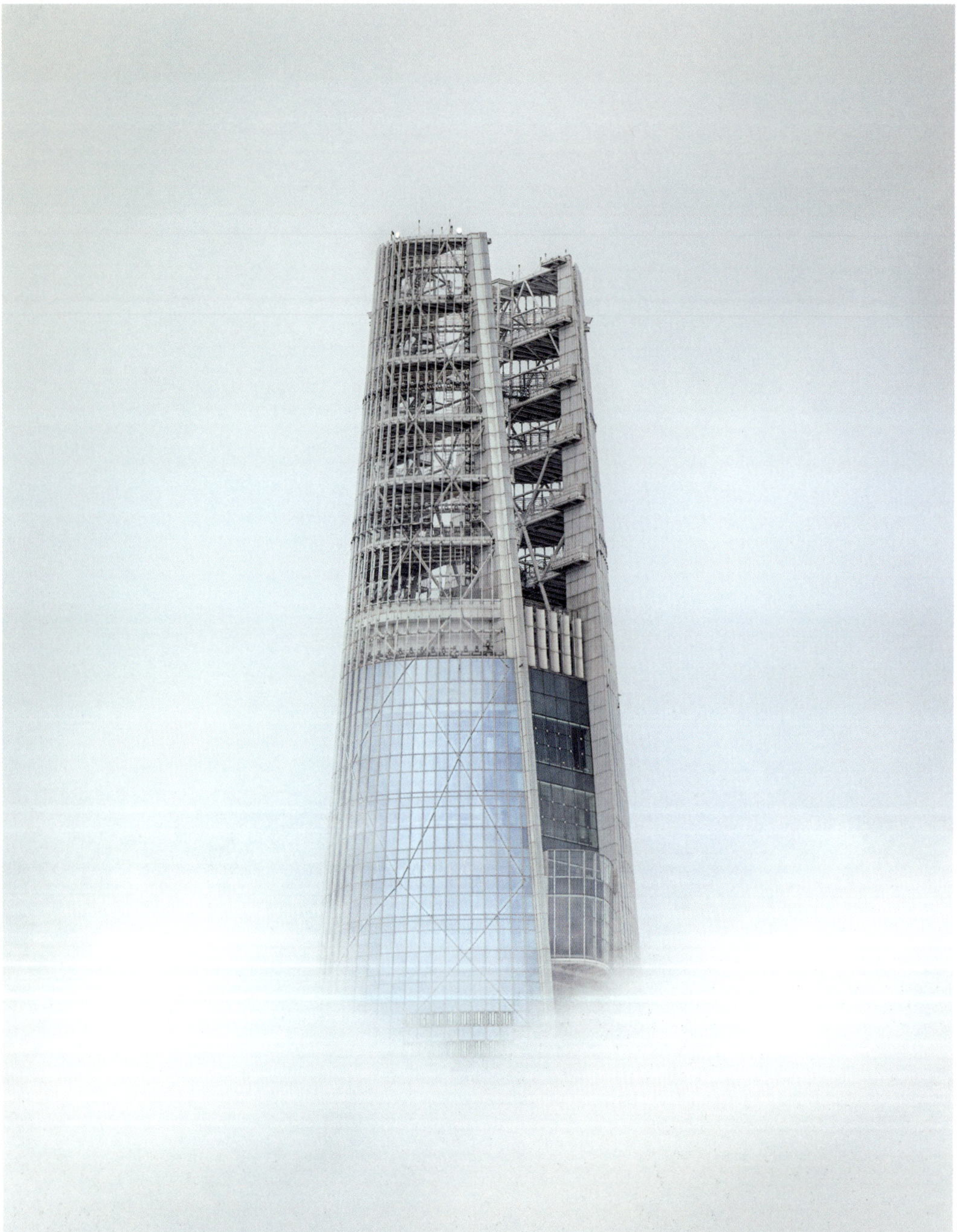

Lotte World Tower, Jamsil-dong, Songpa District

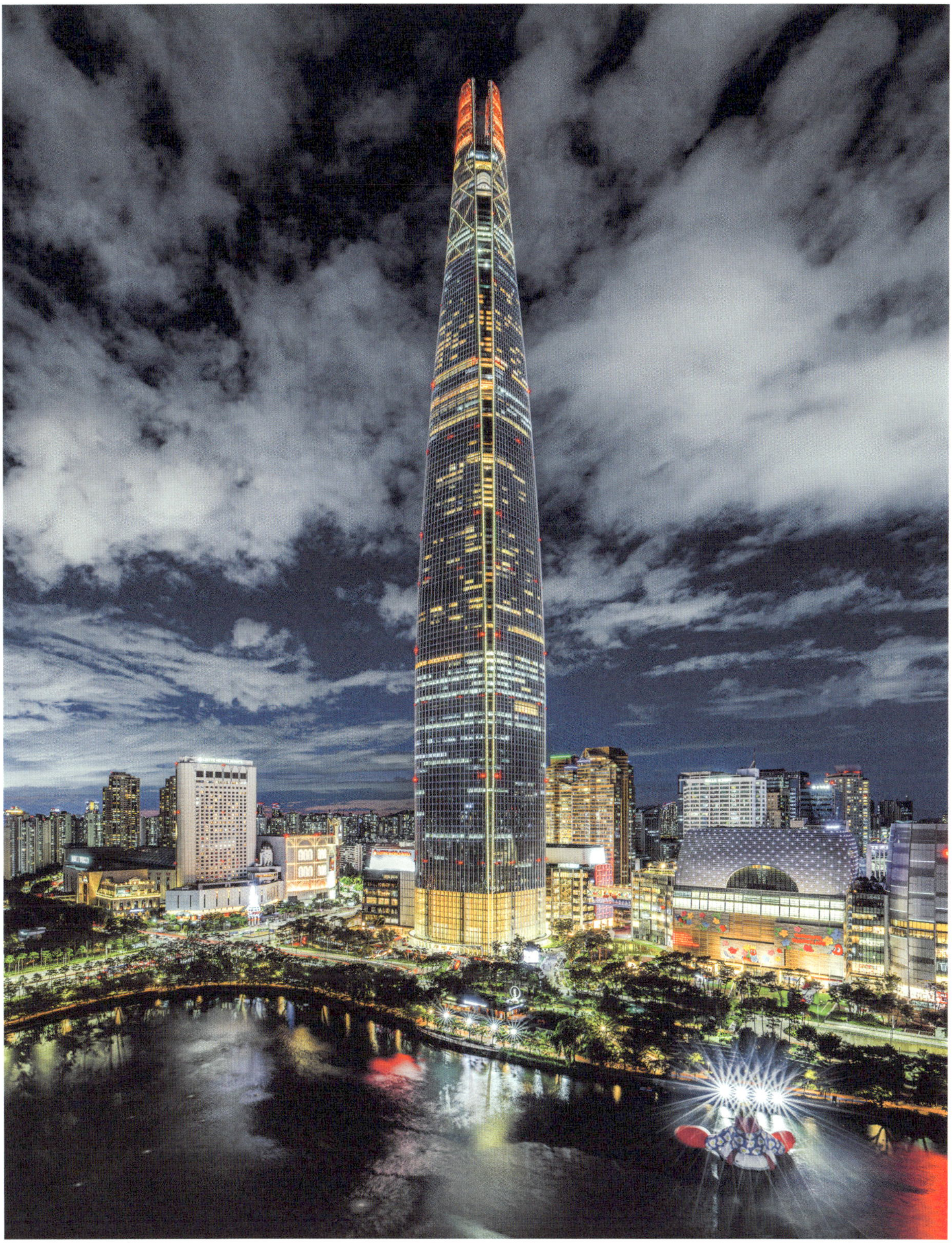

Lotte World Tower, Seokchon Lake, Jamsil-dong, Songpa District

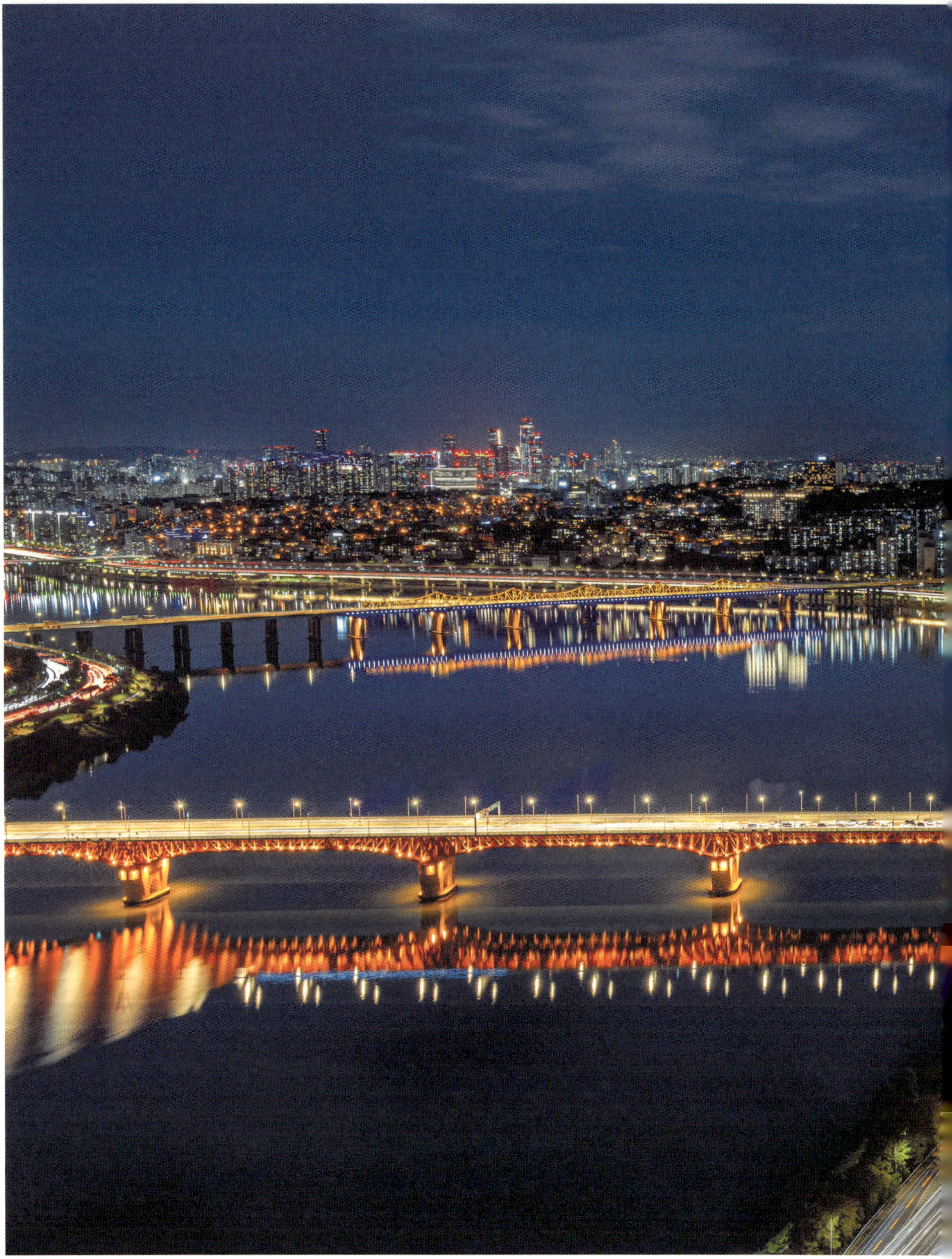

Hangang River > The iconic river crosses Seoul from north to south

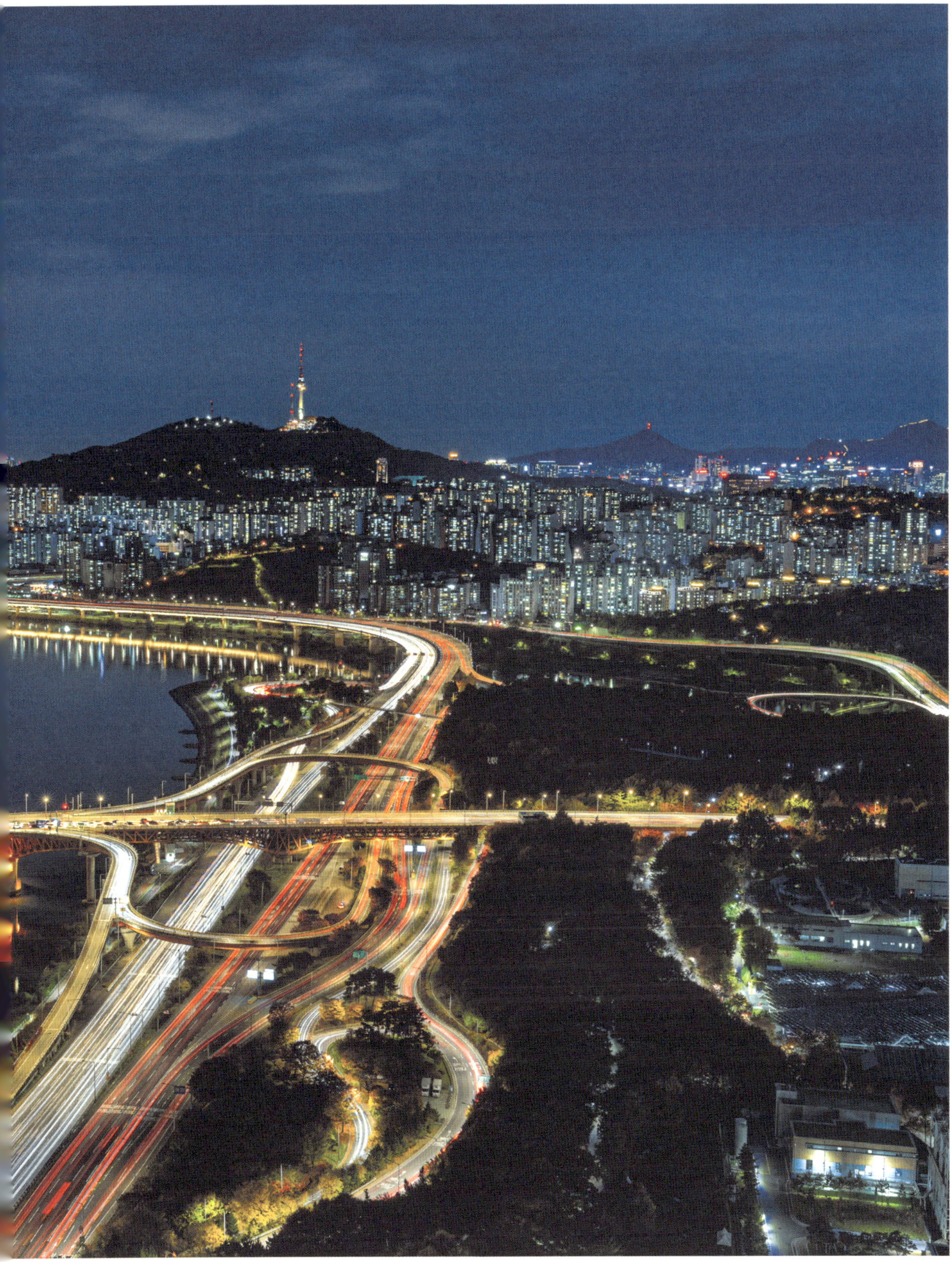

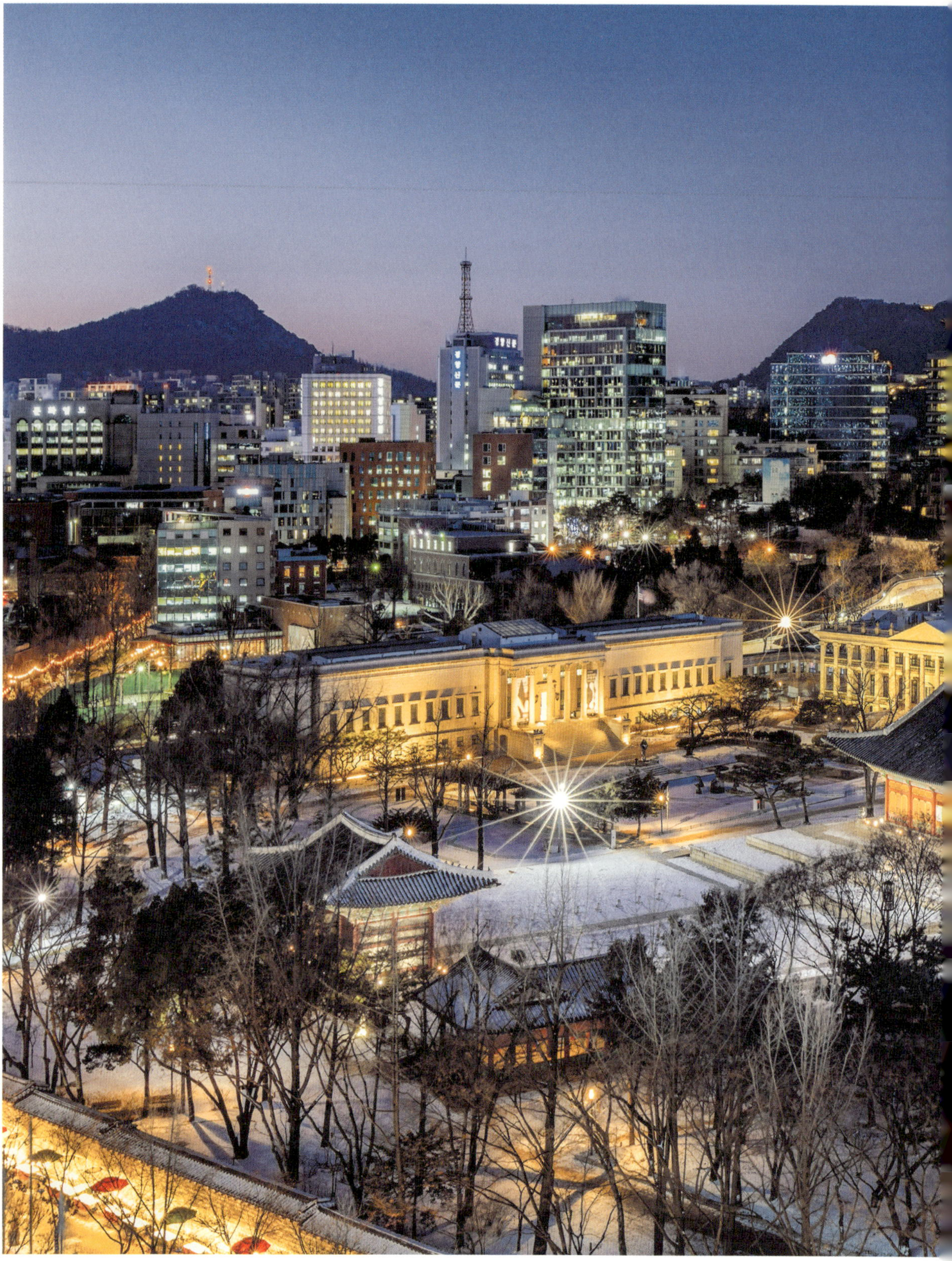

Deoksugung Palace, Jung District

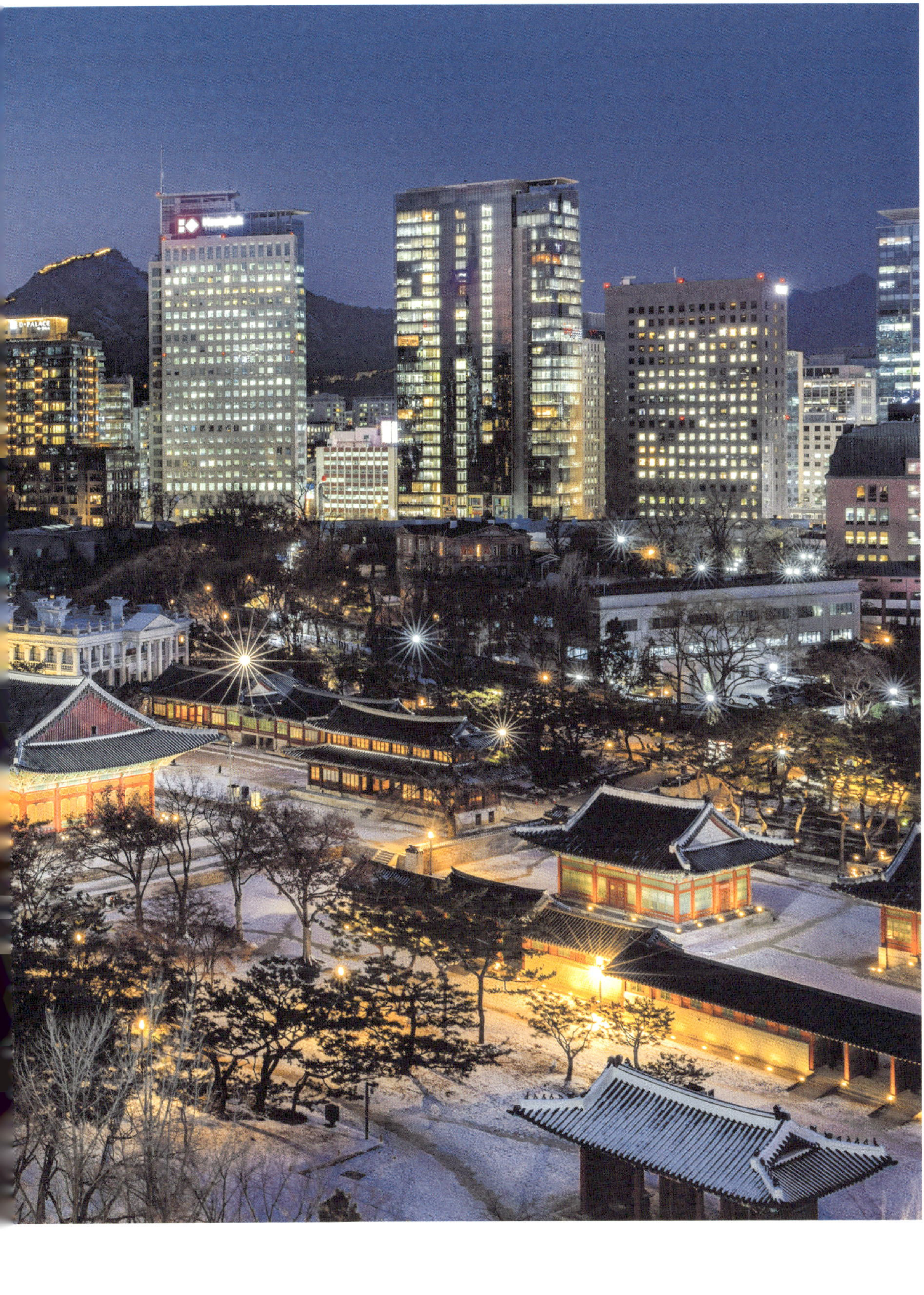

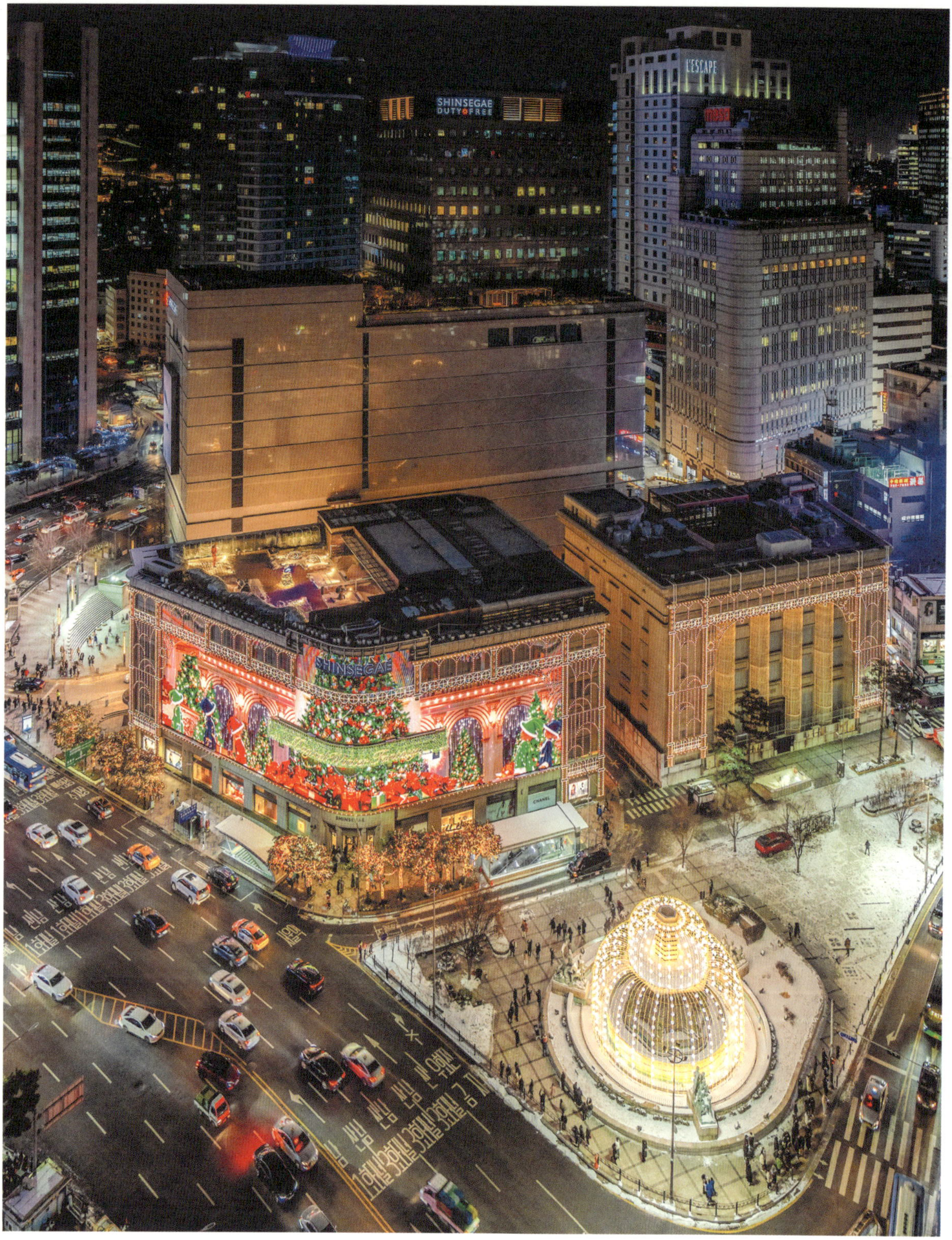


Sogong-dong, Jung District